LIVE & WORK IN

PORTUGAL

LIVE & WORK IN

PORTUGAL

Guy Hobbs

Distributed in the USA by
The Globe Pequot Press, Guilford, Connecticut

Published by Vacation Work, 9 Park End Street, Oxford
www.vacationwork.co.uk

LIVE & WORK IN PORTUGAL
By Guy Hobbs

First edition 2005

ISBN 1 85458 333 6

Publicity: Charles Cutting

Cover design by mccdesign ltd

Title page illustration by Mick Siddens

Typeset by Brendan Cole

Cover photograph: boats at a Portuguese marina

Printed and bound in Italy by Legoprint SpA, Trento

CONTENTS

– SECTION I –
LIVING IN PORTUGAL

– SECTION II –
WORKING IN PORTUGAL

FOREWORD

Despite the fact that over five million tourists flood to Portugal's southern shores every summer, this fabulously diverse country remains largely undiscovered by outsiders. For a relatively small country (it is less than 100 miles wide), Portugal offers visitors an astonishing range of terrain, from the soft, green hills and lush valleys of the north, to the spectacular sandstone cliffs, and secluded coves of the southern coastline. It is no wonder then that the country is increasingly attracting expats, retirees, business-people and second-home buyers in their droves, and this book, Live and Work in Portugal, aims to act as a reference manual to help you steer a smoother and more informed path through the essential preparations.

Until relatively recently, much of Portugal was isolated and villagers enjoyed a rural way of life that had remained unchanged for hundreds of years. Driving through villages away from the coast meant negotiating gravel tracks, narrow bridges and giving way to donkey carts. Whilst EU funds have helped to overhaul the country's infrastructure, part of Portugal's charm is that it has remained remarkably unspoilt. Despite the modern construction in the Algarve, it takes little more than a short drive inland to enjoy wide open spaces, and the sights of cattle grazing amongst cork trees, and fortified towns perched on isolated hills. Portugal has not been ravaged by developers, but has taken its time to accommodate itself to the needs of the modern world.

Portugal has a history as a trading nation, and as such, its people are warm and welcoming to foreigners. Over the centuries, there has been a steady influx of foreigners, and, for the British especially, there is something comforting about the two countries' age-old alliance. Ever since the treaty of Windsor in 1386, England and Portugal have enjoyed close relations. Indeed, it was Catherine of Braganza, the Portuguese wife of Charles II, who introduced such quintessential British rituals as tea drinking and eating toast and marmalade to the UK! And in the seventeenth century it was British families who made their fortunes by producing port in the north of the country. These families maintained a rigid segregation from the Portuguese, forming their own cricket club, and bathing on private beaches. Whilst this attitude can still be found amongst the expatriate ghettos of the Algarve, for many the joy of relocating to Portugal lies in becoming embroiled in the customs, traditions and culture of the locals.

The Portuguese themselves are initially very reserved but those who are able to delve a little deeper will find their hosts to be a remarkably straightforward, courteous, dignified and proud people. Above all the Portuguese are a gentle race (that is until they get behind the wheel of any motorised vehicle!), and live their life at a leisurely pace. Those keen to escape the rat race could do far worse than adopting a fatalistic Portuguese attitude, casting aside notions of punctuality and embracing the simplicity of the Portuguese brandos costumes – gentle ways.

Lower property prices (the average house price on the mainland is just €217,000/£149,000), low-cost airlines, better motorways, a fabulous climate, and lower cost of living are luring a new generation of expatriate to Portugal, made up not just of holiday home buyers, but also those who wish to relocate permanently. With this in mind, developers are building homes that are suitable for year-round occupation and boast many of the luxuries that northern Europeans have come to expect. Marina and golf-course developments are readily available, as are charming inland retreats and modern city apartments. The chapter in this book on *Setting up Home* will help to guide you through the many options available. On the mainland most places are within easy reach of the three main airports of Faro, Porto and Lisbon, on the network of fast new motorways, and these airports are now served by frequent and affordable flights.

On the face of it the biggest obstacle to relocation will be finding a job. English-language teaching and seasonal work in the tourist industry are always available, but for those seeking a more permanent career, the recent economic downturn, and rising unemployment have created a highly competitive job market. Nevertheless, those with a specialised skill and a good level of Portuguese, should be able to apply their expertise to the rapidly modernising economy. The *Employment* chapter in this book gives useful job-hunting advice and provides a comprehensive overview of the Portuguese employment scene. Those with an entrepreneurial mindset will find everything they need to help them realise their dream in the final chapter *Starting a Business*.

All in all, living and working in Portugal will be an adventure, but one which may at times cause confusion and frustration to the unitiated. We hope that you will find this book an essential part of your preparations and that it will serve as a useful reference point along the way, helping you to overcome any obstacles and relax into your new lifestyle.

Guy Hobbs
Oxford
July 2005

ACKNOWLEDGMENTS

The author would like to thank the following people and organisations, in no particular order, for their invaluable help in compiling this book: ICEP (Investment, Trade and Tourism) in both London and Lisbon, The Hispanic and Luso Brazilian Council, The Portuguese Investment Agency (*Agência Portuguesa para o Investimento – API*), Mr Stefano Lucatello of The International Property Law Centre, The Portuguese Embassy in London, the Department of Social Security Overseas Branch, The Portuguese-UK Business Network, Clive Veigas Bennet of Veigas Bennet Consulting, *Portugal* magazine, the network of Business Formalities Centres (*Centros de Formalidades das Empresas – CFE*), the British-Portuguese Chamber of Commerce, the British Embassy in Lisbon, and The Federation of Overseas Property Developers, Agents and Consultants (FOPDAC). In addition, Dan Boothby's *Buying a House in Portugal* has proved an invaluable source for the chapter on setting up home.

Thank you also to all those who provided information and the fruits of their own experience of living, buying property, retiring, working and starting a business in Portugal, especially: John Carey, Lesley and Mike Collins, Sam Dunlop, Maribel Gattey, Michelle Hone, Lesley Keast, Maggie Milne, Emma-Louise Parkes, David Skinner, Mary Sworder, and Patricia Westheimer.

TELEPHONE NUMBERS

Please note that the telephone numbers in this book are written as needed to call that number from inside the same country. To call these numbers from outside the country you will need to know the relevant international access code; these are currently 00 from the UK and Portugal and 011 from the USA.

To call Portugal: dial the international access code +351 and then the number in this book.

To call the UK from Portugal: dial +44 then the number minus the first 0.

Section 1

LIVING IN PORTUGAL

GENERAL INTRODUCTION

RESIDENCE AND ENTRY REGULATIONS

SETTING UP HOME

DAILY LIFE

RETIREMENT

GENERAL INTRODUCTION

CHAPTER SUMMARY

○ **The Portuguese.** Portugal is a mix of influences including Celtic, Roman and Moorish.

   ○ Foreigners are struck by the slightly old-fashioned feel, the relaxed attitude of the locals and the byzantine bureaucracy.

   ○ Most of the modern developments in Portugal are concentrated in the Algarve.

○ **The Capital.** Lisbon is more in the mainstream of cosmopolitan Europe than the rest of the country and has been transformed in the last decade by renovation and prestige building projects.

   ○ Lisbon has great nightlife, steep hills, cheap restaurants and an excellent tram system like San Francisco's.

   ○ The original city was destroyed by an earthquake which killed 30,000 in 1755.

○ **Politics.** For nearly forty years, Portugal was ruled by a military dictator, Antonio de Oliviera Salazar.

   ○ A bloodless military coup in 1974 ended the dictatorship and led to the establishment of democratic government.

   ○ In the elections of 2005, a high turnout of voters gave an absolute majority to one party (the socialist party) for the first time in a decade.

○ **Economics.** It is estimated that Portugal's hosting of Euro 2004 will contribute around €360 million per annum to the economy, mainly through tourism, over the next six years.

○ **History.** Historically Portugal is renowned for its shipbuilding and navigation skills.

   ○ Vasco da Gama and Columbus both studied at the famous Portuguese school of navigation in Sagres.

○ **Language.** Portuguese is spoken by an estimated 200 million people (mainly Brazilians) worldwide.

> o **Demography.** The current population of Portugal is around 10.5 million. Over half the Portuguese population is still rurally based.
>
> o **Communications**. Mainland Portugal has three international airports: Lisbon, Porto and Faro. The budget airline revolution has made flying to Portugal from the UK cheap and easy.

DESTINATION PORTUGAL

The pace of life in the small country of Portugal is slow compared to its neighbour Spain. The inexorable march of tourism has made its impact, largely in the southernmost region, the Algarve, and the coast around Lisbon. As in Spain, where the tourists go the foreign residents usually follow. An estimated 200,000 Britons own property in Portugal, and of these at least a quarter are living and working there full-time. Many more have chosen to retire to Portugal or simply own holiday homes. For years before mass tourism came in the 60's, there were expatriate colonies in Lisbon (Lisboa) and Porto (Oporto) involved mainly in trade. Portugal was never particularly fashionable. Artistic and literary types went to Mallorca, or the South of France, to North Africa, Paris or the Greek islands, but almost never to Portugal, and so for a time the idyllic calm was preserved.

Nowadays, nearly every fishing village in the Algarve has a tourist development, but there is as yet no comparison to the jetset resorts of the Spanish Costa del Sol. Some may prefer it this way and although this southern region is among the most developed, with good (if congested) roads and an abundance of card phones, cash points and other modern items, visitors and foreign residents (*estrangeiros*) are still struck by the slightly old-fashioned feel, the relaxed attitude of the locals... and the bureaucracy. The latter tends to be more accentuated outside the main tourist and city areas. Lisbon nowadays is more in the mainstream of cosmopolitan Europe, with a lively fashion and nightlife scene as well as its picturesque old Moorish quarter. There was a building boom in Lisbon as it upgraded the urban infrastructure for Expo '98, which attracted international focus on the city and increased the numbers of tourists. The event was backed by over one billion pounds of government and private sector finance.

More recently Portugal hosted Euro 2004 (the European football Championship), thrusting this tiny country of just 10 million people into the limelight. The European Championship is the world's third biggest sporting spectacle, after the World Cup and the Olympics, drawing a television audience of 1.5 billion people. The event therefore required massive investment from the Portuguese government, who spent an estimated €4 billion on the country's public infrastructure, investing in new motorways, high-speed rail lines and

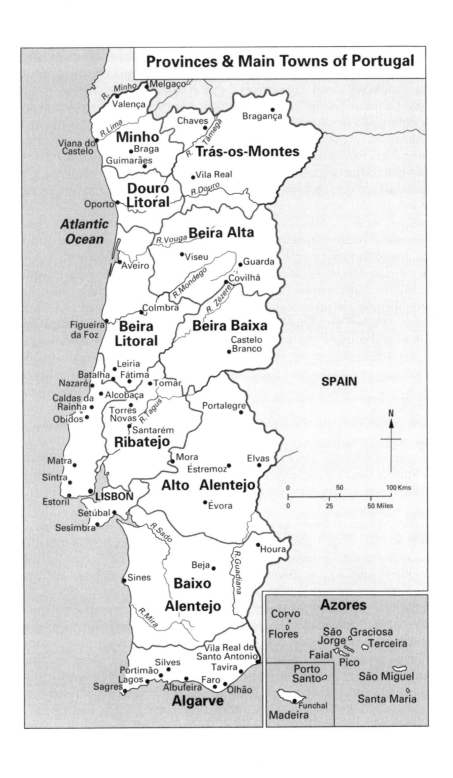

Provinces & Main Towns of Portugal

R. Minho
Melgaço
Valença
R. Lima
Chaves
Bragança
Minho
Viana do Castelo
Braga
R. Tâmega
Guimarães
Trás-os-Montes
Vila Real
Douro Litoral
R. Douro
Oporto
Atlantic Ocean
R. Vouga
Beira Alta
Viseu
Guarda
Aveiro
Covilhá
R. Mondego
R. Zézere
Coimbra
Beira Baixa
Figueira da Foz
Beira Litoral
Castelo Branco
Leiria
Batalha
Fátima
Nazaré
Tomar
SPAIN
Caldas da Rainha
Alcobaça
Portalegre
Torres Novas
R. Tagus
Obidos
Santarém
N
Ribatejo
Matra
Mora
Elvas
Sintra
Éstremoz
Estoril
Alto Alentejo
LISBON
Setúbal
Évora
0   50   100 Kms
Sesimbra
0   25   50 Miles
R. Sado
Houra
Beja
R. Guadiana
Sines
Baixo Alentejo
Azores
Corvo
Flores
São Jorge
Graciosa
Terceira
R. Mira
Faial
Pico
Vila Real de Santo Antonio
Porto Santo
São Miguel
Silves
Tavira
Portimão
Lagos
Faro
Sagres
Albufeira
Olhão
Funchal
Algarve
Santa Maria
Madeira

medical facilities. This was one of the greatest financial outlays ever made in Portugal and many criticised the government for a frivolous investment that they simply could not afford. However, in the short term, the championship certainly brought a massive boost to the economy of around €800 million according to one report, and the massive investment created jobs, boosted wages and shored up the tourist infrastructure. However, the Portuguese were clearly hoping for a long term 'Barcelona effect' (referring to the massive increase in the number of tourists to the city following the 1992 Olympics). Officials predicted a 3%-6% annual increase in tourism and an increased revenue of 350 million euros per annum, due to the tournament raising Portugal's profile internationally. It remains to be seen whether this heightened visibility has had the desired effect.

Portugal's history as an independent country can be traced back to the medieval kingdom of Portuçale (see below), and its roots are in the mingling of the Celtic and then the Roman people who came here. To the south, a Moorish influence is still evident. More recently (and importantly, for Britons wishing to work there) Portugal joined the then Common Market in 1986, the same year as Spain and Greece. Membership of the European Union has accelerated the modernisation of town and country life, with the increased mechanisation of agriculture and aid and investment coming from Brussels for projects like the expansion of the underground railway in Lisbon (the *Metropolitano de Lisboa*) and new motorways which are being driven through the tranquil countryside by the state-owned Brisa company.

These new roads are visual proof of change and the gradual reduction of the numbers of donkey-carts in the countryside, which are still a common form of transport in the more rural areas, like the Minho region, lying between Porto and the Spanish border in the north. But development has seen the tracks worn and plodded by these familiar quadrupeds, widened, asphalted and then motorised with a vengeance.

Its heritage and traditions are sometimes under threat. There was an international outcry recently when a £200 million project to build a new dam and reservoir in the Côa Valley turned out to be threatening the site of Europe's largest Stone Age 'art gallery'. Engravings of animals dating back to the last Ice Age were discovered and the project was stopped before too much damage was done.

Visitors to this remote valley are now welcome and it may become another feature of Portugal's burgeoning tourist trade. The Portuguese are quite keen to encourage tourists to move away from the Algarve, and to see some of the less well-known parts of the country. As a result there are many places in Portugal which still have potential for tourism development, which it is hoped will be carried out in a less environmentally damaging way than it has sometimes been in the past. To the east and north, there are still many villages connected to the outside world only by dirt tracks trodden by the donkeys, an attraction for some visitors with the transport to get there. In Portugal, there are still places to get away from it all and over 60% of the population is still rurally based.

Not everything is changing for the better, though, despite the great strides the country has made in recent years. As more imported goods fill the shops, and services and facilities are upgraded, the cost of living is also rising, especially in Lisbon. Although Portugal is no longer a bargain Eden of retreat, it is still has some of the cheapest living costs in western Europe and an equable climate (rainier in the north). It is also a more relaxed country in which to live and work than some of its Mediterranean neighbours.

Pros and Cons of Moving to Portugal

The strong historical links between Britain and Portugal have long made it a popular and welcoming country for citizens of the UK to retire to. Relations between England and the ancient medieval kingdom of Portuçale go back to at least the time of the Crusades, when a party of English knights bound for the Holy Land stopped off to help King Alfonso Henriques drive out the Moors, and took part in the capture of Lisbon. This was the first action of what is probably England's oldest continental alliance and trade has ebbed and flowed between the two countries ever since. It is unusual that UK imports and exports in Portugal are more or less in balance; today the country is said to be 'a relatively easy market for first time exporters'.

Good relations between the two countries and Portugal's membership of the EU also offer another advantage to the country. Whereas previously legendary Portuguese bureaucracy was a real hinderance, these days British, Irish and other EU citizens have the right to reside, to seek work, to join trade unions, to study, to practice a profession, to own property, to use the health services, to enrol children in schools and so on. However, many expats report that although theoretically there is less bureaucracy to wade through, overall public services are stilled drowning in red tape, and there is a tendency for official information to be written in complicated Portuguese. For those coming from outside the EU, it can take a minimum of six months to get a residence permit. Further details on residence and permits can be found in the chapter which follows on *Residence and Entry Regulations*.

Friendly relations are only one of the advantages. High on the list of priorities of many sun-seeking expatriates is the country's marvelous weather conditions. Portugal's climate compares very favourably with that in northern Europe and in areas such as the Algarve and Madeira, fantastic weather is almost guaranteed all year round. Added to this undeniable perk is the country's picture-postcard beauty. Portugal has always been a favourite with holiday-makers due to its incredibly diverse landscapes, charming towns and villages and miles and miles of largely unspoilt coastline.

Equally attractive to some is the fact that Portugal is such a popular place for expatriates to live and work. Many trail-blazing Britons and Americans have already done the hard work and set up communities that can provide the newcomer with English-speaking services and ready made networks of people with similar interests. Such communities also offer numerous opportunities for work. Those who wish to be a little more adventurous and assimilate themselves into the local way of life will find the Portuguese to be very interested in and friendly towards strangers. Most expats agree that the Portuguese people are polite and hospitable, if a little reserved initially.

While property prices have shot up in the past fifteen years, there are still bargains to be found, even in the Algarve, if one is prepared to go a little inland. The average house price in mainland Portugal is around €217,000 (£149,000), however, this figure is artificially high because of the massive jump in house prices in the Algarve region, where the average is €310,000 (£213,000). In the rest of the country, prices continue to be far lower, the lowest being in Coimbra and the Beiras regions – €161,000   (£110,500).

Unfortunately for those not yet contemplating retirement, there are still far fewer employment opportunities for foreigners in Portugal than in many other countries. In spite of an improved economy, and fairly low unemployment, recent years have seen both of these falter. Unemployment has risen to around 7% and work is becoming increasingly hard to find, other than in well-trodden paths such as English teaching. It is difficult for non-Portuguese speakers to find work because of the language barrier. Also there are the low wages paid to Portuguese employees with which the British find it hard to compete. On the plus side, prospects for seasonal jobs, for holiday company personnel, entertainers, and in bars and hotels, are better than you might expect; while self-employed foreigners generally do extremely well in the Algarve, running businesses catering for their fellow northern Europeans.

Remarkably, 80% of the UK investment in Portugal has gone to the Algarve, mostly into real estate; and UK companies see further prospects here for expansion. This may bring more jobs for those, like lawyers and accountants, involved with these new investments and companies. There is expansion, too, in the engineering and consumer goods sectors.

The business capital of Portugal is Porto, not least because of the port wine trade which began in the Middle Ages. The English exported in return wool from the South Coast to Portugal. Dried fruit, salt, honey and wax – as well as wine – were also traditional imports into England from Portugal. Porto has, since those days, attracted a range of British and other foreign commercial investments, particularly from American and German companies. Siemens, the German electronics and engineering giant recently completed a £300 million memory chip plant near Porto. Other multinationals established there are Opel Portugal, Ford, Volkswagen, Texas Instruments, Alcatel, Yasaki, Borealis, Continental, Bendix, Mitsubishi, Samsung, Pepsico, Nestlé and Pioneer. The financial service sector changes in areas like banking which have helped to bring

Portugal into the European Monetary Union and the adoption of a single currency may also provide useful openings for anyone considering developing business connections with the country.

One of the attractions of Portugal for business is a positive disadvantage for international workers. Although minimum wages are fixed by law, they are dismally low compared with Britain and casual workers can easily find themselves working simply for bed, board and pocket money. Such a disadvantage has to be weighed against the traditional hospitality of the Portuguese people and the comparatively low cost of living.

Despite being spoken by an estimated 200 million people worldwide, it would be a mistake to assume, unless one is a talented linguist, that Portuguese is an easy language to pick up. In written form, it bears more than a passing resemblance to Spanish but in pronunciation it resembles no other tongue. Although a knowledge of Latin, or Romance languages like French and Spanish, will help with word recognition, the difficulty of learning to speak Portuguese may be a drawback for those wishing to live and work there.

PROS AND CONS OF LIVING IN PORTUGAL

Pros

o Portugal is an extremely hospitable country with a long historical association with the UK.

o Procedures for house and property-buying have become well-established over several decades and there is plenty of professional advice to help the uninitiated avoid the pitfalls.

o Portugual has a mild climate all year round, as do the Portuguese islands of the Azores and Madeira.

o Services are well-developed in the areas popular with tourists and expatriates.

o Portugal is fast catching up with its more sophisticated EU neighbours, but its unspoiled picturesque charm is one of the many attractions it still has over them.

o Although prices, especially property taxes, have increased dramatically over the past few years, the cost of living generally and most property prices (except in the most sought after areas) are lower than in many northern European countries.

o New investment also means there are now a wider range of job opportunities.

o Tourism has meant that travel between Britain and Portugal is relatively inexpensive.

o The Portuguese generally are relaxed and easy-going.

Cons

o Despite a thriving economy and low unemployment, openings for foreigners in Portuguese industry are often limited.

o Housing conditions often do not meet Western standards.

o Wages in Portugal are low compared with the rest of the EU.

o Dealing with bureaucracy in Portugal constitutes a test of forbearance and fortitude.

o In remoter regions communications, the roads and utilities are often still poor.

o The climate in the north can be cold and rainy.

o Portuguese life, especially family life, can be closed and inward-looking.

o Development, especially in the Algarve, has made it a less attractive place for those wishing to get away from it all.

o Essential services like hospitals have room for improvement.

o Prices are rising, and imported goods can be expensive.

POLITICAL AND ECONOMIC STRUCTURE

History

Under the Romans, Portugal was part of the province of Lusitania and populated by Celtic tribes who became Romanised and adopted the Latin language. Following the break-up of the Roman Empire the barbarian hordes swept unimpeded through the Iberian Peninsula. Then, conversion to Christianity came (as in Britain) in the sixth century. In the eighth century virtually the whole of the Peninsula was taken over by the Moors. Until the eighth century, in fact, the history of Portugal virtually mirrors that of Spain; but the Moslem occupation of the area later to become known as Portugal lasted two and a half centuries less than in the rest of the Peninsula, a fact that was to have an important effect on its development as a separate political entity later on.

From the twelfth century, Portugal was an independent kingdom and King Alfonso Henriques fought his way down the coast with the help of his Crusader allies to recapture the modern capital Lisbon from the Moors. By the mid fourteenth century, the country had expanded to approximately its present boundaries and in 1386 the Portuguese signed the Treaty of Windsor with the English against their mutual enemies at the time in Spain. So was born a long history of Anglo-Portuguese friendship and cooperation.

To consolidate this treaty, Phillipa, the daughter of John of Gaunt, was given in marriage to King John of Portugal. The third son of this marriage was later to become known as Henry the Navigator. So begins Portugal's history of maritime expansion.

A man of vision and learning, Henry secreted himself on Cape Sagres, the southwest extremity of Portugal, where he founded a school of navigation attended by both Vasco de Gama and Christopher Columbus. Prince Henry also refined the process of boat building which resulted in the Portuguese *caravel*, a vessel designed to withstand lengthy sea voyages and adverse weather conditions.

The most significant result of his navigational researches, though, was the realisation that the route to India and the Spice Islands lay not to the west, as Columbus stubbornly believed until his death, but around the Cape of Good Hope and eastwards, which is where the main focus of Portuguese expansion lay. The Portuguese had long been fishermen and traders. Now they were becoming a world power.

In 1488, Bartholomew Dias set sail from Portugal, rounded the Cape of Good Hope, and sailed into the Indian Ocean. In 1497, Vasco de Gama sailed the same route and landed first in what became Portuguese Mozambique; and then continued to India and the Spice Islands. By the end of the fifteenth century the Spaniards and Portuguese had also become rival colonists in the New World, a problem which exercised world leaders at the time.

The rough east-west division between Portuguese and Spanish territories prompted the Pope's pragmatic solution (over-mighty even by Papal standards). The Treaty of Tordesillas which he devised in 1494 divided the world vertically between Spain and Portugal; and each would claim any land as yet undiscovered in their respective hemispheres. Portugal's half included by chance the yet-to-be-discovered country of Brazil, stumbled upon by Pedro Alves Cabral in 1500.

By the mid-sixteenth century this tiny nation on the western shores of Europe (with a population of only about one million at most) had become the first world power, acquiring a vast empire which included Morocco, parts of East Africa and the islands along its coast, the enormously rich prize of Brazil, and the East Indies. Thus over-extended, Portugal found it impossible to protect her overseas interests from the ravening English and Dutch navies, or, on her own doorstep, to protect herself from the designs of Philip II of Spain. He seized the Portuguese throne in 1580 and thus initiated sixty years of Spanish rule. During this period the disintegration of overseas Portuguese interests continued, including the loss of the East Indies to the Dutch.

In 1807, during the Napoleonic wars, the Portuguese royal family were saved by the British from impending capture by the French, and borne off to Brazil with an escort provided by a British naval squadron. Brazil declared her own independence in 1821.

The intended unification by Portugal of her two African colonies of Mozambique and Angola (which was successfully prevented by Cecil Rhodes in Rhodesia) was a sticking point in late nineteenth-century relations between Britain and Portugal – one of the rare disagreements between the two countries. Following the declaration of the Portuguese Republic in 1910, the British navy provided its customary rescue service for beleaguered Portuguese royalty, this time removing Manuel II to Gibraltar.

Relations between Britain and Portugal prospered once again when Portuguese soldiers fought on the Allied side in the First World War. In the Second World War, Portugal remained neutral; but the British invoked the fourteenth century Treaty of Windsor to enable the Americans to build bases on the Azores. From here they pursued German submarines which were attacking the Atlantic convoys.

Economics

Until the 1950's the majority of Portuguese led a lowly and largely agrarian existence. Wealth was enjoyed by a small minority of the population; and the rest lived in conditions reminiscent of eighteenth century (i.e. pre-revolutionary) France. The Salazar regime ran the economy hand-in-glove with a small circle of magnates whose riches were largely accrued through massive colonial exploitation. Basically five families were involved: Champalimaud, Mello, Quina, Queiroz, Pereira and Espiríto Santo. The unions in Portugal having been rendered toothless by the regime, a plentiful supply of cheap, subdued labour ensured that industrial wheels ran smoothly for the benefit of this small section of society.

Additionally, and with equal complicity of the industrial barons, the regime practised protectionist policies which precluded the setting up of any rival companies to upset the monopolies of the five leading families. The effect of this was to ensure the Portuguese nation remained in the economic dark ages, by preventing much needed modernisation and industrialisation.

A belated spurt of industrial development in the fifties caused the exodus of rural populations to the towns in search of jobs, leaving behind in the villages only the old and the very young, which resulted in severe agricultural decline.

In 1975, the Agrarian Reform Law was passed with the aim of breaking up the large estates south of the river Tagus, whose ownership had been maintained by the same social stratum through exploitation of the mass of miserably paid farm workers. By restricting the size of estates, expropriating the surplus land, and encouraging its occupation by these workers, the Agrarian Reform achieved a redistribution of ownership which resulted in a rush of people attempting to earn a living through agriculture. However, the achievements of the reform were diminished when Barreto's Law of 1976 partially reversed the earlier legislation by increasing the permitted size of estates, thus enabling landowners to claw back some of their former property. This resulted in thousands of farm workers being thrown off the land they had been occupying and caused mass unemployment in the countryside. The effects of Barreto's law can still be seen today, although Portuguese agriculture is now moving out of the dark ages with the help of EU subsidies and the Common Agricultural Policy.

1974, the year of the coup (which was otherwise known as the Carnation

Revolution), was not an auspicious one for the economy. Faced with the dual horror of revolution and a world recession, many Portuguese businessmen fled the country (having first emptied their bank accounts) leaving their factories rudderless behind them. To aggravate matters, tourism and foreign investment both slumped. In an effort to stabilise the economy the government nationalised the banks, insurance companies and transport; and some major industries including petrochemicals and brewing. They also began to dismantle the old industrial monopolies.

It is probably a measure of the state of the economy that nine constitutional governments came, wrestled with the economy, and went, in the six years between 1976 and 1984. Economic austerity became the watchword of the late seventies; and negotiations for IMF and European bank loans were continuously on the agenda. In addition, negotiations for entry into the Common Market began, although it was to be ten years before they came to fruition.

In 1983, the budget included a 28% retrospective increase in income tax; and an exit tax was levied on anyone leaving the country, a means of raising cash more often encountered in third world countries. The situation since Portugal joined the European Union in 1986 has improved immensely. The years between the late eighties and late nineties have been called the 'Prodigious Decade'. This was when Portugal began to catch up with its European neighbours, gaining enormous ground in the first few years of EU membership. Portugal deftly used the Expo '98 exhibition in Lisbon to attract foreign investment and improve facilities, much as Barcelona achieved when that city made urban improvements to hold the Olympic Games in 1992. EU funding provided for new motorways, bridges and dams and helped to bring the country's infrastructure up to date. As a result there was an unprecedented boom in consumer confidence and new shopping centres sprang up around Lisbon and Porto to provide for those with new-found wealth. Membership of the EU has brought Portugal many economic benefits and the institution is still seen as a guarantor of the country's relatively recent democratic institutions. During the prodigious decade the Portuguese economy grew at rates higher than the EU average, around 3.7% per year and by 2001 unemployment was as low as 4%.

Prime Minister Gutieres successfully engineered Portugal's official entry to the Euro in 1999, partly by privatising 22 companies and so reducing the public deficit. Income from tourism has been steadily increasing: no less than two hundred and fifty tour operators currently feature Portugal (including Madeira and the Azores) amongst their destinations. American investment has also been significant.

The Current Economic Situation

Despite the economic progress of the *Prodigious Decade*, Portugal began to experience a slowdown in economic activity during 2001 and inflation rose to a rate over 4%. By 2002 Portugal's budget deficit had reached 4.1%; seriously above the 3% ceiling permitted by the EU's Stability and Growth pact. At the same time unemployment has steadily been rising from just 4% in 2001 to around 7% in 2005. Portugal's economy is not looking terribly healthy, with real GDP growth at just 0.5% in 2002, and in 2003 the economy actually shrank by 1.3%.

On top of these worrying trends is the looming threat that by 2006 EU funds are likely to have been completely cut and the government will be forced into greater self-sufficiency. Whilst membership of the EU was Portugal's saviour in the late 1980s, the benefits are now being reaped by the EU's newest members, who are also taking trade away from the Portuguese economy. Throughout the 1990s, Portugal was able to attract many multinational investors, with extremely low labour costs, as little as €7 per hour in 2001. However, the new EU members have stolen that mantle from the Portuguese, offering even lower labour costs, and the same level of qualified staff.

Whilst low labour costs may well have been useful bait for attracting foreign investors, for those living in Portugal it meant low wages and a low standard of living. The average salary in Portugal is currently just €12,000 per annum, and whilst living costs are lower than in Northern Europe, they are certainly not low enough for a satisfactory standard of living on such low wages.

One of the main challenges for the Portuguese economy in the coming years is therefore to accelerate the convergence of productivity growth and living standards. The economy's trade specialisation has typically been in low-skill, labour-intensive sectors, in which it faces rising competition from new EU members. Therefore the government must raise the skills of the Portuguese workforce and shift towards more competitive products within industry. Policies are required that facilitate labour mobility, intensify the use of information and communication technology, raise managerial efficiency and create a favourable climate for private investment. However, achieving this, whilst simultaneously bringing the budget deficit under control, stemming rising unemployment and boosting growth in the economy, is no mean feat.

The spiralling budget deficit mentioned above is a chronic problem that must be addressed with urgency. Rapid growth of primary spending over more than a decade has placed Portugal amongst the higher-spending countries, despite its low-income level. Nevertheless, government spending is decreasing (although still high at around 46% of GDP in 2004) and the new government's plans to create a more efficient public sector will hopefully permit more resources to go to the development needs of Portugal.

After Portugal joined the EU, the development of a service-based economy was an inevitability. Agriculture and fishing have almost died out in terms of their importance to the economy (representing 3.3% of GDP), although the primary sector still employs 12% of the working population. One of the most important service sectors is tourism and this is an area of the economy that continues to increase in importance year on year. However, the industry is changing gradually as the government attempts to shift the emphasis from pie and chips beach holidays towards higher spending cultural tourism. One of the aims of hosting the high-profile Euro 2004 tournament in Portugal was to put the country in the spotlight and remind potential holiday-makers across Europe that there is much more to Portugal than just the Algarve. ICEP Portugal has estimated that Euro 2004 will have contributed around €360 million per annum to the economy through tourism over the next six years.

All things considered, the Portuguese economy is in need of an enormous boost to drag it out of the current malaise. However, it is possible that the new socialist government, complete with a parliamentary majority, will be able to successfully navigate the country's economy from a path based on public consumption and public investment to one focused on exports and private investment.

Government

The monarchy was abolished in 1910; and the First Republic lasted from 1910 to 1926. Portugal had emerged from the First World War in economic and political chaos. During 1920 alone seven consecutive governments were formed and dissolved. This was followed by a period of changing military governments in 1925. In 1926, a right-wing military coup led by General Gomes da Costa overthrew the republic and established a military dictatorship which was itself overturned by General Carmona in 1928. Carmona survived as president of Portugal until 1951.

Like Portugese bullfighting, Portuguese coups have tended to be bloodless. In 1928, President Carmona appointed a young law professor from Coimbra university as minister of finance. The name of the new minister was António de Oliveira Salazar. By 1933, Salazar had become prime minister and instigated a new constitution, the New State (*Novo Stado*), under the guise of which the democratic rights of the Portuguese were slowly whittled away. Political opposition was neutralised and workers' rights were nullified by the introduction of state-controlled union organisations.

By 1956, there were penal colonies for dissidents and arrests of citizens for an unlimited period in the interests of national security were commonplace. In short, the apparatus of dictatorship was firmly in place. Salazar retained his post for nearly forty years by rigging the various presidential elections so that only candidates who supported him achieved office: they then naturally reappointed him prime minister.

Cracks appeared in Salazar's regime when the 'winds of change' that were stirring the African colonies of western nations to strive for their independence were resisted by the Salazar regime. The deeply unpopular Colonial Wars, launched in 1961, were to be one of the main contributory factors to the eventual downfall of the regime.

Salazar was forced to retire in 1968, following a fall on the head that incapacitated him permanently. He was succeeded as prime minister by Marcello Caetano, who had no intention of relinquishing the colonies of Angola, Guinea-Bissau and Mozambique. The main guerrilla liberation movements of these lands were UNITA, PAIGC and FRELIMO who, between them, took up a good deal of foreign news space during the thirteen years that Portugal waged war in Africa. The refusal of Caetano to make a settlement with the rebels in Angola caused deep resentment in the ranks of the military. General António Spínola, the governor general of the colony who had prepared the ground for a settlement, had argued that the only way forward was for the colonies to be formed into a Portuguese-speaking federation with a measure of self-autonomy. He was subsequently sacked for expressing such views.

Following the increasing politicisation of the military and a split in ideology between the upper and lower ranks (effectively the older and younger officers) the seeds for a military coup were sown. The younger officers rallied around the figure of Spínola, who was later jettisoned in favour of Major Otelo Saraiva de Carvalho, who took charge of the Movement of the Armed Forces which eventually staged a coup on April 25th 1974, thus ending fifty years of dictatorship. The first constitutional parliament was elected democratically on 25th April 1976.

Under the constitution, a president is elected by popular vote every five years, and the parliament, the Assembly of the Republic, every four years.

Political Parties

By 1976, power had been returned to civilians and four main political parties had emerged: the PCP, the PS, the PPD/PSD and the CDS. The oldest is the PCP, the Portuguese Communist Party. Founded in 1921, it went underground during the dictatorship. Its main areas of influence are amongst the industrial working class and the farmers of the Alentejo region. The PS (Socialist Party) was founded in 1974 with Mário Soares as its general secretary. Vigorously anticommunist, it has strong links with the German Social Democratic Party. The PPD/PSD was the right-wing party whose leader, Sâ Carneiro, became prime minister in 1979 and 1980. Supported by the professional and managerial cadres of Portuguese society it also finds favour with the lesser bourgeoisie and is roughly comparable with the Liberal Democrats in Britain.

The CDS is a conservative party founded by Freitas do Amaral. Its influence is strongest in the north of the country, where its support is based amongst the professional and property-owning upper middle classes and right-wing Catholics.

After the 1985 elections, President Ramalho Eanes asked Dr Anibal Cavaco Silva to form a government when Mário Soares stood down as prime minister.

Mário Soares took over the presidency in 1986. In 1995 Portugal elected the PS (Socialist Party) into government headed by Dr Antonio Guterres a Christian Socialist and 'moderniser' in the mould of Tony Blair. For many years he enjoyed high popularity at home and international respect. He even adopted the British Prime Minister's law and order prescription 'Tough on crime, tough on the causes of crime'. The Guterres government combined higher public spending in some areas (like education) with rigorous fiscal and economic policies which favour deregulation and privatisation.

After winning a large re-election victory in 1999, the Guterras government gradually lost its popularity. Despite overcoming economic problems to bring Portugal into the Euro, in December 2001 Dr Guterres resigned. A heavy defeat for his party in local elections aggravated a perception of drift and errors. Seventy people had earlier lost their lives when a bridge over the River Douro in northern Portugal collapsed, reinforcing a belief that the government had failed to address the country's declining infrastructure. Following national elections in March 2002, Portugal's new government reflected a move to the right when the centre-right Social Democrats, led by Durão Barroso formed a coalition with the smaller conservative Popular party. However, in June 2004, Durão Barroso resigned in order to preside over the European Commission in Brussels and the political crisis that ensued led to Lisbon's mayor, Pedro Santana Lopes succeeding as Premier: a government that was to last just seven months.

The Current Government and the Future

In February 2005 the general election, called more than a year earlier than necessary, decisively installed Portugal's fourth government in three years. President Jorge Sampaio called the election just four months after the centre-right government had taken office, and stated in his address to the nation that the country was in crisis and that he had lost faith in the centre-right coalition government.

Certainly the coalition had become incredibly unpopular due to constant internal squabbles and the fact that Lopes had never managed to convince voters that he was the man to reinvigorate Portugal's ailing economy. Hence, the Portuguese, echoing the President's fears, gave an absolute majority to one party for the first time in a decade. An unexpectedly high turnout of voters, around 67%, gave the Socialist Party, led by Prime Minister José Sócrates, 120 of the 230 seats in parliament, suggesting that not only had they lost faith in the previous government but also that they wanted a clear socialist majority in power to try and pull the country out of the economic mire. Although Sócrates will have his work cut out for him, Portugal finally has a government with the parliamentary means to take decisive action.

The huge public vote of confidence obtained at the election has placed an enormous amount of responsibility on the shoulders of the socialist government.

The electorate will demand a very clear programme of action, with concrete objectives and Sócrates is now charged with, as a bare minimum, putting into practice his core election promises such as raising to three per cent Portugal's meagre growth rate (now around 1%), reducing public expenditure, and creating jobs. Portugal has for many years been accustomrd to a very low rate of unemployment. However, following the failure of a low-salary, unskilled labour economic model, this figure has crept above seven per cent.

The previous governing coalition had attempted to deal with the problem of enormous public expenditure by imposing wage freezes on public sector workers and other real cuts. However, this simply enraged the voting public and had little significant impact. Economists have warned that the new government may have to take similarly unpopular measures in order to get the economy back on track. However, Sócrates promises to draw Portugal out of its deep economic crisis by doubling state investment in research and development (in line with that of Spain), a strategy he calls the technological shock plan.

Other proposed measures include an attempt to instill public faith in the functioning of the institutions. The public administration is considered to be bloated and inefficient and the new government promises to eliminate 75,000 jobs over four years. This move does not really tally with his concurrent promise to recover the 150,000 jobs lost under the outgoing government.

Other headline-grabbing election promises include a one-off payment to the 300,000 pensioners below the poverty line, and a programme to place young managers in business. However, the new government has been conspicuously vague about how it intends to put any of these policies into practice. It remains to be seen whether the Socialist Party government, with its popular mandate, and a parliamentary majority will be able to deliver the eagerly anticipated results it has promised the nation.

GEOGRAPHICAL INFORMATION

Mainland and Offshore Portugal

Portugal occupies the southwestern extremity of Europe and covers an area of 34,340 sq miles/88,941 sq kms or approximately 15% of the Iberian Peninsular. Around the the west and south of Portugal stretches 500 miles/804 kms of Atlantic coastline, while in the north and east is the border with Spain. The Minho river, which rises in the Spanish province of Galicia and flows across Portugal to the sea, forms the northern boundary. The other great Portuguese rivers are the Douro, which forms part of the eastern Spanish border and flows through the port wine region on its westward course to Porto, and the Tejo river which cuts Portugal in half and effectively divides the more mountainous north from the plains of the south.

The Tejo river flows into the Atlantic at Lisbon. The plains are again interrupted in the south by the Monchique and Caldèirão Mountains which provide the backdrop for the Algarve.

Madeira, made up of two inhabited islands Madeira and Porto Santo, and two groups of uninhabited islands – all of volcanic origin – lies west of Morocco and 535 miles/861 kms southwest of Lisbon. The total land area of the Madeira Islands is 307 sq miles/796 sq kms. The island of Madeira itself is steep, rising at its highest point to a height of 6106 feet/1861 metres.

The Azores, located about 900 miles/1,448 kms due west of Portugal, comprise nine islands also of volcanic origin (last eruption on Faial 1973), and are divided into three groups, with a total area of 902 sq miles/2,335 square kms. The central group of islands consist of Terceira, Graciosa, São Jorge, Pico and Faial. To the east of these lie São Miguel and Santa Maria; and to the west Corvo and Flores. The largest is São Miguel and the smallest, Corvo is only ten miles square.

Regional Divisions and Main Towns
Portugal is composed of eleven provinces. North to south these are:

MINHO – Braga
TRÁS-OS-MONTES – Braganca, Vila Real
DOURO LITORAL – Porto
BEIRA ALTA – Viseu, Guarda
BEIRA LITORAL – Aveiro, Coimbra, Leiria
BEIRA BAIXA – Castelo Branco
ESTRAMADURA – Lisbon, Sétubal
RIBATEJO – Santarém
ALTO ALENTEJO – Portalegre, Evora
BAIXO ALENTEJO – Beja
ALGARVE – Faro

Population
The current population of Portugal is approximately 10.5 million with an annual growth rate of about 0.4%. The average density of inhabitants is around 275 per sq mile; in some areas it is as low as 60. The most densely populated regions are unsurprisingly Estramadura, Douro and Minho, since they embrace the main industrial and business centres: Lisbon, Sétubal and Porto. Lisbon, the capital, has a population of approximately 3.3 million. The north is more populated than the south, the Algarve being one of the least inhabited regions with an indigenous populace (excluding expatriates) of around 350,000.

It is said that the Portuguese north and south of the Rio Tejo are of different ethnic origins: the people of the north are descended from Celtic and Germanic tribes, while the southerners are known as *moreno* (dark skinned) not because of the hotter climate, but as a legacy of their Roman and Moorish antecedents (the south being the area most resolutely occupied by these respective invaders).

During the 1960s and early seventies, when the colonial wars were in process, it is estimated that over a million Portuguese left the country, most of them illegally, to escape army conscription. Many of them made new lives in North America and Venezuela. The departure of such a large number of able-bodied workers contributed to the decline of Portuguese agriculture by aggravating the depopulation of the countryside. Today it is estimated that over four million Portuguese are emigrants, spread throughout Western Europe, Brazil, Australia and South Africa. There are approximately 100,000 Portuguese citizens of black African descent who emigrated to the mainland after the Portuguese colonies gained independence.

Climatic Zones

Portugal is well-known for its mild climate, which is of the Mediterranean-type on the southern coasts, and is influenced by the Atlantic and the Gulf Stream on the northern ones. The littorals, whether south (the Algarve), or west (Costa Prata and Costa Verde) have similar summer temperatures, which rarely exceed the low 70s Fahrenheit (22°C). However there is a considerable difference in the amount of rainfall between north and south, the latter having a dry Mediterranean climate all year round. Winters become progressively cooler and wetter towards the north.

Greater extremes of temperature are found inland: in the mountains of the northeast, the regions of the Trás-os-Montes and Beira Alta are either blitzed by cold or hammered by sun depending on the season. In the south the temperatures of the plains (roughly the area south of the inland town of Évora) are also ranged at opposite ends of the temperature scale, depending on the season.

In the far south there is a noticeable difference in climate between the most westerly and the eastern part of the Algarve coast. Cape St Vincent, which juts into the Atlantic, understandably takes the brunt of the winter gales. The fact that from Lagos eastwards is package-tourist-land is indicative of the fact that this is the balmiest climatic zone with Mediterranean warmth and dryness.

Madeira and the Azores, which the Portuguese refer to rather inappropriately as the *Adjacente* (Adjacent Isles), have their own exotic climates. Madeira is subtropical, which means it is has a pleasant climate year through. It also claims an average of 2,000 hours of sunshine annually. The rainy season is from October to March and the misty season (*capacete*) lasts through most of August. Dry winds from Africa (*leste*) intermittently deposit a small part of the Sahara on Madeira. The pleasures of the Madeiran climate however vastly outweigh the minor irritations of the capacete, leste and the odd tropical cloudburst.

The Azores have a surprisingly mild climate considering their location. Their position on the map is vaguely unexpected: isolated in the Atlantic they are reminiscent of a convoy which dropped anchor on the way to America, and decided to stay put. Temperatures in this exposed archipelago are mild in summer and rarely go below 58°F/14°C in winter.

TEMPERATURE CHART								
Area		Jan/Mar		Apr/June		July/Sept		Oct/Dec
		Air	Sea	Air	Sea	Air	Sea	Air	Sea
Monte Estoril	°C	17°	15°	22°	17°	26°	19°	17°	16°
(Lisbon Coast)	°F	63°	59°	71°	63°	79°	67°	63°	60°
Quarteira	°C	17°	16°	22°	19°	27°	23°	18°	17°
(Algarve)	°F	63°	61°	72°	67°	81°	73°	64°	63°
Santa Maria	°C	17°	17°	20°	19°	24°	22°	919°	20°
(Azores)	°F	63°	63°	67°	66°	75°	72°	67°	69°
Funchal	°C	19°	9°	22°	20°	25°	23°	21°	21°
(Madeira)	°F	67°	65°	71°	68°	77°	73°	70°	70°

REGIONAL GUIDE

A sked to perform a word association exercise, the chances are that the average Briton will say Algarve, (or possibly sardines), as a response to 'Portugal' (with port wine a close third). The Algarve is undoubtedly the spot that most foreign would-be residents would choose to buy a home, attracted by the mild climate and the relatively good facilities and infrastructure that have already grown up around the expatriate communities. It is also likely to be the most obvious place for jobseekers to pick up temporary work related to the tourist industry. Summer tourism monopolises large chunks of the coast from Lagos to Faro. The western and eastern extremities are, however, surprisingly empty.

Other expatriates, perhaps wishing to escape the intrusion of holiday-makers into their idyll, have made their homes in and around Lisbon. The Estoril coast north of Lisbon, and the Lisbon coast south of the city, both have their champions (the peripatetic Lord Byron among them) who rate the combination of a superb climate and the attractions of the capital as unbeatable. Byron put it more picturesquely, and added that one cannot expect comfort to be always attendant on pleasure. Perhaps, however, in modern Portugal, it is possible to attain both simultaneously.

Other foreign residents, in particular business people of various types, not just those in the port wine trade, have made their homes in Porto. Porto is probably the only city in Portugal where one is likely to encounter the frenetic atmosphere characteristic of big business centres everywhere. The commercial life of Porto has received a boost since Portugal joined the single currency. Thus the remaining trade and employment restrictions with the rest of the EU are ended.

Beyond the main tourist and urban areas, Portugal offers remarkable scenic variety. If the character of the Portuguese has been shaped by the sea, then its landscape must have been moulded by rivers, a multitude of which crisscross the length of the land. The result of such a watery abundance, is a pastoral landscape of great beauty and variety. This ranges, northwards, from lush vine-covered valleys, vast pine forests and fields of corn and root crops, to the baked plain of the south, where citrus groves, cork forests and fig plantations give a more Mediterranean aspect to the scenery.

Some adventurous foreign residents have bought properties at knockdown prices in the remoter regions of Portugal. For reasons best known to themselves they are prepared to live without mod cons, including plumbing and mains electricity, in what has been called, without exaggeration, the 'third world of Europe'. Nowhere, in western Europe at least, do such extremes of poverty and relative prosperity exist side by side. For this kind of existence not only is a Byronic attitude to comfort essential; a pioneering streak and an ability to mix with locals will help.

This regional guide is not intended to give an idea of the employment prospects of each region. This topic is covered, region by region, in the *Employment* chapter.

Information Facilities

Basic information on Portugal can be obtained from the Portuguese Tourist Office in your own country. In London this is 22-25a Sackville Street (2nd Floor), London W1X 1DE; ☎020-7494 1441; fax 020-7494 1868; www.portugal.org). This is also the head office of ICEP (Investment Trade and Tourism of Portugal), an unusual organisation, which combines the functions of promoting trade, tourism and investment in the country. The Tourist Office provides fact sheets and leaflets on the different regions (as well trade and commercial information). The head office of ICEP/Turismo in Lisbon can be found on Avenida 5 de Outubro, 101, 1050-051 Lisbon (☎217-909500; fax 217-935028; www.portugalinsite.pt). The main Tourist office in Lisbon is in the Palacio Foz on Praca dos Restauradores (☎214-63314). The tourist offices (*Turismo*), located in all the main tourist towns can prove invaluable, once you are in the country.

THE SOUTH

THE ALGARVE
Main city: Faro
Main tourist office: Rua da Misericordia, 8-12 8000 Faro; ☎289-803604.
British Consulate: Largo Francisco A. Maurício 7-1, Portimāo; ☎282-417800.

The Algarve takes its name from the Moorish word *al-gharb* which means west. The famous sandy Algarve coast is a familiar one to tourists and foreign residents alike. At the southwestern point of the Algarve is Cape St Vincent whose illustrious maritime associations include not only Prince Henry the Navigator's fifteenth century school of seamanship, founded at the tiny port of Sagres on the Cape's east side, but also several naval battles including Nelson's daring victory against the Spanish in 1797.

Faro is the administrative centre of the province. The airport, situated four miles/six km from the city centre, operates around the clock during the summer to shuttle sunseekers to the resorts west of Faro including Quarteira, Albufeira, Carvoeri and Praia da Rocha. East of Faro, the coast with its offshore sandbanks has remained, a fairly quiet place where sheep graze and fishermen and farmers still make a modest living, though this is changing as this part of the Algarve becomes developed.

The tourists tend to home in on the ancient town of Tavira, which, with its castle, Roman bridge and dozens of churches, is one of the region's picture-postcard sights. So attractive is the town that a couple of smart housing developments have materialised in the vicinity. These developments apart, property prices drop dramatically once you are in the eastern Algarve. Another picturesque inland town is Silves, once the hilltop capital of the Moors, and with an impregnable-looking fortress at the summit. Both the castle and the thirteenth-century cathedral, built on the site of a former mosque, survived the terrible earthquake of 1755 which caused widespread devastation. It is possible to rent apartments in Silves, a useful base to prospect the region away from the hubbub of the coast. Further inland from Silves is the beautiful mountainous area of Serra de Monchique based around the spa town of Caldas de Monchique.

The Algarve has a total area of 5,500 sq. km and a population of approximately 400,000 permanent inhabitants rising to over a million people at the height of the summer. There are good roads throughout the Algarve and a single track railway line running from Lagos to Vila Real do Santo António that also links to the line running to Lisbon and the north. The old main road, the EN125, runs along the length of the coast and a new motorway, the Via do Infante, now runs parallel linking Lagos in the west with the Spanish border in the east (about an hour's drive time). This road also links with the motorway to Lisbon near Albufeira.

The Algarve has around 100 sandy beaches washed by the Atlantic, which, due to the maritime shelf and water currents, remains surprisingly warm even during the winter. Away from the immediate coastal plain are the foothills leading up to the highest point Foia (902 metres) above the village of Monchique. Central Algarve is at the heart of the explosion in property development in Quinta do Lago, Vilamoura and Vale do Lobo. This part of the Algarve is home to the majority of expats who have settled on the coast.

PROPERTY HOTSPOTS

Lagos (Western Algarve). Lagos in an important tourist town these days and with the development of this western side of the Algarve property prices have been rising. However, there are still many architectural signs of the town's ancient past, including a building dating back to around 1445 believed to be Europe's first slave-market. Much of the walled town remains intact and a recently erected statue commemorates the Algarve's only Saint, São Gonçalo de Lagos, who was born in 1360 and died in 1422 in Torres Vedras and canonised by Pope Pio VI in 1778. Lagos' new marina has helped change the Lagos of old and the municipal council has constructed a modern Cultural Centre in which various exhibitions and culturally related events are held during the year. In the Marina different boat tours and deep sea-fishing outings can be booked.

There is an enormous demand for property in Lagos and as it is a coastal resort complete with attractive beaches and dramatic coastline, property is fairly expensive. A two-bedroom house costs an average of €206,000, while a two-bedroom apartment can be found for around €129,000 (cheaper than other western Algarve resorts). However, there is a strong market for holiday rentals here and the resort is busy all year round.

Vilamoura (Central Algarve). Vilamoura is an area rather than an actual town. It is one of the largest single tourist complexes in Europe and covers some 2,000 hectares of land. The landscaped countryside here is varied – there are areas covered in pine forests, other stretches have been left as open marshland. The company owning the complex is environmentally conscious and every effort is being made to protect nature within Vilamoura's continued planned development. Due to the size of the resort area, Vilamoura offers many forms of sport and entertainment, and in addition, on the southern border is a long sandy beach. Amongst the many attractions and facilities are four different golf courses, a large marina, a lawn bowling club, a tennis club, a sports club, a shooting club, five-star hotels, tourist apartments, self-catering villas, nightclubs, an international casino, a cinema, and a riding school. As a location specifically designed for tourism Vilamoura has proved very successful and property nearby is sought after. Those with buy to let intentions should certainly investigate Vilamoura as it offers year round rental potential due to the tourist activity generated by the marina and the golf courses. New-build two-bedroom apartments with garden and communal pool start at around €220,000.

Tavira (Eastern Algarve). Tavira is a lovely old town situated on either side of the river Gilão; its two halves connected by a seven-arched Roman bridge. A small, medieval castle on a low hill presides over the centre of the town and next to the castle is the Church of Santa Maria do Castelo containing the tomb of Tavira's liberator, Dom Paio Peres Correia, during the Christian reconquest of the 13th century. Just offshore, easily reached by boat, is a long sandy island – Ilha de Tavira – great for kids. Tavira has 37 churches and many fine 18th century buildings. Grapes are grown in the surrounding vineyards and salt is produced from seawater in nearby pans.

Tavira's original economic reliance on the fishing industry has now faded due to the change in the migration patterns of the tuna fish which bought wealth to the town. The surrounding area is still very rural and undeveloped though this is changing due to the demands of the tourist industry and the opening of golf courses close by. Close to Tavira are the small beachfront villages of Cabanas and Pedras del Rey, while Santa Luzia is a very small unspoilt village with a castle.

Property on the eastern Algarve is still relatively inexpensive. A two-bedroom property here costs an average of €160,000 and with demand rising, this is an excellent place to invest.

BAIXHO ALENTEJO & ALTO ALENTEJO (THE PLAINS)
Main towns: Beja, Evora, Portalegre.

These two provinces, lower and upper Alentejo respectively, account for over 25% of the total surface area of Portugal. Sparsely populated and mainly agricultural, most of the region is a vast tableland, stretching south of Evora to the borders of the Algarve. Lower Alentejo is the less scenic of the two provinces, offering virtually no visual variant from sun-baked wheat fields. The coast of Baixho Alentejo gets pummelled by the Atlantic (unlike the more tranquil Algarve coast) and has the beginnings of tourism and the southern part of the province, between Sines and Cape St Vincente, is likely to become a modest tourist centre of the future.

The northern half of Baixho Alentejo, from just below the industrial port of Sétubal, is virtually deserted and is likely to remain so now that a giant oil terminal has been built at Sines. The one bright spot in this otherwise bleak province is the hilltop city of Beja, a UNESCO-designated area of special cultural interest, which has become something of a tourist honey pot. Founded by Julius Caesar as a resting place for pensioned-off legionnaires, Beja was later occupied by the Moorish invaders. In the thirteenth century a castle was built by Dom (King) Dinis directly over the Roman site. Beja's Convent of the Immaculate Conception is renowned in Portugal for the seventeenth-century nun, Mariana Alcoferado, whose rather scandalous letters to the Chevalier de Camily, who daily passed her window at the convent, caused some controversy when they were published in translation in Paris in 1669.

The province of Alto Alentejo is scenically more rewarding than it neighbour and has vestiges of Roman architecture and fortified towns such as Elvas and Estremoz – the latter is known as the 'marble town', the source of its prosperity extracted from nearby quarries. Alto Alentejo is also full of prehistoric sites, including standing stones and stone circles. Évora is the main town, formerly invaded by Moors and now by tourists. Évora's population of 40,000 is double that of Beja. The other main town of Alto Alentejo is Portalegre, a town set amongst rolling countryside and which is famous for its old tapestry factory, and it is said that 5,000 shades of wool are used in the reproduction of centuries' old designs.

PROPERTY HOTSPOT

Vila Nova de Milfontes. One of the most popular destinations in Alentejo, largely due to its stunning beaches and relative proximity to the Algarve. The town, whose name translates as 'new town of 1000 springs', lies on the estuary of the Rio Mira and has stunning beaches on both sides of the estuary. Ferries operate between the two banks. Despite the sprawling new developments that have sprung up in the area, this is still a relatively tranquil area retaining its traditional charm. However, the town can become overcrowded during high season.

The resort is considered by estate agents to be an up-and-coming area with the foreign market – as yet there is no real expatriate community as the majority of buyers has traditionally been wealthy Portuguese from the north. It is possible to find a one-bedroom apartment for as little as €100,000.

The Alentejo area is often thought of as the bread basket of Portugal, with its wide open countryside, plains and low hills and its rich fertile soil. With few exceptions, all the major towns are mainly reliant on agriculture, livestock and wood and exploring this area is a pleasure with its storks nesting on top of telegraph poles and pylons and chimneys and the smell of pine and eucalyptus. Topographically the countryside varies considerably, from the open rolling plains of the south to the granite hills bordering Spain in the northeast. To the east of Portalegre the beautiful Nature Park Area – the Parque Natural da Serra de São Mamede – includes medieval villages that have changed, architecturally, very little over the centuries. In the south, near Mértola is another Nature Park – the Parque Natural do Vale Guadiana – which is pretty much uninhabited. To the west, the coastal strip running from the port of Sines down to Cape de São Vicente is also a reserved area.

The Alentejo region has until recently been overlooked by property buyers, who have mainly sought property along the coast further south. This is (perhaps unfortunately) changing and prices are rising in the Alentejo. Expats are buying and renovating properties here, above all in the southern and eastern reaches of the region where they can have fast access to the west and southern coasts in addition to the shopping centres of the more well trodden areas in the Algarve.

RIBATEJO
Main town: Santarém

On the northwest edge of the plains region Ribatejo, meaning beside the Tagus, is a fertile province where large estates produce figs, olives and citrus fruits in great abundance. Another agricultural speciality is rice which is grown in specially flooded meadows along the banks of the River Tagus. Ribatejo is also cattle country, where you can see the Portuguese cowboys (*campinos*) wearing traditional dress and carrying lances. Their charges are the grazing bulls and horses, as yet blissfully unaware of their fate in the bullrings of Portugal. The Portuguese version of this sport does not match the barbarity of its Spanish counterpart: in deference to the sensibilities of a former royal patron who saw his son gored to death before his eyes, the bulls are not killed in the bullring, but outside afterwards.

The capital of the province is Santarém, which was one of the the six great Moorish strongholds of Portugal. Set high above the Tagus river, it makes an impressive sight from the surrounding countryside. The best view from the city itself is from the Moorish tower, the Portas do Sol. Throughout the fourteenth and fifteenth centuries it was the meeting place of the royal parliaments. Nowadays, perhaps the most famous meeting is the two-week fair which starts on the fourth Sunday in May.

ESTREMADURA
Main towns: Lisbon, Setúbal.
Main tourist office: Palacio Foz, Praça dos Restauradores, Lisbon; ☎213-463658
British Embassy: Rua de São Bernardo 33, 1249-082 Lisbon; ☎213-924000; www.uk-embassy.pt.

The narrow coastal province of Estremadura encompasses the southern part of the Costa de Prata in the north, and the estuary of the River Sado in the south. Wine production and the growing of fruit and vegetables are of importance to the region. The province has attracted a large expatriate community, in part due to the excellent coastline around Lisbon to the south and the Estoril coast to the north, and of course also to the bright lights of Lisbon itself. There are two nature reserves near Lisbon: the Reserva Natural do Estuário do Tejo and the Reserva Natural do Estuário do Sado.

PROPERTY HOTSPOTS

Sintra. Singled out for praise by Lord Byron amongst others, Sintra has many buildings of architectural merit, and is dominated by the two conical chimneys of the *Palácio Nacional da Vila* with its backdrop of beautiful sub-tropical vegetation – the summer residence of the royal family since the 15th century. Sintra has a microclimate, temperatures range from 4°C to 30°C (the average is 18°C) caused by the cold sea current and the forested Serra di Sintra. Cold air from the sea hits the trees and causes the *Bafo da Duquesa* (literally, the Duchess's fart) – low clouds to form over the area. At night this causes a tropical climate, by day a humid southern Atlantic climate. Sintra is a UNESCO World Heritage Site and has many historic, architecturally interesting buildings and gardens. There is also a restored tram connecting the town and the beach resort of Praia da Maças, and the craggily perched coastal village of Azenhas de Mar. To the west of Sintra is the village of Colares, famous for its white wine. To the north is the imposing Monastery at Mafra.

This area is extremely popular with property buyers, due to that fact that it is less than 30km from Lisbon, yet remains relatively unspoilt. A two-bedroom apartment here can be bought for around €116,000. At the top end of the market, luxury villas in Sintra are highly sought after and prices start at €725,000.

Cascais. Cascais, once a small fishing port, is located at the mouth of the Rio Tejo and became a very fashionable area when King Luís I started using the 17th century Citadela as his summer residence in the 1870s. The wealthier Portuguese started building the palaces and mansions that still exist today and with the electrification of the Lisbon-Cascais railway line in 1926 the small fishing port grew in size and prestige. During World War II exiled royalty and heads of state sought refuge in Cascais, and in nearby Estoril, and between 1939 and 1946 the population of the area increased by some 20,000. Today Cascais is seen as a sophisticated place and home to a wealthy Lisbon and international set and a stylish summer resort with numerous restaurants, bars and nightclubs. Cascais boasts a smart new marina and the Parque Palmela, created by the Duques de Palmela, where open-air concerts are often held. Nearby is the windswept Guincho beach, where surfers and windsurfers congregate. The capital Lisbon, Estoril with its casino, and Sintra, are within easy reach of Cascais.

The most popular properties for sale in Cascais are villas and apartments close to the beach and the golf course. Luxury villas can cost upwards of €1 million. However, it is possible to find a two-bedroom apartment for around €180,000.

Lisbon has been a thriving port since Roman times; its importance grew under the Moors who called the city *Lishbuna*, and again during the time of the great Portuguese colonial expansion of the late fifteenth and sixteenth centuries. Largely destroyed by the earthquake of 1755, the city was rebuilt on a grid pattern in less than ten years, under the frenetic direction of the Marquess of Pombal. Some quarters of the city survived the earthquake, most notably Belém and Alfama. In more modern times Lisbon has acquired a huddle of run-down suburbs, as housing became a major problem when ex-colonials flooded back home following the liberation of Portugal's African colonies after the 1974 Portuguese Revolution. A cosmopolitan and lively place, Lisbon is built on a series of hills, most of which can be negotiated by ancient wooden trams – one of the city's hallmarks. The *Alfama* is the old Moorish quarter of the city. The towns and villages around Lisbon are another highlight of this region:

Three-bedroom apartments with shared pools on the Praia D'El Rey Golf and Country Club on the Atlantic coast north of Lisbon start from €190,000; plots cost from €140,000; a three-bedroom villa with pool will set you back around €205,000. A typical modern golf resort, the Club consists of a new course surrounded by new build homes. This area is not the hottest part of the country, and winters can be cool and wet.

THE NORTH

BEIRA LITORAL
Main towns: Leira, Coimbra, Aveiro.
Main tourist office: Largo da Portagem, P-3000 Coimbra; ☎ 239-855 930.

The coast of Beira Litoral is a continuation of the Costa de Prata, which is untroubled by tourism except for a few minor resorts; and therein lies its charm. The outstanding centre of the province – the ancient, cobble-stoned city of Coimbra, the former capital of Portugal in the twelfth and thirteenth centuries – is inland. Piled high above the right bank of the Mondego river, its crowning glory is the tower of the historic university, one of the oldest in Europe and referred to in the tourist literature as 'the Oxford of Portugal'. The university was founded in 1290 and one of its major later additions is a magnificent Baroque library containing well over a million volumes. There is no doubt that Coimbra would be a delightful place to live, with its atmosphere of scholarly traditions and reputation for poetry and music. Elsewhere in the province, local industry was traditionally seaweed harvesting and sea salt production, in and around the port of Aveiro. Inland, the region is economically mainly reliant on small and medium size industries and, importantly, the production of wine.

North of Lisbon the Costa de Prata consists of long stretches of sandy beaches exposed to the Atlantic Ocean surf. Due to its location, north of Lisbon, the tourist season doesn't last as long as that further south due to the wetter and colder climate. With a fast motorway connecting Lisbon and Coimbra, the area is likely to develop faster than it has been doing. Coimbra lies midway between Lisbon and Porto.

PROPERTY HOTSPOT

Aveiro. Aveiro was once a great seaport until the mouth of the river silted up, closed the harbour and created a shallow lagoon. Today the area is a centre for industry but Aveiro has its charms with its canals and Art Nouveau mansions and the *barcos moliceiros* – the boats used to collect seaweed from the lagoon to fertilize the surrounding land. The houses lining the beach have distinct colourful facades, painted in various hues. This is a good location for those who dream of finding a property to renovate. A two-bedroom apartment in the area costs around €115,000.

BEIRA BAIXA
Main town: Castelo Branco

The parched landscape of the plain of Beira Baixa is on the whole as unproductive as it looks, though it manages to produce a modicum of cork and fruits; you can drive for miles through this rolling and sometimes mountainous landscape without seeing another car or person, before reaching the whitewashed walls of the next sleepy village. The main town of Castelo Branco has a population of 15,000 souls. The neglected remains of its castle are a reminder of its frontier town origins. From Castelo Branco it is possible to visit mountain villages barely touched by modernity, including Monsanto and Idanha-a-Velha. The latter was once an important Roman town, parts of which have not greatly changed from that time: the walls are still standing; the Roman bridge is still viable and the more durable vestiges of daily Roman life, including inscribed and sculpted marble, are just lying casually about the place.

BEIRA ALTA
Main towns: Viseu, Guarda.

The province of Beira Alta embraces the wooded and largely unfertile valleys of the lower Douro in the north, and a stretch of the granite mountains (the highest in Portugal) of the Sierra da Estrela in the south. Viseu, which from its high plateau dominates the surrounding landscape, was once the heart of Roman Lusitania. The remains of the Roman garrison camp, built at a crossroads, are still visible on the outskirts of the medieval city. Viriatus, the Iberian rebel, and symbol of Lusitanian independence, supposedly made his last stand against the Romans at Viseu. The other main town of the region, the aptly named Guarda, is pitched high in the north east of the Estrela mountains at 3,400 feet/1057 metres and commands outstanding views into Spain. As you would expect from its location Guarda was intrinsic to defence against Spanish acquisitiveness.

Largely unexplored, this region is suitable for walkers and those of an adventurous bent.

DOURO LITORAL

Main town: Porto (Oporto)
Main tourist office: Rua Clube Fenianos 25, Porto; ☎ 223-393470.
British Consulate: Avenida da Boavista 3072, P-4100 Porto; ☎ 226-184789; fax 226-100438.

This, the smallest province of Portugal, is also the most bustling and industrial. The valley of the Rio Douro (Golden River), which rises in western Spain and once foamed and frothed its way across northern Portugal, dominates the scenery of the Douro Litoral. Damming has now curbed its wilder excesses, however, it nevertheless remains an impressive sight as it cuts a swathe through a series of spectacular gorges. Between Mesão Frio and Pinhão lies the stretch of the Douro where the valley sides are lined with terraced vineyards that produce the famous Port wine. Atop the northern bank of the final gorge, where the Douro meets the Atlantic, is piled Portugal's second largest conurbation, Oporto (Porto to the Portuguese), with its population of over 400,000.

Prosperity here has agricultural and trading origins and dates back to the beginnings of the port wine trade. In the eighteenth century, the king's minister, the all-powerful Marquis of Pombal, strictly delineated the zone in which the grapes for port wine could be grown. In effect, this became a strip varying in width from ten to thirty miles either side of the Douro. As with all wines of character, it is the fortuitous combination of soil qualities, climate, grape, and centuries of expertise, which produce the unique and much-prized end result. Casks of port are transported from the valley to Vila Nova de Gaia, the port wine-dealing suburb of Porto, on the opposite side of the Douro from the main city. Surprisingly the British have dropped to second place, after the French, in the league table of port tipplers, while American demand is growing at the luxury end of the market. Porto was also the birthplace of Henry the Navigator, has an international airport, and has all the charms of a large, old, faded, riverside community. Property in the city is more expensive than anywhere in the northern region, due to the city being a hub of business and educational institutions. A two-bedroom town-house will set you back around €255,000.

In tourist office parlance, the coast of Douro Litoral is also the southern half of the Costa Verde (Green Coast). North of Porto is Póvoa de Varzim, an elegant sea resort where traditional industries such as fisheries and silversmiths co-exist with tourism. There are also natural spas in this area, as well as beaches and a native pine forest stretching along the coast. The Costa Verde stretches north from Porto to the Spanish border and is an area with a large, young population. A coast road runs north past beautiful beaches and summer resorts such as Caminha and Vila Nova de Cerveira from Porto to Valença do Minho on the Spanish border. Inland and to the north, there is the huge national park area covering the mountains of Peneda, Soajo and Gerês.

MINHO
Main town: Braga
Main tourist office: Corner of Praça da República/Avenida da Liberdade; ☎253-262550.

There are few tourists in Minho and the province is the place to go for those who appreciate more remote places. It is a province of wooded river valleys, vineyards and wild coastline and Minho has remained isolated and mistrustful of change. In the north of the province the Rio Minho forms a watery frontier with Galicia, in northern Spain.

The main city, Braga, was originally the Roman, Bracera Augusta. Destroyed by the Moors, it rose again from the rubble under the auspices of King Ferdinand of León, who liberated it in 1040. Braga became an important archbishopric and ultimately the religious centre of Portugal and its archbishop's palace and cathedral are of monumental proportions and considerable interest. Outside the city is the Bom Jesus – a highly ornate granite and marble staircase with resting places dedicated to Christ, the five senses, and the virtues, in ascending order. Although a marvellous Baroque concoction, the site has seen no religious miracles, however, this does not prevent the devout from climbing it on their knees.

The province possesses a number of unbelievably romantic-looking towns. Guimarães was the first capital of Portuçale – the land between the Lima and Douro rivers, which was the starting point for the reconquest of the lands occupied by the Moors. Minho's other great attraction is the 70,000-hectare Parc National da Peneda-Gerês, in the northeast of the province. Although popular with campers it is large enough not to seem crowded.

PROPERTY HOTSPOT

Viana do Castelo. Lying at the mouth of the Lima estuary on the Costa Verde, Viana do Castelo has a long relationship with the sea and seafaring. The town gained importance in the 15th century when João Velho, who was to chart the Congo, and João Álvares Fagundes, who charted the rich fishing grounds off Newfoundland, set out from here. The town is a busy fishing port and is the Minho's main resort. In August every year a three-day festival is held in honour of Our Lady of the Sorrows (Nossa Senhora da Agonia), which draws thousands of visitors to the town and the surrounding villages. Up above, and dominating the town, is the Basilica of Santa Luzia, from which you get a fantastic view of the town, the river and the Atlantic Ocean beyond.

A ferry and road bridge across the river link the town to the sweeping sandy beach at Praia Cabedelo that stretches as far south as the holiday resort of Esposende. To the north is the popular holiday resort of Vila Praia de Âncora. Some distance inland, along the River Lima, are the pretty towns of Ponte de Lima and Ponte de Barca.

The Minho Coastline is considered to be a major up-and-coming destination. Property here is still affordable, but demand is on the increase and the area is becoming increasingly popular. Two-bedroom apartments in the area sell for as little as €70,000, whilst a two-bedroom house should cost you no more than €250,000.

TRÁS-OS-MONTES
Main towns: Vila Real, Bragança.

The poorest province in Portugal is the northeastern one of Trás-os-Montes (Behind the Mountains). It has half the number of inhabitants of the Minho, in twice the area, and traditionally people here have had to move abroad or into the cities to find work, send money back to their families and save for their own future. The lower reaches of the province embrace the upper reaches of the Douro, where fertile valleys allow the growing of grapes for the production of port wine. In addition citrus and succulent fruits flourish there. The upper part of the province is a complete contrast; the most inhospitable mountainous terrain and harshest climate of Portugal can be found there. Left more or less to themselves, the inhabitants of the region have evolved their own traditions and dialects and, in harder times, provided a refuge for those fleeing religious persecution. The largest industrial town of the region, Vila Real, is situated amidst the foothills of the Serra do Marão. The building depicted on the wine labels of Mateus Rosé is the Solar de Mateus – situated a couple of miles from Vila Real.

Bragança, the remote, brooding capital of the province, is the royal seat of the family of that name who ruled Portugal from 1640 to 1910. Rising from the splendid medieval citadel set above the new town is a massive keep, the Torre de Menagem, a symbol of the city's impregnability in days gone by. An architectural curiosity within the citadel is the Domus Municipalis, constructed in the shape of an irregular pentagon. Anyone in the citadel on Ash Wednesday will see a sinister, caped figure representing death stalking through the narrow streets. The children of the town throw stones at him as part of this traditional but macabre ritual. The region is a perfect place for mountain trekking, canoeing or taking it easy up in the spa towns of Carvalhelhos, Chaves, and Pedras Salgadas.

OFFSHORE PORTUGAL

MADEIRA
Main town: Funchal
Main tourist office: Avenida Arriaga 18, 9004-519 Funchal; ☎291-211900; www.madeiratourism.org.
British Consulate: Apartado 417EC Zarco, 9001-956 Funchal; ☎291-212860.

Funchal is the main town of the Ilha de Madeira, the largest island of a small archipelago located in the middle of the Atlantic Ocean some 600 km from the coast of Morocco. Ilha de Madeira is 56 km long and about 20 km wide, however due to volcanic peaks that soar up to 1,862 metres in places, and drop sharply into the ocean in others it would take a day to drive around the island. The impressively dramatic beauty of the peaks set against the lush semi-tropical vegetation around its coastline makes Madeira a fascinating place to live.

Although it is certain that the Phoenicians knew of its existence, the 'discovery' of Madeira in 1419 is attributed to Zarco and Vax Teixeira, young adventurers from Prince Henry the Navigator's entourage. Named from the Portuguese word for wood, the main island, steep and uninhabited, was first colonised by emigrants from the Algarve and the inmates of the Lisbon prisons. Sugar cane was the first principle crop grown on the island and by 1514 there were already some 5,000 permanent inhabitants living in Madeira. After losing control of the islands to both the French and the Spanish, it was repossessed by the Portuguese in 1662. By the 1890s the island was attracting tourists to its verdant shores and Madeira has remained a very popular destination. Over the centuries the painstaking construction of hillside terraces has helped to make the island richly productive in grapes for the famous Madeira wine, sugar and fruits, especially bananas.

The island's airport is at Santa Cruz, 12miles/19km from the capital, Funchal. Nearly half the island's inhabitants live in and around Funchal – a sheltered town that has long been a discreetly elegant resort, probably best epitomised by the world-renowned Reid's Hotel, which stands amidst twelve acres of glorious gardens. A large number of swimming pools on the island compensates for the fact that steep-sided Madeira has no sandy beaches, however, a two-hour journey by boat or a fifteen minute journey by air will take you to the island of Porto Santo 25 miles away, which possesses the beaches that the main island of Madeira lacks. Two groups of uninhabited islands: the Desertas and the Selvagens (nature reserves) can also be reached by boat. Madeira lies 621 miles southwest of Lisbon and has an exceptional climate (between 16°C and 25°C/61°F and 76°F). Although the internal combustion engine has long reached Madeira, there are other, quieter varieties of local transport, including ox-carts.

The international airport on the main island provides a fairly easy and regular connection with the continent. The assortment of plants and tropical fruits, mild temperature of the surrounding ocean, the cultural heritage, luxurious hotels and Funchal's cosmopolitan life (not forgetting the wine) could make this a great place to live in. However, space on an island is limited and prices are not the cheapest to be found in Portugal.

THE AZORES (AÇORES)

Main tourist office: Rua Ernesto Rebelo 14, 9900-112 Horta, Azores; ☎292-200500; www.drtacores.pt.
British Consulate: Rua Domingos Rebelo, 43A, 9500-234 Ponta Delgada, S. Miguel, Azores; ☎296-628175.

Unfortunately, the charming notion that the Azores may be the vestiges of the lost city of Atlantis is highly improbable as this mid-Atlantic archipelago of nine islands was formed gradually by seething volcanoes.

The Azores lie about 900 miles from the coast of Portugal, far out in the Atlantic Ocean and cover an area of about 900 sq. km. Although perhaps too far away for most of us to consider buying a second home there, they could be a charming place to retire. The first of the islands to be discovered was Santa Maria, which was given the name 'Azores' after the Portuguese word for 'goshawks' in the first half of the 15th century. The islands of Flores and Corvo were discovered by Diego do Teive, which is the name applied to the archipelago of nine islands (Santa Maria, São Miguel, Faial, Graciosa, Ilha do Pico, São Jorge, Terceira, Ilha do Corvo and Ilha das Flores).

During the 15th and 16th centuries settlers from both Portugal and Flanders began to cultivate crops and rear cattle on the islands. During Phillip II of Spain's reign of Portugal (1580-1640), the Azores prospered and the ports of Angra do Heroísmo on Terceira, and Ponta Delgada on São Miguel developed into important centres of trade. In the early 19th century the Azores also became an important staging post for whalers. The Azores are beginning to be visited by tour operators and holiday-makers and have always been popular with the sailing fraternity.

The islands' estimated 240,000 inhabitants include a large proportion of fair-haired, blue-eyed Azoreans descended from the Flemish Knights of Tomar (in mainland Portugal). A traditional stopping-off point for transatlantic sea traffic, the Azores are not the easiest chunks of land to get to though there are frequent two-hour flights from Lisbon to the three Azorean airports at Ponta Delgada (São Miguel), Lajes (Terceira) and Horta (Faial). Ponta Delgada is also served by regular flights to Funchal (Madeira) and, during the peak season, to Porto and Frankfurt. Charter flights fly between North America and the Azores. Inter-island air services are run by SATA (*Servicio Açoreano de Transportes Aeros*); there are also regular inter-island ferry services. Corvo, the only island without an airstrip, can be reached by helicopter.

The Azores are volcanic and there have been fairly constant eruptions, either on the land or from the bed of the sea, throughout the islands' known history. In the 20th century the islands played a strategic role as a military air base between the USA and the rest of the world. The islands lie on the same latitude as Lisbon and are an integral part of Portugal and so are part of the EU. With sapphire blue and emerald lakes, fertile prairies, volcanic cones and craters, medieval churches and manor houses, the Azores enjoy year-round mild temperatures (between 14°C and 22°C) and could be the place to buy if you are looking to get away from it all, completely and utterly. Living on the islands may be an option for the truly self-sufficient who have discovered the unspoilt scenery and sub-tropical climate. Prices in the Azores are very affordable – a two bedroom house can be found for as little as €100,000.

USEFUL WEBSITES

o **www.portugal.com:** provides travel resources and booking for visitors to Portugal and the islands.

o **www.portugal.org:** a comprehensive guide to Portugal published by ICEP, the national tourist and investment agency.

o **www.portugal-live.net:** accommodation, culture, gastronomy, shopping, sport and travellers' tips.

o **www.portugal-info.net:** Who? What? Where and When? in Portugal – from jobs and property to food and films.

o **www.portugalvirtual.pt:** A directory of contacts.

o **www.alltravelportugal.com:** The European Travel and Tourism Bureau's site.

o **www.portugalinsite.pt:** Portugal's official tourism website.

GETTING TO PORTUGAL FROM THE UK AND IRELAND

By Air

Mainland Portugal currently has only three international airports – Lisbon, Porto and Faro. However, there are plans for a further international airport at Ota. It is predicted that there will be an enormous increase in the number of visitors to the country in the next few years, so the Portuguese government aims to constantly improve and expand the country's airport infrastructure. In 2005 work on Lisbon's Portela airport is due to begin. The aim is to increase the airport's capacity by 2008. The islands are served by Funchal Airport (Madeira) and Ponta Delgada Airport on the island of São Miguel (Azores).

From the UK, it takes less than three hours to get to the three mainland airports. Faro airport tends to be the most popular as it serves the Algarve, where the majority of expatriates and second-home owners are based. Madiera takes around 3 hours and 40 minutes from the UK. Getting to the Azores is more complicated and currently involves changing in Lisbon. Flying time from Europe to the Azores is over four hours. However, the Portuguese airline *SATA Internacional* has plans to launch a new April-October service direct from London to the Azores, which will cut travelling time considerably.

The budget airline revolution has had an enormous effect on the cost and ease of getting to Portugal. There have never been so many flights between the UK and Faro, Lisbon and Porto and the number continues to increase. In 2005, *Easyjet* apparently plans to add new services from Newcastle to Faro and from London Stansted to Porto, to its existing routes to Faro. *Ryanair* has also added a new service to Porto; *Jet2* has added a Faro service from Leeds-Bradford; and *Flybe* intends to run a summer service from Exeter and Birmingham to Faro.

Nor has flying to Portugal ever been so cheap. Ryanair was offering return flights to Porto for under £50 for a week in May 2005, and return flights in the height of summer for as little as £65. The main airlines flying to Portugal are currently Ryanair, Easyjet, Jet2, BMIBaby, MyTravelLite, and Monarch Airlines, but the airlines, routes and prices are constantly changing, so it is always best to keep an eye on the travel pages of *The Guardian* and *The Independent*.

There are of course down-sides to the low-cost airlines, such as long check-in times, delays, extortionately priced food and drink on board, inconvenient travel times, and the incomprehensible taxes and charges that are levied at the last minute of booking, making prices higher than the ones that are advertised. There is also a strong tendency for these airlines to fly mainly to Faro, which is of little use if you live in the north of Portugal. Nevertheless, for many people, the availability of such low-cost flights more than makes up for these inconveniences, and because the tariffs are constantly changing, depending on special offers and when you choose to travel, there is an addictive quality to finding the cheapest possible fares online. Prices often change daily and it is generally cheaper to fly midweek, and at unsociable hours. Booking well ahead is also a good way to get the best fares.

Depending on when you wish to travel, the no-frills airlines are not always the cheapest, and because they have created such fierce competition in the market-place, some of the mainstream carriers such as *British Airways* and *TAP Air Portugal* have been forced to drastically reduce their prices. These national carriers also offer flights at more civilised times of the day and with a greater degree of comfort. *BA* flies daily from Gatwick to Lisbon, Porto and Faro and six times a week to Funchal. BA also operates a service to Lisbon from Heathrow. Return flights to Lisbon and Porto start at around £100. Flights to Madeira are more expensive, starting at £140 return, and return flights to Faro can be as little as £70. However, flight prices vary dramatically according to the time of year, availability of seats, and how far in advance you book.

Portugal's national carrier, *TAP Air Portugal,* flies three times a day to Lisbon from Heathrow (from £128), twice a day from Gatwick(from £125), and once a day from Manchester. They also fly twice a day to Porto (from £98) and once a day to Faro, from Gatwick/Heathrow. Flights to Funchal cost around £178 from Gatwick and £192 from Heathrow. Those coming from Ireland should try *Aer Lingus*, who operate three scheduled flights a week from Dublin to Lisbon and Faro.

Prices change rapidly, so it is always a good idea to shop around online and try to find the best deals. Airlines often have special offers available and online deals so, for those on a budget, it pays to spend some time researching the various possibilities before booking a flight. Useful websites that search for the cheapest flights available at any time include www.skyscanner.net and www.airfares.net.

A reliable, independent booking service for low cost flights on scheduled and charter services to Portugal is available from *Flightclub* (Guildbourne Centre, Chapel Road, Worthing, West Sussex BN11 1LZ), who are members of ABTA. Telephone ☎0845-880 1808 for further information, or book online at www. flightclub.co.uk.

The Airlines
Please note that airline services can and do change frequently, so it is best to check current routes on the internet and to keep an eye on the travel press.

Aer Lingus: Flies from Dublin to Lisbon and Faro three times a week. ☎0845-084 4444; www.aerlingus.com.
BMI Baby: Flies from Cardiff and East Midlands to Faro. ☎0870-264 2229; www.bmibaby.com.

British Airways: Flies daily from Gatwick to Lisbon, Porto and Faro and six times a week to Funchal. BA also operates a service to Lisbon from Heathrow. ☎0870-850 9850; www.ba.com.

Easyjet: Flies to Faro from Bristol, East Midlands, Luton, Gatwick and Stansted. New routes from Newcastle to Faro and Stansted to Porto are planned for 2005. www.easyjet.com.

EU Jet: Flies to Faro three times a week (Mon, Thurs, Sat) from Kent International Airport Manston and twice a week from Shannon Intnerational Airport (Thurs, Sun). ☎0870-414 1414; www.eujet.com.

Excel Airways: Flies to Faro from Birmingham, East Midlands, Glasgow, Gatwick, Manchester and Newcastle. ☎0870-169 0169; e-mail flight. bookings@excelairways.com; www.xl.com.

First Choice Airways: Flies from Birmingham, Bristol, East Midlands, Exeter, Gatwick, Glasgow and Manchester to Faro and Funchal. Also flies to Faro from Stansted and Luton. ☎0870-850 3999; www.firstchoice.co.uk/flights.

Flybe.com: Flies to Faro from Birmingham and Exeter. ☎0871-800 0535; www. flybe.com.

FlyGlobespan: Flies to Faro from Edinburgh and Glasgow. ☎0870-5561 522; www.flyglobespan.com.

GB Airways: (formerly Gibraltar Airways, now owned by BA). Flies from Gatwick to Porto daily and to Faro up to twenty-one times a week (return fares to both destinations start at £69). ☎0870-850 9850; www.gbairways.com.

Jet2: Flies from Leeds Bradford and Manchester to Faro. ☎0870-737 8282; www.jet2.com.

Monarch: Flies from Birmingham, Gatwick, Luton and Manchester to Faro; and from Gatwick to Lisbon. ☎0870-040 5040; www.flymoarch.com.

MyTravelLite: Flies from Birmingham to Faro. ☎0870-156 4564; www. mytravellite.com.

Portugalia: Flies from Manchester to Faro, Lisbon and Porto on weekdays. Also at weekends to Faro and Lisbon. ☎0870-755 0025; www.flypga.com.

Thomson Flights: Flies to Faro from Bournemouth, Coventry, Glasgow, Gatwick,

Manchester and East Midlands. Flies to Funchal from Birmingham, Bristol, Exeter, Glasgow, Luton, Manchester, Newcastle and East Midlands. ☎0800-000747; www.thomsonflights.com.

TAP Air Portugal: Flies three times a day to Lisbon from Heathrow (from £128), twice a day from Gatwick(from £125), and once a day from Manchester. They also fly twice a day to Porto (from £98) and once a day to Faro, from Gatwick/Heathrow. Flights to Funchal cost around £178 from Gatwick and £192 from Heathrow. ☎020-7828 0262; www.tap-airportugal.co.uk.

Charter Tickets

The immense changes in the European flight industry in recent years have had a knock-on effect on charter flights, which traditionally have been tied in with package holidays. These days there are very few differences between charter and scheduled flights as it is possible to buy flight-only tickets, in many cases all year round. These can be booked direct through companies such as Monarch (www.flymonarch.com) and Excel (www.excelairways.com), who also offer scheduled flights (see above) or through an agent. The only real difference with flight-only charter tickets is that they are still usually issued for a fixed period, such as 7 days or 14 days.

The largest UK purveyor of flight-only charter tickets is *Avro* (☎0870-458 2841; www.avro.com), offering flights to Faro from Birmingham, Bristol, Edinburgh, Glasgow, Leeds-Bradford, Gatwick, Stansted, Manchester and Newcastle. They also sell flights to Funchal from Gatwick and Manchester; and flights to Lisbon from Gatwick. Another charter ticket provider to check is *Airtours* (☎0870-238 7788; www.airtours.co.uk), who offer charters to Faro from a variety of UK airports.

Discount Travel

Flightclub: Guildbourne Centre, Chapel Road, Worthing, West Sussex BN11 1LZ; ☎0870-880 1808; www.flightclub.co.uk. A reliable, independent booking service for low cost flights on scheduled and charter services to Portugal.

Websites selling flights

www.airflights.co.uk
www.avro.co.uk
www.cheapflights.com
www.dialaflight.com
www.ebookers.com
www.flightline.co.uk

www.lastminute.com
www.opodo.co.uk
www.statravel.co.uk

By Car/Ferry

Obviously having your own car whilst in Portugal is useful and something that many will want to consider, especially if you are bringing possessions over. However, those moving to Portugal permanently may find it more practical to buy a car locally than to register a foreign vehicle (see *Daily Life*). Realistically you should aim to spend 3-4 days driving to get to Southern Portugal, as it is a very long drive – the distance from Calais to the Algarve by road is well over 2000km. Remember that if you stick to the motorways in France, Spain and Portugal you will have to pay a hefty amount in tolls (the cost of getting from Calais to the Spanish border alone is around £50). It is therefore better to stick to the main trunk roads and take your time, take in the scenery and acclimatise yourself to the Portuguese way of life ahead of you. For information about the current toll rates, the state of roads, road works, and weather conditions you can consult the following websites for France: www.autoroutes.fr; and for Spain: www.dgt.es.

There are a number of cross channel ferries to consider as well as the Channel Tunnel, though the time and money saved by taking say, a ferry from Portsmouth to St. Malo rather than from Dover to Calais is debatable. Getting into a port further south in France will cut out the Paris traffic, but you will have to head through the countryside for a time before picking up the main arterial motorways. The main ferry services are *P&O Ferries* (☎0870-520 2020; www. poferries.com); *Hoverspeed* (☎0870-240 8070; www.hoverspeed.com); *Brittany Ferries* (☎0870-566 5333; www.brittanyferries.com); *Seafrance* (☎0870-571 1711; www.seafrance.com); *Transmanche Ferries* (☎0800-917 1201; www. transmancheferries.com). All ferry services and the Channel Tunnel (☎0870-5353 535; www.eurotunnel.com) alter their prices depending on the season, the time of travel, the number of passengers, size of vehicle etc. Some of the operators offer frequent-user discount schemes and packages aimed specifically at foreign home owners. As with the airlines it is worth shopping around to see which service best suits your particular needs. Try www.channel-travel.com and www. cross-channel-ferry-tickets.co.uk for discounted channel crossings.

There is another alternative to this long and tiring drive, which is to take the ferry as far as Spain, thereby reducing the number of hours spent behind the wheel. However, tickets are not cheap and travel time can be up to thirty-six hours. P&O run ferries between Portsmouth and Bilbao twice a week, which take around 36 hours one way. Contact P&O Eurpean Ferries (☎0870-520 2020; www.poportsmouth.com). Ferries operated by Brittany Ferries (☎0870-366 5333; www.brittany-ferries.co.uk) run between Plymouth and Santander twice weekly and take around 18 hours. As a rough price guide, a family can travel at peak times to Spain and back, with a car, for around £1000. However, prices do fluctuate dramatically depending on the time of year. Bear in mind however that the added cost may be compensated by the fact that you will pay far less on petrol, tolls and accommodation during the journey to Portugal. These routes are fairly popular, so it is necessary to book well in advance, especially in the summer.

Once in Portugal, you will be pleased to find that the quality of the road network has improved dramatically over the last ten years due to heavy government investment. However, these improvements are ongoing and some of the work is severely behind schedule. For example, a new link from Lisbon to the Spanish border (towards Valladolid), which should have opened in 1998, has barely been started.

By Train and Coach

With the ease and low cost of flying to Portugal from the UK, very few people choose to go all the way by coach or train. However, these options are still available. *Eurolines* (☎020-7730 0303; www.eurolines.co.uk), operated by *National Express,* offers coach services running from London Victoria to various destinations in Portugal. The price of a return ticket will undoubtedly be more than a budget flight, at around £148 return to Lisbon and £168 return to Faro. The journey time is a hefty 35-38 hours depending on your destination and travellers have to change bus once in Spain and once in France. Alternatively if you travel by Eurolines or some other method as far as Paris, there are daily buses to Lisbon and Porto, leaving from the Porte de Charenton terminus.

Travelling from the UK to Portugal by train will cost a minimum of £200 and will take somewhere between 24 and 40 hours. Nevertheless a surprising number of Brits choose to travel this way and are treated to some fantastic scenery along the way as a result. The cheapest (and longest) method of getting to Portugal by train is to take the London-Lisbon route from Charing Cross, which involves taking a ferry across the Channel and then changing in Paris (and having to change from Nord to Austerlitz station). However, the advantage of this method is that the tickets are valid for two months and you are able to stop off anywhere that takes your fancy along the route.

Alternatively, it is far quicker to take the eurostar from London Waterloo to Paris Gare du Nord, change onto the *TGV* from Paris Montparnasse to Hendaye (another change is required at the Spanish border) and arrive in Lisbon's St. Apolonia station around 24 hours after setting off. Alternatively you could change in Portugal at Pampilhosa for Porto. It is also possible, on the final leg of the journey on the *Sud-Expresso* from Hendaye to Lisbon, to order a sleeping car (couchette) on the overnight train, which makes the last part of the journey far more bearable.

GETTING TO PORTUGAL FROM THE USA AND CANADA

Those travelling from North America to Portugal have several options open to them. The only direct flights are from New York, so anyone travelling from any other US city will have to fly into New York and change, or go via a European city. The direct flight time from New York to Lisbon is around seven hours and the cost is usually under $1,000 in high season. However, those flying from a central or west coast city should expect to add $300 to the price and a minimum of three extra hours travelling time. The shorter the connection time, the more you can expect to pay. Some of the best deals are to be found by travelling via a European city, for example via London, Paris or Munich with *BA*, *Air France* or *Lufthansa*. Those flying into London may be able to organise a very cheap connecting flight with one of the budget airlines (see above).

There are no direct flights from Canada. So, anyone travelling from Canada will have to change in either New York or a European airport, depending on the carrier. Flight times from Montreal and Toronto to Lisbon are around 10-12 hours, and from Vancouver, around 14-15 hours. High season returns from Toronto, via New York, with Continental start at around CDN$1500.

The Airlines

Air France: (☎1-800 237 2747; www.airfrance.us/. Flies from New York, via Paris to Lisbon and Porto for around $1060 in high season (flight time approx. 11 hours).

American Airlines: (☎1-800 433 7300; www.aa.com). Direct non-stop service from New York to Lisbon, daily.

British Airways: (☎1-800 247 9297; www.ba.com). Various US cities and Vancouver to Lisbon, Porto and Faro via London.

Continental Airlines: (☎1-800 231 0856; www.continental.com). Flies from Newark to Lisbon via London.

Delta: (☎1-800 241 4141; www.delta.com). New York to Lisbon (not direct).

Lufthansa: (☎1-800 399 LUFT; www.lufthansa-usa.com). Flies to Lisbon, Porto and Faro via Germany.

Northwest/KLM International: (☎1-800 447 4747; www.nwa.com; www.klm.com). Flies from Vancouver to Lisbon with only one stop.

TAP Air Portugal: (☎1-800 221 7370; www.tap-airportugal.pt.). Flies in conjunction with Continental from New York to Lisbon and from Montreal to Lisbon in conjunction with United and Air Canada.

Discount Travel

Air Brokers International Inc: 685 Market St., Suite 400, San Francsico CA 94105; ☎1-800 883 3273; e-mail websales@airbrokers.cmo; www.airbrokers.com.

Airhitch: (☎1-800 326 2009; e-mail info@airhitch.org; www.airhitch.org).

Stand-by seat brokers. For a non-refundable $29 registration fee, they guarantee to get you a flight as close to your destination as possible. For a flight from the east coast to Europe, costs are currently just $165.

Airtech: (☎212-219 7000; e-mail fly@airtech.com; www.airtech.com). Standby seat-brokers.

Flightcentre: (US: ☎1-866 967 5351; www.flightcentre.us. Canada: ☎1-888 967 5355; www.flightcentre.ca). Very low price fares and last minute offers.

Orbitz: (☎1-888 656 4546; www.orbitz.com). Useful website offering comparisons of fares from the US to Lisbon on all the major airlines.

STA Travel: (☎1-800 781 4040; www.sta-travel.com). Specialists in youth and independent travel.

Travel Cuts: (☎1-888 FLY CUTS; www.travelcuts.com). Canadian company that organises cheap student travel.

Worldtek Travel: 111 Water Street, New Haven, CT 06511; ☎1-800 243 1723; fax 203-865 2034; e-mail info@worldtek.com; www.worldtek.com. Discount travel agency.

GUIDES AND LITERATURE

Guides

Azores: The Bradt Travel Guide, David Sayers (Bradt Travel Guides, 2003). The first general travel guide to the islands.

The Blevins Franks Guide to Living in Portugal (Blevins Franks, 2002). Useful financial guide to Portugal by international financial advisers, Blevins Franks. New edition due 2005/6.

Buying a House in Portugal, Dan Boothby (Vacation Work Publications, 2004). Comprehensive guide to buying property in Portugal.

Eyewitness Guides: Portugal, Martin Symington et al, (Dorling Kindersley, 2004).

Fodor's Exploring Portugal (Fodor's, 2005).

A Hedonist's Guide to Lisbon, Sarah Marshall (Filmer, 2004). Targeting youthful city breakers who need to know where the most in vogue bars and clubs are.

Living in Portugal, Anne de Stoop (Flammarion, 2005). Not as much a guide as a glossy book filled with beautiful photographs of life in Portugal.

Lonely Planet Portugal, Charlotte Beach et al. (Lonely Planet, 2005). See also *Lonely Planet Lisbon,* Julia Wilkinson (2001).

Madeira and Porto Santo, Rodney Bolt (Cadogan Guides, 2003).

Rough Guide to Portugal, Mark Ellingham et al. (Rough Guides, 2005). Best general handbook to Portugal. See also *Mini Rough Guide to the Algarve,* Matthew Hancock (2002), *Algarve Directions,* Matthew Hancock (2005), *Lisbon Directions,* Matthew Hancock (2004), *Mini Rough Guide to Madeira,* Matthew Hancock (2001).

Special Places to Stay: Portugal, Alastair Sawday (Alastair Sawday Publishing, 2005).

Time Out Guide to Lisbon, (Time Out, 2005). Very good for nightlife.

Walking in Portugal, Bethan Davies & Ben Cole (Pili Pala Press, 2000). Step by step guides to thirty-three walks through Portugal's countryside.

General Background and History

A Concise History of Portugal, David Birmingham (Cambridge University Press, 2003). An introduction to the people and culture of Portugal. This second edition brings the story up to the turn of the century.

Contemporary Portugal: Politics, Society and Culture, Antonio Costa Pinto (East European Monographs, 2003).

The Developing Place of Portugal in the European Union, Jose M. Magone (Transaction, 2003). Examines how Portugal became a part of the European Union as a political system and its development towards Europeanisation and domestication.

History of Portugal, A.D. de Oliviera Marques (Columbia University Press, 1976). Very readable general history.

Portugal: A Companion History, Jose Hermano Saraiva et al. (Carcanet Press, 1997). Brief illustrated history.

Portugal: A Traveller's History, Harold V. Livermore (The Boydell Press, 2004). Historical guide drawing on personal experience, and combining insights on the country's history with a look into architecture, painting, music and wildlife. Most recently published history available.

The Portuguese: The Land and Its People, Marion Kaplan (Penguin 1998). Portuguese history, families, football, poetry, port and pousadas. New edition due in 2006.

The Blue Shirts: Portuguese Fascism in Interwar Europe, Antonio Costa Pinto (Columbia University Press, 2000). One of the few English-language studies of the rise of Salazar to power.

They Went to Portugal, Rose Macauley (Penguin, 1985). A history of British travellers to Portugal. See also: *They Went to Portugal Too* (Carcanet, 1990).

Unknown Seas: How Vasco de Gama Opened the East, Ronald Watkins (John Murray, 2004). Fascinating and very readable story of Vasco de Gama's voyage.

Literature Associated with Portugal

A Small Death in Lisbon, Robert Wilson (Harper Collins, 2000). Atmospheric thriller set in war-time Lisbon from a British author who lives in Lisbon.

Backwards out of the Big World: Voyage into Portugal, Paul Hyland (Flamingo, 1997). Paul Hyland meets contemporary writers and probes the nation's psyche with talks with fishwives, bullfighters, businessmen and gypsies.

Ballad of Dog's Beach, José Cardoso Pires (Everyman, 1986). Detective thriller set in the last years of Salazar's dictatorship. Subsequently made into a film.

The Book of Disquiet, Fernando Pessoa (Penguin, 2002). One of the few pieces of prose from Portugal's best known poet, this collection of musings and ramblings is considered a classic.

Journey to Portugal, Jose Saramago (The Harvill Press, 2002). Portuguese novelist, Saramago, crosses his native land from northeast to southwest, exploring the towns and villages of Portugal. A personal voyage of discovery and a delightful travelling companion.

The Lusiads, Luís de Camões (Oxford Paperbacks, 2001). One of the greatest epic poems of the Renaissance. Tells the story of the creation of the Portuguese Empire through the feats of Vasco da Gama, as he recounts his voyage to India in 1497.

The Maias, José Maria Eça de Queiroz (Penguin, 1988). Story of the declining fortunes of a landowning family over three generations, portraying the corruption rife within the clergy and high society.

The Return of the Caravels, Antonio Lobo Antunes (Grove Press, 2003). One of Portugal's most respected contemporary writers. Other works include *Act of the Damned, The Natural Order of Things* and *The Inquisitors' Manual.*

The Year of the Death of Ricardo Reis, José Saramago (The Harvill Press, 1998). Set in Lisbon in 1936. One of the most accessible books by Saramago, the nobel prize winning Portuguese writer. Other novels include *All the Names, Baltasar and Blimunda, Blindness, The History of the Siege of Lisbon* and *The Gospel According to Jesus Christ.*

Travels in My Homeland, Almeida Garrett (Peter Owen, 2005). Sparkling narrative of a ramble around the country by the classic nineteenth century Portuguese writer.

Useful Addresses

The European Bookshop, 5 Warwick Street, London W1B 5LU; ☎020-7734 5259; fax 020-7287 1720; e-mail mrg@esb.co.uk; www.europeanbookshop. com. Portuguese and other foreign language publications, including guides.

The Travel Bookshop, 13-15 Blenheim Crescent, London, W11 2EE; ☎020-7229 5260; fax 020-7243 1552; e-mail post@thetravelbookshop.co.uk; www. thetravelbookshop.co.uk.

Stanfords, 12-14 Long Acre, London WC2E 9LP; ☎020-7836 1321; fax 020-7836 0189; e-mail sales@stanfords.co.uk; www.stanfords.co.uk. One of the largest map shops in Britain, with a wide range of maps for Portugal.

RESIDENCE AND ENTRY
REGULATIONS

CHAPTER SUMMARY

- The first step, upon arriving in Portugal is to apply for a foreigner's identification number – the *número de identificação fiscal* (NIF).
- **Residence Card.** The *Autorização de Residência* is required by any EU citizen who moves to Portugal, including paid workers, sole traders, the self-employed, students, those who intend to live off savings and family members of any of the above.
    - Residence permits should be applied for at the local *Serviço de Estrangeiros e Fronteiras*.
    - The residence permit should be carried at all times for possible inspection.
- **Work Permits.** EU citizens do not need a work permit. Non-EU citizens should organise their work permit before moving to Portugal, at their local Portuguese consulate.
    - Non-EU citizens must be able to prove that they can offer skills that could not be offered by a Portuguese or EU citizen before they will be offered a job.
    - A work permit for long-term employment is usually granted for six months, after which it can be renewed.
- Identity cards (*bilhete de Identidad*) are also available. They are not compulsory, but allow the holder to apply for a driving licence and can be used in lieu of a passport for identification purposes.
- **Tax Residence.** If you spend more than 183 days in any calendar year in Portugal, then you automatically become resident for tax purposes.
- Once resident in Portugal it is advisable to register with your embassy or consulate, who will keep you up to date with any information.

OVERVIEW

Portugal is a full member of the EU and one of the founding members of the Eurozone. Consequently many of the complications regarding visas and work permits which affect American and other non-EU entrants do not apply in the case of British and Irish citizens. For applicants from non-EU countries, however, the Iberian love of paperwork is strongly in evidence in Portugal and the bureaucratic demands involved in your application for a work or residence permit can be painfully slow and plentiful.

British visitors to Portugal do not need a visa, but other visitors who do should make their application to the nearest Portuguese Consulate in their country of origin. Remember that if you are planning to extend your visit to Portugal and you do need a visa, that your passport will have to be stamped on entry to Portugal so that the authorities will be able to determine the date of entry. This does not apply to Britons and other EU nationals.

Applying for a residence visa for Portugal directly from abroad is possible, but this can be both complex and time-consuming. However, non-EU nationals may find it more convenient to apply for a residence visa before they arrive in Portugal in order to avoid becoming embroiled in Portuguese bureaucracy once there – and it is not unknown for non-EU nationals to be forced to return to their own country and apply for residence from there, or to have to travel to the nearest Portuguese Consulate (in Spain) in order to apply from outside the country.

To work in Portugal EU citizens will need a residence visa. No other work permit is required.

FISCAL NUMBER (NIF)

The first step for anyone moving to Portugal is to apply for the foreigner's fiscal identification number. The *número de identificação fiscal (NIF)* is essential for work, to do business, or to buy anything substantial in Portugal, e.g. a house, land, or a car. Residents and non-residents with any financial dealings in Portugal must obtain this number.

The application process is the same for both EU and non-EU citizens, although non-EU citizens must have entered the country with the correct visa. The NIF is available to tourists or residents on presentation of a current valid passport at the local tax office *(finanças)*. You will be given a temporary fiscal number, which will be replaced by a permanent number and card *(Cartão de Contribuinte)* after a few months. The fiscal number will then appear on all your tax returns and on any formal documentation involved in the buying or selling of property or on any business transactions.

RESIDENCE PERMITS FOR CITIZENS OF THE EU

Once ensconced in Portugal, EU citizens, EEA citizens and the Swiss, wishing to settle in Portugal and who have not already made their residence permit arrangements must apply immediately to their local *Serviço de Estrangeiros e Fronteiras* – Immigration and Border Control Department (SEF – Rua Conselheiro Jose Silvestre Ribeiro 4, 1649-007 Lisbon; ☎217-115000; fax 217-140332; www.sef.pt) – for the *Autorização de Residência*, the vital document which confers residence status on the holder. This residence card is required by all categories of immigrant, including paid workers, sole traders, the self employed, those who intend to live off their own means, students, and family members of any of the above.

UK citizens will need to visit their local British Consulate where for a small fee a certificate will be issued to certify that you are a British citizen. Next, take your passport, the consular certificate, three passport photos, and a copy of your most recent bank statement to the Serviço de Estrangeiros e Fronteiras and they will process the Autorização de Residência in just a few weeks. It is possible to speed up your application by obtaining the application form in advance of your trip to the foreigner's office (the form can be downloaded as a PDF from www.sef.pt). You may also require a document proving that you are covered for health care, such as an insurance policy or a social security card. Different categories of immigrants to Portugal will also require certain other documents: Employed workers should take the original and a photocopy of their work contract; sole traders must be able to prove that they have established a company as a sole trader; the self-employed should provide a declaration of self-employment; those living by their own means will need to prove that they are able to do so (i.e. demonstrate a means of income or savings); students must provide proof of their registration at an institution in Portugal. This information must be provided when applying for a residence authorisation in your home country or when applying for the Autorização de Residência in Portugal.

The residence document is a red and green card bearing the applicant's photograph and signature (and sometimes thumbprint) which must be carried by the holder at all times for possible inspection. A small fee is charged for the document (currently €2.54).

In the case where one spouse is an EU citizen and the other is not, in order to receive a residence permit the non-EU citizen will need to produce a document issued by the competent authority in their country of origin proving the status of the relationship.

VISAS & PERMITS FOR NON-EU CITIZENS

Holders of Canadian or American passports may reside in Portugal for 60 days without a visa; those holding Australian passports are allowed an extra 30 days, and can stay in the country for 90 days. Canadian and US passport holders still require a visa to visit the Azores. Non-EU nationals can apply for a visa to the Portuguese Embassy or Consulate in their home country before leaving for Portugal. Portuguese embassy and consulate addresses in some of the English-speaking countries of the world are included in the *Useful Addresses* section below.

For those looking to stay in the country longer, apply to the district police headquarters, in Lisbon to the Serviço de Estrangeiros (address above). If possible, find someone already resident in Portugal (a national or foreign resident) who is willing to act as your referee. You will also need a pile of passport-sized photos, your passport, proof that you have some kind of housing arranged in Portugal, evidence of good financial standing, and a medical certificate.

Although some non-EU residents manage to avoid applying for the residence permit by simply leaving the country every few months and getting their passport stamped on re-entry for a further visit, this is not really advisable; and anyone intending to live permanently in Portugal will find that it is virtually impossible without having the *Autorização de Residência* and the privileges which it brings.

Work Permits for Non-EU Citizens

Non-EU citizens who intend to work in Portugal on a long-term basis will need a work permit and for this they must be able to present proof of having a job, e.g. a contract of employment from the prospective employer, along with the approval of the Portuguese Ministry of Labour. Be warned that this process can be long and laborious. Applications are made to your country's nearest Portuguese Consulate at the same time as the initial request for a residence visa. A completed contract of employment will be sent to your employer in Portugal, who must then submit this to the Ministry of Labour for approval. The entire procedure is likely to take a few months, so preparations should be made well in advance.

Anyone planning to work in Portugal for a temporary period of less than 30 days is not required to have a work permit, but must gain written consent from the Work Inspection Institute (IDICT – *Instituto de Desenvolvimento e Inspecção das Condições do Trabalho*) in the area in which he or she wishes to work. The head office, in Lisbon (Praça de Alvalade, 1-1º, 1700-073 Lisbon; ☎ 217-924500; fax 217-934047; www.idict.gov.pt), will be able to provide a list of all of the regional offices for anyone who has difficulty in locating their nearest IDICT office.

Although some people, who may only want to work in Portugal temporarily (but for longer than the 30-day exemption period), go to Portugal without a work permit, find a job, and then apply for a permit later, this way of doing things is not recommended, as the Portuguese authorities are clamping down on such cart-before-the-horse tactics.

Applying for a work permit in Portugal tends to be quite difficult and a labour market that has been thrown open to workers from other EU countries is now quite difficult for Americans and others from outside the EU to enter – though not impossible, especially for those who have specific skills to offer. The Work Inspection Institute in Portugal must be convinced that the job for which you are applying could not be done equally well by a Portuguese or EU national; and this decision will depend heavily on the amount of unemployment in the particular area where the job exists. In addition, an employer resident in Portugal is restricted by law to employ only one foreign (i.e. non-European Union) employee in every ten. A work permit for long-term employment is usually granted for six months, after which time it can be renewed at half-yearly intervals. The only people from non-EU countries exempt from applying for a work permit are au pairs, academics employed by Portuguese universities and private English tutors. It should be emphasised that British and other EU citizens coming to work in Portugal do not need a work permit and do not need to go through these procedures.

Entering to Start a Business

A work permit is not required for those who enter Portugal to set up their own business and are self-employed. A residence permit, however, will be required. Professionals (e.g. doctors, lawyers, etc.) must first have their qualifications checked by the relevant Portuguese body which will grant permission to practise based on the authenticity of these qualifications (and whether they are considered equivalent to Portuguese qualifications). Although the need for a work permit is waived for the self-employed, many of those who fall within this group will be forced to obtain a licence before setting up in business; this includes any concern which deals with food, the maritime industries, or renting out property in Portugal.

Extending Work Permits and Other Procedures

Visits can be extended for up to six months by applying to the Serviço de Estrangeiros e Fronteiras (the Foreigners' Department of the Ministry of Internal Affairs, address above) once you are in Portugal; branch offices can be found in most major cities (including Coimbra, Faro, Porto, Madeira and the Azores). When the times comes to renew the card you will need to give proof that you can support yourself for the coming year, e.g. current bank statements showing a regular income. After following this process for five years, non-EU residents are entitled, like those from within the European Union, to the five-year *Autorização de Residência*, which saves a phenomenal amount of annual hassle.

IDENTITY CARDS

A part from a residence permit (*Autorização de Residência*) and a fiscal number (*Cartão de Contribuinte*) prospective residents may require an identity card (*Bilhete de Identidad*) which must, by law, be carried at all times by Portuguese nationals. Application forms for these should be available at the nearest British Consulate. You will need to produce your passport, a few photos, and the Autorização de Residência. Completed forms must be submitted to the President of the local district council (*Junta de Freguesia*) whose responsibility it is to certify the authenticity of your address and to certify the card. After this, your application is in the hands of the Portuguese authorities and will take anything between one day and one month to process.

Although to many of us the mention of identity cards evokes sinister images of totalitarianism, the Portuguese version of these is useful (though not compulsory) for foreign residents. The identity card works in much the same way as in France and other European countries. The ID card entitles the holder to apply for a Portuguese driving licence and can be used in lieu of a passport when registering at hotels and for identification purposes, even for travel to other European countries.

RESIDENCY AND CITIZENSHIP RIGHTS

O nce a UK national has obtained the residence permit, he or she is entitled to the same rights as a Portuguese national, with the exception that he or she is not allowed to vote in Portuguese elections. However, UK nationals living abroad still retain the right to vote in UK elections and remain British citizens even though they are resident in a foreign country.

If at any time you decide to leave Portugal permanently, then simply hand in your Autorização de Residência at the local police station before your departure.

Registering with your Embassy

Once resident in Portugal, as anywhere in the world, it is also advisable to register with your embassy or consulate: a list of these is provided below. This registration enables the authorities to keep emigrants up to date with any information they need as citizens resident overseas and, in the event of an emergency, helps them to trace individuals. Your embassy or consulate can also help with information regarding your status overseas and advise with any diplomatic or passport problems, and offer help in the case of an emergency, e.g. the death of a relative overseas. However, consulates do not really function as a source of general help and advice.

As a rule, British embassies and consulates interpret their role helping British citizens overseas more strictly than those of many other countries. As those who have needed their help in an emergency have found, diplomats tend to keep within the letter if not the spirit of their duties. Appeals for assistance in matters that fall outside these duties – explained in a leaflet available from embassies/consulates or the *Foreign and Commonwealth Office* (Consular Division, Old Admiralty Building, London SW1A 2PA; ☎020-7008 0232; www.fco.gov.uk) – often fall on deaf ears.

TAX & RESIDENCY

Residents in Portugal are liable to income tax on their worldwide income. You are deemed to be a resident of Portugal if:

○ You remain in Portugal for more than 183 days in any calendar year; or
○ You visit Portugal for a shorter period in any year and you have a place of abode available to you in Portugal on 31st December of that year, which it is your intention to keep and occupy as a permanent residence; or
○ If your centre of economic interest is in Portugal, i.e. if your main source of income, investments or business interests lie in Portugal.

In addition, remember that all members of a family unit are considered to be resident in Portugal if the person who is responsible for the family is resident there. The Portuguese tax year runs from 1 January to 31 December. If you find that you may be liable to pay tax in both Portugal and your country of origin you may find that you are covered by a Treaty of Double Taxation, which depending on the provisions, will prevent you being taxed twice.

USEFUL ADDRESSES

Serviço de Estrangeiros e Fronteiras – Main Offices

Head Office: Rua Conselheiro Jose Silvestre Ribeiro 4, 1549-007 Lisbon; ☎217-115000; fax 217-140332; e-mail sef@sef.pt; www.sef.pt.

Lisbon Regional Office: Avenida António Augusto de Aguiar 20, 1069-119 Lisbon; ☎213-585500; fax 213-144053; e-mail dir.lisboa@sef.pt.

Central Portugal Regional Office: Rua Venâncio Rodrigues 25-31, 3000 Coimbra; ☎239-824045; fax 239-823786; e-mail dir.centro@sef.pt.

Algarve Regional Office: Rua Luis de Camões n°5, 8000-388 Faro; ☎289-805822; fax 289-801566; e-mail dir.algarve@sef.pt.

Madeira Regional Office: Rua Nova da Rochinha 1-B, 9054-519 Funchal; ☎291-232177; fax 291-231918; e-mail dir.Madeira@sef.pt.

Azores Regional Office: Rua Marques de Praia e Monforte 10, Apartado 259, 9500-089 Ponta Delgada; ☎296-302230; fax 296-284422; email dir. acores@sef.pt.

North Regional Office: Rua D. João IV 536, Apartado 4819, 4013 Porto Codex; ☎222-207813; fax 225-104385; e-mail dir.norte@sef.pt.

Note: Further local offices are listed at www.sef.pt/contactos.htm.

Portuguese Embassies and Consulates Abroad

United Kingdom

Portuguese Embassy in London: 11 Belgrave Square, London SW1X 8PP; ☎0870-005 6970; fax 020-7245 1287; http://portugal. embassyhomepage.com.

Consular Section: Silver City House, 62 Brompton Road, London SW3 1BJ; ☎0870-005 6970.

Portuguese Honorary Consul, Jersey: Burlington House, St. Saviour's Road, St Helier, Jersey JE2 4LA; ☎01534-877 188; fax 01534-625 005.

Portuguese Consulate, Belfast: Hurst House, 15-19 Corporation Square, 72 High Street, Belfast BT1 2AJ, Northern Ireland; ☎01232-242 242; fax 01232-235 776.

Ireland

Embassy of Portugal, Dublin: Knocksinna Mews, 7 Willow Park/Westminster Park, Foxrock, Dublin 18; ☎01-289 4416; fax 01-289 2849.

USA

Portuguese Embassy: 2125 Kalorama Road, NW Washington DC 20008; ☎202-328 8610; fax 202-462 3726. Consulates in Boston; New Bedford; Providence; New York; Newark; San Francisco and Los Angeles.

Canada

Embassy of Portugal: 645 Island Park Drive, Ottawa, Ontario, K1Y 0B8; ☎613-729 0883; fax 613-729 4236; www.embportugal-ottawa.org.

Portuguese Consulate: 438 University Avenue, Suite 1400, Box 41, Toronto, Ontario, M5G 2K8; ☎416-217 0966; fax 416-217 0973; www. cgportugaltoronto.com.

Portuguese Consulate: 2020 Rue de University, Suite 2425, Montreal, Québec, H3A 2A5; ☎514;499 0359; fax 514;499 0366; www. cgportugalmontreal.com.

Portuguese Consulate: 904 Pender Place, 700 West Pender Street, Vancouver, BC, V6C-353; ☎604-683 3674; fax 604-685 7042.

Portuguese Consulate: 167 Lombard Avenue, Suite 908, Winnipeg, Manitoba, R3B OV3; ☎204-943 8941; fax 204-943 1159.

Portuguese Consulate: 13915, 96 Street, Edmonton, Alberta, T5E 5Z1; ☎780-476 9099; fax 780-475 6757.

Portuguese Consulate: 775 Avenue Murray, Apart.710, Québec, G1S 4T2167; ☎418-681 8650; fax 418-656 2019.

Australia

Embassy of Portugal: 23 Culgoa Circuit, O'Malley ACT 2606, Canberra (PO Box 9092, Deakin ACT 2600); ☎612-6290 1733; fax 612-6290 1957.

Consulate General of Portugal in Sydney: Level 9, 30 Clarence Street, Sydney NSW 2000; ☎02-9262 2199; fax 02-9262 5991; www.consulportugalsydney.org.au.

Melbourne: Honorary Consul, 846 Toorak Road, Hawthorn East, VIC 3123, Melbourne; ☎613-9822 7140; fax 613-9822 7379.

Perth/Freemantle: Honorary Consul, GPO BOX 780, 22 Cliff Street, Freemantle WA 6160; ☎618-9335 9458; fax 618-9430 6448.

Darwin: Honorary Consul, 15 Colster Crescent, Wagaman, Darwin NT 0810; ☎618-8927 1956; fax 618-8927 7288.

Brisbane: Honorary Consul, 21 Scrub Road, Carindale, Brisbane QLD 4152; ☎07-3324 8351; fax 07-3324 9429.

Adelaide: Honorary Consul, PO Box 8070, Station Arcade, 3rd floor, 25 Peel Street, Adelaide SA 5000; ☎618-8110 0999; fax 618-8110 0966.

New Zealand

Consulate of Portugal in Auckland: Honorary Consul, 16 Fisher Crescent, Mt Wellington, Auckland; ☎649-259 4014; fax 649-259 4013.

Consulate of Portugal in Wellington: Honorary Consul, PO Box 1024, Suite 1, 1st floor, 21 Marion Street, Wellington; ☎644-382 7655; fax 644-382 7659.

South Africa

Portuguese Embassy: Barclays Square, 296 Walker Street, Sunnyside 0132, Pretoria; ☎012-341 5522; fax 012-341 5690.

Portuguese Consulate: Portuguese House, Ernest Oppenheimer Blvd, Bruma, Johannesburg 2198 (PO Box 5092, Johannesburg 2000); ☎011-622 0645; fax 011-622 0661.

Portuguese Consulate: Suite 1005, Main Tower, Standard Bank Centre, Hertzog Boulevard, Cape Town 8001; ☎021-418 0080; fax 021-418 0084.

Portuguese Consulate: Suite 1612, 16th Floor, 320 West Street, Durban 4001 (PO Box 315, Durban 4000); ☎031-305 7511; fax 031-3046036.

Foreign Embassies and Consulates in Portugal

United Kingdom

British Embassy: Rua de São Bernardo 33, 1249-082 Lisbon; ☎213-924000; www.uk-embassy.pt.

British Consulate, Porto: Avenida da Boavista 3072, 4100-120 Porto; ☎226-184789; fax 226-100438.

Honorary British Consulate, Madeira: Apartado 417, EC Zarco 9000-956, Funchal, Madeira; ☎291-221221; fax 291-233789.

British Consulate, Portimão: Largo Francisco A Mauricio 7-1°, 8500-535 Portimão; ☎282-417800; fax 282-417806.

Honorary British Consulate, Azores: Quinta do Bom Jesus, Rue das Almas 23, Pico da Pedra, Riberia Grande, 9600 Azores; ☎296-498115; fax

296-498330.

Ireland

Embassy of Ireland: Rua da Imprensa a Estrela 1-4, 1200-684 Lisbon; ☎213-929440; fax 213-977363.

USA

United States Embassy: Avenida das Forças Armadas, 1600-081 Lisbon; ☎217-273300; fax 217-279109.

American Consulate, Azores: Av. Príncipe do Mónaco, 6-2º Frente, 9502 Ponta Delgada; ☎296-282216; fax 296-287216.

American Consular Agency in Madeira: Rua da Alfândega, No.10, 2nd Floor, Rooms A&B, 9000-059 Funchal, Madeira; ☎291-235636; fax 291-229360.

Canada

Canadian Embassy: Avenida da Liberdade, 198-200, Third Floor, 1269-121 Lisbon; ☎213-164600; fax 213-164693.

Canadian Honorary Consul, Faro: Rua Frei Lourenço de Sta Maria Nº1-1º, Apartado 79, 8001, Faro; ☎289-803757; fax 289-880888.

Canadian Honorary Consul, Azores: Rua António José de Almeida Nº27 1ºEsq, 9500 Ponta Delgada, Azores; ☎296-281488; fax 296-281489.

Australia

Australian Embassy: Avenida da Liberdade, 200-2º, 1250-147 Lisbon; ☎213-101500; fax 213-101555; www.portugal.embassy.gov.au.

South Africa

South African Embassy: Avenida Luis Bivar 10, 1069-024 Lisbon; ☎213-192200; fax 213-535713.

South African Honorary Consulate in Porto: Rua Antonio José Da Costa, 78-1, 4150-090 Porto; ☎226-076010; fax 226-099820.

South African Honorary Consulate in Funchal: Hotel Madeira Carlton, Largo Antonio Nobre 9000, Funchal, Madeira; ☎22-3521; fax 22-3514.

Further Assistance. In all your dealings regarding residence and entry requirements, whether to start a business, work, or retire, you should find the process nowadays is relatively straightforward, if at times somewhat time-consuming. Where difficulties do arise while you are in Portugal you should seek out lawyers or financial consultants who are fluent in English (ask other foreigners for recommendations). In this way rather than getting lost in any Portugese legalise/bureaucratic jargon thrown your way you will get a translation of it.

A leaflet entitled *Some Hints on Taking Up Residence and Living Conditions in Portugal* is available from the British Embassy in Lisbon (address above). A couple of other useful addresses are the *British Portuguese Chamber of Commerce* (Rua da Estrela 8, 1200 Lisbon, Portugal; ☎213-961586) and the *Tourist Office ICEP Investment Trade and Tourism of Portugal in London* (2nd Floor, 22 Sackville Street, London W1S 3LY; ☎020-7494 1517; ww.portugalinbusiness.com).

SETTING UP HOME

CHAPTER SUMMARY

- The **average house price** in mainland Portugal is around €217,000, however, this figure is artificially high because of the massive jump in house prices in the Algarve region, where the average is €310,000.
  - Those looking for property bargains are now investigating the previously overlooked Alentejo region due to the relatively cheap price of property and proximity to Faro airport.
  - Buying in Portugal offers a stable property investment – prices are rising steadily.
- **Estate agents.** In Portugal all estate agents must be authorised to operate by one of the recognised professional associations.
  - **Inspection trips:** although there will be no obligation to buy, expect a certain amount of pressure.
- The overall costs of **conveyancing** (including the fees charged by lawyers, the land registry, the notary, taxes, bank charges and so on) come to around 10% of the cost of a resale property.
  - All urban properties have a *caderneta urbana* – an identity card giving the size and location of the plot and giving the rateable value for the property.
  - In mid-2003, the rules and rates of the old property transfer tax (SISA) were changed, so that now the aqcuisition of dwellings is subject to a 6% municipal property transfer tax (IMT).
- **Buying land.** Because of the rapid growth of urban developments in recent years, certain building restrictions have been introduced. Get your lawyer to check this for you before buying land.
- **Renting property.** When you sign a contract for a long-term let you will usually need to pay between one and three month's rent as a deposit to cover damage to the property.

  Removals. The approximate charge for removals from the UK to Portugal is £120-£150 per cubic metre, plus a fixed administration charge.

OVERVIEW

It may seem ironic to the Portuguese that thousands of foreigners have cheerfully set up home on their doorsteps, or where their doorsteps would be if they could afford them, around Lisbon and the Algarve. Only about 40% of Portuguese own their own home and in Lisbon, Porto and Funchal (Madeira) the percentage is little more than 20%. In fact, Portugal faces an acute housing shortage, particularly in the main industrial areas, where property prices and rents are excessive for those on Portuguese salaries. The foreign resident population (for whom such considerations are often remote) may salve their consciences by reflecting that they make a contribution to the prosperity of the country and provide work for Portuguese builders, handymen, caretakers and domestic employees. In the case of domestic employees, incidentally, Portugal is one of the few European countries where house servants are commonly employed.

How Do the Portuguese Live?

In response to this question, one Portuguese replied 'beyond their means'. This is understandable, in view of the high cost of housing and rents relative to the generally low Portuguese wages and the rising cost of living, which means that Portugal is not a prosperous country in the same sense as its western European neighbours. Because of the general housing shortage, there is a tendency for offspring to live with their parents until they get married. Even after marriage, newlyweds will often live with one or other set of inlaws; a situation that gives rise to its own set of problems. In country areas especially, several generations of one family will live under the same roof and even go on Sunday outings together.

In common with their European counterparts, many urban Portuguese tend to live in apartments in suburbs from which they can commute to work. Life in the cities is much more like that in London, Paris or Rome. Traditional Portuguese architecture includes gracious nineteenth century porticoed villas, terraced town houses with tile decorations on the outside walls, and thick-walled rustic farm dwellings with either no windows, or very small ones, designed to protect the inhabitants from the molten summers and icy winters.

Owing to the tendency of the Portuguese to try to make a better living in the two main cities, or to move where job prospects are likely to be better, country properties are often abandoned and can make interesting homes for foreign buyers keen on restoration and conversion work, and who have the time and money necessary. At present, the Algarve accounts for 90% of all sales in Portugal to foreigners and 50-60% of these are estimated to be to the British. The Portuguese themselves are moving away from the country and into towns, meaning that the bargains are to be found outside the built-up areas.

Thus, there are all types of property available in Portugal. The only foreseeable problem is that a country as small and as much in demand with foreign residents may reach saturation point in certain areas, if immigration continues at current levels. Development is another factor. The government of Portugal is seeking, with the aid of EU initiatives, to attract business development to even the remotest province of Trás-os-Montes, which may make even this northeastern corner of Portugal more conveniently inhabitable in the future. Maybe remote districts like this will become the Algarve of the future, for those present-day expats still in search of property bargains, and a life away from the tourist crowds.

Owing to their distance from Europe, both Madeira and the Azores tend to attract more timeshare residents than permanent ones. One estimate puts the number of expatriates living permanently in the Azores at less than one hundred: these have certainly yet to become Portugal's answer to the Canary Islands. Setting up home in mainland Portugal, though, is far less of an adventure than it used to be.

Rent or Buy

On the whole, if you can afford it, it is better to buy your home rather than renting if you intend to stay long-term. Not only is this likely to prove a sound investment, but renting in the main towns and cities can be as expensive as rents in Britain, if not more so. The paradox of renting in Portugal (and one which is not fully understood even by the locals) is that doing this on your own account is becoming more expensive every year; but the income to be derived from renting your property out is somehow not so lucrative. Lisbon remains one of the cheapest cities in Western Europe in which to rent property, but it is no longer a bargain.

It is usual for foreigners working for large companies or in the international schools (of which there are many in Portugal) to have their accommodation provided free. However, those doing shorter-term jobs (e.g. English-language teaching) or who have temporary or summer jobs, or who, for some other reason, are unable to afford high rents, may prefer to bypass their local estate agents and look in the *alugamse* (to rent) columns of newspapers like the *Diário de Notícias*, where it is possible to find something cheaper, either in the suburbs or perhaps in one of Lisbon's picturesque but crumbling eighteenth-century buildings.

One central Lisbon resident explained his surroundings thus
Every one of these old buildings has a UNESCO preservation order on it. You cannot even install a new lift without a committee approving it. The landlords can't be bothered to go through all the procedures necessary to get permission for the repairs and they can't charge high rents, so the buildings are falling down.

Terms likely to be used in newspaper rental advertisements include *quarto* (room), *cozinha* (kitchen), *bahno* bathroom, *terraço* (terrace). As there is such a shortage of accommodation in Lisbon, Porto and the Algarve anyone landing a job there should try to get their housing provided if possible, or at least help with finding accommodation at a price they can afford. The minimum rental is usually six months. It may also be possible to rent part of a house – look for *Partes de Casa* advertisements. In the Algarve, holiday accommodation is rented out by the foreign owners at exorbitant prices in summer. It is not usually feasible to rent a villa for a year as the owners will probably want to inhabit their property for some summer weeks, and Christmas, Easter etc. It may be possible to find a country property for rent but own transport will be essential. Sometimes those working in the tourist industry manage to rent flats in the large apartment blocks inhabited by the Portuguese in the main Algarve towns. Such accommodation is best found by asking on the spot, in bars and restaurants, or consulting the advertisements in the *Anglo-Portuguese News*. Those who have building or handyman/woman skills should not neglect the possibility of negotiating lower rentals as a quid pro quo for maintenance work. This method of finding accommodation may also suit those who eventually intend to buy their own property and do it up, as it gives them a chance to look around and not pay through the nose while they are doing so. Further information on renting property is given below

Portugal has been a long time favourite with buyers of property abroad and there has always been more of a demand for properties on luxury developments than is the case in Spain. Since the new POOC planning law was introduced in 1993 (see box below), development has decreased, especially along the most popular area – the Algarve – and as a consequence property prices have risen. However, the planning laws have also ensured that new developments have been tastefully and stylishly designed and tend to fit into their surroundings, rather than assault them, as has so often been the case in neighbouring Spain. Portugal remains a charming and conservative country and the architecture of the country, throughout the country, is one of the reasons why people decide to own property there. It is possible to find older properties in the country to renovate, both large estates and tumbling down dwellings, but until recently the majority of prospective buyers were looking for new developments and modern resale properties within reach of the beaches, services and amenities of the Algarve. Property prices vary, but tend to be higher than those in Spain due to higher land prices and, generally, superior quality of build.

Because of the varied climate and topography of Portugal there has always been a lot of choice in terms of location and climate available to the prospective property buyer, from the golf course, marinas and holiday resort atmosphere of the Algarve to the quiet cork groves of Alentejo; from the mountain scenery of the north-east to the gently rolling plains of central Portugal with its medieval walled towns and sparsely populated countryside; from the cosmopolitan atmosphere of Lisbon and Porto to the wild crashing surf of the Atlantic seaboard. Portugal is bisected by its famous rivers; and bounded by the sea and mountains. The sun-drenched southern region with its sardines and blue fishing boats give way to the wet and misty north with its vineyards and storks and mountains. Portugal is a small country and it has retained its charm and its sense of history, and has preserved its finest buildings and kept the building of new edifices controlled.

POOC LAW

Coastal zones in Portugal have had, increasingly, problems related to the growing human pressure in terms of changes in land use associated with urban and industrial occupation, new accessibility (ports, motorways) and traffic. These problems have been further intensified by recreational use (beaches, water sports) and excessive fishing. The deterioration of water quality and sediments together with the alteration and degradation of natural habitats, major landscape changes and the rapid changes in habits and way of life of the local population led to an EU Directive on the management of interface areas between land and sea.

Plans for the Management of the Coastal Zone (POOC) have been developed which together cover the entire coast of Portugal and move towards an integrated management of the Portuguese coastal zones. What this has meant for property developers is that further coastal development in certain designated areas is restricted – the law enforces a 200m distance from the coastline on any new developments. What this means for potential buyers of property in Portugal is that properties with beach frontage in many locations are seeing above-average price rises as demand exceeds supply.

Trends. As the Algarve has become more built up over the years, and restrictions on development have halted a building frenzy, existing property on this coast has become more expensive and new buyers have started buying and building further inland, in the hills behind the coast. Alentejo, a previously overlooked region is attracting buyers due to the relatively cheap price of land and property and its proximity to Faro airport, Lisbon, and the beaches.

Whereas much of the development along the Algarve coastline had been more or less centred around the 'Golden Triangle' of Vilamoura, Quinta do Lago and Vale do Lobo in the central Algarve, both the eastern and western reaches are now becoming increasingly popular places to buy. Buying along the Eastern Algarve puts you in easy reach of Spain; while the Western Algarve remains one of the most beautiful stretches of coastline in Europe, with small secluded beaches and rocky outcrops.

Luxury complexes built around golf courses have long been a feature of development in Portugal, and developers continue to produce these sought-after properties. At least when you live by a golf course you can be sure that that precious view over the greens will never be invaded by further developments. However, such beauty comes at a high price and a luxury villa on such a development can sell for as much as £3 million or more.

The Atlantic seaboard, also previously overlooked by foreign buyers (apart from the well-heeled seaside resorts of Cascais and Estoril close to Lisbon) is now attracting buyers other than native Portuguese, as is Madeira, which has undergone a transformation in recent years and has become a mainstream tourist destination.

Buying in Portugal offers a stable property investment. Prices are on the increase, but the increase is steady rather than rampant in the traditional areas where expats have bought. Buying-to-let is also a very feasible option.

Comparative Costs. The average house price in mainland Portugal is around €217,000 (£149,000), however, this figure is artificially high because of the massive jump in house prices in the Algarve region, where the average is €310,000 (£213,000). In the rest of the country, prices continue to be far lower, the lowest being in Coimbra and the Beiras regions - €161,000 (£110,500). New homes are more expensive than old, and developments aimed solely at overseas buyers are the dearest of all. Buying a resale property in a popular location will cost around €100,000 for a small apartment, and anything up to and over €1 million for a family-sized detached villa close to a beach. Prices have risen only moderately over the past couple of years, though the Algarve has seen the highest increases. Remember that in the more remote regions of the country communication lines and systems are still not great, and travelling time between airport and property will increase, often to an impressive amount, the further away you are from the main centres of population. Hours of driving along slow, poorly surfaced switchback roads to get to your mountain eyrie can be exciting and interesting over the first few trips but pretty soon the journey time will get to you. Although, on the positive side, prices of property in such isolated places will be cheaper than those that are closer to towns.

Prospective buyers can keep up with the latest trends and developments by reading the property and travel sections of some of the broadsheets and Sunday newspapers.

WHAT YOUR MONEY WILL BUY		
The following is for guidance only:		
€14,000	Farm property close to Guarda, Beira.	
€30,000	Detached property near Viseu in need of renovation/ modernisation.	

€40,000	Two-bed traditional stone cottage in need of renovation, set in countryside close to Coimbra.
€57,000	Odemira, Alentejo; plot of land 5,400 sq. metres with planning permission already granted.
€60,000	Ruin with stunning views of surrounding countryside with utilities already connected, near Ourique, Alentejo.
€80,000	Ruin within easy reach of Obidos, sea views, restoration or new build project.
€92,000	Two-bed apartment in centre of Albufeira with terraces, shared swimming pool and garden.
€105,000	Plot of land, 1,776 sq. metres, with two ruins, Tavira, Algarve.
€110,000	Farmhouse plus ruins on 1,500 sq. metre plot, Tavira, Algarve.
€110,000	Two-bed country villa near Calheta, western Madeira.
€118,000	Old watermill in need of complete renovation, Ourique, Alentejo.
€130,000	Plot of land located on Atlantic coast 5km from Nazaré, in a protected area, 1,650 sq. metres with planning permission for one or two dwellings.
€136,500+	Marina apartment (1/2/3-bedrooms) with 96 sq. metres of living area, air conditioning and terraces, Lagos, Algarve.
€150,000	New-build two-bed apartments on beachfront near Sines town centre.
€164,000	Restored 2-bed, 1-bathroom townhouse in Albufeira, Algarve.
€195,000	Two-bed property within easy reach to beach, motorway, and Lisbon, São Martinho do Porto.
€225,000	Three-bed cottages on resort complex, shared swimming pool, sea views, Praia da Luz.
€250,000	Semi detached, 4-bed, 3-bathroom villa close to beach, with grounds in Lagos, Algarve.
€343,048	Three-bed semi detached villa on outskirts of Loulé town, Algarve.
€460,000	Two-bed, 2-bathroom traditional townhouse with views over Monchique mountains.
€517,000	Two-bed, 2-bathroom villa in lakeside village complex in Quinta do Lago, Algarve.
€825,000	Villa overlooking Praia d'El Rey golf course, close to Lisbon.
€1,600,000	Five-bed country estate with swimming pool, tennis court in 12,000 sq. metres of land, Sintra.
€1,600,000	Riverside mansion over three floors, living space of 1000 sq. metres in need of renovation, central Porto.
€1,1600,000	Four-bed villa overlooking golf course in Vilamoura, with swimming pool.

The rest of this chapter aims to guide the prospective resident through some other issues relating to house buying or renting in Portugal, and through some of the steps necessary to complete the various buying or renting formalities and procedures. It is not however a substitute for professional and local advice, which is easily obtainable both from property agents and in the UK and in Portugal; or from lawyers (you can find a list in the *Directory of British Employers in Portugal* in the *Employment* chapter); or from those who have already set up home in Portugal and have their own tales to tell, cautionary or otherwise.

FINDING PROPERTIES FOR SALE

Estate Agents

As Portugal has become a more and more popular place in which to buy a holiday home more and more estate agents dealing in properties in Portugal are being established, both in the UK, and Portugal, and elsewhere. Estate agents dealing in property abroad can be found advertised in local telephone directories, on the internet and in international property magazines such as *Homes Overseas* (www.homesoverseas.co.uk) and *International Homes* (www.international-homes. com). Estate agents' websites and advertisements can give you a rough idea of the types and prices of property dealt with by a certain agent but will often not be bang up to date and will only show a small proportion of the properties on the books.

Discuss, in depth, your requirements with estate agents; sound them out about want you want – is such a property available locally? Or are your ideas are unrealistic? Agents will be more than willing to offer advice on the costs involved in purchasing and to help handle the property buying transaction for you. Remember that estate agents are looking to sell the properties already on their books, for their existing clients. However, if they are bona fide, they may well tell you honestly that you might do better by going to see their sister company, or another estate agency altogether, which may be more likely to have the kind of property that you are looking for. Giving an estate agency a clear idea of what you are looking for will hopefully save both you and them time and money. You don't want to end up traipsing around being shown totally unsuitable properties and discussing your requirements with an agency will allow you to find out about what alternatives there are. You may think you want a particular kind of property but an estate agent may come up with other types of property or localities that you hadn't considered previously.

Agents can arrange for you to view properties in Portugal, and many agents based abroad work in co-operation with locally-based agents who take care of the day-to-day business in Portugal. If you decide to go on an inspection trip to see a certain property or properties make sure that you arrange an appointment to view far enough in advance of your trip out there. If you are going out to Portugal on a house-hunting trip and will be viewing a number of properties it is a good idea to take a camera and a map of the area along with you. Take photographs to help you remember salient points about each property that you view; mark the property on a detailed map of the area so that you can then scout around and get to know whether a particular location is right for you. If an agent is showing you the wrong kind of properties let them know so that you, and they, can get back on to the right track. If you are on a house-hunting trip your time will be precious, though in many cases the right property turns up on the last day of such trips ('Well, there is this other property, but we didn't think it would suit you!') necessitating an extension of your trip, or a return to Portugal as rapidly as possible.

The bigger international outfits can lay on every service you can think of once you have invested in one of their properties – from an initial inspection trip to arranging a removals service, money matters, residency, etc.

Whether you buy through a Portuguese or UK estate agent it is essential that the company, and agent, is properly qualified and holds a licence. In Portugal estate agents must be qualified, in the UK this is not yet the case. The official status of an estate agent will be indicated on their stationery and their licence should be displayed on the premises.

Depending on the time scale you have allowed yourself to find and buy a property, before dealing with estate agents you should decide first on the area where you want to buy. By all means look in estate agents' shop windows, check out price ranges and property on offer in different parts of the country through property magazines, local English-language newspapers, the Internet, property exhibitions, etc., but don't tie yourself immediately to one or several estate agencies before you are sure about where you are hoping to buy. It will also be far more productive for those looking for an individual property rather than a new build one to research properties (and estate agents) on the ground in Portugal. Once there, you will be able to get a feel for the reliability and efficiency or otherwise of a particular agent as well as being able to see the most recent properties that have come onto the market and research local services and amenities. Flights are cheap these days and doing your research can save you time and money in the long run. Forewarned is forearmed.

Portuguese Estate Agents (Imobiliários)

In Portugal all estate agents must hold qualifications from and be authorised to operate by one of the recognised professional associations, either the *Associação de Mediadores Imobiliários de Portugal* (AMIP), or the Association of Portuguese Estate Agents (*Associação Portuguesa de Empresas de Mediação Imobiliários* – APEMI). Agencies that have been authorised to operate will display their certificate of registration and identification number (*mediador autorizado*) on the premises, and seeing these should give you some confidence in moving forward with that agency. Make sure that all staff, or at least those representatives that you are dealing with, are AMI or APEMI members – not just the owner of the business.

As in the UK, estate agents in Portugal operate in various ways with some dealing with only top end properties or they may only concentrate on the area around where their office is based. Those that deal with local properties will have a good knowledge of the possible problems associated with planning regulations, utility provision etc., in their locality. Estate agents dealing with properties on the Algarve are very likely to speak English, and may even be British, or German or Dutch (both the Germans and the Dutch have bought in numbers in Portugal). Imobiliários away from the tourist areas and off the beaten track may not be used to dealing with English-speakers, though agents will still bend over backwards in order to make a sale. Some estate agencies may be one-office outfits, or part of a large chain, or only deal specifically with the selling of their own developments and properties.

Portuguese estate agents in general provide far less detailed descriptions of property than that which we are used to at home and are somewhat less pro-active. Photographs of properties and details will be of varying quality, though in general the more expensive the property the better the marketing will be.

The chief role of the Imobiliário is to sell any property that has been placed with the estate agency, most of which will be resale properties. An estate agent's allegiance is with the vendor, from whom they draw their commission, and not with you the buyer. However, estate agents will be able to advise on aspects such as mortgages, residency, the tax system, etc., but such services will of course come at a cost. Once a deal has gone through, any issues that arise over the property will have nothing to do with the agents. It is therefore imperative to get a lawyer (an independent lawyer, rather than one recommended by the estate agency or the vendor) to check all contracts thoroughly before buying a property.

Because of the sometimes cash in hand nature of things in Portugal, you may be asked to sign a document before being shown a property or properties which protects the estate agent's interests, and ensures that he or she will be paid the commission should you go ahead and buy one of the properties on his or her books. This is because a property may be placed with several agents all of whom are after making their commission from the sale.

Note that many properties in Portugal are sold privately, so if you are driving through a village and see a 'vende se' – for sale – sign on a particular property that catches your eye it is permissible to call the owner, whose telephone number will be painted on the for sale sign.

UK Estate Agents

Because estate agents in the UK do not need to be qualified or members of a professional body, anyone can set up and call themselves estate agents. They can work from home, or have an office on a high street. They may market their services through advertisements in the local free presses, through English-language newspapers and magazines in Portugal, and on the internet. They may act as agents or middlemen for Portuguese estate agents who do not have the contacts, the marketing know-how or reach, or the fluency in English, that a British estate agent has. Because they may well have an office in the UK, contacting such agents can be a good starting place for sounding out the prices and property available, above all if they deal with the region/s where you are interested in buying.

Because these international agents have experience of dealing with Portuguese property law, regulations and red tape they can be very helpful for anyone who is wary of dealing with estate agents in Portugal direct. The initial suspicion and worry that comes with doing business in a foreign country where you do not know the rules and regulations, or have the native's know-how, can be circumvented by dealing with UK-based agents. However, this fact is well recognised by the more dishonest agents, who can play on people's fears and offer services that will cut down the interaction between the prospective buyer and the Portuguese agents to a minimum.

Prospective buyers of property should make sure that they are aware of and very clear about everything that is taking place 'on their behalf' during negotiations and try to remain in control of proceedings. Before entering into a contract with any estate agent check to see what their commission will be and ask for a breakdown of costs so that you can see what charges are going to be levied for services rendered. It may work out to be far more expensive going through an estate agent back home than dealing with a Portugal-based estate agent direct.

Commission

The commission rate charged by estate agencies can vary from 5% to 15%; the majority of the agents in the Algarve charge 5% + VAT. A higher commission is payable on cheaper properties than on more expensive ones, and the rate will also vary from region to region – higher rates being charged in more popular resort areas. Commission is paid by the vendor. Theoretically, if you are dealing with an agent based in the UK who works as an intermediary for a Portuguese estate agent then the commission charged on the sale of a property should be shared between the two of them, rather than you being charged commission twice.

Inspection Flights

If you know the type of property you want to buy and where you want to buy it, some property firms can arrange inspections flights to Portugal. A typical deal involves the estate agency booking the flight to Portugal, collecting and returning you to the airport and free accommodation for the duration of your trip. A consultant will take you round various properties on a one-to-one basis, showing you the area and the facilities on offer. Normally you will only have to pay for your flights (prices will depend on whether you are booked with a budget airline, or a more expensive scheduled flight) and these will be refundable if you eventually decide to buy a property with the agents.

Although there will be no obligation to buy on these inspection trips obviously the agency is hoping that they aren't wasting everyone's time by showing properties to someone who has no intention of buying with them. An inspection trip is not a free tour of the country, but is intended for those seriously wanting to purchase at the time of the inspection.

Before booking a special inspection visit, it is a good idea to have a clear idea of the location/s you would like to buy in and the kinds of prices property sells for in that location. You will also need to have talked through the ways in which you can finance your purchase – and the estate agent will want to know that you have the financial backing to be able to pay a deposit there and then should you find a suitable property on the inspection trip.

If you are sure of the area where you wish to buy, a three- or four-day visit is often adequate, though a longer trip leave room for the unexpected to turn up. To begin with you will be shown the various locations that you are interested in – be able to examine the infrastructures, school and medical facilities, leisure facilities, etc on offer. You will get a good idea of the type of properties available in these locations and be shown round a number. Towards the end of an inspection trip you will have time to review any properties that you think might be suitable. If you decide to buy a property that you have seen then the agency will be able to introduce you to a local lawyer who will be able to advise on the contracts, etc., should you decide to ask them to act on your behalf. Once back home the estate agency will continue to liase between your lawyer, the vendor and yourself.

WHEN ON AN ARRANGED INSPECTION TRIP:

- Don't be rushed around by the agent, but take your time and get a measured response to all properties that you view.
- Try and get some time away from the consultants to go off and explore on your own. Some companies may insist that you spend all of your visit under their direction and frankly these are to be avoided as a certain amount of pressure may be brought to bear. You need to be able to hear your own intuitive thoughts about a property and location without the interruptions of a salesman.
- Avoid mass inspections where you are shown a whole load of unsuitable

properties. Such an inspection will be a waste of your time and money. Don't waste time looking at properties you have no interest in buying.

o Have a clear notion of what you are looking for in a property in terms of size, location and price and let the agents know.

o If you decided to buy a property while on an inspection trip it may be difficult to ask to use (or to find) a lawyer other than the one that the agent offers you. You will be under a time limit, and a certain amount of pressure, to close the deal on the property before your return flight leaves.

o Inspection trips take the business relationship between a prospective buyer and an agent into a more complex area. Rather than being able to walk away should you decide that an agent hasn't got what you are looking for, going on an inspection trip means that the agent is investing time and money in you as a client and you therefore become more important to the agent. They will want a return on their investment.

Estate Agent Addresses

Algarve Real Estate Centre: Rossio Grande, Alto do Poço, Lote E/F Loja A, Apartado 110, 8501-906 Alvor; ☎282-420970; fax 282-420979; www.algarve-real-estate-centre.com.

AlgarImob: Urb. Porte da Vila Lote 2-T, 8600-642, Lagos, Algarve; ☎282-769362; fax 282-763612; www.algarimob.com.

Algarve Realty: Rua 25 de Abril, 7 r/c, 8300-184, Silves; ☎282-442471; www.algarverealty.com.

AT&T: Conjunto Monumental Infante, Avenida Arriaga nº 75, 3rd floor, Office 302, 9000-060 Funchal, Maderia; ☎291-220880; www.att.pt.

Bonau & Filio: Av. 25 de Abril, Bloco D, r/c Esqº., 8700-011 Fuzeta, Portugal; ☎289-791485; fax 289-791488; www.bonaulda.com.

Caldeira & Stevenson: Rua da Carreira, 92, 9000-042 Funchal, Madeira; ☎291-228435; fax 291-220206; www.caldeirastevenson.com.

Central Portugal Properties: Tras de Figueiro, Alvorge 3240-402, Ansiao; tel/fax 236-981717; www.centralpor tugalproperties.com.

CerroNovo: Centro Comercial, Cerro Grande, Albufeira; ☎289-510790; fax 289-510799; e-mail sales@cerronovo. com; www.cerronovo.com and www.cerronovo.co.uk; UK Office 01380-831411. CerroNovo is a long established family run company, the directors of which have been working in the Algarve since the 1970s. A government-registered estate agent, Cerro Novo have offices in Cerro Grande on the west side of Albufeira, and specialise in quality villas, apartments and land throughout the Algarve.

Cicerone, Lda: Av. Bombeiros Voluntários, 4, Estoril; ☎214-680389; email cicerone@mail. telepac.pt.

Country Homes Portugal: ☎+31 (035) 691 8418 (the Netherlands); www. rusticportugal.com.

Engel & Völkers: Rua 25 de Abril 38, 8600-763 Lagos, Algarve; ☎282-770980; fax 282-760720; www.engelvoelkers.com.

Esaguy Propriedades, Lda: Av. 25 de Abril, 6, 7670-250 Ourique, Alentejo: ☎286-516124; fax 286-516185; www.property-portugal.com.

Escape2portugal: Salisbury House, 228 Bury New Road, Whitefield, Manchester, M45 8QN; ☎0161-351 2160; fax 0161-767 8404; www.escape2portugal.co.uk.

Finespo: Rua Joaquim Martins Rodrigues, 107, 8200-448 Guia, Algarve; ☎289-560261; fax 289-560269; www.finespo-algarve.com.

Gameiro & Graça: Rua das Margaridas, 9, Birre Centre, Cascais; ☎214-850405; fax 214-872397; email gameiroegraca@clix.pt.

George Knight: Edifício Avis, Av. Fontes Pereira de Melo, 35, 18º B, 1050 Lisbon; ☎213-540001; fax 213-541914; www.georgeknight.pt.

Gold Real Estate: Largo Sta Maria da Graça, 12-14, 8600-518, Lagos, Algarve; ☎282-770640; fax 282-768319; www.algarve-gold.com.

Hamptons International: Avenida das Comunidades Portuguesas, Edifício Lapinha A, 8600-501 Lagos; ☎282-789336 & 0870 414 0444; fax 282-788184; e-mail portugal@hamptons-int.com; www.hamptons.co.uk. Also have offices in London: 18/21 Cavaye Place. London SW10 9PT; ☎020-7244 4740; fax 020-7244 4701.

Harrison Stone: PO Box 41, Petworth, Hampshire GU28 0YZ; ☎01798-342776; www.harrisonstone.co.uk.

Headlands International: Station Road, Nene Park, Irthlingborough, Northants NN9 5QF; ☎01933-654000; fax 01933-654099; www.headlands.co.uk. Also have offices in Portugal on the Algarve: *David Headland (Portugal) Lda*, Edifício Twin Stars, Rua Cristovao Pires Norte, 362, Almancil 8135-117; ☎289-351790; fax 289-391079.

Homelife: Rua de Bernardo Lima 35-2ºB, 1150-075 Lisbon; ☎213-570500; fax 213-570502; www.homelife.co.pt.

Homes For Sale in Portugal: Couchel, 085-3350 Vila Nova de Poiares; ☎239-423362; fax 239-422627; www.homesforsaleinportugal.com.

Iberus: Av. 25 de Abril, 5, 8200-012 Albufeira, Algarve; ☎289-583000;

fax 289-588162; www.iberus.com.

Imatico, Lda: Av. Manuel Remigio, Ed. Palmar, 2450-160 Nazaré; ☎262-551552; fax 262-551501; www.real-estate-portugal.com.

IMObarlavento: Rua D. Vasco da Gama, nº 11 r/c, 8600-722 Lagos, Algarve; ☎282-763879; fax 282-763879; www.imobarlavento.com.

IMOrainbow: Rua Comandante Henrique Tenreiro, Loja A, 8800-591 Cabanas, Tavira, Algarve; ☎966-246691; fax 966-119694; www.imorainbowcabanas.com.

João Paulo & Cidália: Rua Dr. Nunes da Silva Lote 6, r/c, Loja G, 8600-387 Lagos, Algarve; ☎282-761359; fax 282-761 362; www.jpsite.com.

Jones Homes: Emerson House, Heyes Lane, Alderley Edge, Cheshire SK9 7LF, United Kingdom; ☎01625-588 460; fax 01625-588 490; www.joneshomesportugal.com.

Knight Frank: Edifício Taurus, Campo Pequeno nº 48 - 4 Dt, 1000-081 Lisbon; ☎217-999960; fax 217-999965; www.knightfrank.com.

Maria Matos: Largo N. Sra. das Dores, nº 1, Zambujeira, 2530-323 Lourinhã; ☎261-414349; fax 261-423879; www.mariamatos.com. Agent in the

UK: *Undiscovered Portugal*, Howell Doug, 149 Preston Drove, Brighton BN1 6FN; ☎01273-546256.

MGA Imobiliaria: Largo Ribeiro do Amaral, 13B, 3400 Oliveira do Hospital; ☎238-601422; www.mgaimobiliaria.com.

Martina & Associadas Propriedades, Lda: Rua Frederico Arouca, nº24-2º, 2750-353 Cascais; ☎214-821373; fax 214-821359; www.map.com.pt.

Neves & Terlouw, Lda: Estrada Nacional nº109, nº69 Montijos, 2425-618 Monte Redondo; ☎244-689160; fax 244-689159. Also at Rua Dr. Sá Carneiro, Venda da Esperança, 3420-069 Covas, ☎238-671513; fax 238-671514; www.nevesterlouw.com.

North Portugal Estate Sales: Casa das Flores, Quinta do Regueiro, Bogadela, Barbeita, 4950-044 Moncao, Alto Minho; ☎914-128345; fax 251-531211; www.north-portugal-holiday-rentals.com.

Portogoa Construções, Lda: Rua dos Carros, Loja 2, Apartado 174, 8400 Lagoa, Portugal; ☎282-341035; fax 282-341285; www.portogoa.com.

Premier Properties International Group: Great Street, Norton sub Hamdon, Somerset TA14 6SG, UK; ☎01935-

881199; fax 01935-881762; www. premierpropertiesonline.net.

Quadrant Overseas: 50 Brackendale Road, Camberley, Surrey GU15 2JR; ☎01276-507513; fax 01276-507514; www.quadrant-property. com. Quadrant Overseas Property is a real estate agent with 25 years' experience in the sale of property in Portugal, from luxury villas, holiday apartments etc. to something a little more unique from their collection of historic buildings. Most areas are covered including Algarve, Madeira, Lisbon, Cascais and the Estoril coast.

Realestate Algarve: Rua Dr. Paulo J. Godinho, Lote 5 - Loja C, 8600-774 Lagos, Portugal; ☎282-768821; fax 282-768827; www.realestate-algarve. com.

Remax Global: Rua dos Pescadores, 129 Loja B, Praia do Carvoeiro, Algarve; ☎932-484563; fax 912-231210; www.remax-portugal.com.

Rentavila: Rua Marques Leal Pancada 24, 2750-430 Cascais; ☎214-827075; fax 917-327188; www. rentavila.com.

Rose Real Estate: Avenida General Carmona, 13, 2765-207 Estoril; ☎214-665100; fax 214-665095; www.rrrlda.com.

Sanotomero: Largo Nossa Senhora da Guia, 14, 8200-443, Guia, Algarve; ☎289-561345; fax 289-562026; www.santomero-algarve.com.

Silver Holidays Real Estate: Rua do Brasil, Casa Italiana, Loja 5, 8125-479 Vilamoura, Algarve: ☎289-314312; fax 289-314260; email silver.holidays@clix.pt.

Sociedade Imobiliária Balancal: Sitio du Balancal, São Gonçalo, 9050-296 Funchal, Madeira: ☎291-795161; fax 289-395249; www.madeira-real-estate.com.

Sunny Homes: EN124, Vivenda Quintue r/c, Carvoeiro, 8400 Lagoa, Algarve; ☎282-359062; fax 282-359064; www.sunnyhomesportugal. com.

Sunseaker Properties: Apartado 89, Praia da Luz, 8601-926, Lagos; ☎282-697413; fax 282-697413; www. sunseaker.co.uk.

Sunshine Villas: Buganvilla Plaza, Loja 17, Quinto do Lago, 8135 Almancil, Algarve; ☎289-398564; fax 289-398590; www.sunshinevillas.com.

Vieiranima, Lda: Centro Comercial Monumental Lido, 1º, Loja 17, 9000-101 Funchal, Madeira; ☎291-765023; www.vieiranima.com.

Vilagente: Edifício do Cinema, Loja 3, Vilamoura, 8125-432, Quarteira, Algarve; ☎289-314486; fax 289-315578; www.vendavilla.com.

Warren International (UK): Grenville Court, Britwell Road, Burnham, Buckinghamshire SL1 8DF, UK; ☎01628-660885; fax 01628-662845; www.propertyinportugal. uk.com.

Other Useful Contacts

Names of other agents dealing in property in Portugal can be obtained from the *National Association of Estate Agents*, Arbon House, 21 Jury Street, Warwick CV34 4EH; ☎01926-496800; www.naea.co.uk (select the international section). They can send a list (ask for their 'Homelink' department) of members specialising in Portugal. Or contact the *Royal Institute of Chartered Surveyors*, Surveyor Court, Westwood Way, Coventry CV4 8JE; ☎0870-333 1600; www.rics.org.

The *Association of Portuguese Estate Agents* (APEMI): Associação Portuguesa das Empresas de Mediação Imobiliária, R. D. Luís de Noronha, n.º4-2º, 1069-165 Lisbon; ☎217-928770; fax 217-958815; www.apemi.pt. Also has regional offices in Porto, Coimbra, Vilamoura, Funchal in Madeira and Ponta Delgada in the Azores.

The *Associação de Mediadores Imobiliários de Portugal* (AMIP) has its office on Rua Júlio Dinis, 728 - 2º.Esqº. S/226, 4050-321 Porto; ☎226-069312; fax 226-068831; www.amip.pt.

The *Association for Foreign Residents and Visitors to Portugal* (AFPOP – Associação de Proprietários Estrangeiros em Portugal, Apartado 728, 8501-917, Porimão, Algarve; ☎282-458509; fax 282-458277; www.afpop.com) was founded in 1987 with the objective of helping its multinational membership make the most of out of living and working in Portugal. An annual fee of €60 and €75 – for single and joint membership respectively – provides access to the latest information concerning Portuguese laws, assistance with issues that are of concern to members, meetings and events, as well as financial benefits from car purchase, insurance and leisure facilities to discounts at restaurants. AFPOP has a voluntary Management Council and Area Representatives throughout Portugal.

The CEI (*Confédération Européenne de l'Immobilier*: European Confederation of Real Estate Agents, Sainctlettesquare, 11-12, B-1000 Brussels, Belgium; ☎+32-2-219 4008; fax +32-2-217 8841) is one of Europe's largest professional organisation of estate agents, now counting well over 25,000 members from hundreds of cities in thirteen European countries, Austria, France, Germany, Greece, Hungary, Ireland, Italy, the Netherlands, Portugal, Romania, Spain, the United Kingdom and the Slovak Republic, representing a total of over 60,000 operators in real estate. The CEI website (www.webcei.com) has a search facility.

The *Federation of Overseas Property Developers, Agents & Consultants* (FOPDAC) is a membership organisation restricted to agents, developers and consultants active in the international property markets. The federation can be contacted at 618 Newmarket Road (1ˢᵗ Floor), Cambridge CB5 8LP; ☎0870-350 1223; fax 0870-350 1233; www.fopdac.com.

Adverts

When you begin looking into the possibilities of buying a property in Portugal you will very quickly become aware of the vast number of companies out there who are looking to persuade you to do business with them. Take out a subscription to one of the property or lifestyle magazines such as *Portugal* or *Algarve Property Advertiser* or *Homes Overseas* and you will find pages of space given over to advertisements placed by property developers, estate agents, removals firms, lawyers and insurers and accountants. The property pages of weekend national newspapers in the UK almost always have articles on buying property abroad and these pieces will include sample prices of properties and details of the companies interviewed. Many of these property advertisements will include details of the size of the property (and/or land) in square metres which allows the interested to compare prices regionally or nationwide. Another good resource, for both prospective property buyers and service companies is the internet.

The Internet

Although you won't be able (and won't want) to buy properties over the Internet there is a growing number of websites that deal with property – from estate agents' home pages, to those of property developers, mortgage lenders, letting agencies, and websites aimed at expats and house-hunters. Estate agents and property developers are increasingly using the World Wide Web as a marketing tool – as a relatively cheap way to get their name out there. There are now internet portals (websites dedicated to one area of information and/or commerce), which deal exclusively with properties for sale about from thousands of leading agents and developers. Using a search engine such as www.google.com or a web directory such as www.yahoo.com will lead you into a selection of websites dealing solely with Portuguese property for sale.

Because of the vast amount of information (as well as misinformation and downright junk) that is posted on the internet you will need to narrow down any search that you make using a web directory or search engine. Rather than just typing in for example, 'property + Portugal' or 'villas for sale + Algarve' name the specific area or town you are looking to buy in. If you have a name of a property developer or estate agent that you are thinking of doing business with, then use the web as a research tool. Find out as much as you can about their company. You can make initial contact with vendors of property which interests you by using e-mail (you can get a free e-mail address at such places as www.hotmail. com, or yahoo.com) but be very wary of any company or individual who asks for payment of any kind over the internet. Although e-commerce has come a long way and although those who have the money to invest in internet security have made it virtually impossible for a hacker to get hold of clients' credit card details that are given over the web, smaller operators may not have. If you decide to continue with negotiations after initial contact over the Internet better to set up a face to face meeting as soon as possible. Anyone can be anybody they want in cyberspace.

The internet can be a great marketing tool – the Hamptons International website for example has reported getting 150,000 hits (visitors to its website) in one month alone. A few sites worth viewing, especially for those looking to buy at the top end of the property market, are Knight Frank (www.knightfrank.com), Hamptons (www. hamptons.co.uk), www.primelocation.com (which includes details of over 80,000 properties for sale), www.propertyfinder.com and newskys.co.uk. Property portals such as www.okapa.com, www.myimo.com, www.bescasa.pt, www.bpiimobiliario. pt, www.cidadebcp.pt, www.habinet.com and www.lardocelar.com are also worth investigating. The best of these websites will allow you to search for suitable properties by specifying search criteria such as whether you want a villa with or without a swimming pool, its proximity to the beach, hospitals etc., as well as the desired region in Portugal, and of course purchase price. Increasingly, agencies are linking up to property portals.

The Press

Daily and weekend newspapers all carry adverts for property abroad – mostly in the property sections, but also sometimes at the back of the travel pages. You may want to take out a subscription to some of the English-language newspapers published in Portugal – some of which are regional rather than national in scope. There are also a number of free sheets available from establishments such as bars, estate agents and tourist offices, which carry property advertisements. Another place to look for both property advertisements and articles on living, working and buying property in Portugal is in the rising number of glossy magazines published both in the UK and in Portugal. Below is a list of some of the newspapers and magazines dealing with property in Portugal:

Algarve Property Advertiser: Vista Ibérica Publicações Lda, Urb. Lagoa Sol, Lt 1-B, 8400-415 Lagoa; ☎282-340660; fax 282-343088; www.vista-iberica.com.

Homes Overseas Magazine: Blendon Communications Ltd., 1st Floor, 1 East Poultry Avenue, West Smithfield, London EC1A 9PT; ☎020-7939 9888; fax 020-7939-9889; www.blendoncommunications.co.uk.

International Homes Magazine. 3 St. John's Court, Moulsham Street, Chelmsford, Essex CM2 0JD; ☎01245-358877; fax 01245-357767; www.international-homes.com.

Portugal Magazine: Merricks Media Ltd, Cambridge House South, Henry Street, Bath BA1 1JT; ☎01225-786 800; fax 01225-786 801; www.merricksmedia. co.uk.

Private Villas Magazine: C.I. Tower, St. George's Square, New Malden, Surrey KT3 4JA, UK; ☎020-8329 0170; fax 020-8329 0101; www.privatevillas. co.uk.

The Portuguese Property Journal: Apartado 118, Santa Barbara de Nexe, 8001-501 Faro, Portugal.

World of Property: Outbound Publishing, 1 Commercial Road, Eastbourne, East Sussex, BN21 3XQ; ☎01323-726 040; fax 01323-649 249; www. outboundpublishing.com.

FINANCE

Buying a property abroad is going to involve, apart from a fair amount of money, getting to grips with a whole new culture of doing business. You will have to learn about the Portuguese tax system; the way the banks there operate; how you can use your money to bring increased dividends and the best way to finance and insure your property and protect your assets from the tax authorities. What follows is a brief outline of this side of life in Portugal to help you to familiarise yourself with the kind of financial bureaucracy and possibilities you will encounter in the country. Much of what follows will be explained to you by your lawyers and agents at home or once in Portugal and you will also learn a great deal about the financial side of life in Portugal through just being there.

However complicated tax systems seem, however convoluted and impossible these systems appear, if you find yourself a good, reliable, English-speaking accountant and lawyer (they are will be well worth the money they charge) you should find your introduction to Portuguese bureaucracy if not exactly a breeze, at least manageable. After all, there are hundreds of thousands of foreigners living in Portugal (including some 200,000 Britons), all filing their tax returns, paying off their mortgages and investing their savings as wisely as possible. Unless you have decided to relocate to a mountain village in one of the more remote provinces of the country you will not be the first foreigner to walk through the door of the local Portuguese bank, tax office, or insurance company, and you are unlikely to be the last.

IMPORTING CURRENCY

Purchasing a foreign property involves sending large amounts of money abroad to cover the costs involved. When you find the right property to buy, you will be given the price in euros or the foreign currency. However, until you have bought all of the currency, you won't know the total costs involved. Depending on the exchange rate fluctuations between your home currency and the foreign currency during the conveyancing procedures, the property could eventually cost you more or less than you had originally thought. Importing money into another country can take time and there are various ways of going about transferring funds. Some solicitors can transfer money between accounts held at home and abroad, and for many potential buyers this may be the quickest and easiest way of doing things.

Another method of transferring funds is to obtain a banker's draft from your UK bank. This is a cheque guaranteed by the bank, which can be deposited into your bank account anywhere in the world. When making the final payment on the purchase of a property at the notary's office it is advisable to hand over a banker's draft made payable to the vendor. Note that a banker's draft works along the lines of a cheque, and once it is paid into an account there will be a short period of waiting before it is cleared and you are able to access the money. You can also transfer money by SWIFT electronic bank transfer. This procedure can take several days and rates of exchange will vary.

Because of currency fluctuations converting currency, for example sterling to euros, will always be something of a gamble. If the pound falls against the euro you will end up paying more than you budgeted for. If, as soon as you sign the contract to begin the process of buying, you convert the total cost of the property into euros you may be happy with the conversion rate but you will lose the use of the money while further negotiations take place over the settlement of the property.

To avoid this, a specialised foreign currency provider such as *Currencies Direct* (Hanover House, 73-74 High Holborn, London WC1V 6LR; ☎020-7813 0332; fax 020-7419 7753; www.currenciesdirect.com) can help in a number of ways, by offering better exchange rates than banks, without charging commission, and giving you the possibility of 'forward buying', i.e. agreeing on the rate that you will pay at a fixed date in the future, or with a 'limit order', i.e. waiting until the rate you want is reached before making the transaction. For those who prefer to know exactly how much money they will need for their purchase, forward buying is the best solution, since you no longer have to worry about the movement of the pound against the foreign currency working against you. Payments can be made in one lump sum or on a regular basis. For example, it is usual when purchasing a new-build property to pay in four instalments, so called 'staged payments'.

There is a further possibility, which is to use the services of a law firm in the UK to transfer the money. They can hold the money for you until the exact time that you need it. However, remember that law firms will also use the services of a currency dealer themselves, so you may be better off going to a foreign currency provider yourself to avoid any excess legal fees.

Intra-EU Credit Transfers. In July 2003 a new system of transferring funds in euros between accounts within the EU was launched using an account holder's unique International Bank Account Number (IBAN) and Bank Identifier Code (BIC) which is also known as the 'SWIFT' code which is a unique code issued to every bank. Banks are obliged to provide bank statements with the IBAN and

BIC printed on them. Firms issuing invoices within the EU now have to print their IBAN and BIC numbers on their invoices.

Exchange Control

Inward investment from external sources (within the EU) has been unrestricted since 1990. With the creation of the Single European Market in 1993, there is now virtually free movement of capital between Portugal and its EU partners; and no limit in value on the entry of foreign currency and payments from the EU into Portugal. Portuguese customs expect visitors to declare all money (in local or foreign currency) imported or exported from the country equivalent to a sum exceeding €4,987,98, whether it takes the form of notes, gold, travellers' cheques or securities. This is so the government can monitor cash flows and prevent potential money laundering.

One important point to remember is that anyone importing money into Portugal to buy property should do so legally as, when or if they subsequently sell the property and wish to transfer the proceeds out of Portugal, they will not be able to do so unless they can prove that the funds were legally imported in the first place.

MORTGAGES

There are several options available to anyone wanting to purchase a property with a mortgage: taking out a mortgage/second mortgage through a bank or building society back home, or borrowing from a Portuguese bank or setting up an offshore company to buy the property. There is also the question of whether to obtain a mortgage in Euros or in Sterling to consider.

Although taking out a euro mortgage on a Portuguese property provides better security against fluctuations in currency values, fluctuation in interest rates may serve to counteract this advantage. One of the main difficulties of Portuguese-based mortgages is actually finding a bank that is willing to lend the money to you, especially if you are not already resident in Portugal. In addition the maximum mortgage in Portugal is usually around 75% of the purchase price, less than is usual in the UK, in addition to allowing a shorter repayment schedule.

Sometimes taking out a fixed UK mortgage will be a better bet, and is usually quite easy to organise. Among those who can arrange a mortgage are UK building societies like *Halifax* (Head Office: Trinity Road, Halifax, West Yorkshire HX1 2RG).

It can be easier to borrow money at home and be a cash buyer abroad. If you use your home as equity to fund buying a property in Portugal you won't have to deal with overseas lenders and brokers and won't have to worry about the mortgage increasing should the euro appreciate against the pound. If you borrow in euros then when currencies move (which they will do), your asset (the home in Portugal) will move in the same direction as the mortgage. It also makes sense to keep your debts in the same currency as your income.

If you are thinking of taking a mortgage with a lender in Portugal remember that there are fewer fixed, capped and discounted schemes operated on the Continent and terms can be more restrictive than those offered in the UK – a high deposit and a maximum repayment term of 15 years is standard.

Hove-based *Conti Financial Services* (204 Church Road, Hove, East Sussex BN3 2DJ; ☎01273-772 811; fax 01273-321 269; www.mortgagesoverseas.com) deals with overseas property mortgages and currently offers a variable interest rate for properties in Portugal of approximately 1.50% above LIBOR (London Interbank Offering Rate – the rate of interest at which banks borrow funds from other banks, in marketable size, in the London interbank market) on a variable rate basis in Sterling or approximately 2.75% in Euros. As an example of the type of mortgage Conti offers, you would be paying approximately €397.50 capital and interest per month for a repayment mortgage of €72,500 over a period of 20 years, at an interest rate of 2.75%; this would make the total approximate amount payable over the 20-year term €98,252, including capital, interest, arrangement and survey fees.

Another overseas mortgage is broker is PropertyFinance4Less (160 Brompton Road, London SW3 1HW; ☎0207-594 0555; fax 0207-594 0550; www.propertyfinance4less.com).

You can, and should, obtain an agreement in principle from a lender for any mortgage finance you may need before agreeing to purchase a property. If you are purchasing a plot and having a villa built lenders will make payments in stages as construction proceeds.

UK Mortgages

If you are planning to buy a second home in Portugal it is possible to arrange loans in the UK – perhaps by taking out a second mortgage on your UK property and then buying with cash in Portugal. Alternatively, it is now also possible to approach the banks for a sterling loan secured on a property in Portugal. If you are considering borrowing in the UK, then the method of calculating the amount that may be borrowed is worked out at between two and a half and three and a half times your primary income plus any secondary income you may have, less any capital amount already borrowed on the mortgage. Sometimes the amount that may be borrowed is calculated at two and a half or three times joint income, less outstanding capital. Your credit history will also be checked to assess whether you will be able to manage increased mortgage payments. It is most usual for buyers to pay for their second home with a combination of savings and equity from re-mortgaging an existing property.

Naturally, the mortgage will be subject to a valuation on the UK property, and you can expect to borrow, subject to equity, up to a maximum of 80% of the purchase price of the overseas property (compared with the availability of 100%

mortgages for UK properties). If you are going to take out a second mortgage with your existing mortgage lender then a second charge would be taken by the mortgage company. Note that some lending institutions charge a higher rate for a loan to cover a second property.

IMPORTANT NOTE

You should ensure that if a loan is arranged in the UK then all of the details of this are included in the Portuguese property contract deed (*escritura*).

Portuguese Mortgages

Portuguese mortgages are all 'full status', which means proof of incomings and outgoings is required and can be arranged for purchase, construction and renovation. For buyers living and working in Portugal, mortgages are obtainable from Portuguese banks for up to 90% of the property value, subject to income verification (tax returns will be required). These loans are based on a variable rate in euros and are from 1%-3% over the prevailing LISBOR or EURIBOR rate. Portuguese banks will also often offer low fixed rate interest repayments for an initial period.

For non-residents, mortgages are available in any major currency from a number of specialist lenders for up to 80% of the property value, subject to income verification. Income can comprise earned income together with pension, investment or rental income, however, different mortgage lenders have different criteria when it comes to relating sources of income to the maximum loan available.

Loans are based on joint net take home income and are calculated on an affordability basis. As an approximate guideline, other existing liabilities, including any mortgage or rental payments, personal loan repayments and maintenance payments, together with your proposed Portuguese mortgage payment, should not generally exceed 40% of your net monthly income.

You may borrow in a currency other than the currency in which you receive your income but the amount of liability is only fixed in the mortgage currency. If you take out a euro mortgage, then your liability may increase in the future if converted to sterling, due to exchange rate movements. Banks operating in Portugal and offering mortgage finance information and help over the internet include Barclays (Av. Barbosa du Bocage, 54 D, 1000-072 Lisbon; ☎217-911301; fax 217-911390; www.barclays.pt, plus branches in Porto and Cascais); Banco Espírito Santo (www.bes.pt), Millennium BCP (www.millenniumbcp.pt), Caixa Geral de Depósitos (www.cgd.pt) and Crédito Predial Português (www.cpp.pt).

MORGAGE COMPARISON TABLE		
	UK Mortgage	**Portuguese Mortgage**
Types available:	repayment, endowment, pension, etc.	capital or interest, plus foreign currency mortgages available
Max. % of value advanced:	95%	typically 70%
Max. compared to income:	2.5 x joint or 3.5 x 1	typically 30%
Period of Mortgage:	5-25 years	5-25 years
Interest rate:	fixed, variable, capped, discounted	fixed, based on Euribor
Repayments made:	monthly	1,3 or 6 monthly

Euro Mortgages

Arranging a mortgage whereby you are borrowing in the local currency minimises the risk of exchange rate fluctuations. Many international banks are happy to lend to non-residents and overseas mortgage brokers have a choice of such lenders. Euro mortgage rates are determined by the European Interbank Offered Rate – Euribor, which is currently approximately 2%. The borrowers monthly disposable income will determine the size of the mortgage. However, in Portugal lenders are not always prepared to lend as high salary multiples as they are in the UK with maximum loan to value ratios of 80%. Borrowers will need proof of income, outgoings and bank statements. Borrowers will also need to budget for bank arrangement fees (about €1,500), lender valuation (approx. €430) in addition to solicitor's fees. Broker arrangement fees range from 0%-0.75%.

Offshore Mortgages

The principle of offshore companies involves turning a property into a company, the shares of which are held as collateral against a mortgage of up to 75% for a repayment term of up to 20 years by an offshore bank based in a tax haven such as Gibraltar or the Channel Islands. The property owner's name is confidential and the property company is administered on the owner's behalf by the offshore trustees. Previously, the advantage of offshore property purchase was that it reduced tax liability in the country of purchase, as, if and when the property was resold, it merely became a question of transferring the shares confidentially to a new owner, thus avoiding transfer taxes and VAT in the country in question.

However there are risks. For example, due to new legislation thousands of Britons who bought property in Portugal through offshore companies now face potentially huge tax bills in the eventuality of either their selling the property, or of their death. Although, in the majority of cases, offshore property purchase has resulted in the legitimate avoidance of wealth tax, succession duty, transfer tax and capital gains tax, a minority of cases has clearly crossed the fine line between tax avoidance and tax evasion at the cost of the state coffers. You should certainly not try to enter into such an arrangement without the advice of an accountant, solicitor, or other professional adviser.

Clampdown on Tax Avoidance

Using an offshore company has traditionally been viewed as the most tax-efficient way of owning property abroad, and until recently it has been. For whereas those who own property have to pay UK income tax on rental income and UK capital gains tax on profits made on the sale of a property, corporation tax is usually lower. Offshore companies are used to avoid problems with local and inheritance taxes abroad, and in Portugal buying through an offshore company was often the only option offered to prospective buyers by property developers. Using an offshore company circumvented the need to pay the stamp duty (of up to 10% of the value of a property) and meant savings on capital gains tax as the company is deemed to be the owner of the property, not the individual/s. However, if the individual was deemed to be a shadow director of the offshore company and was UK-domiciled then the property is classed as a benefit in kind by the tax authority.

However, new Portuguese property laws that came into effect on 1 January 2004 have meant that any property owned by an offshore company now has to pay an annual tax of 5% of the value of the property. Only those companies registered in the exclusion zones of Malta, New Zealand and Delaware are exempt from this ruling, though these zones are likely to be brought into line in the future. The new tax laws will mean that if you buy a property in Portugal for £250,000 you will need to find an additional £12,500 annually to keep the tax man happy. Much has been made of these changes to the law in the British press.

Those who already own property in Portugal through an offshore company have three options: to sell the property; transfer ownership of the offshore company to one of the exclusion zones by setting up a new trust (at a cost of around £5,000); or pay the 10% purchase tax to bring the company onshore.

For those who are looking to buy property in Portugal it now seems a better option to pay the one-off charge of stamp tax at the time of purchase rather than having to pay an annual levy on the price of your property.

THE PURCHASING & CONVEYANCING PROCEDURE

FEES

Conveyancing costs are likely to come to around 10% of the purchase price of a resale property. Costs include the fees charged by lawyers, the land registry, the notary, taxes, bank charges, associates fees, in addition to valuation and arrangement fees payable to the mortgage company. The cheaper the property, the more the likelihood of the 10% rising to a higher figure due to the minimum charges imposed by lawyers and others involved in the conveyancing.

LAWYERS

Vendors of property in Portugal do not necessarily need to hire a lawyer, but buyers most certainly will. It is very important to employ an *advogado* to look after your personal interests. A lawyer should check that the vendor of the property is the legal (and sole) owner of the property and whether there are any outstanding debts on it. They should be able to check that the property has been, or is being, built with proper planning permission and has all the necessary licences. They should check that the terms of the contract are fair and reasonable and prepare a report of their findings for the potential buyer's information. Given the go ahead, the solicitor can then arrange for currency to be transferred to Portugal, the title deeds (*escritura*) to be transferred into the buyer's name and registered with the Land Registry and for fees and taxes to be paid.

An independent lawyer should be either a specialist lawyer from home or an English-speaking Portuguese *advogado*. Be wary of using the services of a lawyer recommended by the vendor or their estate agent, as their impartiality may be, though probably isn't, questionable. Also, should you use a Portuguese lawyer, even if they speak fluent English, they may be unfamiliar with UK law and the ramifications that buying a property overseas may have on your tax or legal situation back home.

Most *advogados* are found through recommendation. If your grasp of Portuguese is shaky then you should definitely find a lawyer who speaks English. The lawyer will be able to:

- ○ Advise a client whose name should be registered as the owner of a property as ownership will have knock-on effects with regards taxation.
- ○ Advise on how to pay for the property – whether through a mortgage, re-

mortgaging, forming a company, cash, etc., and how to minimise costs.

O   Arrange for Power of Attorney should it be necessary (see below).

O   Arrange for the signing of the *escritura* and making purchase payments, and may also be able to organise currency exchange and the transferral of funds from a buyer's home bank account into Portugal.

O   Check that there are no cases pending against the property with regards to planning permission not having been obtained when the property was originally built.

O   Draw up the contract for the sale of the property or between a builder, architect and client.

O   Guide a client through the legal processes involved in buying property in Portugal.

O   Look after the conveyancing procedures.

O   Make payments for the conveyancing costs, taxes etc, on behalf of the buyer.

O   Obtain an NIF number on behalf of the client (this number is needed for the payment of taxes and the purchase of property in Portugal).

O   Recommend local tradesmen, surveyors, agents, mortgage brokers and banks that will suit a clients needs.

Advice for first-time buyers: Use a lawyer! – Patricia Westheimer
Always have a lawyer look over your contract. Even though they tell you it isn't necessary, it is. I did and my lawyer helped me in many important ways. It's worth the extra cost. Use a lawyer whom others recommend and who speaks your language fluently. In fact, I have a rule: I do all of my business dealing, money matters, health issues and anything contractual in English. That way I am less apt to make mistakes. I understand Portuguese, but I will never understand it as well as English.

In the Algarve and in the more cosmopolitan areas of Portugal finding a lawyer who speaks English will not be a problem. Lawyers in these areas will be used to dealing with foreigners looking to buy property in their locality and may well advertise their services in local free sheets and the English-language press. They will be well aware of potential areas of conflicting interests and will be able to smooth your way to the best of their ability within the confines of Portuguese law.

If you are hoping to buy property with land attached in a rural part of Portugal then your lawyer will be useful in finding out about what the planning restrictions are in the area and if there are local bylaws in force with regards to water, grazing or hunting and access rights on the land. You will also want your lawyer to check out where property boundaries end and begin as these may differ from what has been written in the *escritura*, what the owners of the property believe to be the case, and what is registered in the Land Registry. If you are buying a property in an apartment block where you will be part of the *comunidade de propietários* you will also want the rules and regulations checked by a lawyer.

You should get your lawyer to check everything that is put on the table by the estate agents before signing anything. Don't rely on a notary to do the work that a lawyer would normally do. Another good reason for getting a lawyer is that they may well be able to advise you on the most financially beneficial way to deal with the conveyancing process, saving you money by guiding you through the taxation systems of Portugal and the UK. It is a good idea to find a lawyer and get their advice before even starting on the house-hunt. An international lawyer will be able to give you pointers and tell you about the possible pitfalls. They will also be ready to look at contracts before you sign – you may be able to fax them over while you are in Portugal and wait for their appraisal before going ahead and signing and committing yourself to something that you may later regret. Remember that you will need to find either a lawyer from home versed in international law and the laws pertaining to property in Portugal in particular, or an English-speaking Portuguese lawyer versed in the taxation system of your home country. Without this knowledge a lawyer may not be able to organise your affairs to your best advantage.

UK-Based Lawyers

Bennett & Co Solicitors: 144 Knutsford Road, Wilmslow, Cheshire SK9 6JP; ☎01625-586937; fax 01625-585362; e-mail: internationallawyers@bennett-and-co.com; www.bennett-and-co.com. Bennett & Co. provides a comprehensive legal service to private and commercial clients who require legal advice and assistance overseas. Geographically their areas of specialisation include Portugal amongst other countries in Europe and beyond; they have associated firms in most of these countries providing a high standard of expertise in their chosen field.

John Howell & Co: The Old Glassworks, 22 Endell Street, Covent Garden, London WC2H 9AD; ☎020-7420 0400; fax 020-7836 3626; e-mail info@europelaw.com; www.europelaw.com. John Howell & Co is a highly specialised firm of English lawyers which deals only with work in continental Europe and Dubai. It has been dealing with European legal work since 1986 and employs its own fully-qualified foreign lawyers (including Portuguese lawyers) to work alongside its English lawyers, all of whom are bilingual.

The International Property Law Centre: Unit 2, Waterside Park, Livingstone Road, Hessle, HU13 OEG; ☎0870-800 4565 fax 0870-800 4567; e-mail internationalproperty@maxgold.com; www.internationalpropertylaw.com. Specialists in the purchase and sale of Portuguese property and businesses, wills and probate, and litigation.

Lita Gale Solicitors (43-45 Gower Street, London WC1E 6HH; ☎020-7580 2066;

www.litagale.com). Lita Gale Solicitors have associated offices in Lisbon Faro and Madeira and specialise in all matters to do with Portugal and Portuguese Law as well as English Law. Visit their web site for a detailed guide to Buying Property in Portugal and information on their services.

Fees. The fees charged by a lawyer for their work on buying a new or resale property are likely to be about 1% of the price of the property, although there may be a minimum charge (around £1,000). You will need to be aware that apart from the basic fee, should additional negotiations need to be undertaken on your behalf you will be charged. For example there may need to be further clauses added to a contract, or negotiations over the price of a property; if there are irregularities in the *escritura* these will need to be corrected before change of title can take place. There will also be correspondence generated between the solicitors and a mortgage company if you are taking out a mortgage and all these matters will incur further fees.

For properties that have not yet been built, lawyers will generally charge around 1% of the property value plus an hourly rate on work done on your behalf while the construction continues. Because, as is the way of all things, there can never be a 100% definite completion date, more work may need to be done on your behalf as projects and the legalities involved unfold. The solicitor should give you an estimate of the likely charges to be incurred once s/he has seen the existing paperwork relating to the project.

Consulates and embassies in Portugal will hold lists of English-speaking lawyers in your locality. In the UK *The Law Society* (113 Chancery Lane, London WC2A 1PL; ☎020-7242 1222; www.lawsoc.org.uk), also holds lists of registered English-speaking lawyers in Portugal.

Inspections and Surveys

It wouldn't be prudent to buy a property in the UK without having it checked over by a qualified surveyor, so it makes sense therefore to get a property surveyed that you are interested in buying in Portugal. That said, the surveying of property before purchasing is not a legal requirement in Portugal and many people buy on sight. However, the old adage, 'when in Rome do as the Romans do...' shouldn't apply when it comes to something as financially risky as buying a house. If you are buying a property on a mortgage, the lenders may well require a survey, even if it is only to provide an appraisal of the purchase price.

For new properties, and property that is less than five years old the structure will have been guaranteed by the original builders or developers as all builders must guarantee their work against major structural defects for this amount of time in Portugal. However, should you be buying an older resale property, or even a derelict building that you are hoping to renovate, you would be wise to get a

structural survey done.

When you initially view a property that you are interested in, give it the amateur eye and check for any signs of subsidence, bowing walls, damp patches or strange smells. Check for dry rot (stick a knife into windowsills and other likely areas where damp may have struck), a leaking roof (stains on the ceilings), cracks or fractures in the walls. You will want to make sure that all plumbing, electrics, and water heating systems are in good working order, as well as the drainage and water provision. If there is a well on the land ask the vendor if it has been tested recently. Be on the look out for any signs of rising damp or signs of condensation/humidity. While viewing a property take your time and get a feel for the place – you will usually be able to tell if there are any major structural problems.

If you are still not sure, you could arrange for a local estate agent (other than the one showing you the property of course) to give their opinion of the place and of the price asked. Alternatively a local builder may be able to give their opinion of the structural soundness or otherwise of the property. In any case, should you be looking to buy a derelict property for renovation you will want to get a quote from a few builders as to the likely cost of renovation. A builder will also have local knowledge and be able to comment on the purchase price asked by the vendor. All of these opinions will of course come at a cost but will be worth it to set your mind at rest.

All the above people will be able to give you their 'expert' opinions on whether your desired property is sound or not but they are unlikely to be backed up by a professional report. A trained surveyor on the other hand will be able to cast a professional eye over the property and give you a full and detailed report on it. Such a survey will cost you around €500 depending on the surveyor and the size of property. Portuguese surveyors used to dealing with foreigners are likely to provide you with a report similar to what you would expect to get back home. Be sure to get any report that is presented to you in Portuguese translated into English.

You will find qualified British surveyors through the Royal Institute of Chartered Surveyors (RICS Contact Centre, Surveyor Court, Westwood Way, Coventry, CV4 8JE; ☎0870-333 1600; www.rics.org). The equivalent professional body in Portugal is the Associação Portuguesa dos Chartered Surveyors (RICS Portugal, Rua dos Ferreiros à Estrela 73, 2º Esq., 1200-672 Lisboa; ☎213-978307; fax 213-959679). British surveyors who have moved out to Portugal to practise and are able to carry out professional surveys and valuations often advertise their services in the local English-language newspapers and property magazines.

In some cases surveys – to be paid for by the vendor – can be tied into the contract as a condition of purchase, and some mortgage lenders will want to see a surveyor's report before agreeing to any loan, in fact many lenders will insist on nominating their own surveyor.

Conveyancing

Once you have found the right property, you should act swiftly (yet prudently) to ensure that you get it. There is currently a sellers market in Portugal – people are looking to buy property yet there aren't nearly enough properties for sale. It is advisable to never sign anything without having first sought independent legal advice. If there is for some reason such a pressing time limit that you may lose a property that you are interested in unless you sign NOW, then at least try to fax over a copy of the contract to your legal representatives. All buyers, whether individual or corporate, must obtain a fiscal number from the Portuguese tax office *(Finanças)* and this can be arranged by your Portuguese lawyer.

Contracts

When you are satisfied that the property won't be falling down in the near future, having been able to negotiate a structural survey, or you have decided, 'to hell with the expense, it's what I've always wanted…' then you will be ready to sign contracts with the vendor. Note that there may be potential tax advantages as well as other savings at a later stage by registering the property in the joint names of a wife and husband or partner, or in the name of your child or children, or in the name of the person who will stand to inherit the property, or in the name of a limited company.

The contract will be prepared by either an estate agent or developer or, if you decide to buy privately from an individual, by the vendor's lawyer. It will state all relevant information about the sale of the property including the full names and addresses of both the buyer and the vendor and a full description of the property including its title number at the tax office and the land registry. It will state the price to be paid, any fixtures and fittings to be included in the sale, and the completion date when the balance on the sale is to be paid and the *escritura* signed.

Whichever contract is offered to you, have it presented to you in your mother tongue as well as in Portuguese, and make sure that you have your lawyer check it before you sign. There may well be clauses that either you or the vendor will not accept and these will need to be negotiated, as will the purchase price and the amount of deposit payable.

There are strict conditions relating to the repayment of deposits. Make sure that you are informed of these by your lawyer. When paying a deposit ensure that the money is kept by the estate agent or legal representative of the vendor in a bonded escrow account until the sale has gone through. This will guard against a crooked vendor, or estate agent, taking your deposit and then deciding to sell the property to another instead. Though they will be acting illegally, should they do such a thing getting your money back through the courts may take quite a time and will certainly leave a nasty taste in your mouth – perhaps putting you off ever buying in Portugal.

Purchase Contracts for Resale/New Properties

Whether you are buying a finished property or choosing a plot to have a villa built, the first step is to sign the Reservation Agreement. This document legally reserves your property for up to two months while you appoint a lawyer and arrange a mortgage if necessary. The Reservation Agreement becomes effective with the payment of a deposit, which should be held in an escrow account. If you then decide within the reservation period not to proceed with the purchase, the deposit ought to be refunded in full.

The next step is for both parties to enter into a Promissory Contract of Purchase and Sale *(Contrato de Promessa de Compra e Venda)*, which is legalised at the Notary's Office. The buyer will pay a deposit of 20% of the total purchase price (less any reservation deposit already paid) and the parties will agree with the Notary and record a date for completion of the purchase. If a vendor withdraws from the sale, he or she is required by law to repay twice the deposit. Likewise, if the buyer fails to complete the purchase, then the buyer forfeits the total of the deposit.

If a buyer is having a villa built the Promissory Contract will record the promissory commitments of buyer and seller to enter into a building contract, which specifies the terms under which the villa will be constructed, including plans, the timing of the various stages of the project, and the stage payments to be made.

Purchase Contracts for Off-plan Properties

For properties that are still under construction at the time of purchase, stage payments will be required during the construction period. It may be possible to arrange the payment schedule to suit the purchaser's individual needs and a typical payment schedule could be as follows:

- O On the signing of the contract: A deposit of 20% payable by bankers draft, personal cheque, cash, traveller's cheques or credit card.
- O After a set period, or on completion of a certain phase in the building work (e.g. completion of the exterior walls and roof): 25% of the agreed purchase price.
- O After a set period, or on completion of another phase in the building work (e.g. completion of interior, fitting of interior furniture and windows and doors: Another 25% of the agreed purchase price – the timing of this payment may vary and is generally dependent upon the building project completion date.
- O On completion or signing of the *escritura*: Outstanding balance payable. With such contracts it is advisable to negotiate a clause in the contract that allows you to withhold a certain percentage of the cost price – say 10% – for a certain period after you have moved into the property as a guarantee against possible defects.

This will ensure that the builders will come back to rectify any problems that crop up, and a good firm should be happy to provide this type of insurance. You may also want to alter the specifications of fixtures and fittings, type and style of tiles, etc., that have been specified by the builders/developers. If you do alter specifications there will be changes needing to be made to the price structure and also to the completion date. Make sure that the developer is the legal owner of the land, has obtained the required building regulations and that the required payments are held in a bonded account until completion and your taking possession of the property.

Property Status

All properties, whether plots or residences, have an entry in the Land Registry *(Conservatória do Registo Predial)* in the name of the owner, showing the history of the property and whether any charges or debts exist against the property. In addition, all urban properties have a *Caderneta Urbana* (akin to an identity card for the property) from the tax office *(Finanças)*. This gives the article number, size and location of the plot, defines the borders of the plot, and gives a rateable value *(valor patrimonial)* for the property. This is the property value upon which the annual municipal property tax, payable to the local Town Hall is based. When purchasing a property, it is advisable to do a search in *Finanças* as well as in the *Conservatória*, as there may be actions pending against the property not yet advised to the *Conservatória*. All residences in Portugal must also have a Habitation Licence *(Licença de Habitação)* issued by the local *Câmara*.

Checks that Should Be Made on a Property Before Completion
Resale Properties:

O Are fittings and/or furniture included in the purchase price?
O Are there any planning restrictions pertaining to the property and/or location which will affect your plans should you wish to build on or alter the property?
O Are there community charges to be paid on the property? Do you understand the statutes of the *comunidade de propietários*, and are you happy to comply with them?
O Are there restrictions on the uses that can be made of the property?
O Boundaries, access, and public right of way bylaws are clearly defined and understood.
O Check the description of the property in the Land Registry.
O Check the property is free of any debts or charges; that all utility and community bills, and taxes (including the IMI tax) have been paid up to date. Remember

that debts on a property are 'inherited' by the new owner.

O   Has there been a completion of a survey to your satisfaction?

O   Has there been any alteration done to the property that has not been registered with the authorities and for which a *Licença de Habitação* exists?

O   How much are the local taxes and charges?

O   Is there adequate water, drainage, electricity and telecommunication provision?

O   Is the vendor the legal registered owner of the property?

Additional checks that should be made on off-plan and new build property:

O   A full breakdown of the materials, fixtures and fittings used in the building of the property.

O   Be clear what you are paying for. What are the finishings? Will the surrounding land be landscaped? What will the property look like (have you seen a show home to gauge this)?

O   Make sure that all building completion licences have been obtained.

O   Make sure that the developers or builders have obtained the necessary planning permissions to build upon the land.

O   Make sure that the payment schedule and completion date are clear.

O   Make sure the developers or builders are the legal owners of the land they are developing.

O   Protect yourself and insure against the possibility of the developer or builders going bankrupt before completing the property.

O   Make sure the property has been registered with the local authorities for real estate taxes.

Additional checks that should be made on plots of land for self-build projects:

O   Will you be given a permit to build (*Licença de Obras*) from the town hall.

O   How much will it cost to build on the land and can you afford the costs – get quotes from architects and builders.

The Notary

A notary (*notário*) although a lawyer, does not give legal advice to either the vendor or the purchaser of a property. The job of a notary, who is a government official, is to witness the signing of the Promissory Contract of Purchase and Sale *(Contrato de Promessa de Compra e Venda)* and of the title deeds *(Escritura Publica de Compra e Venda)* in his or her office located in the area where the property is being purchased, and to deal with other administrative matters.

Before preparing the *escritura* a notary will ensure that the purchaser has received the property as stated on the contract and that the vendor has received the correct purchase price. The notary will also advise on taxes that are due on the property. Once the *escritura* has been signed, the purchase price of the property is then handed over to the vendor, or the vendor confirms that payment has already been received. Proof of payment is then noted down in the *escritura,* which is then registered in the local Property Register.

Notaries collect their fees from the vendor and the purchaser and these fees are charged in accordance with a sliding scale of charges set by the Portuguese government. These will vary depending on the price of a property and the amount of work the notary has done on behalf of the two parties in preparing documents. Note that not all notaries will speak English and you may therefore need to be accompanied to meetings by a speaker of Portuguese.

Power of Attorney

A Portuguese lawyer will need a power of attorney *(Procuração)* to be able to act on your behalf. If you are staying in Portugal, this can be arranged in the Notary Office. Otherwise, it can be prepared by the Portuguese Consulate in your country of residence, or by a notary working in your home country, in which case it must be accompanied by a Notary Certificate of Apostille of the Hague Convention and translated into Portuguese.

THE SIGNING OF THE ESCRITURA

Once other formalities are completed, the sale can proceed with the signing of the Deed of Purchase and Sale *(Escritura Publica de Compra e Venda),* which is carried out before a notary and officially recorded at the same time as the balance of the purchase price is paid, according to the terms of the Promissory Contract. The notary will check that stamp duty has been paid on the property and ask for receipts proving that all taxes on the property have been paid. The signing of the *escritura* is the Portuguese equivalent of completion or closing.

If a buyer is having a villa built on a plot of land, the *escritura* will be for the sale of the plot, and the buyer and seller will execute the building contract at this time.

Some days later, the notary's office issues a stamped photocopy of the entry of the *escritura.* Upon showing proof of the *escritura* at the *conservatória,* the property can then be registered in the name of the new owner. It can take several months for the process of registering the change of title deeds as all taxes and fees must be paid before a property can be registered in the new owner's name. Once a certificate has been issued stating that the name of the owner of the property has been registered, the purchaser's lawyer should collect it and forward it on to the new owner.

BUILDING OR RENOVATING

SELF-BUILD

Self-build entails buying a plot of land and then building a house on it yourself. Unfortunately, it isn't as simple as that and there are bureaucratic hoops to be jumped through in order to erect that edifice. Potential builders can spend quite some time waiting for the necessary licences to be granted before being given the go ahead to start building. Finding a site with potential can also be very difficult and time consuming and finding land to develop along Portugal's coastline is practically impossible these days. Even if a plot of land being sold is advertised as coming with planning permission there may be pitfalls so you will need to do your research before buying. Owners of land for sale in Portugal often produce evidence of planning permission for a plot that was actually granted several years ago, believing that permission is still current or is renewed automatically on application. Unfortunately this is not always the case – permission to build is not automatically renewed or updated each year.

Before buying a plot you should run checks on the general status of the land – is it on a conservation area where there will be tight regulations on planning permission? Are there public rights of way over it?, by-laws pertaining to water, hunting, grazing, harvesting rights? Are there likely to be objections to the building schemes that you may have? How costly will it be to install services such as sewerage, a telephone, electricity, or a water supply? Are the ground and resources suitable should you want to put in a swimming pool or tennis court? Get a lawyer, an architect and a surveyor to check over the plot before you buy and get price ranges for the area in which you are interested. If you are buying the plot through an estate agent then he or she should already know what type and size of property would be allowable.

You will want to consult the town plan (*planos directores municipais*) at the local town hall. This plan outlines the areas that have already been given over to development where planning permission should be relatively easy and straightforward to obtain. Furthermore, the town plan will tell you at a glance whether the piece of land you are interested in developing has major restrictions imposed on the size or height of proposed building projects. If your grasp of Portuguese is not great then take along an English-speaking lawyer or surveyor who will be able to explain the technical jargon on the plan. Also check the details of the separate plots around the one that you are interested in. Are they set for further development? Find out what types of regulations pertain to the surrounding land? These will give you a good idea of what regulations will pertain to your piece of land. Is the planned view of the sea or spectacular mountain scenery from your planned home liable to being blocked by an *urbanização* planned for completion a few years down the line?

Once you have checked out that planning permission for what you intend building is definitely likely to be forthcoming you can go ahead and buy the plot of land. The vendor must be in possession of an *escritura* or other officially recognised deed of title. It is at this stage that you will want to get boundaries sorted out and marked on the *escritura*, if they aren't already. You will also want to get your land surveyed by an independent surveyor.

When you are happy that all these points have been cleared up to your satisfaction you can sign the *escritura* for the land at the notary's office and hand over the money for the land. You will then need to apply for a building permit (*Licenças de Obras*). To obtain this you have to submit the plans for the building to the Town Hall, however, it is likely to take several months for plans of the building project to be ready for submission to the authorities.

To get a plan for your house you will need to get in touch with a firm of builders or an architect. If you are buying a plot on an *urbanização* then the developers will be able to give you details of local builders, or you can enquire locally. A builder will be able to provide you with details of the type of houses he could build for you and together you can work out any variations you may want, interior designs, etc.

Alternatively you can find an architect and work together to come up with an original design that will answer your needs and pass the building regulations. An architect's fee is typically 6%-10% of the total cost of the build – which means that they will be in no hurry to design you a cheap house. It is a good idea to use the services of an architect who is a member of the AAP, the professional body of Portuguese architects. Once approved, a building licence will be issued and a fee will be due.

With planning permission granted you can now look for a builder to take on the contract to build your house. Get several estimates. The builders will look at the plans and the building specifications and tell you how much they think it will cost them to complete the job. Estimates will vary – both for the time it will take to complete the job and the fee asked for by the builders to do the job. You will need to weigh up the prices as well as the individual builders' reputations. Having decided upon a builder get your lawyer to look over the contract and make sure that any changes and amendments that arise over the course of the building work (there may be quite a few) are added to the contract and signed by both parties. This will avoid any problems when it comes to the reappraisal of the initial estimate and the final demand for payment. Changes to the initial specifications will also prolong the build time and delay the completion of the work. This will need to be taken into consideration, as the original completion date clause in the contract will have to be changed.

As with all purchases it is advisable to get a solicitor who speaks fluent English and get all documentation completely translated into English. Don't just settle for a précis or summary of contracts.

Once building starts it is advisable to be on site as often as possible, if possible. If you can't be there to oversee the building process personally then try and find someone who you trust to keep an eye on things, or employ a professional to supervise and troubleshoot. Builders everywhere can occasionally be unreliable, or decide not to turn up for work if something more lucrative can be had that day by doing a spot of building elsewhere. You should also check the plans, make sure that the footings are laid correctly – it would be a great shame if your house ended up facing the wrong way for example – and check on type and costings of materials. Do you want cheap, chic, expensive, or flash? This is your house that is being built and you will want to be on hand to choose materials and fixtures and fittings. Keep in mind that things rarely go exactly to plan – for instance there may be rock where the footings should go and blasting this out of the way will increase the labour cost, or you may decide that you want changes made to the original designs. It is therefore a good idea to factor in at least 10-30% on top of the original estimate. Building costs are usually quoted per square metre of build. Be realistic about what you can afford and though a quote may seem high remember that the value of your land will increase before the building work is complete.

Stagger the payment schedule to the builder (for example make payments on: the signing of the contract, the completion of the exterior walls and roof, the completion of the interior, the completion of plumbing, installation of electricity etc., on completion of exterior landscaping) and negotiate to hold back a final payment until a certain period has passed once the house has been completed so that should cracks in walls appear, or there be problems with drainage, plumbing, electrics, etc., you will have some clout should you need to call the builders back in to repair defects.

Depending on the size and design of the house expect a wait of about eight months to a year before being able to gaze upon your dream home. Even after the completion of the house it could take an additional year or two to knock the garden and surrounding land into shape. Plan the start date of construction taking into consideration the climate in which the builders will be working – a blazing sun during the summer is unlikely to be conducive to feverish activity, while winter rains may wash out the project and lose days and weeks from the schedule.

After the house has been built the final instalment of the architect's fees will need to be paid and the property inspected by the authorities to ensure that the building work has kept to the original permitted plans. A habitation licence

(*Licença da Habitação*) will then be issued by the town hall (*câmara*). The completed building will have to be registered with the local Land Registry and with the local tax office for the Municipal property tax (IMI).

Because many foreigners are interested in self-builds there are a number of clued up agents and developers buying up plots of land, often with services and planning permission already obtained, to sell on to clients. A piece of land becomes far more valuable as soon as planning permission has been granted. Property developers also sell plots on their housing schemes for buyers to build their own house on.

A prospective self-builder should look into ways to minimise the amount that will need to be paid in VAT and property taxes over the period of the project from its inception to its completion and the registration of the property. Be aware that IVA (VAT) will need to be paid on building land. IVA will also be added on to building costs.

In the past, when life was more laid back, many home owners would build or carry out extensive alterations to their property without visiting the town hall or applying for planning permission. Then, once the building work was complete they might put in the plans and, in time, the permission would be granted and the habitation licence issued. Nowadays, with strict new building regulations affecting almost every aspect of construction work, if a new build isn't up to scratch, or doesn't have the necessary habitation licence, when it comes to selling, there will be delays, modifications and even possible demolition to contend with.

LOCAL AUTHORITIES

There are several local authorities that will need to be visited when it comes to buying a property or a plot of land in Portugal. In the first instance you will need to register for a residence permit (*autorização de residência*) from the local *Serviço de Estrangeiros e Fronteiros*, which can take up to 60 days to be issued. Additionally you will also need to apply for a tax card (*cartão de contribuinte*) and a Portuguese tax number or NIF (*Número de Identificação Fiscal*). This is an obligatory document to have if you are going to buy property in Portugal and can be obtained from the local tax office (*finanças*). If you are going to be living in Portugal on a full time basis you will also need to eventually obtain an identity card (*bilhete d'identidade*) from the local council (*Junta de Freguesia*).

Once you have found a property you will want your lawyer to run checks on it to find out if you will be permitted to carry out such building work as you have planned. There are several local authorities that will need to be referred to.

The Town Hall (Câmara Municipal)

The local town hall is the place to go to seek out information about whether planning permissions and building permits will be granted. The town hall also houses the municipal plans (*planos directores municipais*) which will tell you if the land is located on an existing and approved area where building is permitted (in which case planning permission should not be a problem), and the nature of the restrictions on the land. Because of the rather rapid growth of urban developments in recent years certain restrictions have been put on building, especially on the Algarve coastline so be sure to check this, or get your lawyer to check it for you. Also use the municipal plans to check the plots of land surrounding the one that you are hoping to buy. See what developments are in the pipeline, if any – these could be possible housing developments or planned roads commercial enterprises.

Permits

If you are going to be carrying out major building work, either erecting a new building or renovating an existing property you will need to get a building permit (*licença de obra*) from the town hall. Before buying a property in need of renovation or a building plot make sure that the vendor, and notary are aware that you will only buy subject to the planning permission and building licence being granted.

Once everything has been checked out by your lawyer to your satisfaction you can go ahead, buy the land and sign for it at the office of the notário. The registration of the land or property can be left to your lawyer, together with the paying of taxes due. Once the building is completed you will need to apply for a Habitation Licence (*licença de habitação*) before being able to move in.

THE PORTUGUESE WAY

Buying land for building or an old wreck in need of renovation should be approached with as much caution as when buying a resale property that is ready to move into. You will want to make sure that any plot of land can actually be built on, and that planning permission has been granted or will be granted without too much trouble. As is often the case in Portugal, it is quite usual for properties to be built or alternations made to existing structures without first obtaining the necessary licences. In the old days, a fine would be imposed once the authorities found out, and there the matter would end. Today, things are tighter and fines are likely to be horrendously large and, depending on the authority, a property could theoretically be pulled down if it has been erected without planning permission. You will want to ensure that the building plot is in fact large enough for the size of house you are planning to have built, and that the land is suitable for building, i.e. that it is easy enough to sink foundations, that subsidence is not going to be a problem and that the land is relatively easy to level off.

Depending on what you are going into, and how much time and money and patience you have, you might decide to hire an architect to design you a villa. In such a case you will be able to have complete control over the specifications of everything from the kitchen sink to the veranda's ironwork surround. Alternatively, you could hire a local builder and use one of their standard designs. Either way you will need planning permission and will need to jump through a few hoops wrapped in red tape.

If you are thinking about building your own home, during the planning stages you will need to take into account all the associated costs that will crop up during the building – e.g. the cost of extending services such as water, electricity and telecommunications lines to the property, road access and drainage, etc., and remember that most quotes can only really be estimates. The true cost of a building project will escalate due to modifications that may need to be made to overcome unforeseen hurdles, or the changing of minds about what is wanted in the way of interior fitted furniture, tiling, bathroom appliances etc.

It is always advisable to discuss your ideas with your lawyer, a builder and an architect or surveyor before going ahead and buying a plot of land or a property in need of renovation.

If you are looking to renovate rather than build from scratch, then ask yourself whether you have the know-how yourself to renovate a tumbledown property or whether you have the necessary funds to hire builders who do. Depending on the amount of work involved in renovating a property, new build often tends to work out cheaper, by up to a third, than renovation. When you have found a property that you are interested in get a survey or local builder to come and look at it. Make sure that the external walls at least are sound. Before starting on any major renovation or building work, employ an architect. Shop around and get several quotes as these will vary a lot, and will depend on the size of the property, or the planned building work, and perhaps on how *au fait* you are with Portugal and your ability to negotiate in Portuguese. Employing an architect to design and oversee the building of a property may come to between £800-£1,600 for a small house, much more for a large villa. Even though it may seem easier to deal with an architect from home, or someone who's mother tongue is English, a Portuguese architect familiar with local building rules and regulations, and the local climate, is likely to more helpful to you in the long run.

An architect's fees will include the price of the plans (make sure that you are completely satisfied with them), the supervision of the building project and should also include the cost of preparing the list of building specifications. This states such things as the quantity and sizes of tiles, bricks, pipes etc, that are needed for the project, the type of concrete and cement needed, and the rest of the building materials to be used. It is likely that you will want to be involved in deciding on the type of electrical and bathroom fixtures and fittings, the colour and type of the tiles for the kitchen and bathroom, etc. Windows and doors and the kitchen units can all be discussed with the architect or builder while the building specification is being compiled.

Once the architect has completed the plans they will then be given to the builder/s in order to get a quote for the cost of the building work involved. This quote will obviously be given after having taken into consideration all the materials needed for the project and though these may change a bit as work proceeds, any variations you decide to make later on will cost you extra – and you will need to amend the contract that you have with your builder accordingly. Sift through several quotes from builders who you have found through recommendation. Recommendation really is the only way to 'vet' a builder, though make sure that such praise comes from independent parties. Ask around among locals and expats and if a builder comes highly recommended then meet him and ask to be shown some of his work. Quotes that come in will vary and the highest quote will not necessarily guarantee the best results, just as a low quote doesn't necessarily mean that the work or materials will be second-rate. Also be advised that there are plenty of expats living in Portugal who are looking for work without having registered with the tax authorities. If you employ such a person and the authorities find out you and your employee may both face heavy fines.

When you sign a contract with the builder get your lawyer to check it to see whether there are any clauses included that may work to your detriment. The contract should include the total price for the job with a payment schedule and work to be carried out. The cost of the job, at the end of the day, will need to be negotiated with the builder. Builders will often ask to be paid 50% before they start work with the balance payable in stages as the work progresses. Try and negotiate with them and if possible include a clause in the contract whereby you hold back say 10% of the total for a period to insure against possible building flaws or defects. Such things may not be evident until the house has managed to 'settle'.

BUILDERS

Any builder you employ should be covered by an insurance policy so that if they go bankrupt while in the middle of working on your house you will be able to claim compensation. By law, a builder in Portugal must guarantee any work carried out for a period of five years. Arrange to pay builders by instalments, never in one lump sum – all in one go. It is also advisable to remain, if possible, in situ or nearby, while the builders are at your property. This isn't to say that you should be on hand to continually interfere and direct operations, but to check that the builders are actually turning up for work and doing the hours that you are getting billed for. Also being aware of what is going on will ensure that the architect's original plans are being adhered to and that the fixtures and fittings are those that were originally agreed on. There are good and bad, reliable and unreliable people all over the world, but if you are trusting someone with a hefty investment of your time and money you need to make sure that your investment is safe in their hands. Because of the amount of continued construction work going on in Portugal, skilled tradesmen are in short supply. Builders often contract to take on several jobs at a time so that should interruptions occur on one project they can turn to the next. Be sure to get several quotes on any major job that you need doing. But there are many reliable and very professional builders in Portugal who will build an individually designed house on your plot of land exactly as you wish, or will sell you a plot of land and build a house chosen from a range of standard designs.

Local tradespeople are on the whole very good and extremely helpful – Lesley & Mike Collins.

Lesley and Mike Collins spent months looking for a holiday home before they found their dream house situated near to the town of Lagoa. Unfortunately it was in a sorry state and has needed a lot of renovation.

We have used mainly Portuguese tradespeople – the builder was recommended to us by our now good friends who were the agents we went through to buy the house. We have been very pleasantly surprised at just how good and sympathetically the builder has done the works to the house. All other tradespeople have also been local except for the heating company who have put in our central heating and hot water systems, which is English owned. All have been very good. You hear such horror stories! We have had some arguments with the local plumber to get the pipework done to our standards and not 'local' standards. On the whole we have found everyone we have dealt with very good and extremely helpful, although they are as expensive as tradespeople in UK.

RENTING PROPERTY

If you are intending to live in Portugal permanently, it is always a good idea to initially rent a place rather than buying too quickly – just in case you find that the reality of life in Portugal doesn't quite meet up to your expectations. Renting property means a less permanent commitment and will allow you time to make up your mind about where you want to live, to see if you like the area, the climate and the amenities and decide what kind of property will best suit your needs. If you are thinking about buying a holiday villa or an apartment to live in on a permanent basis remember that such properties, both along the coasts and up in the mountains, are mainly built for summer only residence. Marble floors can be unpleasantly frigid on the feet over the winter months and anyone considering buying one of these holiday properties with an idea to moving in permanently should spend a winter renting such a property first before buying.

The disadvantage of renting property in Portugal is that, generally, price-wise, it can be a fairly expensive business, with prices in sought-after locations such as Cascais, Estoril, Lisbon and Porto among the highest in Europe and uniformly expensive – a furnished one-bed apartment in São João near Estoril (Lisbon) was recently being advertised for €600/month; while €250/month was being asked for a room in a shared house in Cascais. Rental prices in the Algarve are cheaper than those being asked in the main cities and the more rarefied airs of places like Sintra, Estoril and Cascais.

Prices depend on the size of the property, the time of year, and the location – city centre, beach and golf properties command premium rates and, as elsewhere, the cheapest rents are to be found in the smaller towns and villages. Rents on short-term accommodation will be at their highest in July and August (and often over Christmas and Easter), and at their lowest in late autumn and over the winter.

Advertisements

You will find advertisements offering property for rent in international property magazines such as *Portugal* magazine and *Algarve Property Advertiser*, in local area newspapers; national newspapers and magazines (both English- and Portuguese-language versions), in Portugal, as well as in newspapers and magazines back home. Some estate agents handle properties for rent and many now market themselves through the internet. A quick search on the web using a search engine such as google (www.google.com) will bring up a number of sites offering short- and long-term rents all over Portugal. Websites about a specific area or region often have links to sites offering rental accommodation and many owners of property now have their own websites in order to attract customers.

There are many companies offering self-catering holiday lets though these will invariably work out to be more expensive than renting privately as such companies are looking for a high turnover of clients throughout the high season rather than longer-term tenants. Although these companies may offer out-of-season lets at a cheaper rate, such lets are often impractical for those seeking to remain in one area for some time as the rental period is only as long as the low – winter – season.

As elsewhere when looking for a place to rent, personal recommendation and the 'friend-of-a-friend' approach may be the best way of avoiding unexpected problems, as well as helping you to find the best deal. The locals may know of someone who has accommodation available for rent. Check the noticeboards of local supermarkets and churches and bars where expats congregate. Clubhouses on golf courses, shops in marinas and in kiosks also often have small noticeboards, which may turn up a suitable property.

One of the best places to look is in the small ad sections of local newspapers (both the Portuguese papers and the English-language papers), and free sheets. If you find a property that sounds good, be prepared to act quickly – buy the newspaper in the morning of that day that it is published and make contact with the person who has placed the advertisement immediately to organise a time to view the property. Advertisements in Portuguese newspapers for property to let are listed under *Aluga-se*.

Rental Agents

Increasingly tourists are looking to stay in self-catering accommodation rather than in hotels in order to save money and retain a semblance of an 'at home with the family' atmosphere. This is especially true of the older tourists who often decide to spend more than the usual one or two weeks away from home, especially during the winter months. For this reason some of the major tour operators such as *Thomson* (www.thomson-holidays.com) and *First Choice* (www.firstchoice.co.uk), as well as other operators such as *Worldwide Holiday Homes* (www.holiday-rentals.uk.com) offer many such longer-term self catering stays, particularly for older people. The *Portuguese Tourist Office* (22-25 Sackville Street, London W1X 1DE; ☎020-7494 1442; www.portugalinsite.com) can supply on a list of many companies that offer self-catering holidays.

Once on the ground in Portugal there are many estate agencies that deal with rental properties, in addition to properties for sale. Such agencies will ask for a month's rent in advance, and will charge a commission for the services they provide (usually of a week's rent). Using an agency to find an place to rent tends be more expensive than some of the other options, but offers more security in the long term (rental contracts will be standard and tried and tested) and is a way to avoid the interminable search for the 'right' place. Also, establishing a relationship with an estate agency is a good way of being kept informed of any likely properties for sale that may come onto their books. Be aware that in some resort areas it can harder to find a long-term rental due in part to the high demand for such properties, but also because property owners prefer the higher returns they can get from short-term holiday lets.

The Rental Contract

A rental contract is a prerequisite to renting any kind of property in Portugal and you will find that both short-term (for a period of six months or less) and long-term lets are available. Long lets will generally give tenants more rights than a short-term let. Longer-term contracts often require tenants living in blocks of flats to pay *comunidade* fees. However, if these charges are not mentioned in the contract then they are wholly the landlord's responsibility and the tenant is under no obligation to pay them or to have them imposed subsequently.

Contracts are drawn up through standard, state-sponsored tenant/landlord agreements and it is your responsibility as the tenant to make sure that the contract is fair and correct before signing on the dotted line. A contract will include personal details of the tenant and the landlord together with information about the property (location, size, and inventory of furnishings, fittings etc.), the terms of the lease and payment and expenses details. It is advisable to have the contract checked by a solicitor or someone who really knows about rentals before signing. The written contract should clearly state the amount of rent payable and when the tenant should pay it (usually within the first five days of every month). Many rental contracts ask for rent to be paid by direct debit into the landlord's bank account.

When you sign a contract for a long-term let you will usually need to pay between one and three month's rent as a deposit or bond to cover damages to the property. When the contract is terminated the deposit is returned in full or in part depending on the state of the property. Sometimes the tenant and landlord may agree to use up the deposit in lieu of rent at the end of a lease. You will need to agree on whether the landlord or tenant pays the property taxes and any community fees but you will almost certainly have to pay the bills for electricity, water, gas and the telephone. It is advisable to ask to see previous bills for the property to give you an idea of how much you will need to pay each month and also to make sure that all utility charges have been paid up to date.

The landlord's obligations include maintaining the property in good order and offering the services stated in the contract. For long-term lets, tenants will need an NIF number (*número de identificação fiscal*) and a bank account. If you do not have these, a landlord could ask for as much as six-months rent in advance.

On leaving a property at the end of a lease the landlord will check the inventory of the contents of the property and has the right to charge the tenant from the deposit for any missing items breakages. Note, however, that the landlord is obliged to replace and repair items such as water heaters, kitchen appliances and washing machines, at a cost to himself, that have broken through general wear and tear. Additionally, when you leave a rented property the landlord may levy a charge for cleaning.

Short-term Lets

Short term lets differ from longer lets in that the rental price will usually include all utilities such as electricity, gas and water. Renting for longer than a month may have reduced weekly rates but you may have to pay utility bills separately.

You will usually be required to sign a contract and pay a deposit in order to secure a property. Before you hand over any money or sign the contract, check the terms and conditions of the property rental very carefully. The deposit may be refundable either in whole or in part up to one month before your booking. However, if you cancel within a month of your booking, the deposit is rarely returned. Some travel insurance policies may refund your deposit if you have to cancel your accommodation owing to unforeseen circumstances such as family illness but others may not. Before you can move into a property you are usually required to pay for the rental accommodation in full, although if your rental is for longer than four weeks you may be able to pay in monthly instalments. Depending on how long you will be staying you may also be required to pay a deposit in case of breakages or damage to the property. If the property needs extra cleaning after you have left, the deposit may be used to pay for this otherwise, all being well, the deposit will be returned to you after you have moved out of the property.

If you are booking a short-term let from outside Portugal check that the company or individual you're planning to book through is reputable before parting with any money/deposits etc. Be wary of parting with large sums of money to unidentifiable individuals.

LETTING OUT PROPERTY

Increasingly there has been a tendency for visitors to Portugal to book self-catering holidays – staying in furnished accommodation where they can save money by cooking meals in their apartment rather than relying on restaurants, and living in a more homely type way. Along the Algarve this is becoming an increasingly common option for those looking to spend the winter months in the sun as a cheap alternative to living back in northern Europe. There is therefore plenty of scope for those who are looking to get some financial return from their investment and letting a property is often a good way of accruing an income on that investment, or simply helping to repay the monthly mortgage.

When renting out your property it is advisable to, as one estate agent has put it 'lock away the emotion and look at the maximum return available'. The requirements of the rental and residence markets are very different and it is worth remembering if you intend to buy in the north of Portugal that the holiday rental period is really only a summer one, as the winters can be cold and rainy. Hotter weather in the south means of course that the season can extend into spring and autumn – and even through the winter – so the potential income you may earn from property there is much higher. In the south of the country the high season for renting out property includes the Easter school holidays, Whit Bank Holiday week, July, August, September, October half-term and over the Christmas and New Year period. Top-notch properties can charge up to €225 per day in the high season (€110 per day in the low season) for a two-bedroom apartment with shared pool with views. A large villa with private pool can charge up to €375 and €225 per day in the high and low season respectively. Most letting agents calculate a 30-week letting year. The low season is October-April; the high from July-September.

Because of the amount of property out there looking for short-term, holiday only tenants, there can be quite a bit of competition in the rental market, with hundreds of companies renting out villas and offering similar services. A good head for business and the right choice of property will be of great importance if you want to make money from your property in Portugal. Word-of-mouth may bring some custom (let neighbours, local shop owners and businesses know that you have property to let), as will advertising or asking friendly shop owners to advertise your holiday home in the window of their premises. Placing an advert in supermarkets, marinas and golf clubs and even in shop windows back home is a cheap or usually free form of advertising your property and can often bring in clients.

Many properties are now advertised for rent on the internet, and placing ads in local and national newspapers is another option. If you can design your own webpage, or hire someone to do so, sign up with as many internet sites as possible, get regional sites to provide internet links to your home page, and register with search engines. Dependent on the budget available include the location, size and price of the property and talk up the main selling points. Local estate agents may keep properties for rent on their books and it will be a good idea to register with those that do, but be sure to check their credentials. Make sure that you are dealing with people who are competent and whom you can trust. All too often you can find that extra fees and charges from the agency begin to mount up, or that maintenance of the property is not attended to properly in your absence. Additionally, some estate agents arrange lets for property in the areas of the country in which they specialise (and advertise in expatriate newspapers and elsewhere). Placing an advert in the local yellow pages will also bring custom. The more time and energy you spend on advertising, the more people will be aware of what you have to offer.

The amount of rental income that can be expected from a property will depend to a large degree on the property concerned. Buying a property in a pleasant, out-of-the-way location will often have an advantage over many other properties for those looking to rent on a long-term basis. Villas, with pools especially, attract well-heeled families, and can often command rents in excess of €1,500 per week at the height of the summer season depending on location. If you are buying specifically to rent you should find out about neighbouring properties if you can, and their letting potential. For holiday rentals, a good position within sight and sound of the sea will also obviously be an advantage. Seafront apartments also generally have easy access to shops and leisure facilities which is an added attraction for prospective tenants. If your property is in a major tourist area then demand is likely to be high. Demand is likely to be much lower for properties in some of the lesser known resorts, or tucked away inland. Grouped houses or apartments in low-rise complexes also tend to do better than individual villas.

Many of the golf courses in Portugal are surrounded by residential developments, and although villas or apartments on these are expensive to buy, they can provide a healthy return on your investment. Golfers flock to Portugal to improve their handicap on these courses, especially during the northern European winter. In addition, the golfing fraternity tend to be fairly well-off and will pay a good price for the convenience of staying in course-side properties rather than having to travel too far to a course. For those looking to rent property out as an investment only, and not looking to make use of the property themselves, buying an apartment in Porto or Lisbon though expensive, will guarantee a regular source of tenants.

It is standard practice when letting out any property to charge prospective tenants rent in advance for their stay and to ask for a deposit against possible damage. Telephone and electricity bills can often cause friction between tenant and landlord and it may be as well to remove or lock the phone, or install a payphone while renting out property and to include electricity, water and gas charges – whether this be for two weeks, two months, or longer – in the advance payment to avoid misunderstandings later on. To avoid disputes, it is also a good idea to make a fairly exhaustive inventory of the contents of the property, including a description of their condition. Before you sign a contract, make sure that the details on the inventory correspond exactly with what is in the property at the time. If something is missing, broken or not as stated on the inventory you should agree with the tenant to change the inventory. At the end of the lease, check the inventory and, if items are missing or broken, you have the right to use the deposit to replace or repair. For short-term rentals the price charged should also include cleaning and linen provision.

Theoretically those letting out property on short-term lets should register with the tourist authorities. Subject to the property being deemed suitable for letting by the tourist authorities you will be issued with a permit. Although many owners are not registered, there are fines imposed for non-registration. Remember that whether or not you are a resident of Portugal, Portuguese income tax will have to be paid on earnings from rental.

Rental Contracts
Short-Term Rentals. Rental returns on short-term holiday lets are high, and this kind of contract is probably the best option for foreign property owners since your property can be available for personal use during the year and it is likely to be less difficult to evict problematic tenants. However, it may also mean that during the low season your property will remain empty and you are receiving no

income from it.

Short-term lets require a lot of management time spent on them, as tenants may be coming and going every week or fortnight, especially during the high season. Obviously, if you are resident in Portugal and live near the property then this may not cause much of a problem and the cheapest option will be to manage the property yourself. You will need to be on hand to clean the property before new visitors arrive, welcome the visitors and hand over the keys, troubleshoot and provide information about the area (where to hire a car, find a bank, the best bars, restaurants, beaches, leisure parks etc). If you also have other work or run other businesses then managing your own rental business on top of this may become onerous.

Bookings for short-term rentals tend to vary according to the season and the highest rates, both of booking and rents are during the months of July and August. Some owners often also charge peak rates at Christmas and Easter. If you decide to let your property through a management company then they will be able to tell you what the going rates are. If not, you can always check adverts in the local newspapers or ask other landlords.

Bear in mind that short-term rentals usually mean a lot of wear and tear on fittings and furnishings, and items will have to be replaced on a regular basis. Because short-term tenants are very often on holiday and in a holiday spirit they will probably take less care of the property than a long-term tenant would, so don't furnish your property with anything valuable or irreplaceable. However, this statement may be qualified if you are looking to attract very wealthy tenants with sumptuous décor.

Long-Term Rentals. Long-term rentals are really only a good idea if you are not looking to make personal use of your property for several years at least. Tenancies lasting from six months to a year or more will pay you a lower return than short-term tenancies, but tenants are normally responsible for paying their own utility bills, cleaning costs, etc and there is altogether much less work involved in this kind of tenancy agreement. Most management companies ask long-term tenants for two months' rent as a returnable deposit plus one month's rent in advance and if you are renting privately you would do well to ask for the same. Think very carefully before going into long-term lets and seek legal advice before committing yourself. Make sure you understand all the clauses in the rental agreement, have the contract checked by a lawyer, and ensure that you are totally happy with any contract you sign with a tenant. Any contract should state who is responsible for the payment of rates, the Municipal Tax (IMI) and any community charges. Usual practice is for the landlord to pay the Municipal Tax and for the tenant to pay the community charges. The long-term tenants should pay all utility bills.

Tenants are expected to pay the rent on time and maintain the property in a good state of repair. They may not sublet the property without the permission of the landlord or use the premises for immoral purposes. Failure to fulfil any of these obligations can lead to eviction. As a landlord you will have the right to inspect the property at any time providing you inform the tenant in good time of your proposed visit. Inspect your property every few months to check the general state of repair. The landlord is also obliged to carry out any necessary repair work and general maintenance to the property, and replace any fixtures and fittings that have broken or worn out through general wear and tear. Additional obligations may also be included in the rental contract. Failure to comply with your obligations as a landlord could lead to a tenant demanding compensation.

PROPERTY MANAGEMENT COMPANIES

There are many rental and property management agencies in Portugal, especially in the Algarve, many of whom advertise their services in the local English-language press as well as in the usual places such as the yellow pages.

Management agencies offer a comprehensive range of services – cleaning, maintenance, and payment of utility bills and may also advertise your property and find and vet tenants for you, though there may be an extra charge for this. Monthly statements are often forwarded on to non-resident owners detailing the income and expenditure pertaining to a property. Rental income may be deposited in the owner's Portuguese bank account, sent to owners wherever they may be, or held for collection.

If you are buying solely to let, rather than buying for your own holiday or permanent use then it is a good idea to contact property management agencies to get an idea of the areas in Portugal where there is most need for holiday properties. Obviously, Madeira and the Algarve offer good scope for rental properties but some locales will experience heavier tourist traffic than others. What about the northern coastline and the mountain ranges where property is cheaper but tourist traffic less dense? Sounding out management companies is always a good idea.

If you decide to hand over the running of your property to a management company take a copy of the contract between yourself and the management company to a lawyer and have it checked for legality before you sign anything. Also ask your lawyer to check the rental contract between the tenant and management company that the company will sign on your behalf. If possible, ask that the management company asks for rent to be paid in advance and that they always collect a deposit before a tenant moves in to the property. If you intend to still use the property occasionally for holidays, etc., make sure that management company is aware of this as soon in advance as possible.

SERVICES OFFERED BY MANAGEMENT AGENCIES

o Paying all routine bills – electricity, water, community charges, insurance, local rates, etc., from their own bank account, billing you at the end of each month.

o Monitoring your local bank account every month and converting your Portuguese bank statements to UK-style bank statements, which you will be sent every month.

o Looking after the general maintenance of the property: routine and emergency, painting, plumbing, etc.

o Pool cleaning.

o Gardening – routine or one-off service.

o Security.

o All year round supervision of property.

o Spring-cleaning and laundry service.

o Providing maid service during holiday-let tenancies.

o Welcoming holiday-let tenants.

o On hand to offer tenants advice, or in case of emergencies.

o Finding and vetting tenants for your property.

Useful Addresses

Borboleta Property Management: Sesmarias Country Club Lote 28, Casa Borboleta, 8400-565 Sesmarias Lagoa, Algarve, Portugal; tel/fax: 282-353365; www.borboleta-property-management.com.

CerroNovo: Centro Comercial, Cerro Grande, Albufeira; ☎289-510790; fax 289-510799; e-mail sales@cerronovo.com; www.cerronovo.com and www.cerronovo.co.uk; UK Office ☎01380-831411.

Ennis Property Management: Apartado 1, Foz do Arelho, 2504-908 Caldas da Rainha, Portugal; ☎262-979419; fax 262-978478; www.villa-management.com.

Exklusive Property Management and Servicing: Apartado 706, 8125-909 Vilamoura, Portugal; ☎914-460002; email exclusive@sapo.pt.

Gameiro & Graça: Rua das Margaridas, 9 Birre Centre, Cascais, Portugal; ☎214-850405; email gameiroegraca@clix.pt.

Hamptons International: Avenida das Comunidades Portuguesas, Edifício Lapinha A, 8600-501 Lagos; ☎282-789336 & 0870 414 0444; fax 282-788184; e-mail portugal@hamptons-int.com; www.hamptons.co.uk. Also have offices in London: 18/21 Cavaye Place. London SW10 9PT; ☎020-7244 4740; fax 020-7244 4701.

holidaylets.net: NetSquared Ltd, Cranfield Innovation Centre, Cranfield, Bedfordshire MK43 0BT; ☎01234-757281; fax 01234-756021; www.holidaylets.net.

MAP: Rua Frederico Arouca nº 24-2º, 2750-353 Cascais, Portugal; ☎214-821373; www.map.pt.

Maxcountry Rental & Property Management: Loja 14, Largo S. Francisco, 8100 Loulé, Portugal; ☎289-463322; fax 289-422873; www.maxcountry.com.

Prestige Properties: Rua dos Pescadores, Edif. Galeao, Loja 2, 8400-512 Praia do Carvoeiro, Portugal; ☎282-357623; www.algarve-prestige-rentals.com. Rental and villa management services.

Private Villas / Daltons Weekly: 8th Floor, CI Tower, St George's Square, New Malden, Surrey KT3 4JA; ☎020-8329 0222; fax 020-8329 0104; www.daltonsholidays.com.

rentavillaabroad.com: 208 London Road, East Grinstead, West Sussex RH19 1EY; ☎01342-312626; fax 01342-312212; www.rentavillaabroad.com.

Silver Real Estate and Villa Rentals: Rua do Brasil, Casa Italiana Loja 5, 8125-479 Vilamoura, Portugal; ☎289-314312; fax 289-314260; e-mail silver.holidays@clix.pt.

Villas & Vacations: Apartado 3498, 8135-906 Almancil, Algarve, Portugal; ☎289-390500; www.villas-vacations.com.

villasandrentals.com: 11 Priory Mall, Market Square, St Neots, Huntingdon, Cambs. PE19 2BN; ☎01480-477 773; fax 01480-473 156; www.villasandrentals.com.

INSURANCE

Some considerations that need to be taken into account while looking for an insurance policy on your new property include:

O Is your villa or flat covered by insurance in the event of your letting the property to someone who accidentally burns the place to the ground/floods the bathroom/steals all the electrical appliances and locks a dog in before vacating the premises?

O Is the property covered for insurance purposes even if it remains empty for part of the year?

O Does the insurance policy allow for new-for-old replacements or are their deductions for wear-and-tear?

It is always a good idea to shop around to see what options and premiums are available. Ask neighbours in Portugal for recommendations and remember to always, *always*, read the small print on any contract before signing. Do not under-insure property and remember that insurance will also be needed if a property is being built to order by a developer or builder.

It may be better to go with a large insurance company than a small independent company that may be less amenable when it comes to paying out on a claim. Most companies will anyway demand that any claim is backed by a police report, which may need to be made within a specific time limit after the accident or burglary. If such an event takes place while the house is empty this may be impossible, which is one of the reasons why you should check the small print carefully on all contracts.

In areas where there is heavy flooding or risk of forest fires each year, premiums will be much higher than back home, and also may not be as comprehensive as those offered back home. Additionally, buying cover from a Portuguese company while in Portugal is likely to cost a lot more than taking it from an insurance company back home. Insurance premiums will be cheaper in rural areas than in the larger towns and cities and, wherever your property, you may be required by the company to install certain security arrangements which will need to have been in place should a claim be made.

Some high street companies in the UK will ensure a second home abroad if you are already insured with them. *Norwich Union* (www.norwichunion.co.uk), for instance, place a premium on the value of a prospective client's main home, while *Saga* (www.saga.co.uk) has special premiums for those over 50 (£2 million liability for property, loss of rent provision, full cover of 60 days for untenanted properties, emergency accommodation cover, etc.). Other companies, such as

Schofields (Trinity House, 7 Institute Street, Bolton BL1 1PZ; ☎01204-365080; fax 01204-394346; www.schofields.ltd.uk) include public liability of up to £3 million. *Towergate Underwriting Group* (Towergate House, 2 County Gate, Staceys Street, Maidstone, Kent ME14 1ST; ☎0870-242 2490; fax 01622-754 999; www.towergate.co.uk) and *Copeland Insurance* (230/234 Portland Road, London SE25 4SL; ☎020-8656 2544; fax 020-8656 2544; www.andrewcopeland.co.uk) also offer a wide range of travel-related policies and schemes as well as dealing with general insurance, private cars, commercial insurance and homes insurance. The head office addresses of several major British insurance companies that have operations in Portugal are given below, and these may be worth contacting on arrival.

Insuring through a company back home with representatives in Portugal will mean that claims will be processed in English rather than Portuguese and this can be a great help and means that reading the small print will present no problems. Premiums vary depending on the size, location and age of the property, in addition to other factors such as security arrangements, the amount of time it will be occupied over a period of a year, the value of the contents, distance from emergency services, etc.

If you are going to let your property to holiday-makers getting good insurance cover is a necessity that you must not overlook and you must inform your insurers, otherwise the policy may be void or an extra premium may be payable. As well as covering the villa or apartment and its contents, you will need to cover your own liability in the event of the unforeseen occurring. It also makes sense to try and find a policy that will cover you for loss of earnings from rentals if your house becomes impossible to rent through problems arising from flooding, fire and Acts of God. Policies will also need to be updated should your property rise substantially in value. Note that your property will not be covered for theft by a tenant unless you take out a policy which covers larceny. Additionally, the policy will only pay out on theft it there are signs of forced entry. Furthermore if the property is to be used as a holiday home only, where the property will be left empty for months at a time you will need to inform the insurance company to ensure that you are covered throughout the year whether in residence or not. It is also useful to get emergency travel cover so that if there is an emergency concerning your property your travelling costs to Portugal will be covered.

With long-term rental agreements either the owner or tenant should always arrange appropriate insurance for a property to cover the cost of rebuilding should it be necessary, contents insurance and third party liability. Apart from being a sensible precaution, third party insurance for property is also a legal requirement. Most insurers prefer a multi-risk policy covering theft, damage by fire, vandalism, etc. If the insurer has bought into a development, it may well turn out that the building as a whole is already covered. It is advisable to check this before taking out an individual policy. In any event, it is unlikely that the existing cover will include the private property of individual inhabitants.

Anyone who has purchased a resale property may find that the seller's insurance may be carried on by the next owner. However, the new owner will have to check whether the policy is transferable.

Useful Addresses

American Life Insurance: Av. da Liberdade, 36-4, 1250, Lisbon; ☎213-475031; fax 213-474612.

Axa Portugal: Praça Marquês de Pombal, 14, 1250-162 Lisbon; ☎213-506100; fax 213-506136; www.axa.pt. Has associated offices throughout Portugal.

Commercial Union Assurance Co: Av. da Liberdade, 38-4, 1250 Lisbon; ☎213-475570; fax 213-423920.

David Hills Insurance Agency, Rua Vasco de Gama no. 259, 8135 Almancil, Algarve, Portugal; ☎289-399774; fax 289-397215; e-mail info@davidhills. com; www.davidhills.com. Specialists in property, health, commercial, travel, motor, marine and personal insurance in Portugal.

Royal Exchange Assurance: Av. Marques de Tomar, 2, 1050 Lisbon; ☎213-155235; fax 213-531567.

Saga: The Saga Building, Middelburg Square, Folkestone, Kent CT20 1AZ; ☎020-8282 0330 / 0800-015 0751; www.saga.co.uk/finance/holidayhome/.

THE COST OF RUNNING A PROPERTY

The cost of living in Portugal isn't as cheap as it once was but is still cheaper than the UK and a couple wouldn't end up on a starvation diet if they had a joint monthly income of €1,000/£660. Wages are significantly lower than those in the UK, which keeps the cost of services down. For a nuclear sized family expect to pay monthly electricity costs of between €40-50/£25-35, depending on usage, and around €10 per month water charges. Gas is cheap (€50 approx. for a 45 kg bottle or around €40 per month for piped gas) and telephone charges are comparable to those in the UK.

The annual property tax will depend on the rateable value of your property, while community charges depend on the size of the property, the number of properties in a *comunidade* and the services provided. These charges could cost around €25/£15 per month in a larger community.

TYPICAL ANNUAL RUNNING COSTS OF A PROPERTY IN PORTUGAL

Community Fees:	Controlled by the committee of owners (*comunidade de propietários*) and based on a percentage of the cost to maintain the facilities provided, relative to the size of your property. Will vary depending on property size and value.
Municipal Tax (IMI):	Typically 0.2%-0.5% of property value for individual owners/5% of property value for offshore owners.
Insurance:	0.5%-1% of value of property.
Water, Electricity, Telephone & Gas:	A standing charge and metering slightly higher/ equivalent to that in the UK.

Plus additional costs on any mortgage repayments, travel expenses, heating, and sundries.

UTILITIES

It is important to give the utility companies notice of a second address should you have one, or set up a standing order from your bank account so that you remain in credit with the utility service companies at all times. If you are not punctual with payment of bills you are likely to have services cut and will incur reconnection charges (which can be costly).

You will also need to notify the local Town Hall (*câmara municipal*) that you own property within their jurisdiction, and register with the municipality for the local property taxes. Make sure that all bills have been paid up to date before you move into a property. If the previous owner has left without paying them then you will be responsible for clearing the debt.

Electricity

The domestic electricity supply in Portugal is 220v AC and plugs on electrical appliances are of the continental two-pin type. Appliances originating in the UK (where the voltage is 240v), will work quite satisfactorily, if a little sluggishly, once they have been re-plugged; alternatively adaptors can be used.

Electricity Portugal is provided by the national electricity company EDP (*Electricidade de Portugal:* ☎ 800-505 505; www.edp.pt) and is relatively expensive in relation to the average salary received by the majority of the population. Usage of electricity is metered and there is a standing charge along with a charge for each Kilowatt hour (KWh) of electricity consumed. Bills are issued monthly and can be paid by direct debit – a good option if you are an infrequent visitor to your property or tend to be unpunctual when it comes to paying bills. Bills are based on estimates as meters tend to be read by the electric company once a year (when adjustments for over/under-readings are made).

It is important to try to organise meter installation or reconnection (if necessary) through your local branch of the EDP well in advance, as the waiting lists for both services can be long. New owners of a previously occupied property will need to present to the EDP the deeds of the property (*escritura*) and some form of identification document (a passport or residence card). The EDP will come and inspect the electrics on the property and if it needs updating you will need to have this done before you can transfer the contract for electricity from the previous owners into your name. Owners of a new property that isn't already connected to the electricity grid will need to register with the EDP and arrange to have cabling laid and a meter installed.

It is worth noting that in some regions the power is given to tide-like fluctuations which can damage expensive electronic equipment, so it is worth contemplating the purchase of a voltage stabilizer – costly but probably less so than replacing damaged equipment. An electricity meter should be installed outside a building if possible, where it can be read regardless of tenants or owners being at home.

It is advisable to pay bills promptly as, unlike in the UK where a couple of warnings are issued before the electricity company finally pulls the plug, in Portugal no such liberal benefit-of-the-doubt attitudes exist. All the above assumes of course that a property has been connected to the electricity supply in the first place as outside the regions of Lisbon, Porto and the main towns and villages of the Algarve, there are still some areas that are not yet connected to the electricity grid. How easy it is to get connected depends entirely on whether pylons have reached the area near the property.

Eventually mains electricity will be available anywhere in Portugal, but until this happens one can install a private generator, or do without. Many Portuguese are accustomed to living without electricity. Over the summer months relatively little hardship is involved, though in the north of the country winters can be cold and damp, and a source of heating will need to be investigated. Electricity is rarely used for cooking due to the expense and bottled gas is the usual alternative. Water can be heated by gas and there are even gas-powered refrigerators. Petrol, oil fired and wood burning stoves, log fires, and tilly lamps are all used as a means of providing heat and light in the more remote areas of the country.

Gas

Piped gas is scarce in Portugal, and is limited to Lisbon and the main conurbations. It is supplied by *Galp Energia* (☎ 217-242500; www.galpenergia.com). There are plans afoot to extend the gas network, but it will take several years. Bottled gas (propane and butane) is inexpensive and widely available throughout the country from local stores. Both types of gas are sold in domestic-sized containers of 11 kilograms and 45 kilograms. Most householders place a regular order with a local supplier, who collects a deposit for the first canister and thereafter charges only for the contents. Normally one has to collect the canisters, but it is also possible to arrange delivery.

Those in more secluded areas may have to collect their gas supplies from the local depot. As with electricity, if you are in an area where piped gas is provided you will need to sign up with the gas company and arrange to pay the standing charge and gas bills by standing order. The gas companies are likely to come and inspect your appliances for safety every few years. Gas bills (for piped gas) are rendered monthly and VAT (IVA) is included in the bill.

Because gas is generally a cheaper form of energy than electricity many properties run as many household appliances as possible on it and it is commonly used for cooking and heating in most homes in Portugal. There are safety issues when using gas, make sure that the property has adequate ventilation, that pipes are checked regularly to ensure that they haven't perished and regulator valves are in good order. Leaked gas sinks and lingers in a room where a spark or a dropped match will ignite it with disastrous results if there isn't the ventilation to disperse it. Bottled gas has a tendency to run out at the most inopportune times and so it pays to always make sure that you have an adequate supply ready for such eventualities.

Water

Even if a property in Portugal is connected to the main water supply, a continuous output is not always necessarily the result. The normally baking summers dictate that the supply will be periodically cut off as a water conservation measure. This is especially likely to happen in the south, though less likely in the mountainous north, which means that properties there should have an emergency cistern installed in order to cover such eventualities. Due to the hardness of the water in many parts of Portugal it is useful to have filters installed, preferably within the system (rather than on the outlets only), to prevent the furring up of pipes, radiators, etc. Water drawn from wells should be tested periodically for purity and reliability as a health precaution.

Those without any form of water supply will want to have a water deposit (*cisterna*) built and arrange for a water tanker to make regular visits. The local fire brigade often provides such a service. Alternatively a borehole can be sunk, but you will need authority from the town hall before going ahead.

Undoubtedly it is less hassle if a property has its own water supply and in some instances it is not unheard of for those without a water source to summon the services of a dowser. The ancient art of water divining is alive and well in Portugal and there are expert practitioners who can locate a source with pinpoint accuracy. A well (*poço*) then has to be sunk to the depth of the water table in that area. Water diviners can be found more easily by word of mouth than by consulting the yellow pages. Those looking to be linked to the mains water supply should ascertain at the time of purchase how easy and costly this will be. You will need to present copies of documents proving ownership of the property (the escritura) and identification when applying.

For those connected to the mains water supply, water is metered and bills are payable, on a bi-monthly basis, on the amount consumed, together with a standing charge. Bills can be paid when the meter reader calls or in person at the câmara municipal (Town Hall).

Although a swimming pool is something that most holiday homes require, due to the cost of water, especially in the south of Portugal, the upkeep can be a costly business.

Heating & Air Conditioning

Although the climate of Portugal is far, far better than that of northern Europe, the winter months, even in the south, will have their cold days and evenings will be cooler after sunset during these months. In the north of the country, and high up in the mountains, some form of heating will be wanted, and necessary, at certain times of the year. However, with the notable exception of these areas of Portugal, the provision of heating has not been at the forefront of most builders' and developers' minds up to now. Older properties may not be too well insulated, and it will be well worth the investment to insulate your property as well as possible, as it will keep the place cooler in the summer, and warmer in the winter.

Often the cheapest options of heating, if you live near a ready supply of logs, is to install a wood-burning stove, which can also be used as a water heater and from which radiators can be run. Alternatively portable gas or electric heaters can be used, though electric heaters are less common due to the high cost of the power source. Surprisingly, solar heating is still relatively uncommon, although becoming less so, in most areas of the country, and it is possible to obtain certain tax allowances and even grants for the installation of such systems. Solar systems are also a very good alternative to a generator for rural properties. Apartment blocks may have central heating systems running through the building, the cost of which is paid for by the community charges.

Bear in mind that if you decide to live in a purpose-built summer holiday villa through the winter months, your heating bill is going to be substantially higher than if you reside in a well-insulated house.

Many modern air-conditioning units will also incorporate warm air heating systems. If you can't afford air conditioning then installing either ceiling or portable fans is a good idea. Some form of air conditioning will be a good selling point for anyone hoping to rent out property.

REAL ESTATE TAXES

Buying property is an expensive business. Rather than being a deal struck between two individuals, where someone hands over a sum of money to someone else in return for an apartment or a house or a plot of land, there are all sorts of additional payments that have to be made to various individuals and institutions. These payments (taxes, stamp duties, lawyers' fees, notary fees) are likely to add another 10-15% onto the purchase price of your chosen property. These fees will be dealt with elsewhere in this book but included here are the taxes that are associated with property.

Municipal Property Transfer Tax (Imposto Municipal sobre as Transmissões Onerosas de Imóveis – IMT)

This is a tax levied on transfer of ownership of real estate located in Portugal. From 1 June 2003 the rules and rates of the old property transfer tax (SISA) were changed (and increased) so that now the acquisition of dwellings is subject to a 6% municipal property transfer tax (*IMT*) on its acquisition value or its tax registry value, if higher. In the case of rural land, the tax rate is 5%. The acquisition of other urban properties and other acquisitions are subject to 6.5%. Any property acquired by an offshore company will incur a tax of 15%. This tax is based on the higher of the purchase price and the registered value of the property.

Transfers below €80,000 are exempt from IMT; there is a sliding scale of tax for transfers of property priced between €80,000 and €500,000; and a maximum tax of 6% for purchases over €500,000. In the Azores and Madeira these rates are: below €100,000 – exempt; €100,000-€625,000 – sliding scale; and a maximum rate of 6% for purchases over €625,000.

To stop any under-declaration of price the Portuguese Government exercises a right of purchase where they consider and can prove that the declared price of acquisition was understated by 30%, or €5,000. In addition, the vendor of a property is obliged to produce to the Notary, on completion, the Promissory Contract of Purchase and Sale to show that the sale price stated in the contract is the same as that declared for the purpose of the Deed of Purchase. Which means that transfer tax will be payable on the true sale price, not on a lower sum declared by the owner.

IVA (VAT)

Property transactions such as acquisition and letting are normally VAT exempt, however, VAT of 19% is payable on all new properties – i.e. those that have recently been completed by developer or builder and are being sold for the first time. There are currently plans to raise the standard rate of IVA to 21%. Note that IVA in the Azores and in Madeira is charged at a rate of 13%.

Municipal Tax (Imposto Municipal sobre Imóveis – IMI)

The old Municipal Property Tax or rates known as *Contribuição Autárquica* that was payable by all owners of property in Portugal (both residents and non-residents) on 31 December annually has now been replaced by a new Municipal Tax, the levies of which will differ depending on the type of property and the value of the property; on whether the property is a country property or an urban property or a building plot. The rateable value of a property is assessed on the fiscal value of a property as registered in the local tax register. As many of these values are out of date, a re-valuation process has been set in motion and any property changing hands will be automatically revalued. New taxable values under the new IMI are likely to equate to 80%-90% of a property's market value. Because the re-valuation process is likely to take several years to complete all property taxable values will be corrected in accordance with inflation and adjusted according to regional market swings. A taxable rate of between 0.4%-0.8% of the corrected taxable value will be payable, with a yearly ceiling on increases until 2008. In 2004, Municipal Tax could not be increased by more than €60. Once revaluation has occurred the IMI will be between 0.2% and 0.5% of the value given to the property.

These new tax rules, effective from 1 December 2003, have meant a significant increase in Property Tax payable by offshore companies owning property in Portugal and real estate owned by offshore companies is now taxed at a whopping 5%.

Capital Gains Tax (Imposto De Mais Valias)

In 1989 the application of Capital Gains Tax was widened from being purely a tax on businesses, to include profits made by individuals on various transactions: 10% on any profits from the sale of shares held for a period of less than two years; 20% on the sale of non-residential property and 24% on the sale of land for development.

In common with France, Capital Gains Tax is not charged on the sale of an individual's sole residence provided the proceeds of such a sale are reinvested in another property (or land) within two years, otherwise 50% of the gain is added to the regular income. A capital gain on the sale of shares held for more than one year is tax exempt, for holding of less than one year the tax rate is 10%. A capital gain is usually added to regular income and therefore included in the calculations of the yearly tax return. In addition, in calculating a capital gain, account is taken of the rate of inflation from the date of purchase until the date of sale. There is a flat rate of 25% for non-residents.

REMOVALS

Moving house is one of the most stressful times in a person's life and, considering that you will not be just moving down the road, or to another location a few hours' drive away, but to another country with an alien culture, it is as well to plan your move with as much precision as possible. For citizens of the European Union there are now very few restrictions on living and working in the EU, and there are no customs duties to pay on personal effects. However, for those citizens of non-EU member states you will need to check with the nearest Portuguese embassy or consulate to find out the current regulations relating to your native country. With the cheapness and availability of flights between Portugal and most other countries in Europe there is no longer that feeling of great distance between say, Albufeira and Aberdeen that there used to be. These days most of us are used to travelling relatively large distances at least once a year and separation from our family and friends for varying periods of time is a natural part of day-to-day living.

Whether you are moving to your property in Portugal for a trial period in order to see whether you wish (and can afford) to live there full-time, or whether you are moving some of your belongings there in order to set up a business, it is advisable to make a trip out to your property first, unencumbered with belongings. Check that all services are connected and that all papers and permits are in order. While you are in Portugal you could look into the costs involved in hiring removals men or hire cars or a van from the Portuguese end. Organise your financial affairs in Portugal, set up direct debits to pay the utility companies, and organise the transferral of funds from your bank account at home to your account in Portugal. Then go home, let your house, either privately or through a management company, or sell it, and begin your journey into a new life.

MAKING THE MOVE

The amount of moveable possessions that any prospective foreign resident will take with them will vary considerably. But generally speaking anyone moving to Portugal on a long-term basis to take up a leisurely expatriate existence will need the professional services of a removals firm to transport their most treasured possessions and basic necessities.

Ideally anyone setting up home in a foreign country should take as little as possible as transport charges are high – for larger items such as wardrobes and beds the costs can run to hundreds of pounds per item. Before asking a removals firm to give an estimate of removal costs it is a good idea to have a thorough turnout and try to reduce the mountain of personal or family possessions as much as possible. Think through carefully which items really are essential in your new home. The less furniture you take with you from your old house to Portugal, the more interesting it will be to furnish your new house with locally acquired items. The cost of hiring a removals firm to take everything from a home in the UK to a home in Portugal will typically cost between £2,000-£3,000/€3,000-€4,500 and take a couple of weeks.

The British Association of Removers (3 Churchill Court, 58 Station Road, North Harrow, London HA2 7SA; ☎020-8861 3331; fax 020-8861 3332; www. removers.org.uk) can provide the names and telephone numbers of reputable removals companies throughout the country that are members of BAR and specialise in overseas operations and can provide advice on removals procedures. BAR members offer a financial guarantee, through BAR, if they go out of business. The addresses and phone numbers of some of the companies which deal with Portugal, whether directly or by sub-contracting to other agencies, are given below.

General Conditions of Import

All reputable international removals firms should be fully aware of the regulations concerning the transport of personal and household items. Anyone thinking of taking their household effects out to Portugal in a private truck or van should first consult their nearest Portuguese embassy or consulate for the most up to date regulations and advice. Much of the paperwork involved in importing goods will have to be in Portuguese. The Association of Translation Companies (Suite 10-11, Kent House, 87 Regent Street, London W1B 4EH; ☎020-7437 0007; fax 020-7439 7701; www.atc.org.uk) will be able to put you in touch with translation services specialising in translating documents relating to removals abroad, property purchase, residence, import/export etc. Translation service companies are also listed in the yellow pages.

The conditions for importing personal effects into Portugal are in line with regulations in force in other EU countries, namely that citizens of the EU countries (including Britain and Ireland) may apply to take any household goods and effects that they have owned for at least six months into Portugal tax and duty free.

IMPORT PROCEDURES FOR NON-EU CITIZENS

The basic all-important document for importing personal goods into Portugal, Madeira or the Azores is the *Certificado de Bagagem* (Baggage Certificate). Initially one should contact the nearest Portuguese consulate to make the application. Consulates charge a small administration fee and will require the following documents:

- ○ Either a copy of the *escritura* (title deeds) of the Portuguese property purchased, or if the applicant has had a house built, a copy of the applicant's residence certificate (*Autorização de Residência*) issued by the *Serviço de Estrangeiros*.
- ○ Two copies in Portuguese of an inventory of all the belongings that you intend to import, including the make and serial numbers of all electrical items.
- ○ Two copies of a declaration of ownership, in Portuguese, of goods and personal effects.
- ○ A full passport.

From the moment of being granted residence in Portugal an individual is allowed a period of one year to import all household goods in as many trips as are needed (although it is often more economical to transport all possessions in one go). For those who have bought a second home or holiday residence the procedure for importing personal effects and furnishings is similar to that for more long-term and permanent residents, except that the documents required by a Portuguese consulate can also include a photocopy of the deeds, or *Caderneta Predial* (Property Register), or *Título de Registo de Propriede*.

On arrival in Portugal, the individual must draw up a notarised declaration that he or she will not sell, hire out or otherwise transfer ownership of the property or personal goods within the twelve months following importation. Note that it is extremely difficult to import any goods that have not been included on the manifest after the expiry of the one-year period allowed for importation. It can take up to a year to get a separate import licence from the *Ministro de Finanças* for an individual item, and the duty can be high.

Finally, it is a commonly-held misunderstanding that if you buy an item in Britain (or another EU country), pay VAT (sales tax) and then subsequently export it to another country in the EU, there is an entitlement for a refund of the VAT paid on purchase – this is simply not true. The misunderstanding arises from the fact that if you are buying anything to take with you, such as a fridge or stereo, it can be supplied *VAT free* if the goods are delivered direct to the remover as an export shipment from the dealer.

CHECKLIST FOR MOVING HOUSE

- Confirm dates with the removals company.
- Sign and return contract together with payment.
- Book insurance at declared value.
- Arrange a contact number where you can be reached at all times.
- Arrange transport for pets.
- Dispose of anything you don't want to take with you.
- Start running down freezer contents.
- Contact carpet fitters if needed.
- Book disconnection of mains service.
- Cancel all rental agreements.
- Notify dentist, doctor, optician, vet.
- Notify bank and savings/share accounts of change of address.
- Inform telephone company.
- Ask the post office to re-route mail.
- Tell TV licence, car registration, passport offices of change of address.
- Notify hire purchase and credit firms.
- Make local map of new property for friends/removals company.
- Clear the loft/basement.
- Organise your own transport to new home.
- Plan where things will go in new home.
- Cancel the milk/newspapers.
- Clean out the freezer/fridge.
- Find and label keys.
- Send address cards to friends and relatives.
- Separate trinkets, jewellery and small items.
- Sort out linen and clothes.
- Put garage/garden tools together.
- Take down curtains/blinds.
- Collect children's toys.
- Put together basic catering for family at new house.

Removals Companies

Removal companies can take away much of the hassle of moving if you choose the right one; as one successfully-moved expat put it:

> *The secret is to use a really good removal company. Ours was superb and handled everything for us – all the paperwork, form filling, everything we could possibly worry about was handled by the firm.*

It is particularly important to shop around for a wide variety of quotes as removals companies sometimes sub-contract jobs to other firms whose drivers are going to the country in question and charge their client the extra fees picked up along the way. The approximate charge from the UK to Portugal is £120 to £150 per cubic metre plus a fixed fee for administration and paperwork. The amount will vary greatly on either side of this estimate however, depending on where in Portugal the shipment is going and where it is coming from in the UK. The price per cubic metre should decrease with the volume of goods you are transporting.

It is advisable to take out comprehensive insurance against possible damage to your possessions while in transit. A removals company can advise you about cover and make arrangements on your behalf, and the cost is usually quite modest. Another fact to bear in mind for non-EU citizens is that the customs clearance charges involved in exporting and importing goods can sometimes be more expensive than the shipping charges themselves (also something which a good removals company should advise you of and deal with on your behalf).

Make sure that the removals lorry will be able to reach your property with ease (check parking restrictions, access etc.). If goods are held up for days at a time at customs in Portugal it may be that another removals firm could be subcontracted to deliver to the Portuguese address. Check the contract to see what the clauses (and fees) are regarding such delays.

Useful Addresses

A&G Removals: Unit 6, Keld Close, Barker Business Park, Melmerby, Ripon, N. Yorkshire HG6 5NB; ☎01765-640 882; fax 01765-640 985.

Allied Pickfords: Heritage House, 345 Southbury Road, Enfield, Middlesex, EN1 1UP; ☎020-8219 8000; www.allied-pickfords.co.uk. A worldwide network with many branches in Britain.

AIM Removals: Parque Industrial do Infante, Unit 8, EN 125, Torre, 8600-256 Odiaxere; ☎282-799141; fax 282-799146; email algarve.movers@clix.pt.

Andrich International Removals: The Shortwoods, Waterfallows Lane, Linton Heath, Derbyshire DE12 6PF; ☎01283-761990; fax 01283-763965; www. andrichinternationalremovals.com. Offers a regular service to Portugal with full and part loads.

ARTS International: Ditchling Common Industrial Estate, Hassocks, West Sussex BN6 8SG; ☎01212-124546.

Avalon Overseas Movers: Drury Way, Brent Park, London NW10 0JN; ☎020-8451 6336; fax 020-8451 6419 www.transeuro.com. The private removals division of the large firm Transeuro.

Britannia Bradshaw International Ltd: Centrepoint, Marshall Stevens Way, Westinghouse Road, Trafford Park, Manchester M17 1PP; ☎0161-877 5555; fax 0161-888 3372; www.bradshawinternational.com.

Britannia Pink & Jones Ltd: Britannia House, Riley Road, Telford Way, Kettering, Northants. NN16 8NN; ☎01536-512019; fax 01536-410584; www. pinkandjones.co.uk.

Cargo Forwarding: Transit 1, 1 Westbank Way, Belfast, Northern Ireland, BT3 9LB; ☎028-9037 3700; fax 028-9037 3736; www.cargo-forwarding.co.uk. A worldwide service with door-to-door or door-to-depot rates on request and storage facilities.

Clark & Rose Ltd: Barclayhill Place, Portlethen, Aberdeen AB12 4LH; ☎01224-782800; fax 01224-782822; www.clarkandrose.co.uk.

Cotswold Carriers: Warehouse No. 2, The Walk, Hook Norton Road, Chipping Norton, Oxon OX7 5TG; ☎01608-730500 fax 01608-730600; www. cotswoldcarriers.co.uk.

Crown Relocations: ☎freephone 0800-393363. With offices in: Birmingham (0182-726 4100); Glasgow (0123-644 9666); Heathrow (020-897 1288); Leeds (0113-277 1000); London (020-8591 3388); Manchester (0161-273 5337); www.crownrelo.com. A large multi-national removals and relocations company.

Easy Transportation Ltd: Mercury House, Russell Gardens, Shotgate Industrial Estate, Wickford, Essex SS11 BH8; ☎0845-230 9889; www.easy-trans.co.uk.

European Relocations: Unit 3, Beaumanor Road, Leicester LE4 5QD; ☎0116-261 0700; www.europeanrelaocations.com.

Four Winds International Group: Georgian House, Wycombe End, Beaconsfields, Bucks, HP 9 7LX; ☎01494-675588; fax 01494-675699; www.fourwinds. co.uk.

Harrison & Rowley: 34-36 Foster Hill Road, Bedford MK40 2ER; ☎01234-272 351; fax 01234-271 114; www.harrisonandrowley.co.uk.

Harrow Green International: Merganser House, Cooks Road, London E15 2PW; ☎020-8522 0101; fax 020-8522 0252; www.harrowgreen.com. Full removals service, but they can also make arrangements for pets.

Interpack Worldwide Plc: Interpack House, Great Central Way, London NW10 0UX; ☎020-8324 2000; fax 020-8453 0544; www.interpack.co.uk. International company offering pet shipping, full / part house contents, motor vehicles, air freight and storage.

K&R Transportes, Lda: Cerro do Ouro, 8200-468 Paderne, Albufeira, Portugal; ☎289-368879; fax 289-368881; email transporte. algarve@clix.pt.

Luker Bros (Removals & Storage) Ltd: Shelley Close, Headington, Oxford OX3 8HB; ☎01865-762206.

MDS Removals: (UK) ☎01948-667234 / (Portugal) ☎282-574941; email mdremovals@hotmail.com.

MGS Movers & Transport: tel/fax 282-688 056; email mgsnook@bigfoot.com.

New Concept International: (UK) ☎01257-425940; fax 01257-427508 / (Portugal) ☎289-395105; fax 289-395112; www.newconcept.gbr.cc.

Reflex Move: Castlegate Business Park, Old Sarum, Salisbury SP4 6QX; ☎01722-414350; fax 01722-338962; www.reflexmove.com.

Robinsons International Moving and Storage: 1 Hamilton Close, Houndmills Estate, Basingstoke, Hampshire RG21 6YT; ☎01256-465533; fax 01256-859419. They can send a brochure on *International Moving*. Additional branches in London (☎020-8208 8484; fax 02-8208 8488); Birmingham (☎01527-830860; fax 01527-526812); Bristol (☎0117-980 5800; fax 0117-980 5828); Darlington (☎01325-348700; fax 01325-348777); Edinburgh (☎0131-473 2394; fax 0131-473 2309); Manchester (☎0161-766 8414; fax 0161-767 9057); Oxford (01235-552255; fax 01235-553573) and Southampton (☎023-80515 111; fax 023-80515112); www.robinsons-intl.com.

Trans-Portugal European Ltd: Unit 1, Cranfield Way, London N8 9DG; ☎020-7403 1440; fax 020-7403 0093.

UK Algarve Removals: ☎(UK) 02920-862 335/ (Portugal) 289-322 456; email ukalgarveremovals@aol.com.

Customs Office

Lisbon Customs and Excise (Direcção Geral das Alfândegas): Rua da Alfândega, nº 5-r/c, 1100-016 Lisbon; ☎218-813700; fax 218-877035; www.dgaiec.min-financas.pt.

IMPORTING PETS INTO PORTUGAL

Before deciding to take your pet to Portugal, think carefully about the implications for both yourself and the animal.

In 2000, 'Passports' for pets were introduced. These allow people from the UK to take their animals abroad and to return with them without enduring the compulsory six-month quarantine that was formerly in force. Portugal (including the Azores and Madeira) is one of the countries that the UK includes in its Pet Travel Scheme. The Pet Travel Scheme (PETS) allows dogs and cats to visit certain countries in mainland Europe and rabies free areas such as Australia and New Zealand provided that they are vaccinated against rabies. Additionally, they are required to have been treated against tapeworm (*echinococcus multilocularis*) – which can pass to humans – and the tick known as *Rhipicephalus sanguineus* – which also carries a disease transferable to humans.

The latest details of import conditions for taking your pets to Portugal can be obtained by contacting the Pet Travel Scheme (Department for the Environment, Food and Rural Affairs, Area 201, 1a Page Street, London SW1P 4PQ; ☎0870-241 1710; fax 020-7904 6206; www.defra.gov.uk/animalh/quarantine/pets/) and requesting the contact details of your nearest Animal Health Office. Although the 'Passports' scheme makes travelling with animals more straightforward, getting the necessary documentation can be a lengthy process. At the time of writing the *Department for the Environment, Food and Rural Affairs (DEFRA)* – the current name of the old Ministry of Agriculture, Food and Fisheries) was understood to be working to a six-month deadline, so you need to plan ahead.

Some but not all ferry companies and airlines will take accompanied pets, though the list of those that do is growing, so check with your carrier. Travelling by air from the UK to Portugal a pet can travel as excess baggage, however, coming the other way the animal must travel as cargo. Once in the country the animal's documentation will be checked before being taken to the Animal Aircare Centre and then released to the owner. Quarantine is not usually necessary, although regulations may change and you should consult the Portuguese consulate in your home country for up-to-date information well before your planned travel date. Note that in Portugal dogs have to be registered and a dog licence required. Licences are issued for a small fee by the local town hall (câmara).

TAKING PETS OUT OF THE UK

The procedures involved are:

- Vet inserts a tiny microchip just under the animal's skin (cost £20-£30).
- Vet administers a rabies shot, or two, given two weeks apart. (£50 x 2; second shot possibly cheaper).
- Vet takes a blood sample from animal and sends it to a DEFRA-approved laboratory. (£70-£80 including vet's handling charge). Note: If the blood test is negative, your pet must be vaccinated and tested again.
- Vet issues a PETS 1 Certificate, which you have to show to the transport company (e.g. airline, ferry, channel tunnel, etc).
- When taking pets from Britain to Portugal you will need a PETS 5 certificate (this replaces a separate Export Health Certificate) which is issued at the same time as PETS 1 (see above).
- Total cost about £200.

Importing Pets Back into the UK

To get your pet back into the UK you will need a PETS Certificate to show the transport company when checking in your pet at the point of departure. A PETS Certificate is valid six months after the date of the blood test up to the date the animal's booster rabies shot is due (a dog has to be at least three months old before it can be vaccinated). You should obtain the PETS Certificate from a government-authorised vet and you can obtain a list of these from The State Veterinary Service (1A Page Street, London SW1P 4PQ; ☎020-7904 6000) or from one of the Animal Health Divisional Offices whose addresses are available from DEFRA (see address above). Immediately (24-48 hours) prior to leaving Portugal the animal must be treated against ticks and tapeworm by a vet. This has to be done every time your pet enters the UK. The vet will issue an official certificate bearing the vet's stamp with the microchip number, date and time of treatment, and the product used.

Pets Originating Outside Britain

If your pet originated from outside Britain where different systems for identifying dogs and cats are in force it will need a microchip insert for entry to the UK. Pets that have had other forms of registration (e.g. an ear tattoo) must be vaccinated; blood-tested and have a microchip insert. To enter the UK the animal must have the PETS Certificate showing that the vet has seen the registration document.

Pet Travel Insurance

Due to the introduction of the PETS scheme a niche market in pet travel insurance has opened up. *Pet Plan* (Allianz Cornhill Insurance plc, Computer House, Great West Road, Brentford, Middlesex TW8 9DX; ☎0800-107 0204; www.petplan.co.uk), a well-known British animal health insurance company, offers cover for pets taking trips abroad. The minimum 30-day cover costs about £16 for dogs and £10 for cats; 60 days and 90 days' cover is also available. *Petwise Insurance* (Freepost, BDML Connect Ltd., The Connect Centre, Kingston Crescent, Portsmouth PO2 8QL; ☎0800-032 2297; www.petwise-insurance. com), *RapidInsure* (Phoenix Park, Blakewater Road, Blackburn, Lancs. BB1 5SJ; ☎0870-600 7171; www.rapidinsure.co.uk), *Pinnacle Pet Healthcare* (Pinnacle House, A1 Barnet Way, Borehamwood, Hertfordshire WD6 2XX; ☎020-8207 9000; fax 020-8953 6222; www.pinnacle.co.uk) and *MRL Insurance Direct* (Enterprise House, Station Parade, Chipstead, Surrey CR5 3TE; ☎0870-850 0618; www.mrlinsurance.co.uk) also offer travelling pet insurance.

Useful Contacts

Animal Airlines: Mill Lane Cottage, Mill Lane, Adlington, Cheshire SK10 4LF; ☎01625-827414; fax 01625-827237; www.animalairlines.co.uk.

Airpets Oceanic: Willowslea Farm Kennels, Spout Lane North, Stanwell Moor, Staines, Middlesex TW19 6BW; ☎01753-685571; fax 01735-681655; www.airpets.com. Pet exports, pet travel schemes, boarding, air kennels, transportation by road/air to and from all UK destinations.

Littleacre Quarantine Centre: 50 Dunscombes Road, Turves, Nr Whittlesey Cambs. PE7 2DS; ☎01733-840291; fax 01733-840348; www.quarantine1.

co.uk. Pet collection and overland delivery service. Will collect from your home and arrange all the necessary documentation. Also return home service from Europe provided.

Independent Pet and Animal Transport Association International, Inc.: 745 Winding Trail, Holly Lake Ranch, Big Sandy, Texas 75755 USA; ☎903-769-2267; fax 903-769-2867; www.ipata.com. An International Trade Association of animal handlers, pet moving providers, kennel operators, veterinarians and others who are dedicated to the care and welfare of pets and small animals during transport locally, nationwide and worldwide. Citizens of the USA can contact this address for a list of agents dealing in the transport of pets from the USA to Portugal.

GLOSSARY OF TERMS – SETTING UP HOME

administrador	administrator (for a community of property owners/property development)
advogado	lawyer
aluguer	rent
alvará	building permit
alvará de construção	construction licence
arquitecto	architect
Associação de Mediadores Imobiliários	Association of Estate Agents
associação de propietários ou condóminos	community of owners in a community development
autárquica	community rates payment
autorização de obra	planning permission
autorização de residencia	residence permit
caderneta predial	tax registration of a property
calculista de obra	quantity surveyor
casa de campo	country house/chalet
casa de ferias	holiday or second home
casa renovada	renovated house
certidão de registro	property land registration certificate
conservatória do Registro Predial	land registry office
construção	construction
construtor/empreiteiro	builder
contador	accountant
copia simples da escritura	copy of the title deeds
electricista	electrician
escritura	title deeds
escritura de compra e venda	final contract/transfer of ownership to the buyer
escritura pública de compra e venda	notarised deed of sale
hipotecas	mortgage
imobiliária	estate agent
imposto	tax
imposto de mais valias	capital gains tax

imposto de selo	stamp tax
imposto municipal sobre transmissões (IMT)	property transfer tax
imposto municipal sobre imoveis (IMI)	replacement for the *autárquica* (community rates)
imposto sobre de sucessões e boações	inheritance/gift tax
imposto sobre o valor acrescentado (IVA)	value added tax
inventário	inventory
licença de construção	construction licence
licença de obras	town hall building licence
lote (de terreno)	plot (of land)
notario	notary
orçamentos	quote
para cenda	for sale
Plano de Pormenor Urbano	detailed urban plan
predial registro	property registration
propriedade horizontal	freehold title held for a property
quinta	farm/estate
reforma	renovation
regime do arrendamento	law governing property rentals
Registro Predial	Land Registry
seguro de bens domésticos	home insurance
sinal	deposit
SISA	former property transfer tax (now replaced by IMT)
superintendente de vistoria	surveyor
valor tributável ou valor patrimonial	the property's rateable value
vistoria	survey
zona de protecção terrestre	site protected against building development

DAILY LIFE

CHAPTER SUMMARY

- In Portugal the pace is much slower and there are more marked differences between town and country than most western Europeans are used to.
- **The Language.** Portuguese is more difficult to learn than Spanish because the way it sounds diverges from the written form.
- **Schools and education.** Expat parents have three main options for educating their children – boarding school at home, Portuguese state or private schools, or international schools, of which there are many in the greater Lisbon area and the Algarve.
- **Motoring.** Portugal's road system has been transformed into a modern motorway network linking north and south. Unfortunately, driving skills are way behind the technology, with a mortality rate four times higher than the UK.
  - It is illegal to carry an emergency petrol supply in the car.
- **Taxation.** Income tax returns rely on self declarations which must be submitted by 15 March each year.
- **Portuguese health service.** Hospital treatment and the provision of essential medicines are free. There is a nominal fee for general medical consultations.
  - Public hospital standards are uneven. However, recent changes to the health service have allowed for greater input from the private sector. It is hoped that this will improve the management and level of care in public hospitals.
  - Most Portuguese and foreigners take out private health insurance.
- **Social security.** Employees and the self-employed make monthly contributions and in return receive a range of benefits.
- **Social life.** One of the most important events on the festival calendar is *carnaval*, which takes the form of numerous Rio-influenced parades around the country.
- **Shopping.** Portugal has hundreds of specialist open markets for everything from birds to handicrafts. It is worth checking with locals where to go for what.
  - Hand thrown and decorated ceramics are good value and very attractive.

INTRODUCTION

Anyone who decides to become a resident in a foreign country will find that everyday rituals acquire new and in some cases daunting aspects. In the case of Portugal they will find that life moves at a slower pace and that the differences between the town and country are more marked than they are in Britain. Portugal is fast catching up with its more industrialised partners in the EU; but this process is not happening overnight. While the combination of a certain backwardness and high tech may seem to be part of its charm, it should be remembered that Portugal certainly has its own traditions and customs; these often revolve more around family life and the immediate locality. For some, these can be a source of frustration, particularly the tendency to take a more relaxed approach to the minor irritations of everyday life and to getting things done. In some respects Portugal is even more relaxed than the other Latin countries.

Efficiency, however, is becoming more important, as well as customer service. In the workplace, formality in dress and behaviour are often greater than in Britain or the USA and so are traditions of hospitality and courtesy among the Portuguese, who are seen as being more 'laidback' by their more talkative Spanish neighbours. One source of frustration for expats who live there is the tedious paperwork that seems to be generated around everything to do with managing one's day-to-day affairs. These everyday tasks are best delegated, wherever possible, to someone else and assistance should be sought. In Portugal, for emigrants and locals alike, patience is not simply a virtue, it is a necessity. It will take time to adapt to this new way of life and culture, which may however be familiar to some who have already visited the country.

DEALING WITH RED TAPE

As mentioned above, almost all of the interviewees that were approached for this book mentioned that one of the frustrations of daily life in Portugal is dealing with slow and inflexible administrative procedures. As Patricia Westheimer writes: '*You will simply have to be willing to put up with inconvenience and incompetence*' and she advises that the only way to deal with these frustrations is by possessing '*patience, perseverance and a good sense of humour*' in abundance.

The country's love of bureaucracy is one of the last vestiges of decades of dictatorial rule. However, since Portugal joined the EU, slowly but surely, the situation has been improving. These days most of Portugal's bureaucratic procedures can be confronted in a single institution known as the citizen's shop (*loja do cidadão*). Most government departments are represented in these lojas, precluding the need to spend hours queuing at different windows in different parts of town. At the lojas it is possible to pay utility bills, access postal services, pay road tax, draw pensions, obtain a driving licence, pay social security contributions and so on. The service is not intended just for foreigners and although it is possible to enquire about foreigner's matters, applications for residence cannot be processed here.

The service is as yet only available in certain towns, namely Aveiro, Braga, Coimbra, Lisbon, Funchal, Porto, Setúbal and Viseu. However, there are plans to extend the network of lojas and there are also less comprehensive versions of the service (the *Postos de Atendimento ao Cidadão – PAC*) in some smaller towns. As yet there is no such service in the Algarve, Alentejo or the Azores.

You can find your nearest branch on the website (www.lojadocidadao.pt), or by calling the helpline (☎ 808-241107). Most lojas are open from 8.30am to 7.30pm, Monday to Friday and from 9.30am to 3.pm on Saturdays.

Many expats discover Portugal as a holiday destination before they decide to live there permanently. This is only one reason for moving to any country and the day-to-day life we discover on holiday is rarely, if ever, the same as that which is lived by the locals. As well as the affluent middle classes, teachers and temporary workers, Portugal is mainly popular among those who decide to retire there; or to enjoy some rest and relaxation away from cold winters. It is a country which Britons, over the years, have found congenial and welcoming.

The details in this chapter provide basic information on how to deal with the various demands of everyday life. Where opening times and other factual information have been given it is important to note that there are likely to be local variations, to which one should be alert. Those who have written to us with their experiences of living and working in Portugal all agree that there is one crucial preparation which can ease the transition to a new way of life (and is often a test of your true desire to live there). This is to endeavour to speak, however badly, the Portuguese language.

THE LANGUAGE OF PORTUGAL

Although it is possible to get by without speaking the language, especially in the Algarve and in the cities, where there are sizeable numbers of foreigners and international visitors, it seems only a matter of courtesy to be able to converse in Portuguese, however badly, even if your work and daily life is mainly conducted in English. It is also important to understand the written form. English is becoming more widely spoken in business circles, and among the young; but not always by the legendary bureaucracy with which, at some time or another, you will have to deal. So, although this may not seem the highest priority among the many other preparations which are involved, if you do not already speak the language you should certainly try to learn some elements of it before departure.

As well as proving an invaluable accomplishment when the next bureaucratic notice announcing an amendment to one of the endless regulations appears in your letterbox, or the national press, you will discover that speaking the language helps in other ways and can open a whole new window on the country and its people; it will help you settle in, and smooth the process known as 'culture shock'. Speaking the language will help you to come to terms with life in another country and help you to feel more at home.

Of course, language learning – and adapting to life abroad – will take time; but when a bill arrives you can actually make enough sense of it to know whether or not it requires urgent attention; you will be able to understand job advertisements, even to meet and talk with your neighbours. In the end, it will be worth it.

Who does this apply to? Nearly everyone involved in trade with the Portuguese, or anything more complicated than a casual summer job, needs to speak the language. There may be some exceptions: for example, many doctors, dentists and lawyers with a mainly British or northern European clientele can often get by with just English, particularly if they have a bilingual staff and partners. So can English teachers. But generally, in the long run, this is unsuccessful. As regards shopping, you can also probably get by without speaking Portuguese in areas with self-service shops and supermarkets; tourists find they manage in the open-air markets with just sign-language. However for dealing with clients, or socialising, or getting things done and integrating yourself more than superficially into your surroundings, the effort you put into learning Portuguese will be rewarded. There are some signposts on how to do this below. What better way to understand a country and its culture than to speak its language?

The Language

Portuguese is spoken by an estimated two hundred million people worldwide, three quarters of whom are Brazilians. It is the national language of Portugal (including Madeira and the Azores) as well as Brazil and is also spoken in parts of India and Sri Lanka, Angola, Mozambique and Macau. The Galician language of northwest Spain is more closely related to Portuguese than Spanish. As a result of the early Moorish occupation a number of Arabic words were also incorporated into Portuguese. But it is, like Spanish, one of the European languages which evolved from Latin as a result of the lengthy Roman occupation of the Iberian Peninsular. It is a Romance language, like French or Romanian.

Today, as a result of its colonial and imperial history, it has become a truly 'world' language, the next in line in terms of numbers of speakers after English and Spanish. It has more speakers than French.

Learning Portuguese

Unfortunately, though, it is not considered an easy language to master. The vowel sounds seem particularly complicated to native English speakers, and difficult to imitate, especially the diphthongs indicated by the tilde (wiggly mark) over *ã* and *õ*. Initially Portuguese consonants appear even more bewildering than vowels, as the written and oral forms do not seem too closely related, but once the basic rules of their pronunciation have been learned, they will prove easier to cope with than the mouth-distorting vowels. In Portuguese *ch* is pronounced like English *sh*, while *s* is pronounced like English *sh* when it comes before a consonant and at the end of a word, thus Cascais is pronounced '*Kushkaish*'. The letter *x* is pronounced a little like the English *sh*; thus *peixe* (fish), is pronounced 'paysh'. In written form one can see more easily the similarity with Spanish.

Work hard on learning the language before you go – John Carey

The only real challenge I faced was the Portuguese language, especially in a social setting. My lack of practice meant that I found it difficult at times to engage in group conversations. I would recommend that anyone thinking of moving to Portugal should work as hard as they can on learning the language before they go. Many people comment that it is a difficult language to learn, but with lessons, a bit of application and practice, it shouldn't be too hard. I got the sense that a good basic grasp would have helped me more than scrambling to pick it up once I was there.

A knowledge of Latin, Spanish, or French, can help you to recognise the roots of many Portuguese words and to understand them this way; this can be an encouraging start for anyone trying to learn the language. But the main difficulty in learning arises in understanding the spoken form, which sounds more Slavonic than Latinate and is further complicated by the fact that many sounds are slurred, or sound very indistinct until one has developed an ear for them. The secret is to assimilate the pronunciation (that is to say, the rules of its phonology or soundsystem) and then practise listening, then imitating or reproducing these sounds. Country dialects pose yet another problem.

Here are some different ways of learning the language, both before you go and when you are in the country.

Self-Study Courses. These generally consist of a combination of books and cassettes which are usually aimed at holiday-makers and business-people. Such courses include the BBC's *Get by in Portuguese*, a package of two cassettes and a book; also *Discovering Portuguese* consisting of a book and cassettes. *Colloquial Portuguese* is a similar and slightly more expensive 'interactive' book and CD/cassette (Routledge). Useful for self-study, and also with a private teacher or in the classroom, is the excellent *Teach Yourself Portuguese* (Hugo), also comprising a book and cassette. These self-study courses are available in most larger bookshops at prices ranging from £20 to £35; or they can be taken out from the library: nowadays there is often a charge for this. The well-known *Linguaphone (www. linguaphone.com)* Portuguese course can be ordered by telephoning ☎0800-

136973. AA Publishing offers a very reasonably priced *Portuguese Phrase Book.*

An increasingly popular method of language study is to follow an online course. The BBC offers an online course in beginners Portuguese called 'Talk Portuguese' (www.bbc.co.uk/languages/other/portuguese/). There are numerous other online courses that can be found with a simple Google search.

Language Courses in Britain. There are various types of courses held all over the UK to suit different needs and pockets, from local education authority evening classes to the high-powered business person's one-to-one intensive course. Details of some courses available around the UK are published in a leaflet obtainable from the Hispanic and Luso Brazilian Council (Canning House, 2 Belgrave Square, London SW1X 8PJ; ☎020-7235 2303; fax 020-7253 3587; www.canninghouse. com) and although the majority of courses mentioned are London based, there are Portuguese courses held in universities and colleges of further education from Belfast to Bristol.

One of the longest established UK language schools for Portuguese is the *Portuguese Language School,* EBC House, 235 Upper Richmond Road, London SW15 6SN; ☎020-8877 1738. The Hispano and Luso-Brazilian Council also arranges its own term long evening courses at Canning House. Further details may be obtained from the address above. Some up-to-date information on school or private courses may also be found on the HLBC library noticeboard downstairs; see also the *Anglo-Portuguese Society Newsletter* which has news for members and from time to time features information about learning Portuguese (Anglo Portuguese Society, c/o Canning House, 2 Belgrave Square, London SW1X 8PJ).

Other large organisations providing Portuguese classes throughout the UK and Europe include *Inlingua* (Rodney Lodge, Rodney Road, Cheltenham GL50 1HX; ☎01242-250493; fax 01242-250495; www.inlingua-cheltenham.co.uk); *Cactus Languages* (Suite 4, Clarence House, 30-31 North St., Brighton, BN1 1EB (☎01273-775868; www.cactuslanguage.com); and *Berlitz* (Paradise Forum, Birmingham B3 3HJ (☎0121-233 0975; fax 0121-233 1236; www.berlitz. com).

A cheaper option than a full time course is to enroll for evening classes at a local college – there is usually a range of courses open to the general public. Most offer GCSE or A-level Portuguese, although some may have beginners and conversation classes. Contact your local education authority, further education authority or adult education centre for details of courses. Most college courses tend to coincide with the academic year.

Private Tutors in the UK. This can be a pricey option – the going rate is anything from £20 to £30 per hour – but offers advantages for those who are lucky enough to find the right tutor. London especially has its floating population of Portuguese and Brazilian students who will be willing to eke out their existence by giving a few language lessons. The main source for this kind of tuition is the Canning House library noticeboard mentioned above. More officially, the *Institute of Linguists* (Saxon House, 48 Southwark Street, London SE1 1UN; ☎020-7940 3100; www.iol.org.uk) keeps a register of private language tutors all over Britain and has about twenty Portuguese tutors on its list. A free database is operated on the Institute's website. If the Institute is unable to put you in touch with a tutor in your area, an alternative is to enquire at your local library or see your own local press or newsletters where you may be allowed to post a 'tutor-wanted' advertisement; or enquire at local universities or colleges which usually have departments of modern languages and noticeboards to find Portuguese students in your locality.

Portuguese people resident in the UK who are learning English may also be willing to 'exchange' conversation or lessons with a similarly minded English person; universities – or even your local language school – are the places to post such an ad (or the Hispano and Luso-Brazilian Council noticeboard – see above).

Language Courses in Portugal. There are a large number of courses in general conversational or business-orientated Portuguese available through various organisations in the main cities and towns of Portugal. A good place to start looking is the *Instituto Camões* (Rua Rodrigues Sampaio, 113, 1150-279, Lisbon; ☎213-109100; fax 213-143987; www.instituto-camoes.pt), an institution charged with promoting the language and culture of Portugal around the world, much like the British Council. The following is a necessarily truncated list of language schools and organisations offering such courses:

Centro de Iniciacão e Aperfeicoamento de Línguas (CIAL): Avenida da República 41-8º Esq., 1050-187 Lisbon; ☎217-940448; fax 217-960783; e-mail portuguese@cial.pt; www.cial.pt.

CIAL – Centro de Línguas: Rua Almeida Garrett 44 r/c, 8000-206 Faro; ☎289-807611; fax 289-803154; e-mail algarve@cial.pt.

Euro Academy: 67-71 Lewisham High Street, London SE13 5JX; ☎020-8297 0505; fax 020-8297 0984; www.euroacademy.co.uk. Offers courses in Lisbon and Faro suiting both young people and adults. Executive courses at all levels are available beginning on any Monday throughout the year.

Instituto Camões: Rua Rodrigues Sampaio, 113, 1150-279, Lisbon; ☎213-109100; fax 213-143987; www.instituto-camoes.pt.

inlingua Language Centre: Rua Sá da Bandeira, 605-1º Esq., 4000 Porto; ☎223-394400; fax 223-394409; www.inlinguaporto.com.

ILA – Instituto de Línguas de Algés: Avenida Bombeiros Voluntários, 29-2º 1495-024 Algés; ☎214-102910; e-mail info@ila-lisboa.com.

International House: Rua Marquês Sá da Bandeira 16, 1050-148 Lisbon; ☎213-151496; fac 21-3530081; www.international-house.com. Schools in nine

locations in Portugal including Porto, Braga, Aveiro.
Mundilingua: Apartado 361, 8501-913 Portamão; ☎282-483 637; fax 282-485
058; www.mundilingua.com.

SCHOOLS AND EDUCATION

Education in Portugal

A long with the public health system, the education system in Portugal, where until recently compulsory attendance in schools was only up to the age of fourteen (the minimum working age), is also not yet working as it should, and it is something of a surprise to discover that the illiteracy rate of those of the population over the age of fifteen is 9% – twice that of Greece and three times that of Spain. Many of those without the three Rs are elderly women from rural areas and youngsters who have dropped out of school.

Illiteracy among the elderly can be blamed squarely on the Salazar regime, which regarded education as the privilege of the upper and middle-classes only and branded academics who opposed this view as dangerous liberals. Right up until 1970, over 60% of urban and regional councils in Portugal did not possess the facilities for providing secondary education. The situation with regard to primary schools was somewhat better and 10,000 primary schools were established, along with new universities in Lisbon, Braga, Aveiro and Évora and Lisbon technical university, over the 48 years of the dictatorship. The Revolution of 1974 made education the right of all Portuguese.

Despite an uneven quality, the education system has improved immeasurably in the last few years thanks largely to the vision of Roberto Carneiro, the minister of education in the late 1980s, whose spending on education provision was only exceeded by that spent on Portugal's number one priority, public works. Carneiro's programme of reforms was sweeping and included the opening of hundreds of well-equipped new primary and secondary schools, and a revamping of the curriculum. However, according to a recent report 46% of Portuguese children abandon their studies without finishing compulsory education.

The Structure of Education

In addition to the state schools, which are free (although parents are charged for books and stationery) there are private schools, which are partly funded by the state. Compulsory state education in Portugal lasts until a child is 15 years old.

Infant Education. Pre-primary education in Portugal is not compulsory but there are many free, state-run institutions that allow your children to get a head-start in Portuguese and make friends. Places in a *jardim de infância* are limited and their quality can vary. However, an alternative is one of the many private kindergartens of varying quality in the main cities. Charges are upwards of €180 a month. Those who work for the larger companies are often provided with free crèche facilities.

Primary Education. Compulsory basic education in Portugal consists of three stages lasting for eight years. State primary education begins at six years old and lasts for four years (*Ensino Basico – 1 Ciclo*). This is followed by a two-year attendance at a middle school (*Ensino Básico – 2 Ciclo*) followed by three years' secondary schooling (*Ensino Basico – 3 Ciclo*), with the option of continuing for another three years at a post-secondary school (on a fee paying basis).

At the end of the third stage students are awarded with a certificate of basic education (diploma de ensino básico), assuming that they have passed exams on all of the curricular subjects (the equivalent exams to British GCSEs).

Secondary Education. Education from the age of 15 to 18 is optional and only available to those who have successfully completed the compulsory basic education. Secondary education is made up of two types of courses: general education (*cursos gerais*) or technical/vocational courses (*cursos tecnológicos*) for those who are less academically minded. Regardless of course, all students engaged in secondary education must study the following core subjects: Portuguese, one foreign language, philosophy, PE and personal and social education. Beyond this, the courses are organised into four areas of study: arts, economic and social sciences, humanities, and science and natural sciences. The equivalent to the British 'A' levels are taken at the end of the secondary phase at age 18, and are a prerequisite for access to higher education. Successful general students receive the *diploma de ensino secundário.*

Further Education

In 1970 Portugal had only five universities: two in Lisbon, one in Porto, another in Coimbra and the private Universidade Católica Portuguesa (faculties located in various cities); this number has increased dramatically and institutions now include the autonomously run, public universities of Aveiro, Minho, Évora, Alto Douro, Trás-os-Montes, Beira Interior, Azores, Madeira and the very small University of the Algarve. In 1988 Portugal launched its version of the Open University. Other institutions of further education include fifteen technical colleges (*Politecnicas*) and specialised public and private institutes for the teaching of dentistry, fine arts, management, etc.

The well-connected traditionally attend the Catholic University, which has faculties spread over several cities. University entrance is by an exam, the *Prova Geral*, a general test taken in addition to the Portuguese version of 'A' levels. Adults over the age of 25 without formal entrance qualifications may enter university subject to succeeding in an ad-hoc aptitude test. The degrees awarded by Portuguese universities are the *licenciado, mestre* and *doutor* (the equivalents of a BA, MA and PhD respectively). In 2003 the Minister for Education announced that students would have to pay higher tuition fees than previously which is likely to reduce the number of prospective students at university level.

The first university in Portugal, Coimbra, was founded in 1290, yet although this ancient university has a revered place in the university system it is not necessarily the best and many consider the University of Lisbon to be a superior institution. Foreigners interested in studying at a Portuguese university should consult *Study Abroad*, an annual publication priced €18.50 and available from UNESCO Publishing (7, place de Fontenoy, 75352 Paris 07, France; ☎+33 1 45 68 1000; fax +33 1 45 67 16 90; www.unesco.org/publishing), which gives details of courses for which grants are available. The Calouste Gulbenkian Foundation (The Education Department, Avenida de Berna 45A, 1067-001, Lisbon; www. gulbenkian.pt) also provides grants for artists and those wishing to study Portuguese culture and language. The International Association for the Exchange of Students for Technical Experience (IAESTE) is a reciprocal training scheme providing student exchanges from one month to one year in many countries of the world including Portugal. Those interested should contact IAESTE in their home country (in the UK the address is 10 Spring Gardens, London SW1A 2BN; ☎020-7389 4771; fax 020-7389 4426; www.iaeste.org.uk).

Further information on Portuguese universities can be obtained from the Ministry of Education in Lisbon (Gabinete Relacoes Internacionais, Ministério da Educação, Avenida 5 de Outubro 107-13, 1069-018 Lisbon; ☎217-950330; fax 217-933618; www.min-edu.pt).

If you have children and are hoping to send them to university in the UK you should be aware that there are rulings on whether a student is classified as being a home or a foreign student. Depending on the prospective student's circumstances this can make a difference to the fees payable and the financial support available. The main criterion is that for three years prior to the first day of a university course the prospective student must have been resident in the UK and that no part of that three-year period has been spent wholly or mainly for the purpose of receiving full-time education. Eligibility criteria for university places are set out in detail on the website of the Department of Education & Skills at www.dfes. gov.uk/gfees. The Department of Education & Skills also publishes a number of guides, including the useful *Student Support for those Living or Working Overseas* at www.dfes.gov.uk/studentsupport.

Study and Exchange Schemes. There are a number of such schemes for those already studying or intending to study at a British university and wishing to spend up to a year at college in Portugal as well. The *Erasmus* scheme is part of the EU's Socrates programme, intended to encourage cooperation between universities as well as student exchanges. Students and UK institutions should contact the *UK Erasmus Students Grants Council,* (e-mail erasmus@ukc.ac.uk; www.erasmus.ac.uk). In Portugal contact the *Agência Nacional para os Programas Comunitários Sócrates e Leonardo da Vinci* (Avenida D. João II, Lote 1.07.2.1, Edifício Administrativo da Parque Expo, Piso 1 – Ala B, 1990-096 Lisbon; ☎218-919909; fax 218-919929; e-mail agencianacional@socleo.pt; www.socleo.pt.

However, Maribel Gattey found studying in Porto under the ERASMUS scheme to be a frustrating experience

Studying in Porto was a very different experience from studying in England. On the whole the general feeling of the foreign students was that there was a real lack of organisation at the university. For example I have been studying Portuguese for 2 years and when I enrolled in a Portuguese course for foreign students at the university, they put me and other people from my university in the beginners class, as there were no spaces in the more advanced classes. Bettering my Portuguese was the main reason for studying in Portugal, so I am sure you can imagine how frustrated I felt. I even knew of one English student at the university who could not even get on the course.

Portuguese Schools

Expatriate parents living in Portugal have three main options for educating their children: send the kids to a boarding school in Britain; send them to a Portuguese state or private school or, the most popular option, send them to an international school, of which there are many in the greater Lisbon area and the Algarve. Sending a child to boarding school in the UK is going to be the most expensive of these options as it involves not only paying the school fees but also the cost of flying children between Portugal and the UK. By being separated from their parents children will also miss integrating fully into an international or Portuguese community and the broader perspective and linguistic advantage that such an opportunity brings.

The second option suggested above is increasingly popular and a number of expats, particularly in the Lisbon area, send their children to the local Portuguese school. The best way to find out which schools are the most respected academically is by asking for recommendations. Be aware that there are few Portuguese state or private schools where English is taught by a native speaker and bear in mind that prospective pupils will need to speak Portuguese in order to follow the curriculum, so especially for older children, it is important to ensure that they learn enough Portuguese before beginning school.

There is a range of international schools in the main areas where expats tend to congregate. The majority are day schools, but some will make boarding arrangements, usually on a weekly basis, for children whose parents live too far away from the school to make regular school runs, or who for other reasons would prefer their offspring to board. Some schools operate a school bus service to collect children from local addresses. Age ranges accepted by international schools vary – some schools take children from four to thirteen years; others will take children up to sixteen years, i.e. until they have sat their GCSEs; others take pupils up to age eighteen and include in the curriculum preparation for university entrance. Amongst the international schools, syllabuses on offer include the British and American curricula and the International Baccalaureate. Nearly all international schools are co-educational. *The Council of International Schools* (21A Lavant Street, Petersfield, Hampshire GU32 3EL ☎01730-263131; www. cois.org) keeps a directory of International schools in Portugal and elsewhere in the world.

Further information on schooling in Portugal, including lists of Portuguese state and private schools, can be obtained from the Ministry of Education in Lisbon (see details above).

Useful Addresses
International Kindergartens:
Boa Ventura Montessori School: Rua Nunes dos Santos 5, 2765 São Pedro do Estoril; ☎214-688023. Ages 2-5 years.

CLIP – Colegio Luso-Internacional do Porto: Rua de Vila Nova 1071, 4100-506, Porto; ☎226-199160; fax 226-196196; e-mail clip.porto@clip.pt; www.clip. pt.

The Cascais International School: Rua das Faias. Lt.7 Torre. 2750-688 Cascais; ☎214-846260. Montessori based. Age bands: 1-3 years and 3-6 years.

International Preparatory School: Rua do Boror 12, Carcavelos, 2775-557, Carcavelos; ☎214-570149; e-mail info@ipsschool.org; www.ipsschool.org. From age 3. British National Curriculum.

St Dominic's International School: Outeiro da Polima, Rua Maria Brown, 2785-518, São Domingos da Rana,; ☎214-440434; fax 214-443072; e-mail school@dominics-int.org; www.dominics-int.org. Catholic school. Age range 3-18 years. International curriculum.

St Julian's School: Quinta Nova Carcavelos, 2776-601, Carcavelos (near Lisbon); ☎214-585300; fax 214-585312; e-mail mail@stjulians.com; www.stjulians. com. One of the oldest and best known schools. Takes pupils from 3 to 18 years.

Queen Elizabeth's School: Rua Filipe Magalhães 1, Alvalede, 1700 Lisbon; ☎218-486928; fax 218-472513. Ages 3-11.

International Schools:
The British School, Madeira: Rua dis Ilhéus 85, 9000-176 Funchal, Madeira;

☎291-773218; fax 291-932288; www.britishschoolmadeira.com. Ages 3-12.

Carlucci American International School of Lisbon: Rua António dos Reis 95, Linho, 2710-301, Sintra; ☎219-239800; fax 219-239899; e-mail info@caislisbon. com; www.caislisbon.com. American curriculum.

CLIP – Colegio Luso-Internacional do Porto: Rua de Vila Nova 1071, 4100-506, Porto; ☎226-199160; fax 226-196196; e-mail clip.porto@clip.pt; www.clip. pt. Kindergarten to Form 12.

Escola Internacional São Lourenco: Caixa Postal 445N, Sitio Da Rabona, 8135, Almancil, Algarve; ☎289-398328; fax 289-398298; e-mail eisl@mail. telepac; www.eisl-pt.org. Teaches an adapted version of the English National Curriculum. Ages 3-18.

International Christian School of Cascais: Avenida de Sintra Lote 1, 1154, 2750, Cascais; ☎214-861860; fax 214-861860. American curriculum.

International Preparatory School: Rua do Boror 12, Carcavelos, 2775-557, Carcavelos; ☎214-570149; e-mail info@ipsschool.org; www.ipsschool.org. From age 3. British National Curriculum.

International School of the Algarve: Apartado 80, 8400-400 Lagoa, Algarve; ☎282-342547; fax 282-353787; geral@eialgarve.com; www.eialgarve.com. UK curriculum.

International School of Madeira: Calcada do Pico nº 5, 9000-206, Funchal; ☎291-225870; fax 291-225870; www.Madeira-international-school.com. Ages 3-10.

International School Vale Verde: Apartado 125, Luz-Lagos, 8601-907; ☎282-697205; fax 282-471761; e-mail valeverde@sapo.pt. UK curriculum.

Oporto British School: Rua da Cerca 326/350, 4150-201, Porto; ☎226-166660; fax 226-166668; www.oportobritishschool.com. Founded in 1894. IGCSE's and IB.

Queen Elizabeth's School: Rua Filipe Magalhães 1, Alvalede, 1700 Lisbon; ☎218-486928; fax 218-472513. Ages 3-11.

St Dominic's International School: Outeiro da Polima, Rua Maria Brown, 2785-518, São Domingos da Rana,; ☎214-440434; fax 214-443072; e-mail school@dominics-int.org; www.dominics-int.org. Catholic school. Age range 3-18 years. International curriculum.

St George's School: Avenida do Lidador 322, São João do Estoril, 2765-333 Estoril; ☎214-661774. Primary/preparatory school.

St Julian's School: Quinta Nova, 2776-601, Carcavelos (near Lisbon); ☎214-585300; fax 214-585312; e-mail mail@stjulians.com; www.stjulians.com. One of the oldest and best known schools. Takes pupils from 3 to 18 years. Offers International Baccalaureate and UK curriculum.

Vilamoura International School: Apt. 856, 8125-911. Vilamoura; ☎289-303280; fax 289-303288. UK and international curriculums.

THE MEDIA AND COMMUNICATIONS

The Press

Despite the small size of its population, an astounding number of newspapers and journals are published in Portugal. There are over a dozen daily papers and around eight weighty weeklies to satisfy the Portuguese passion for discussing politics, business and sport.

Daily papers include *Público* (www.publico.pt), which has become a reference for expatriate as well as Portuguese readers, *Diário de Notícias* (www.dn.pt), *Jornal de Notícias* (jNotícias.pt), *Expresso* (www.expresso.pt) and *Correio da Manhã* (www.correiomanha.pt). Magazines include *Visão* and women's magazines like *Caras* and *Maria*.

English-language Newspapers and Magazines

To keep the expatriate community informed about their parochial concerns there are several excellent English-language newspapers, notably the *Anglo-Portuguese News* (Rua Melo e Sousa 33A, 2765-253 Estoril; ☎214-661431; fax 214-660358.) It is published weekly on Thursdays and includes a Property supplement with every issue. Generally, the Anglo-Portuguese News is sold at news-stands where foreign newspapers are also on sale. *The Portugal News* (PO Box 13, Lagoa 8401-901; ☎282-341100; www.the-news.net) is the country's largest circulation English-language newspaper and costs €1. *The Resident* (Edifício Paris, 1st Floor, Shop 8, Parque Empresarial 8400 Lagoa; ☎282-342936; www.algarveresident. com) costs €1.25 and is published every Friday and is available in hotels as well as news-stands and places like pubs and clubs in the Algarve, which are frequented by expatriates. If you wish to have any of these publications mailed to your Portuguese address you can take out a subscription. In addition to these newspapers, there is an English-language weekly newspaper, *The Euro Weekly News* (Head Office: Avenida de la Constitucion, Edificio Fiesta, Locales 32 & 33, Arroyo de la Miel, 29630, Benalmadena, Spain; ☎0034 952-561245; www. euroweeklynews.com), which though published in Spain, issues an Algarve and Lisbon edition.

On Madeira you will find the *Madeira Times* and there are several glossy magazines published for the expat community in Portugal including the bi-monthly *Essential Algarve* (HDP Algarve, Parque Empresarial Algarve 7, EN125, Apartado 59, 8400 Lagoa; ☎282- 341333; fax 282-341360; www.essential-algarve.com).

For those who cannot do without newspapers from home it is possible to buy the main international dailies from international newspaper stands in the main towns and in the tourist areas.

Before leaving for Portugal, there are a few magazines to whet your appetite, that are aimed at expatriates and those who dream of moving to Portugal. These magazines offer a subscription service, so you can continue to receive issues once in Portugal. The main two are:

Destination Algarve: Vista Ibérica Publicacões lda., Urb. Lagoa-Sol, Lt. 1-B, 8400-415 Lagoa; ☎282-340660; e-mail vista.lda@netvisao.pt.

Portugal Magazine: Merricks Media Ltd., 3&4 riverside Court, Lower Bristol Road, Bath BA2 3DZ; ☎01225-786800; www.portugalmagazine.co.uk.

Television

Television in Portugal is surprisingly good. The equivalent of the BBC is RTP (Radiotelevisão Portuguesa), which has two main channels, RTP1 and RTP2. Then there are SIC and TVI, each offering a combination of news and current affairs, films, series, and sport. The bill of fare includes lyrical Portuguese documentaries, an inordinate number of Brazilian soaps, various recycled British series and sit-coms, home-grown costume dramas, American quiz shows, and on RTP1, RTP2 and TVI plenty of sports coverage, including English, Italian and Brazilian football as well as the national football league. Unfortunately, keeping to television schedules does not seem to be a Portuguese strongpoint and programmes are liable to change without notice. Fortunately for expatriates the many old and recent cinema films on the television are rarely dubbed.

Satellite television is popular and parabolic dishes have sprouted across city skylines like mushrooms in a meadow on an autumn night. Dishes cost around £200 and there are various rental packages; and installation companies are cutting each others' throats to cash in on the demand. The television scene was transformed by the introduction of the two private channels in 1990; and now the airwaves are awash with programmes beamed into Portugal by satellite and cable. This is the way for those expatriates who wish to keep in touch with events at home to receive the BBC, Sky, CNN, and other English language services. Cable and satellite dish installation companies advertise in the local expatriate press. Television licences in Portugal were abolished in 1991.

Radio

The choice of radio stations in Portugal is extensive. Over 400 licences have been granted. Portuguese stations are useful if you are trying to learn the language and also for music. Some of these are TSF (89.5 FM) for news, talk and current affairs; RFM (93.2 FM) for news and music; Antena 3 (100.3 FM), mainly music; Nostalgia (104.3 FM), for tracks from the 60s, 70s and 80s; and Antena 2 (94.4 FM) for classical music. Still, many expatriates find themselves drawn inexorably to the BBC World Service whose broadcasts continue 24 hours a day. Radio 4 can also be picked up on long wave in some areas. To obtain the World Service you need a good quality short-wave radio. The frequencies change during the day.

English-language newspapers carry hour-by-hour wavelength guides. Alternatively the BBC World Service's own monthly magazine, *BBC On Air*, keeps you up-to-date with any changes in broadcasting frequencies. The British Consulate and the British Council in Portugal should have copies, or you can write to the *On Air* Subscription Department at PO Box 326, Sittingbourne, Kent ME9 8FA or telephone 01795-414 787, or visit the website at www.bbconair.com.

Books

Bookshops. With the boom in tourism in Portugal there is an increasingly wide selection of English books, magazines and newspapers available. The older traditional bookshops (*livrarias*) have limited foreign language titles, but any FNAC store in Portugal usually has translated Portuguese literature. There are also several English and international bookshops in Portugal, usually advertised in the English-language press. Those listed below are worth trying:

Algarve Book Cellar: Edificio 'O Galeão' Loja 1, Rua dos Pescadores, 8400-512 Carvoeiro, Lagoa; ☎282-085713; fax 282-085714. English language book exchange.

Editorial Notícias: Rossio 23, Lisbon. Some English language books.

Livraria Britanica: Rua de S Marçal 83, Lisbon. Exclusively English language books.

Livraria Britanica: Rua José Falcão 184, Porto.

Livraria Internacional: Rua 31 de Janeiro 43, Porto.

Livraria Bertrand: Rua Garrett 73 Lisbon; ☎213-421941. Lisbon's biggest bookseller (there is another branch in the Centro Comercial Columbo).

Livraria Buchholz: Rua Duque de Palmela 4, Lisbon. Huge multi-lingual collection.

Livraria Portugal: Rua do Carmo 70, Lisbon. Mostly art/history books – some in English.

Magna Carta Bookshop: Quinta da Praia, Lote 4 – Loja 9, Alvor; tel/fax 282-496001; e-mail info@magna-carta.biz; www.magna-carta.biz.

Libraries. Expatriates who are not fluent enough in Portuguese to join a Portuguese library may like to know that the following English libraries are open to the public (although the role of British Council libraries is currently being reassessed, this one is at present still in operation):

British Council: Rua de São Marçel 174, P-1294 Lisbon. Open Monday to Thursday from 10am to 5pm. Closed during August.

Anglo-American Library: Hotel Atlântico, Monte Estoril. Open Mondays, Tuesdays, Thursdays and Saturdays; 10am to 12.30pm.

Telephone

The good news about applying for a telephone in Portugal is that over the past few years a tremendous reduction has been made in the waiting time for instalment, which is now down from something like two years to just a month or less. However, the bad news is that those in the remoter areas will probably have to do without a landline, or get a mobile phone.

Although the Portuguese telephone system has been steadily modernised over recent years, there is at present an extreme reluctance to erect a line of telegraph poles to anywhere that is considered off the beaten track. The telephone system has also retained some idiosyncrasies, including giving a ringing tone even when the line at the other end has been disconnected or is out of order. Faults on the line are most likely to occur during bad weather.

Applications for connecting a telephone line should be made to the local *Portugal Telecom* office (local offices can be found in the Páginas Amarelas or by contacting Telecom's head office at Av. Fontes Pereita de Melo 40, 1069-300 Lisbon; ☎215-002000; www.telecom.pt). You will need to take along copies of your passport or residence card and proof of address (rental contract or property deeds). If you need to have a telephone line installed, rather than reconnected, applications should be made as early as possible and the equipment required (extensions, etc.) should be thought out well in advance as the installation process can still take a while; any changes required after installation are likely to engender the same waiting period as the arrival of the original telephone line. After a long or short gestation period, a representative from Telecom will eventually materialise and shortly afterwards the equipment will be installed. Installation of a telephone line costs about £60; line rental works out around £20 a month. Calls are charged on a table of tariffs depending on the duration of the call and whether it is a local, regional, national or international call. A list of prices and cheap rate periods can be obtained from Portugal Telecom. There are other telecommunications companies, including *novis* (Edifício Novis, Estrada da Outurela 118, 2795-606 Carnaxide, Lisbon; ☎210-10 0000; fax 21-012 9210; www.novis. pt), providing services in competition with Telecom.

Telephone Numbers

There are no codes specifically for towns in Portugal but each area has a code, which prefixes and is included in the nine-digit telephone number that all subscribers receive. The full nine-digit number must be used whether calling from within Portugal or from abroad. Telephone numbers these days are given as three sets of three digits (i.e. 282-624-789), the area code being the first three digits of the telephone number. The country code for Portugal is 351.

To dial abroad from Portugal you will need to dial the international prefix (00) followed by the country code (e.g. United Kingdom – 44; USA – 1; Australia – 61; New Zealand – 64; Eire – 353; Canada – 1; South Africa – 27, etc.) followed by the prefix of the area/town code minus the initial 0, followed by the number of the subscriber.

AREA TELEPHONE CODES

Abrantes	241	Angra do Heroísmo	295
Arganil	235	Aveiro	234
Beja	284	Braga	253
Bragança	273	Caldas da Rainha	262
Castelo Branco	272	Castro Verde	286
Chaves	276	Coimbra	239
Corvo	292	Covilhã	275
Estremoz	268	Évora	266
Faro	289	Figueira da Foz	233
Flores	292	Funchal	291
Graciosa	295	Guarda	271
Horta	292	Idanha-a-Nova	277
Leiria	244	Lisbon	21
Mealhada	231	Mirandela	278
Moura	285	Odemira	283
Penefiel	255	Peso da Régua	254
Pombal	236	Ponte Delgado	296
Ponte de Sôr	242	Portalegre	245
Portimão	282	Porto	22
Porto Santo	291	Proença-a-Nova	274
São João de Madeira	256	São Jorge	295
Santa Maria	296	Santarém	243
Santiago do Cacém	269	Seia	238
Setúbal	265	Tavira	281
Torre de Moncorvo	279	Torres Novas	249
Torres Vedras	261	Valença	251
Viana do Castelo	258	Vila Franca de Xira	263
Vila Nova da Famalicão	252	Vila Real	259

Common services telephone numbers are included in the front pages of the telephone directories, which are available by province. There is a charge made for calls to Directory Enquiries. Some of the more commonly used numbers are:

USEFUL TELEPHONE NUMBERS

Alarm Call	12161
Emergency Services	112

International Directory Enquiries	177
International Operator (Europe)	099
International Operator (Rest of the World)	098
National Directory Enquiries	118
Speaking Clock	12151
Tourist Enquiries	800-296-296 (freephone)
Weather Report	12150

Mobile Phones

If you want to use a mobile phone purchased at home during your time in Portugal, you will need to check with your service provider what the call rates are when using the phone abroad and whether there is coverage for the service. Portugal uses GSM 900/1800 telephones, which are compatible with the rest of Europe, but not with the North American GSM 1900. You may also need to inform your service provider before going abroad to get international access on your handset activated. There may be a charge for this depending on the phone package that you have. Using your mobile phone while abroad is expensive – you will be charged extra for incoming calls and access to your voicemail may also be restricted.

There are three mobile operators in Portugal: Optimus (www.optimus.pt), TMN (www.tmn.pt) and Vodafone (www.vodafone.pt). As elsewhere in the world, mobile phone coverage varies from area to area. Some of the more isolated and mountainous areas of the country will have problems with coverage and you should check with the various operators to see which can provide the best coverage for your home area (as well as the best deals).

Mobile phones are very popular in Portugal – by 2004 there were 9.34 million registered mobile phone users – and phone outlets and agents are not hard to find in the towns and cities. There are two ways of paying for calls: either by setting up an account with a service provider, or by using pre-pay cards bought from supermercados and other outlets. It will be cheaper in the long run to buy a mobile phone from a Portuguese operator but whether you want to do this will depend on how long you intend staying in Portugal each year. Further advice on using mobile phones abroad can be found on the internet at www.gsmworld.com and at www.telecomsadvice.org.uk.

The Internet

There are over 6 million internet users in Portugal with 60% of the population – much higher than the European average – regularly going online. There are internet cafés and cybercafés all over Portugal for you to make use of if you only plan to spend a few weeks a year in the country, but if you are moving to Portugal permanently then you will probably want to get connected to the web. If you have a laptop, remember that the power supply may vary from that in your home country and you will need an AC adaptor as well as an adaptor to fit the plug into a Portuguese socket.

There are a number of International ISPs (Internet Service Providers) such as AOL providing internet access in Portugal along with Portuguese ISPs such as Esoterica (www.esoterica.pt) and the largest provider, Telepac (www.telepac.pt). You will need to connect with one of the ISPs and either register on line or over the phone giving the necessary details required after which you will be given all the necessary information to set up a connection yourself. Telephone companies have special discount tariffs for heavy internet usage and other tariffs for evening and weekend usage.

You will want to get an e-mail address to allow you to stay in contact with friends, relatives and colleagues through the internet. There are a number of ways to get hold of an email address, and it will depend on whether you have your own internet connection or are dependent on using a cybercafé or other public internet access points. Two of the most convenient, reliable and free e-mail account providers accessible from any computer connected to the internet are www.hotmail.com and www.yahoo.com. If you go to their websites you can get a free e-mail account by following the simple signing up process.

Post

CTT (*Correios e Telecomunicações*) is the national company running the postal service. Portugal's postal service has been considerably modernised in the last few years and the service is reasonably efficient – letters sent by airmail should reach their destination in mainland Europe within three days. There are over 1,000 post offices (*correios*) so you do not have to go far to find one. Those living in rural areas where delivery services are infrequent often find it more convenient to collect their mail from the nearest Post Office and this can be done by completing a form and renting a post office box (*apartado*) on a six-monthly or yearly basis.

The price of stamps (*selos*) is subject to continual increase and they are sold at post offices, automatic dispensing machines and at kiosks and other outlets displaying the CTT logo. The *correio normal* service is an ordinary postal service and anything sent this way should be posted in the red post boxes; the more expensive *correio azul* is an express service and items sent using this service should be posted in blue letterboxes. CTT also offers express mail and courier services through its EMS division, and the international courier services such as DHL and UPS also operate in Portugal.

Post office opening hours vary. In the main towns and tourist areas they are from 8.30am to 6pm Monday to Friday and on Saturday mornings until 12.30 pm. Many post offices also offer a fax service and some of the larger post offices will have extended opening hours.

Addresses in Portugal. The majority of addresses in Portugal consist of a building, street name, and number, followed by a storey number e.g. *Rua Sá da Bandeira, 605-1° Esq* means that the office/apartment is on the first floor of number 605 Rua Sá da Bandeira, on the left (Esq is short for esquerda – left; Dir is short for direita – right; r/c is short for rés-do-chão – ground floor). An apartado is a PO Box; Portuguese postcodes are now written as a sequence of seven digits, to the left of the locality name, with a dash between the fourth and fifth digits (e.g. *1050-148*) and replace the old P-1234 coding.

CARS AND MOTORING

Driving Licences

For temporary visits to Portugal (of a continuous period of up to 180 days in any one year) a valid EU or international driving licence may be used. EU-issued licenses are valid in all member countries, regardless of the country of issue. In order to drive on a licence issued in a country outside of the EU you will need to obtain an International Driving Permit. In Portugal an International Driving Permit can be obtained from the *Automóvel Club de Portugal* (ACP), Rua Rosa Araújo 24, P-1250 Lisbon; ☎213-180202 fax 213-159121; www.acp.pt.

You may be required to produce an additional identity document with photograph (e.g. your passport) along with the licence. Those with an EU licence will need to exchange it for one issued in Portugal within 12 months of taking up residence in the country, or when the old licence expires. As driving licences bear the address of the holder, if you take up permanent residence in Portugal you will need to get a licence issued by the Portuguese authorities. Non-EU citizens taking up residence in Portugal are required to exchange their licence for a Portuguese national licence.

To obtain a Portuguese driving licence if you are a non-EU citizen you will need to apply to the district office of the *Direcção de Viação* where you will be issued with the Portuguese version of the EU licence. Portuguese licences must be renewed at the ages of 65 and 70, and every two years thereafter, for which purpose a medical certificate must be submitted.

It is important to carry your driving licence along with all vehicle registration documents with you whenever you are driving in Portugal. If you are stopped by the police and cannot produce these you are likely to be given an on-the-spot fine.

Running a Car

Petrol (*gasolina*) prices in Portugal sit in the middle of the European cost scale and are cheaper than in the UK. Unleaded (*sem chumbo*) petrol costs roughly €1.11 per litre and the national average for a litre of diesel (*gasoleo*) is approximately €0.90.

Many of the best known makes of European car are now sold in Portugal, so you should be able to find an agent for spares in the main areas of population. Finding a reliable garage, or a self-employed mechanic to look after your car is more often a matter of trial and error (and there may be some business opportunities in this field for qualified mechanics from the UK). The Automóvel Club de Portugal (see above), which has a reciprocal agreement with foreign motoring organisations, can offer advice and addresses of motor retail outlets.

The MOT. The Portuguese equivalent of the British MOT (*Inspecção Periódica Obrigatória*) needs to be passed by vehicles over four years old. The tests are carried out every two years for vehicles between four and seven years old, and then annually, at authorised IPO garages. At the garage you will need to provide proof of ownership, your tax card and the car's log book. Once your vehicle has passed the IPO, you will be given a stamp which should be placed, along with your insurance stamp, in the bottom right-hand corner of the windscreen.

Registration & Road Tax. In order to register a vehicle in Portugal, application should be made to one of the 18 regional offices of the *Direcção Geral de Viação* (head office: Av. da República, 16, 9º, 1069-055 Lisboa; ☎213-122100; fax 213-555670; www.dgv.pt) within 12 months of taking up residence in the country, and the appropriate registration tax must be paid. Road tax (*Imposto Sobre Veículos*) can be as much as 80% cheaper than in the UK. The amount of tax you pay is related to the cubic capacity and age of the vehicle. Tax discs can be purchased annually in June from the local tax office or some newsagents. The tax docket is displayed in the top right-hand corner of a vehicle's windscreen.

Insurance. If you are taking your own vehicle to Portugal a Green Card or receipt issued by your insurers is also essential, though if you are using a car hired in Portugal insurance will be included in the hire contract. Third party insurance is compulsory in Portugal. Vehicles carry the insurance docket in the bottom right-hand corner of the windscreen. One useful contact for car insurance in Portugal is *David Hills Insurance Agency*: Rua Vasco de Gama no. 259, 8135 Almancil, Algarve, Portugal; ☎289-399774; fax 289-397215; e-mail info@davidhills.com; www.davidhills.com (specialists in property, health, commercial, travel, motor, marine and personal insurance in Portugal).

Driving

The annual mortality rate from road accidents in Portugal is among the highest in Europe. Twice as many people are killed in their cars in Portugal than in Italy, per head of population, and four times as many as in the UK. Indeed, Portugal spends more on the consequences of reckless driving (such as hospital treatment) than it makes on tourism – one of the country's most lucrative industries. The Portuguese powers-that-be are sensitive to this appalling record and have now introduced measures to improve road safety. For example, the alcohol limit has been reduced to just 0.2 grams per litre of blood – the lowest in Europe. Other measures include medical and psycho-technical tests for drivers of commercial passenger vehicles in addition to the written and practical driving test. Businesses in Portugal are also beginning to recognize the problem. *Galp*, the national oil company is one of the first to have started sending employees on advanced driving courses.

This improved training and testing is making a difference, though many UK residents used to a more sedate driving style would agree that almost all Portuguese drivers are aggressive speed merchants who hate being the last in a convoy of traffic and so tend to tailgate until they can overtake. Looking in the rear view mirror only to observe the bonnet of a car perilously close to the boot of your own, with its driver drumming impatient fingers on the steering wheel is a particularly unenviable thrill. Those living in Portugal will have to judge for themselves whether the Portuguese are extremely hazardous road users with a near fatalistic attitude to death or merely far more used to the rules of their own roads than we others are.

To be fair, the Portuguese are by no means the only culprits for the appalling traffic accident statistics, especially in the Algarve, where a certain number of the drivers are, after all, not Portuguese but foreigners. Groggy tourists arriving in the midday heat and driving off in a hire car without so much as a glance at the unfamiliar instrument panel are a definite source of danger and can be just as lethal as any do-or-die native inhabitant. For those interested in avoiding accident blackspots, the main 'highways of death', as they have grimly become known, are the notorious *Marginal* (coast road) between Lisbon and Cascais, the Lisbon to Porto route and the Algarve coast road. In summary, the watchword when taking to the roads in Portugal is, go cautiously and drive defensively.

Roads. Until quite recently the roads in Portugal were of very poor quality. Entry into the European Union, and the need to have a proper road infrastructure for commercial and tourism purposes, gave the necessary impetus to a spate of road building programmes that have upgraded existing roads and created new motorways. It is no exaggeration to say that Portugal now has one of the most advanced road networks in Europe. New developments include the A25 from Vilar Formosa on the Spanish border to Aveiro. A new road running south along the coast from Porto to Figueira da Foz, is also under construction and is due to open very soon. The flow of traffic through Lisbon has been improved enormously by the relatively new Vasco da Gama bridge across the Tagus and the new ring roads. These programmes are ongoing.

Motorway tolls are payable at various staging points on the motorways. For those who travel regularly on toll roads, an automatic payment system known as the *Via Verde* has been introduced. This allows drivers, whose cars a fitted with an identification device, to avoid the long toll queues and tolls are deducted automatically from their bank account.

Rules of the Road

In common with most of Europe, Portugal drives on the right and overtakes on the left, except when overtaking stationary trams (see below). Road markings include: a broken white line, which may be crossed when clear for overtaking; and a continuous white line, which must not be crossed. Traffic approaching from the right has priority, except when entering a main highway from a side road displaying a 'Stop' sign, or from a private driveway. The majority of roads are without cat's eyes. A complete version of the Portuguese highway code, in English, can be downloaded from the website of the *Direcção-Geral de Viação* (www.dgv.pt).

Speed Limits. These have been reduced recently to 50kph (30mph) in built-up areas (and if towing). Outside of towns on *estradas municipais* the speed limit is 90kph (56mph) for unencumbered vehicles; 70kph (44 mph) for vehicles towing. The speed limit on national highways (*estradas nacionas* and *itinerários principais*) is 100kph (62mph). On motorways (*autoestradas*) the maximum speed for vehicles is 120kph (75mph). If you are towing a trailer or caravan the maximum speed is 100 kph.

Seat Belts and Compulsory Items to be Carried. It is compulsory for both driver and front seat passenger to wear a seat belt. If the rear seats are fitted with seat belts then anyone sitting in these seats must also wear them. All vehicles should carry the following at all times:

- A red warning triangle (to be erected on the road behind the vehicle in the event of an accident or breakdown).
- A first aid kit.
- A spare wheel and carjack.
- The vehicle registration document (*livrete*).
- Road tax disk.
- An insurance certificate (plus your green card if the vehicle is insured outside of

Portugal).

o IPO (MOT equivalent) stamp.

o Your ownership registration document (*titulo de registo de propriedade*).

Prohibitions. It is prohibited to drive with undipped headlights in built-up areas; to carry children less than 12 years of age, or dogs, in the front passenger seat of a car; and to carry an emergency petrol supply. This last injunction is less of a nuisance than expected – petrol stations (*bombas de gasolina*) can be found within striking distance of almost every town of any consequence.

Alcohol Limits. The legal limit is now 0.2 grams per litre, the lowest rate in Europe, equalled only by Sweden. Penalties for being found to be over the limit include a fine and the withdrawal of your driving licence. Anyone found to have in excess of 1.2 grams of alcohol in their blood is prosecuted under criminal law and liable to a prison sentence of up to one year.

Driving in Lisbon and Porto. This is difficult if not hazardous: one must give way to cars and trams (*elétricos*) approaching from the right in squares, and at crossroads and junctions. At official tram stops (*paragem*) overtaking trams is forbidden until passengers have finished boarding and leaving the tram. The overtaking of stationary trams is permitted on the right (i.e. the opposite to usual) only after passengers have finished their external manoeuvres and the way is clear.

In built-up areas use of the horn is prohibited during hours of darkness, except in an emergency. In traffic-clogged Lisbon there is a Blue Zone disc parking system in operation. Free discs are available from the Automóvel Club de Portugal or from the local police. No parking signs are the universal clearway sign: blue, with a red circle and diagonal red slash.

Fines & Traffic Police

If you are caught committing a traffic offence in Portugal you can receive a hefty on-the-spot fine; and unlike in the UK where you do not have to produce your insurance documents for immediate inspection, in Portugal the police will want to see all driving documents including an insurance receipt. If you are driving a vehicle that is not registered in your name it is essential to have the owner's written permission on a special authorisation form issued by the motoring organisations. Due care should be taken not to violate traffic regulations. Traffic cops are ever present all over Portugal and especially on the motorways and faster stretches of road you will often come across craftily placed speed traps. Approaching drivers may flash you to let you know of speed traps. Radars mounted on roadside posts record the speed of any approaching vehicle and may either flash a warning and indicate your speed, or cause a set of traffic lights further along the road to change from green to red.

Breakdowns and Assistance

If you are unlucky enough to break down it is compulsory to display the universal warning triangle on the road behind the vehicle to indicate to other road users that something is wrong. Those who are members of the AA or RAC can call the ACP (Automóvel Club de Portugal) for assistance. The ACP runs a 24-hour towing and breakdown service from offices in Lisbon and Porto (see below), which call the nearest ACP office to you and arrange assistance. The emergency breakdown number is ☎707-509510.

In cases of accident the police (*policia*) must be called. If necessary an ambulance (*ambulância*) should also be requested. Main highways are furnished with orange emergency SOS telephones. To use these, press the SOS button and wait for an answer. If you do not know your exact location, give details of the emergency and the number of the SOS telephone. If reporting an accident from a private telephone the emergency number 112, which is the number for all emergencies in Portugal.

Maps. The Michelin Map for Portugal is No. 733. Automóvel Club de Portugal produces a national road map, which is periodically updated. A list of Portuguese maps (commercial and large scale Ordnance Survey types) is available from Stanfords Travel Bookshops (London: 12-14 Long Acre, London WC2E 9LP; ☎020-7836 1321 / Bristol: 29 Corn Street, Bristol BS1 1HT; ☎0117-929 9966 / Manchester: 39 Spring Gardens, Manchester M2 2BG; ☎0161-831 0250; www.stanfords.co.uk).

Useful Addresses

Automóvel Club de Portugal: Rua Rosa Araújo 24, 1250-195 Lisbon; ☎213-180202; www.acp.pt.

Direcção-Geral das Alfandegas (Director-General of Customs): Rua da Alfandega 5 r/c, 1149-006 Lisbon; ☎218-813700; fax 218-813818; www.dgaiec.min-financas.pt.

TRANSPORT

The amount of investment in infrastructure in recent years in Portugal, largely with the help of EU funding means that travelling in Portugal is now considerably easier than it once was. The network of main roads and motorways has been completely re-developed, as has the rail infrastructure and many new motorways and rail links are currently under construction. Particularly impressive developments in recent years include the rail link running underneath the new

Vasco da Gama bridge, and extensions to the capital's underground network. All of these extensive improvements have upgraded links to areas where access was once difficult. The country's main airport infrastructures are to be modernised and re-equipped to maximise current handling capacity and there are plans to build a new airport at Ota, north-east of Lisbon to meet the anticipated growth in air travel.

All in all getting from A to B in Portugal is now fairly manageable and the links between the main cities and the tourist areas are quick, reliable and fairly cheap.

Internal Air Travel

The Portuguese internal airline is Portugália Airlines (☎218-425500; fax 218-425623; www.pga.pt), a private company. It has regular flights between Lisbon, Porto, Faro and also several towns in foreign countries, and charter flights to Madeira from mainland Portugal. There are charter companies and air taxis which can also provide transport to Portugal's regional airports like Bragança, Chaves, Vila Real, Coimbra, Covilhã, Portimão, and Viseu, as well as the international airports of Lisbon, Porto and Faro.

The Azores have their own airline, SATA (www.sata.pt), which operates regular connections between the islands and charter flights to Madeira, continental Portugal and several countries in Europe.

Rail

The network of the national rail company, Caminhos de Ferro Portugueses (CP), covers most of the country. Train travel everywhere in Portugal is inexpensive and senior citizens (those over 65 years) pay even less – only 30% of most fares. Children under four can travel for free, and those aged 4-11 only pay half the fare. Young people aged 12-26 can buy a youth travel card (*Cartão Jovem*), which offers a 30% discount on most routes. Other discounts are available, such as the tourist ticket (*Bilhete Turistico*) which is valid for 7, 14 or 21 days. All discounts are subject to restriction, so check with Caminhos de Ferro Portugueses (contact details below).

Over 90% of trains are so-called Regional slow trains stopping at every station en route. The medium-fast trains are the Intercidades (Intercities) and the fastest are the Rápidos, which link Lisbon and Porto in under three and a half hours. Since 2001, this high speed service has linked the main cities of Lisbon, Coimbra and Porto, providing one of the most efficient intercity services in Europe. By 2008, this service will also link Porto to Spain via Vigo. High speed connections between Lisbon and Madrid (to be completed by 2011) and between Faro and Seville (2015) are also planned.

Ticket prices on the Intercidades are double that of those on the Regionals.

For the Rápidos there is a supplement payable. In Portugal it is obligatory to buy tickets in advance, which will usually entail queuing, as there is no provision for buying a ticket after boarding a train. However, you can also buy tickets online and by phone, and the Lisbon to Porto tickets can also be purchased from ATM machines. Further information when in Portugal may be obtained from travel agencies or between 7am and 11pm from CP, (☎808-208208; www.cp.pt).

Stations: International trains use the Estação Santá Apolónia station in Lisbon and the Estação de São Bento in Porto. Trains from Lisbon to Sintra depart from Estação Rossio and trains for the Estoril Coast (north of Lisbon) from Estação Cais do Sodré. In the provinces stations can be several miles from town.

Bus

There are local and long-distance buses (*autocarros*). The inter-city buses are the most popular form of travel in Portugal and there are services to most towns and cities, although services are less frequent to more remote areas. The old state-owned bus company, the Rodoviária Nacional, has been disbanded and replaced by a number of smaller private operators, but a national network of express coaches is operated by Rede Expressos (for booking information, reservations and routes call ☎213-581460 or look at the website www.rede-expressos.pt). Bus and coach fares are slightly higher than on the trains, but travel times often quicker. Also, unlike many provincial rail stations, bus stations are nearly always located in town centres.

There are a number of other bus companies running express services (e.g. between Lisbon and the Algarve, and between Lisbon and Porto) and tickets for popular destinations should be bought in advance from bus stations or travel agents. The central bus station in Lisbon is on Avenida João Crisóstomo (nearest metro Saldanha) though some bus companies have other terminuses and it is therefore best to enquire with tourist offices for timetables and terminus information.

In Madeira and the Azores, buses are the only form of public transport. For further information contact the respective tourist boards:

Madeira: Direcção Regional de Turismo de Madeira, Avenida Arriaga 18, 9004-519 Funchal; ☎291-211900; fax 291-232151; www.madeiratoursim.org.

Azores: Direcção Regional Do Turismo Dos Acores, Rua Ernesto Rebelo 14, 9900-112 Horta; ☎292-200500; fax 292-200501; www.drtacores.pt.

Boats

Within Portugal, boat transport is used particularly on the Rio Tejo (River Tagus) estuary around Lisbon where ferries depart from the Sul e Sueste river station (near the Praça do Comércio) and the river station at Cais do Sodré to Cacilhas/ Almada, Trafaria, Barreiro (train station for the south), Seixal, Montijo etc.

South of Lisbon a car ferry crosses the Sado River from Setúbal to the Península de Tróia, a well known playground for the locals which projects into the Sado estuary. There are also ferries across the Rio Guadiana between Vila Real de San António and Spain, and across the Rio Minho from Vila Nova de Cerveira, Monção and Caminha to Spain.

Pleasure Boats. From Porto one can take boat trips up the Douro River past the port wine vineyards; minicruises are also available. The departure point is at Ribeira. Portugal specialist travel agent *Unicorn Holidays* offers short breaks in Porto with a daylong cruise along the Douro River leaving from Porto Quay; an oppportunity to sample some of the wine, port and local cuisine: (☎0173-7812255; www.unicornholidays.co.uk).

City Transport

Both Lisbon and Porto have very good city transport networks, and both are currently undergoing improvements. Investments underway include the expansion of the Lisbon underground, the Porto Light Metropolitan Railway, and the south Tagus Light Metropolitan Railway (in greater Lisbon). Work is also underway on the Light Metropolitan Railway in the centre of Coimbra.

In the smaller cities there are good local buses. Lisbon also has an extensive tram system as well as a good bus system, ferries and the metro, which currently consists of four lines. Porto also has a metro system. In most places you can find discount schemes for those who travel frequently on public transport. These consist of weekly or monthly travel cards and reduced rates for pensioners and children.

Taxis. Taxis are plentiful in the main towns and are distinguishable by their black and green livery. It is, however, usually difficult to hail a taxi; normally one has to queue at a taxi rank (e.g. in front of the Cais do Sodre rail station in Lisbon) or to telephone. Compared with other European countries Portuguese taxis are inexpensive. Hire is as per the taximeter in large towns or by the kilometre in more out-of-the-way places. Be aware that some taxi-drivers will attempt to over-charge you if you look particularly new to the country, as anywhere in the world. From 10pm to 6am there is a 20% supplement to pay; and large and heavy suitcases may mean an additional 50% charged; tipping is as in the UK, i.e. about 10%, although this is not obligatory. The journey from Lisbon airport to the city centre takes about 25 minutes.

BANKS AND FINANCE

Banking

In the aftermath of the 1974 Revolution most of Portugal's banking system was nationalised. Since the mid-80s commercial banking and insurance has been opened to private initiative, with the result that the financial system has evolved towards greater liberalisation, diversification, and internationalisation. Portugal's accession to the EU in 1986 prompted a series of policy measures, which liberalised the sector and as a direct result the Portuguese government's share of total shareholder equity in the banking system declined from 90% to 30% in the ten years following the joining of the EU. The only major financial institution that now remains in Government hands is Caixa Geral de Depósitos (CGD). Four banking groups dominate Portugal's banking sector: Grupo BCP (Banco Comercial Portugues) is by far the largest and most influential; Banco Espirito Santo (BES); Grupo Totta which includes Banco Totta & Acores (BTA), and is now owned by the Spanish banking giant Grupo Santander, and Banco Portugues de Investimento (BPI).

Other banks, including those from Germany, Britain and the USA, have established branches in the main cities. Spanish banks such as BBVA and Citibank have also made a large impression on the Portuguese banking world. The equivalent of the Bank of England in Portugal, the Banco de Portugal, is the only bank authorised to issue bank notes and all credit institutions come under its control.

Portuguese banks remain relatively small by European standards, but the sector has been completely modernised in recent years and electronic and internet banking are now the norm – particularly useful when checking on your account and carrying out transactions while abroad. Foreigners generally find the Portuguese banking system to be similar to that of the US and other Western European countries offering the same banking facilities

Even if you only own a holiday home in Portugal, it is worth keeping a certain amount of money in a Portuguese bank account to pay the necessary taxes and bills that build up on a property. A Portuguese account will also allow any tenants that rent the property to pay rent directly into a local account, from which local rates and bills can be paid. It should also reduce the number of times you convert currency between Sterling and Euros, saving you commission fees.

When choosing a bank, it's a good idea to ask friends and acquaintances for recommendations and to obtain relevant information from a range of banks and compare the charges, services offered, etc. It is worth asking your bank at home for advice: Barclays for instance, has several branches in Portugal and will be able to transfer accounts to their Portuguese branches. Other banks such as Lloyds TSB and HSBC have representatives to whom they can refer you. The advantage of banking with a company that has branches in Portugal is that they will be used to dealing with the requirements of foreign clients. Alternatively one can enquire at Portuguese banks with branches back home who will be able to give details of their nearest branch to your property in Portugal. If you use your property in Portugal as a holiday home only, you can have all correspondence from your bank in Portugal sent to your main home address abroad.

Banks in resort areas and cities usually have at least one member of staff who speaks English, however, those in rural areas generally don't. Service in small local branches is often more personalised than in larger branches and the staff less harried.

Banks in Portugal operate standard opening hours of 8.30am-3pm Monday to Friday and some branches in Lisbon and in the resort towns on the Algarve may also open in the evenings. Most Portuguese banks will be able to give cash advances on credit cards but will charge a fee for this service. The most convenient way to access cash these days is through the ATMs.

ATMs

There are now ATMs (automated teller machines), called *Multibanco*, located throughout Portugal and you can find them outside banks, in supermarkets and hypermarkets in towns, cities and villages throughout the country. Check with your bank to see whether your credit or debit card can be used in the ATMs in Portugal. Most cards are accepted. Remember that a small commission and cash handling fee is usually charged on each withdrawal so it makes sense to withdraw relatively large amounts at any one time rather than a series of smaller withdrawals. ATMs offer you a choice of language of instruction.

Upon opening a Portuguese bank account, you will be issued with a Multibanco card. The Multibanco system allows cardholders to use ATMs at any Portuguese bank, free of charge and in the UK it is associated with the Link ATM system. The card can also be used as a debit card in 95% of shops and restaurants in Portugal as well as at motorway toll booths and payphones.

Bank Accounts

The type of bank account permitted under Portuguese regulations depends on an individual's status (i.e. are they registered as resident or non-resident in Portugal). Portuguese banks levy charges on pretty much all transactions so before opening an account, be sure to ask for a breakdown of any charges that may be forthcoming, including annual fees. If you plan to make a lot of transfers between banks and accounts you may be able to negotiate more favourable terms.

Opening an Account. When opening an account you should fill in the forms appropriate to the type of account (e.g. joint or single; current (*conta corrente*) or deposit (*depósito a prazo*) and in due course you will be issued with a book of cheques (see below). The most common type of account is the current account, although these offer very low rates of interest (around 0.1% is standard). Savings should be placed into a deposit account although currently Euro-zone rates of interest are fairly low. To open an account, those who are 18 or over can simply go to the local branch in person. The banks will require either your passport of residence card as proof of identity, some form of proof of your address in Portugal, and your tax card (*cartão de contribuinte*).

Writing Cheques. These will be unfamiliar to UK cheque users: the payer's signature (*assinatura* comes at the top, underneath which comes the payee's name (*é ordem de*), and the amount (*a quantia de*) is written at the bottom. On Portuguese cheques you also have to write the place (*local de emissão*) where the cheque is issued (e.g. Lisbon, Cascais etc.). When writing figures in Portugal, note that a fullstop is used, rather than a comma, to indicate thousands. As in France it is a criminal offence to write a cheque with insufficient funds to cover it and if you do so your bank can ban you from issuing cheques in Portugal.

Non-Resident Accounts. Non-residents can open tourist (current) accounts in Portugal to which they may transfer funds from their bank back home. Such accounts are useful for paying bills, taxes and general domestic expenses. For those who may be absent from the country at the time certain bills fall due (e.g. water, electricity, television licences, etc.) it would be advisable to arrange to pay these by direct debit. The minimum opening capital varies between banks, but can be as little as €100 for a current account; considerably more for a deposit account. It is generally known that Portuguese banks are not keen to lend money at all. Overdrafts are not permitted on tourist accounts.

Deposit accounts in foreign currency may also be opened in Portugal by non-residents, although there is a time limit, usually one year, that one may hold such an account. The interest rate is fixed by the banks and is taxed at source.

Once the coveted resident status has been conferred the individual is free to join the mainstream Portuguese banking system and open a normal account. Portugal has a double taxation agreement with Britain, which avoids income being taxed twice.

Opening a Portuguese Bank Account from the UK. Although some people may be more confident opening an account with a branch of a UK bank in Portugal, you will find that the Portuguese branches of British banks function in just the same way as the Portuguese national banks. HSBC and Barclays Bank are the most widely represented of the British banks in Portugal with branches throughout the country. Those who wish to open an account with one of the branches in Portugal should contact their local branch in the UK, which will provide the relevant forms to complete. Alternatively, the London offices of the largest Portuguese banks are also able to provide the forms necessary to open an account with their home branches.

The banks which will provide such a service include Banco Totta & Acores (68 Cannon Street, London EC4N 6AQ; ☎020-7236 1515; fax 020-7236 7717; www.bancototta.co.uk) and the Caixa Geral de Depositos (Walbrook House, Walbrook, London EC4N 8BT; ☎020-7280 0200). Alternatively you could contact the Portuguese UK Business Network (1st Floor, 22/25a Sackville Street, London W1S 3DR; ☎020-7494 1844; fax 020-7494 1822; www.portuguese-chamber.org.uk) for details on Portuguese banks in the UK.

Banking Procedures

Bank statements are usually sent out to a customer's home address every month and are available on request at any time. Do not expect to get anything free from the bank. Unlike in the UK, charges are levied on day-to-day banking procedures in Portugal, with charges being made on all credit card and cheque transactions, though all the usual services, such as standing orders and direct debit are available.

Most banks will provide cash on presentation of an international credit card (e.g. Access, Visa, American Express). Cardholders are able to withdraw the credit balance of their personal limit, which only takes a few minutes, but is an expensive way of buying euros and it is cheaper, although not as quick, to pay in a Sterling cheque to the Portuguese bank where commission charges will usually be less. Even if you are moving permanently to Portugal it is a good idea to keep your bank account at home open. This will allow you to transfer money (from a pension, or income accrued from property rentals or a business) between accounts if you wish and will be useful when visiting friends and family in 'the old country'.

If you plan to keep most of your money outside the country, and instead to periodically transfer money from your account back home to your account in Portugal, you will need to enquire how long it will take to clear before you can access it and what the bank charges are for this service. Banks tend to like to take their time transferring money as the longer it swills around in their system the more profit they make.

Offshore Banking

Offshore banking is a favourite topic of conversation all over the world among expats looking for high returns on their savings. Offshore banks offer tax-free interest on deposit accounts and investment portfolios through banking centres in tax havens such as Gibraltar, the Cayman Islands, the Isle of Man and the

Channel Islands. More and more high street banks and building societies along with the merchant banks are setting up offshore banking facilities and the list given below offers only a handful of the most widely-known offering such services. Deposit account interest rates work on the basis that the more inaccessible one's money is, the higher the rate of interest paid.

Banks and financial institutions in Portugal also offer offshore banking services. In return for a tax-free interest, clients are generally expected to maintain minimum deposit levels, which can be very high, and restrictive terms and conditions often apply. The minimum deposit required by each bank will vary, the norm being between £1,000 and £5,000. Usually, a minimum of £10,000 is needed for year-long deposit accounts, while the lower end of the minimum deposit range applies to 90-day deposits. Instant access accounts are also available.

For the expat living along the Algarve the banks in Gibraltar offer a convenient place to stash cash in a tax-free account. However, sound financial advice should be sought regarding one's financial and tax position before placing one's life savings in an offshore account. Buying property through an offshore company has until recently been a common practice in Portugal, but changes in the country's tax laws regarding offshore companies has spread something of a panic among those expats who took this option when purchasing property.

Trusts

If you have reasonably substantial assets, then a trust of one kind or another may be an effective way of reducing taxes; but this should only be done with expert advice. The concept of a 'trust' only exists in countries with common-law legal systems, e.g. the UK, USA, Canada and British colonies. However, there are moves by the government in the UK to make trusts less effective as a way of evading taxes.

The concept of a trust is simple enough: you give or lend your money to a trustee; this money is then treated by the taxman as though it were not yours anymore. The trustees appointed to run the trust invest the money as they see fit, or as you have specified when making the initial gift. Income generated by the trust is taxed under a special regime in the UK depending on the type of trust. The two basic categories of trust are:

O Interest-in-possession trust: this gives a person or persons the right to income from the trust or the equivalent of income (e.g. the right to live in a rent-free property). The trustees have to hand over the income to the beneficiaries stated in the trust.

O Discretionary trust: the trustees decide which beneficiaries should receive income or capital from the trust. Where no money is paid out until the end of the trust, this is known as an *accumulation trust*. If money is paid out for the education, maintenance or benefit of beneficiaries until they get an *interest-in-possession,* then the trust is an *accumulation-and-maintenance* trust.

The income from trusts may be used as decided by the trustees, which means that though you may receive some income from the trust (which will be subject to taxation) other income may be invested or spent by the trust as they wish. If the trust company is based in a place where taxes are low or non-existent then the income from the investments will have low or no tax payable on them. Additionally, on death, the money put into a trust, as it is 'not yours' anymore, will not be subject to inheritance tax.

Useful Addresses

Abbey National Offshore (Isle of Man): PO Box 150, Carrick House, Circular Road, Douglas, Isle of Man IM99 1NH; ☎01624-644 505; fax 01624-644 550; www.anoffshore.com.

Abbey National Offshore (Jersey): PO Box 545, International House, 41 The Parade, Jersey JE4 8XG, Channel Islands; ☎01534-885 100; fax 01534-828 884; www.anoffshore.com.

Abbey National (Gibraltar) Ltd: 237 Main Street, PO Box 824, Gibraltar; ☎76-090; fax 72-028.

Banco Santander Totta S.A.: 68 Cannon Street, London EC4N 6AQ; ☎020-7651 0190; fax 020-7329 8207; www.bancototta.co.uk.

Bank of Scotland International (Jersey) Ltd: PO Box 664, Halifax House, 31/33 New Street, St Helier, Jersey, Channel Islands JE4 8YW; ☎01534-613 500; fax 01534-759 280; www.bankofscotland-international.com.

Bank of Scotland International (Isle of Man) Ltd: PO Box 19, Bank of Scotland House, Prospect Hill, Douglas, Isle of Man IM99 1AT; ☎01624-612323; fax 01624-644090; www.bankofscotland-international.com.

BDO Stoy Hayward: 8 Baker Street, London W1U 3LL; ☎020-7486 5888; www.bdo.co.uk, and associated offices in more than 90 countries worldwide. Fifth biggest accountancy firm in the world providing tax advice from offices throughout Europe and overseas.

Bradford and Bingley International Ltd: 30 Ridgeway Street, Douglas, Isle of Man IMI ITA; ☎01624-695000; fax 01624-695001; www.bradford-bingley-int.co.im.

Brewin Dolphin Securities Ltd: Stockbrokers: 5 Giltspur Street, London EC1A 9BD; ☎020-7248 4400; fax 020-7236 2034; www.brewindolphin.co.uk.

Ex-Pat Tax Consultants Ltd: Suite 2, 2nd Floor Shakespeare House, 18 Shakespeare Street, Newcastle upon Tyne NE1 6AQ; ☎0191-230 3141; fax 0191-261 2956; www.expattax.co.uk.

HSBC Bank International Limited: Esplanade, St Helier, Jersey JE1 1HS, Channel

Islands; ☎01534 616000; fax 01534 616001; www.offshore.hsbc.com.

Lloyds TSB: Isle of Man Offshore Centre, PO Box 111, Peveril Square, Douglas, Isle of Man IM99 1JJ; ☎08705 301641; fax 01624 670929; www.lloydstsb-offshore.com. One of their services is the *Lloyds Bank Overseas Club*.

The Fry Group: Crescent House, Crescent Road, Worthing, West Sussex BN11 1RN; ☎01903-231545; fax 01903-200868; www.thefrygroup.co.uk. Offer a comprehensive tax and compliance service. They publish a useful series of guides including *The British Expatriate*, which can also be downloaded from their website.

TAXATION

If you have ever been faced with completing a self-assessment tax form you will be aware that sorting out one's tax affairs is a far from simple matter and one that isn't made easier by the pages and pages of notes and explanations provided by the tax authorities. If you have ever been sent a tax form in a language that you are less than fluent in then chances are you will have had to seek out the services of a bilingual accountant.

Once you move abroad, unless your financial affairs are simple, and consist of one source of income and no investments or savings or interest payments you will be advised to enlist the aid of an accountant versed in international tax laws – at least for your first year in Portugal. Qualified tax consultants should be members of *The Chartered Institute of Taxation* – CIOT – (12 Upper Belgrave Street, London SW1X 8BB; ☎020-7235 9381; www.tax.org.uk) or *The Association of Taxation Technicians* – ATT – (12 Upper Belgrave Street London SW1X 8BB; ☎020-7235 2544; www.att.org.uk) in the UK. *The Portuguese UK Business Network* (1st floor, 22/25a Sackville Street, London W1S 3DR; ☎020-7949 1844; www.portuguese-chamber.org.uk) also holds a list of chartered accountants who deal with taxation in Portugal.

In Portugal the Directorate General for Taxation (DGCI, Rua da Prata, nº 10-2º, 1178 Lisbon; ☎218-878487; fax 218-877747; www.dgci.min-financas.pt) is responsible for tax assessment and collection.

Moving to Portugal
Procedure for UK Residents. If you are moving permanently abroad, the situation is reasonably straightforward. You should inform the UK Inspector of Taxes, at the office you usually deal with, of your departure and they will send you a P85 form to complete. The UK tax office will usually require certain proof that you are leaving the UK and hence their jurisdiction, for good. Evidence of having sold a house in the UK and having rented or bought one in Portugal is usually sufficient. You can continue to own property in the UK without being considered resident, but you will have to pay UK taxes on any income from the

property.

If you are leaving a UK company to take up employment with a Portuguese one then the P45 form given by your UK employer and evidence of employment in Portugal should be sufficient. You may be eligible for a tax refund in respect of the period up to your departure, in which case it will be necessary to complete an income tax return for income and gains from the previous 5 April to your departure date. It may be advisable to seek professional advice when completing the P85; this form is used to determine your residence status and hence your UK tax liability. You should not fill it in if you are only going abroad for a short period of time. Once the Inland Revenue are satisfied that you are no longer resident in the UK, they will close your file and not expect any more UK income tax to be paid.

Portugal has a double taxation agreement with the UK, which makes it possible to offset tax paid in one country against tax paid in another (see below). For further information see the Inland Revenue publications IR20 *Residents and non-residents. Liability to tax in the United Kingdom,* which can be found on the website www.inlandrevenue.gov.uk. Booklets IR138, IR139 and IR140 are also worth reading; these can be obtained from your local tax office or from: *Centre for Non-Residents (CNR):* St John's House, Merton Rd, Bootle, Merseyside L69 9BB; ☎0151-472 6196; fax 0151-472 6392; www.inlandrevenue.gov.uk/cnr.

Taxation Status

Anyone spending more than 183 days in Portugal in any one tax year (which runs from 1 January to 31 December) will be deemed to be a tax resident in Portugal and liable to Portuguese tax on their worldwide income from the date of their arrival in the country. The 183 days does not necessarily have to be taken in one go, it is the total number of days over the whole period that matters. This ruling holds true whether or not you have a residence card. You will also be deemed to be tax resident in Portugal if you are working in the country or your centre of economic interest lies in the country (your main source of income comes from Portugal). Owning a second home in Portugal does not necessarily make you a tax resident of Portugal, as if you only visit the property relatively rarely, do not rent it out or take an income from it then you will be liable only for the usual local taxes and those associated with owning property.

It is of course possible to be a tax resident of more than one country – different countries have different rulings on tax residency – in which case you will need to find a financial adviser steeped in international tax law to advice you on how you can alleviate some of your tax liabilities. In any case many countries have entered into double taxation agreements so that tax doesn't end up being paid more than once. Each double taxation agreement will have its own set of rules depending on what was worked out between the signatory countries.

For some people it will make financial sense to take up tax residency in Portugal and to abandon their tax residency of their country of origin; for others it may be more sensible to remain a tax resident of their country of origin. Each case will be different and it is therefore in your best interests to seek advice from a financial adviser as early as possible before you actually move to Portugal.

Portuguese Income Tax

Personal Income tax (*Imposto Sobre o Rendimento das Pessoas Singulares*) is a wide-ranging tax in four main bands. Your tax number and *cartão de contribuinte* (tax card) are vital for declaring income tax. These must be obtained from the tax office within 30 days of arriving in Portugal. The tax is levied on nine categories or classifications of income:

CLASSIFICATIONS OF INCOME FOR TAX PURPOSES

(A) From employment
(B) From self-employment
(C) Commercial/Industrial profits
(D) From farming
(E) From investment
(F) From rental of property
(G) Capital gains
(H) Pensions
(I) Other income

Residents (i.e. those who live in Portugal for more than 183 days in any tax year – see above) are taxed on their worldwide income after deduction of specific personal allowances. Total income within the above categories is added together to arrive at an annual base from which income tax is deducted at the appropriate rate: 12% is the marginal rate and income is tax-free up to the personal limit of €4,182 a year. This is then taxed at 14% from €4,183-€6,325; at 24% from €6,326-€15,683; 34% on €15,684-€35,071; 38% on €35, 072-€52,277 and 40% on all earnings over €52,277. In the 2006 budget, a new income tax band of 42% will be introduced for annual incomes above €60,000.

Reductions (up to certain limits) of income tax may be claimed on the following: mortgage interest and housing loan repayments; life insurance and medical and educational expenses including any payments made to the *Caixa* social security scheme. Personal income tax allowances are about €214 for single persons and €178 for each partner of a married couple. There is also an allowance of €142.64 for each child. Some taxes paid overseas are also deductible as expenses.

Non-Residents. Non-residents will need to make an annual tax declaration to the Portuguese tax office (*finanças*) on any income generated from any property owned in Portugal (rental, sale, etc.), any income received from business activities or employment in Portugal, from any pension received, and from any income generated from securities or capital invested in the country. There are certain allowances granted (a personal allowance, payments into social security, some housing costs, expenses, etc.) which are deductible from your total annual earnings, just as there are in the UK tax system. Non-residents are not taxed on their worldwide income, only on any income generated in Portugal.

Tax Returns. The system relies on self-declarations. Tax forms are sent out by the tax authorities in January of the year following assessment and must be submitted either by 15 March, in the case of those earning income only from employment and/or pensions, or by 30 April if other categories of income are involved. Payment is due within one month of receiving the bill.

After assessment, the tax authorities will make any adjustments, upwards or downwards, to the level of taxation; and an additional payment will be requested, or an overpayment refund will be issued. There are some additional deductions which can be made for the various specific categories of income, which is where the services of a Portuguese-speaking accountant will be very useful.

Double Taxation Agreements

Portugal has reciprocal tax agreements with a number of countries around the world, which avoids the possibility of someone being taxed twice on their income from renting property, pensions, gifts, inheritance, etc. – once by the Portuguese and once by the tax authorities in their home country. However, there may be a slight hitch during the initial period of Portuguese residency because, for instance, the UK and Portuguese tax years run from April to April and from January to January respectively and therefore UK nationals in Portugal may be taxed by both the Portuguese and UK authorities in the overlapping months of their first year in the new country.

In this case, you would be able to claim a refund of UK tax by applying to the Inland Revenue through your local UK tax office. They will supply you with an SPA/Individual form (which offers relief at source for tax refunds concerning interest, royalties and pensions) or with the SPA/Individual/Credit form (which provides repayment on dividend income for anyone who has suffered double taxation on moving to Portugal). Once the form has been filled out, take it to the *finanças* (tax office) in Portugal. They will stamp it and then you can return it to the British tax authorities as proof that you have paid Portuguese tax and are therefore no longer liable for British tax. This is a procedure that should be carried out while you are in Portugal and not after your return to the UK.

It is important to keep accounts of your income, expenditure etc., while in Portugal to meet any problems should these arise. Double taxation agreements will differ depending on the country involved and the circumstances of the individual. If a pension is taxed in the UK it won't be taxed in Portugal, although it may be more beneficial to be taxed in Portugal rather than in the UK and financial advice should be sought on this.

COUNTRIES WITH A DOUBLE TAXATION AGREEMENT WITH PORTUGAL

Austria	Belgium	Brazil	Bulgaria	Canada
Cape Verde	China	Cuba	Czech Republic	Denmark
Finland	France	Germany	Greece	the Netherlands
Hungary	India	Iceland	Ireland	Italy
Lithuania	Malta	Luxembourg	Macao	Mexico
Morocco	Mozambique	Norway	Pakistan	Poland
Romania	Russia	Singapore	South Korea	Spain
Switzerland	Tunisia	UK	Ukraine	USA
Venezuela				

Several draft agreements with additional countries are at discussion stage.

VAT

VAT, or IVA (*Imposto sobre o Valor Ascrescentado*) as it is referred to in Portugal, was introduced in 1986 when Portugal joined the then European Community. IVA is levied on a wide range of goods and services transferred within Portuguese territory as well as being levied on imports from outside the EU. The standard rate is 19%, with a medium or intermediate rate of 12% and a lower rate of 5% which increasingly covers less, but still applies to some food products, medicine, educational material, water and electricity, etc. Some food products, restaurants and similar activities as well as diesel for farming are subject to the medium rate. Persons from outside the European Union visiting Portugal for less than 180 days can reclaim IVA by completing a form named *Isenção de IVA,* which is then presented to customs when leaving the country.

In the autonomous regions of Madeira and the Azores the IVA rates are levied in bands of 13% (*genérica* – standard), 8% (*intermédia* – medium), and 4% (*reduzida* – reduced) but otherwise operate in a similar way.

Note: at the time of going to press, the Portuguese government announced an increase in the standard rate of VAT from 19% to 21% as part of measures aimed at reducing the public sector deficit to bring it back below the 3% ceiling set by the EU. No further details of the plans were available at this time.

Inheritance and Gift Tax

In 2003 Portuguese tax authorities introduced reforms to abolish Inheritance Tax and Gift Tax (*Imposto sobre as Sucessões e Doações*). The new ruling came into force from 1 January 2004. Previously, Inheritance Tax and Gift Tax was payable on any assets deemed to be located in Portugal (i.e. real estate, securities) at the time of the deceased's death or at the time of their making of the gift. Rates varied from 3%-50% depending on the relationship between the recipient and the deceased or donor. With the abolition of these taxes a Stamp Duty with a flat rate of 10% will now apply, there will be exemptions available for transfers to spouses, descendants and ascendants. Further information on inheritance and wills can be found in the following chapter, *Retirement*.

Municipal Tax (Imposto Municipal sobre Imóveis – IMI)

The old Municipal Property Tax or rates known as *Contribuição Autárquica* that was payable by all owners of property in Portugal (both residents and non-residents) on 31 December annually has now been replaced by a new Municipal Tax, the levies of which will differ depending on the type of property and the value of the property; on whether the property is a country property or an urban property or a building plot. The rateable value of a property is assessed on the fiscal value of a property as registered in the local tax register. As many of these values are out of date, a re-valuation process has been set in motion and any property changing hands will be automatically revalued. New taxable values under the new IMI are likely to equate to 80%-90% of a property's market value. Because the re-valuation process is likely to take several years to complete, all property taxable values will be corrected in accordance with inflation and adjusted according to regional market swings. A taxable rate of between 0.4%-0.8% of the corrected taxable value will be payable, with a yearly ceiling on increases until 2008. In 2004, Municipal Tax could not be increased by more than €60. Once revaluation has occurred the IMI will be between 0.2% and 0.5% of the value given to the property.

These new tax rules, effective from 1 December 2003, have meant a significant increase in Property Tax payable by offshore companies owning property in Portugal and real estate owned by offshore companies is now taxed at a whopping 5%

Further details on real estate taxes can be found in Chapter 3, *Setting Up Home*.

Capital Gains Tax

In 1989 the application of Capital Gains Tax (*Imposto de Mais Valias*) was widened from being purely a tax on businesses, to include profits made by individuals on various transactions: 10% on any profits from the sale of shares held for a period of less than two years; 20% on the sale of non-residential property and 24% on the sale of land for development.

In common with France, Capital Gains Tax is not charged on the sale of an individual's sole residence provided the proceeds of such a sale are reinvested in another property (or land) within two years, otherwise 50% of the gain is added to the regular income. A capital gain on the sale of shares held for more than one year is tax exempt, for holding of less than one year the tax rate is 10%. A capital gain is usually added to regular income and therefore included in the calculations of the yearly tax return. In addition, in calculating a capital gain, account is taken of the rate of inflation from the date of purchase until the date of sale. There is a flat rate of 25% for non-residents.

Useful Publication

The Blevins Franks Guide to Living in Portugal (Blevins Franks, 2002). Useful financial guide to Portugal by international financial advisers, Blevins Franks. New edition due 2005/6.

HEALTH INSURANCE AND HOSPITALS

In Portugal, the national health system is known as the *Serviço Nacional de saúde*, and is made up of public hospitals and health centres known as *centros de saúde*. Unfortunately the Portuguese state health system is currently facing numerous difficulties. Recent years have seen a wave of stories in the newspapers relating to medical mishaps and complaints about doctor-patient relations. On top of this, waiting lists for crucial operations have been getting longer and longer. The system is incredibly unbalanced – areas such as Lisbon are well provided for in terms of hospitals and medical centres. However, in many more remote areas, thousands of patients are forced to use the emergency services for everyday illnesses due to a severe shortage of doctors in their local centros de saúde.

As a result of having a state-run system that even the Portuguese Minister of Health recently described as a 'national shame', those who can afford it often choose to make use of private health facilities. However, despite private health services being well provided in many of the areas with a high concentration of expats, away from the big cities and tourist resorts, people have no choice but to use the public hospitals as there is not enough wealth to support local facilities.

Despite all of the bad press however the state system does work and the government is currently attempting to tackle some of the issues mentioned above.

Ten new hospitals are currently under construction and many more are in the process of being renovated or replaced. Over the last few years one possibility which has been explored, is that of allowing the private sector to play a greater role in service provision, thereby reducing the burden on public expenditure. The 2002 Hospital Bill allowed for new state hospitals to be managed by private companies and for existing state hospitals to be transformed into public companies. It is hoped that by changing the way that hospitals are managed, they will become more efficient and cost-effective. More than a third of public hospitals have already been incorporated as public companies and according to the OECD, higher production and some productivity gains have already been achieved as a result. The bill also allowed for hospital services to be contracted out to the private sector.

The Portuguese Health System

Many countries, including the 25 member states of the EU, have reciprocal health treatment arrangements with Portugal. EU citizens are entitled to use the health service, mostly free of charge, with some limitations. Those who are working in Portugal will be issued with a *Livrete de Assistência Médica* by their employer or by their local health centre.

Hospital treatment within the Portuguese public health system is free, as is the provision of essential medicines. General medical consultations and GP services are provided in the network of health centres (*centros de saúde*) and their local offices; if treatment cannot be provided in these places you are entitled to consult a registered doctor. There is a nominal fee for a consultation at a health centre (around €3) and charges ranging from 40%-100% are levied for non-essential medicines. Contributions are also required for items such as spectacles, dentures, etc. Exemptions – where payment of such charges is waived – are made for children under 12, pregnant women, pensioners and for those receiving less than the national minimum wage, among others. Any payments you do need to make when dealing with the public health system are tax deductible. If you keep you receipts, these can be taken along to the tax office and written off against your income tax.

Centros de saúde are usually open from 8am to 8pm. When visiting a centro de saúde, it is necessary to produce your fiscal identity number (NIF) and a cartão de saúde (health service card). The health service card can be applied for as soon as you have received your residence permit. It is necessary to register your details with your local health centre as soon as possible. All centros de saúde have an emergency department and will allow you to see any doctor. However, should you wish to see a specialist doctor you may have to pay, unless your GP issues you with a *credencial* – a referral – confirming that you need to see a particular specialist.

As mentioned above, the public health system in Portugal is somewhat chaotic and it can take months to get an appointment and waiting times for hospital admission are on average more than three months. Improvements are being made but those Portuguese who can afford it take out private health insurance to cover the cost of treatment at private clinics and health centres.

UK citizens visiting Portugal (or Madeira or the Azores), i.e. non-residents, are entitled to in-patient treatment in a general ward of an official hospital under EU reciprocal health agreements. Permanent residents may apply for form E109, which provides for your family members who may be resident elsewhere in the EU and entitles them to Portuguese healthcare. The regional social security office (CRSS) is where you go to apply for this. However, if you are treated by a doctor working in one of the state health centres mentioned above you must expect to pay some consultation fees and charges for most prescribed medicines, and for dental treatment, etc.

An important point to bear in mind is that once you have taken up residence permanently in Portugal, you will no longer be entitled to receive non-emergency treatment on the British NHS unless you move back to the UK. In the light of all of the above, it is therefore extremely advisable to take out private medical insurance or, alternatively, if you are working in Portugal, to contribute to the country's national insurance scheme.

Hospitals, Chemists and Emergencies

The British Hospital in Lisbon (Rua Saraiva de Carvalho 49, Estrela, 1250 Lisbon; ☎213-943100 is a small one-ward institution. Patients pay fees but the hospital is strictly non-profit. Other funding comes from public subscription. Although it has a small operating theatre the hospital is not equipped to deal with serious emergencies. The British Hospital also runs an outpatient service of which details are available on request. The International Medical Centre in Lisbon (Av. Antonio Augusto de Agular, 40 r/c, 1015-016 Lisbon; ☎213-513310) is suitable for non-emergencies and is staffed by English speaking medical staff.

Chemists (*Farmácias*). Usual opening hours for pharmacies in Portugal are 9am to 1pm and 3-7pm, Monday to Friday. On Saturdays pharmacies tend to close at lunchtime. In Lisbon and Porto there are several 24-hour chemists, while in other areas there is a rota system of late-night opening – the name of the chemist on duty is usually posted in all chemist windows and in the local press. Many Portuguese pharmacists speak English. Pharmacists can be consulted about the treatment of minor ailments.

Emergencies (*Urgências*). If your condition is serious go to the casualty department of the nearest general hospital or *Cruz Vermelha Portuguesa* (Red Cross hospital). An ambulance can be summoned by dialling the emergency number (*Número Nacional de Socorro*) 112. Although the amount of English spoken by the emergency services' operators is improving, it is in no way guaranteed that you will get through to a bilingual operator – so be sure that you can describe as a bare minimum, you location and the service you require. Ambulances in Portugal are driven by *bombeiros* (firemen), often known as the *voluntários*, who are trained in first-aid. In major cities and tourist areas, the emergency services are fast and efficient, but in more remote areas they can be poorly equipped and do not have an exemplary response rate. Larger hospitals' casualty departments are open 24 hours a day. The majority of private health providers also have their own emergency numbers that can be contacted.

The E111 and the European Health Insurance Card

Reciprocal medical arrangements between the UK and Portugal under EU regulations make it possible for those whose visits to Portugal will last for no more than three months at a time to obtain free or subsidised medical treatment. This arrangement may well prove helpful for those going on a property-searching trip and those who already have holiday homes there. This agreement only covers temporary residence, not the first three months of a permanent residence and applies only to emergency medical treatment.

To qualify for such treatment you need form E111 (known as E one-eleven), contained within the leaflet: *Health Advice for Travellers*. As a result of recent changes to European law, a new E111 form has been introduced. Those planning to travel to Portugal during 2005 should apply for a new E111 as the old forms are no longer valid. This new E111 will be valid until 31 December 2005. However, during the course of 2005, the UK will adopt the European Health Insurance Card (EHIC), which will be automatically issued to those who apply for the new E111 during 2005 and tick the appropriate box. Application forms are available online at the Department of Health website: www.dh.gov.uk or from post offices. Downloaded forms will still need to be taken into the post office for approval.

Happily, the Portuguese authorities have simplified the procedures necessary for foreigners to obtain medical treatment while in Portugal and now you have only to present your E111/EHIC, and a photocopy of this, to the ambulance, doctor or practice when treatment is required. The original E111/EHIC will be returned after it has been checked; the photocopy will be retained. Be sure to carry spare copies of the document, as they will be needed if further treatment is required. If you do not have an E111/EHIC, you will be expected to pay for medical treatment, and it does not cover you for non-emergency treatment, e.g. prescribed medicines and dental treatment. Moreover, the E111/EHIC is not a substitute for travel insurance. On the Portuguese mainland and the Azores a nominal charge is made for treatment at health centres. In Madeira it is necessary to pay for a consultation with a GP and claim a refund from a bank appointed as an agent before leaving Madeira. The charges for prescribed medicines are 40% to 100% of the retail price; basic hospital treatment is free but charges are made for X-rays and some other secondary treatments such as laboratory tests.

An E111/EHIC normally has no time limit but is not valid once you have left the UK permanently, or are employed in Portugal. It can sometimes be renewed and it is also possible to get an open-ended E111/EHIC if you make frequent trips abroad for a period longer than three months. Explanatory leaflet SA29 gives details of social security, healthcare and pension rights within the EU and is obtainable from main post offices and from the Department of Work and Pensions, Overseas Directorate, Tyneview Park, Whitely Road, Benton, Newcastle-upon-Tyne NE98 1BA.

The E101 and E128

The Inland Revenue, National Insurance Contributions Office, International Services in Newcastle issues an E101 to UK nationals working in another EU country to exempt them from paying social security contributions in that country if they are still paying contributions in their home country. The E101 only gives free medical assistance for three months. The E128 entitles you to medical treatment in another EU country where you are working, or if you are a student. You have to obtain an E101 *before* you can obtain an E128. Retirees need to fill in form E121 from the Department of Work and Pensions.

Health Insurance Contributions

Anyone legally employed in Portugal will have health insurance contributions automatically deducted from their salary by their employer for payment to the *Caixa*. Anyone who is self-employed will have to make their own payments which are subject to change but which are currently around 30% of the official minimum wage. Useful leaflets setting out the entitlements of taxpayers in Portugal can be obtained from Jobcentres in the UK or you may contact the Benefits Agency, Pensions and Overseas Benefits Directorate (Overseas Branch, Tyneview Park, Newcastle-upon-Tyne NE98 1BA; ☎0191-218 7777; www.dwp.gov.uk) with enquiries relating to health contributions and pensions, etc., before moving to Portugal. Once in Portugal, if you are still in any doubt about your status or eligibility for subsidised health care, enquire at the local *Centro de Saúde* or International Clinic.

Private Medical Insurance

Although the level of convenience, comfort and attention offered through private insurance schemes is superior to that received by National Health patients, the treatment itself will not necessarily be of a higher quality. However, a growing number of foreign residents in Portugal are opting to remove themselves from the long waiting lists and sometimes chaotic conditions of the Portuguese National Health Service to take out private health insurance. Private clinics are mainly concentrated in popular tourist and expat areas, such as the Algarve and Lisbon. These areas also offer a range of alternative therapy centres, rehab clinics and health farms, all of which are advertised in the English-language press.

Those who only spend a few weeks or months a year in Portugal will still require private medical insurance to cover the balance of the cost not covered by the E111/EHIC (see above). One of the advantages of UK health insurance schemes is that their policies cover the claimants for treatment incurred anywhere in Europe, not just in Portugal itself. With an increasing number of insurance companies offering this kind of cover, it is worth shopping around as cover and costs vary. However, it is worth noting that private healthcare in Portugal is tax deductible, but this does not apply to policies purchased in the UK or indeed anywhere outside of Portugal. The Portuguese government views such products as offshore and therefore offers no tax breaks. Most expats who move to Portugal usually start off by moving their policy with them and then opting for a Portuguese policy a few years down the line. Private Portuguese healthcare policies are often cheaper.

If you are transferring your contribution-based Jobseeker's Allowance to Portugal you are automatically entitled to free health care. Make sure you apply for the appropriate form, the E119, before you leave the UK and take this along with the E303 Jobseeker's Allowance form.

Useful Addresses

AXA PPP Healthcare: Phillips House, Crescent Road, Tunbridge Wells, Kent TN1 2PL; ☎01892-612080; www.axappphealthcare.co.uk.

British United Provident Association (BUPA) International: BUPA House, 15-19 Bloomsbury Way, London WC1A 2BA ☎01273-208181; www.bupa-intl. com. BUPA International offers a range of worldwide schemes for individuals and companies of three or more employees based outside the UK for six or more months.

Community Insurance Agency Inc.: 425 Huehl Road, Suite 22a Northbrook, IL 60062, USA; ☎847-897-5120; fax 847-897 5130; e-mail info@ciainsagency. com. International health coverage agency.

David Hills Insurance Agency: Rua Vasco de Gama no. 259, 8135 Almancil, Algarve, Portugal; ☎289-399 774; fax 289-397 215; e-mail info@davidhills. com; www.davidhills.com. Specialists in property, health, commercial, travel, motor, marine and personal insurance in Portugal.

Exeter Friendly Society: Lakeside House, Emperor Way, Exeter, Devon; ☎01392-353535; 01392-353590; e-mail sales@exeterfriendly.co.uk; www.exeterfriendly.co.uk.

Expacare: Columbia Centre, Market Street, Bracknell, Berkshire RG12 1JG; ☎01344-381650; fax 01344 381690; e-mail: info@expacare.com or visit www.expacare.com. Specialists in expatriate healthcare offering high quality health insurance cover for individuals and their families, including group cover for five or more employees. Cover is available for expatriates of all nationalities worldwide.

Goodhealth: 5 Lloyd's Avenue, London EC3N 3AE; ☎020-7423 4300; fax 020-7423 4301; e-mail enquiries@goodhealth.co.uk; www.goodhealthworldwide.com. Offers private healthcare plans to expatriates worldwide.

Healthcare International: 84 Brook Street, London W1K 5EH; ☎020-7665 1627; fax 020-7665 1628; e-mail enquiries@healthcareinternational.com. Global medical insurance for expats and travellers.

Sickness and Invalidity Benefit

Anyone who claims sickness or invalidity benefit in the UK and is moving out to Portugal permanently is entitled to continue claiming this benefit once in Portugal. Strictly speaking, to claim either benefit, you must be physically incapable of *all* work; however, the interpretation of the words 'physically incapable' is frequently stretched just a little beyond literal truth. If a claimant has been paying National Insurance contributions in the UK for two tax years (this period may be less, depending on his or her level of income) then he or she is eligible to claim sickness benefit. After receiving sickness benefit for 28 weeks, a claimant is entitled to invalidity benefit, which is paid at a higher rate. Anyone currently receiving either form of benefit should inform the Department of Work and Pensions that they are moving to Portugal. Forms will then be sent to the DWP International Services Department (Newcastle-upon-Tyne NE98 1YC) who will then make sure that a monthly sterling cheque is sent either to the claimant's new address or direct into his or her bank account. All such claimants must submit themselves, on request, to a medical examination either in Portugal or Britain.

Doctors and Dentists

In the Algarve and other developed areas of Portugal there are an increasing number of smart new private medical and dental clinics, often run by foreigners or Portuguese doctors with excellent English. The most usual method of finding a reliable doctor or dentist is by personal recommendation; alternatively most doctors and dentists advertise in the English-language publications and in the local telephone directory.

Emergency dental treatment is available anywhere in the EU for its citizens, but you will have to pay for everything else and dentistry is relatively expensive in Portugal. Many expats find that it is therefore sensible to keep their UK dentist and fit in routine dental treatment with regular visits home.

SOCIAL SECURITY AND JOB SEEKER'S ALLOWANCE

Social Security

Portugal has a system of social security (*segurança social*) similar to systems in other EU countries. Employees and the self-employed pay their monthly contributions into a fund (*caixa*) and in return receive a range of benefits including healthcare and pensions, and sickness, unemployment, invalid and maternity/paternity benefits. Non-employed people may pay voluntary national insurance contributions if they so wish.

Employees. It is the responsibility of employers to register their workers for social security payments. Social security contributions are payable by both employer and employee as a percentage of the gross salary earned. At the time of writing, the general contribution is 34.75% of earnings of which 11% is payable by the employee. In return for contributions, employees are entitled to family benefits, sickness benefits, maternity, paternity and adoption benefits, unemployment benefits, invalidity benefits, old age pensions and survivors pensions.

The Self-employed. Self-employed workers (*trabalhador por conta própria*) are entitled to the majority of benefits available to employees, including maternity and paternity benefits, invalidity benefits, occupational illness benefits, old age pensions etc. The contribution rates are 24.5% of your salary for compulsory coverage or 32% which includes optional coverage for sickness benefits and additional family benefits. Neither of these options will cover you for unemployment benefit however.

Social security payments must be made to the treasury department of the local *segurança social* office. Alternatively (as it can be problematic to find an office with a treasury department in your area), it is possible to pay electronically via the Multibanco system. To register at the social security office, it is necessary to take the following documents: ID card, social security card, tax card, a statement of the start of activity for fiscal purposes, and a statement of income. Note that The Ministry of Social Security states that it is only mandatory for those self-employed persons whose gross yearly income is higher than six times the national minimum salary to become affiliated to the social security scheme (the minimum national salary is currently just €356.60 per month). If your gross yearly income is equal to, or less than this figure then affiliation is voluntary. As an incentive for self-employment, you may be exempt from making contributions during the first

12 months of business activity.

All payments should be made by the 15th of the month (for the previous month's contributions). It is a good idea to pay on time as interest becomes payable from the 16th of each month, and interest rates are fairly high.

Further information on social security and your rights as an EU citizen is available from the Ministry of Social Security website: www.seg-social.pt (some of which is in English). Further enquiries should be directed to the Department of International Relations for Social Security (*Departamento de Relações Internacionais de Segurança Social,* Rua de Junqueira, 112-1300-344 Lisboa, ☎213-652300; fax 213-652498; e-mail driss@segsocial.pt). There is also a leaflet (SA 29) available from the Overseas Benefits Office, Newcastle-upon-Tyne NE98 1YX (☎0191-218 7777) and Job Centres which gives details of social security, health care and pension rights within the EU; and is also useful reading for anyone intending to live and work in Portugal.

Healthcare. All those who pay into the *Caixa* and their dependants are entitled to use the scheme. However in some cases, even while on benefit, one may have to pay a substantial contribution towards medical consultations and diagnoses involving the use of sophisticated equipment. Generally speaking, expectant mothers, children and pensioners and emergency cases are exempt from all charges. Further information about Portuguese healthcare is given above.

Sickness. Those who are actually ill, and not simply taking a 'sickie' are provided for by the social security system. The sickness insurance fund provides employees with 65% of their average pay, or 70% if they have not taken any sick days in the 365 days before falling ill. The maximum amount of sick leave that a person may take is 1095 days. Thereafter they must undertake a medical examination establishing their inability to work, in which case they would receive an invalidity pension. Employees (and the self-employed) are covered for all medical contingencies by their social security contributions. Contibutions ensure that you are covered for free visits to your doctor at the local *centros de saúde* (subject to a nominal consultation fee – see above). Essential prescription medicines are also provided free of charge. However, the system is currently suffering from severe under-investment and as a result most people choose to take out private health insurance.

In order to claim sickness benefit, you must obtain a Temporary Incapacity Certificate from your local health centre and send it to the social security office within five working days.

Anyone who is moving to Portugal permanently and who claims sickness or invalidity benefit in the UK is entitled to continue claiming this benefit once in Portugal (see above).

Pensions. Retirement pensions are payable from the age of 65. In order to be eligible the beneficiary must provide evidence of at least 15 years' contributions. The amount of state pension that you will receive depends upon a number of calculations. Pensions are dealt with in greater detail in the next chapter, *Retirement.*

Unemployment. Those whose employer has paid into the caixa on their behalf are entitled to unemployment benefit upon losing their job. There are three types of unemployment benefit available and which one you receive depends on your circumstances. The general unemployment scheme (*subsídio de desemprego*) is available to those who have completed 540 days paid work in the 24 months prior to becoming unemployed. The amount of benefit received is calculated as 65% of your average daily earnings in the past 12 months. However, this amount may not be less than the national minimum wage.

For those who have worked a shorter period of time, social unemployment benefit (*subsídio social de desemprego*) is available. This applies to those who have worked 180 days in the past twelve months. This amounts to between 80% and 100% of the national minimum wage, depending on the size of your household.

Finally partial unemployment benefit (*subsídio parcial de desemprego*) is available to those who have previously received unemployment benefit and have taken on a part time job, with a salary not higher than the unemployment benefit they were previously receiving.

In order to qualify for unemployment benefits you must register as a job-seeker at the local employment center (*Centro de Emprego*) within 90 days of becoming unemployed. A claim for unemployment benefit must also be made at the nearest Regional Social Security Office (*Centro Regional de Segurança Social* – CRSS) within the same time period. Unemployment benefit is not available to the self-employed.

Claiming UK Jobseeker's Allowance in Portugal
One of the advantages of labour mobility within the EU is that it is possible for those who are currently unemployed and claiming benefit, or eligible to claim it, to have it paid in another EU country – if planning to go there to look for work. Those who have been claiming UK unemployment benefit for at least four weeks prior to departure are entitled to receive JSA for up to three months, paid at the UK rate, while looking for work in Portugal. In order to do this, you should inform the UK office through which you are claiming benefit, of your intention to seek work elsewhere in the EU. You will need to do this at least six weeks in advance of your departure. It is helpful if you have a precise date of departure and definite destination, preferably with an address. Note that if you go on holiday to Portugal and decide to stay on to work, the benefit cannot be transferred.

Your local job centre should have a leaflet (ref. JSAL 22) for people going abroad or coming from abroad, plus an application form for transferring benefit. When you have told your local job centre of your plans, they will supply a letter (DLJA 402/402) explaining that you are eligible to claim benefit.

The only tricky part is that as an unemployed person, it is impossible to gain a resident's permit in Portugal – as the Portuguese authorities require that you are employed, able to support yourself, or a pensioner. However, your exportable benefits will be honoured in Portugal.

Your local job centre will inform the Department of Work and Pensions in Newcastle, who will then decide if you are eligible for an E303 which authorises the Portuguese authorities to pay JSA for up to three months. The E303 is sent directly by the DWP to Portugal. The DWP also advises that you take form E104 with you. This shows your National Insurance payments to date and proves that you have been resident in the UK. Further details can be obtained from the Department of Work and Pensions, Jobseekers & Benefit Enhancement, Overseas Benefit Directorate, Tyneview Road, Benton, Newcastle-upon-Tyne NE98 1BA; ☎0191-218 7147 and they can send you a fact sheet if your local job centre has not supplied you with one.

CRIME AND THE POLICE

Crime

Until recently violent crime was outside the experience of most Portuguese. Even in Lisbon and Porto, except for certain areas, there was no feeling of menace on the streets. The list of typical offences: smuggling, fraud, rustling, robbery, drunken brawls (occasionally ending in death) etc. is still small beer compared with serial killings, sophisticated art thefts, assassinations and other headline-grabbing misdeeds common elsewhere.

Traditionally Portuguese criminals have gone in for fraud and deception and these along with bribery and corruption still account for most of the criminal statistics. Unfortunately in recent years nefarious activities have become increasingly connected with the drug trade; Portugal is conveniently situated on the drug route from Latin America and drug taking and laundering of the proceeds have become a major headache for the Portuguese police forces. The problem could be said to begin at street level where the contrast between low police pay and huge profits to be made from illegal drugs often diverts the police from the pursuit of law and order.

A recent headline-grabbing incident in which an English football supporter was stabbed to death by a mugger during Euro 2004, seems to be the exception. Generally Portugal has a very low level of violent crime. A recent UN survey on violent crime rated Portugal as one of the safest countries in the world to live in. If you are unlucky enough to encounter a problem, it is likely to be a petty crime such as pick-pocketing and bag-snatching. Foreigners may be a target for this kind of crime, especially at popular tourist sites, or on public transport. Rental cars and cars with foreign number plates are a target for break-ins. It is therefore unwise to leave anything valuable inside a car. However, although this type of crime is fairly common in the larger cities such as Lisbon and Porto, street crime is still virtually unheard of in smaller towns.

Crime victims should report the incident to the local police, and to their local embassy or consulate, who will be able to provide support and legal advice if necessary.

Police

There are several law enforcing bodies in Portugal and in common with most European police forces they are often armed. As in Spain, there has been a deep mistrust of these authorities left over from the days of dictatorship. However, the Portuguese authorities are working hard to improve their public image. The different types of police that you may come across in Portugal are:

Policía de Segurança Publica: The PSP are the city police of whom there are around 20,000, one third of them in Lisbon. They wear grey uniforms and are responsible for dealing with residency cards, reprimanding and fining those who commit traffic offences (e.g. illegal parking), dud cheques, making out statements dealing with lost or stolen belongings, directing traffic and generally patrolling the streets.

Brigada de Trânsito: The Brigada are the traffic police who apprehend speeding and erratic drivers, stop dubious looking vehicles and elicit on-the-spot fines for various contraventions of the traffic regulations (e.g. failure to wear a seat belt). During the main tourist season they are much in evidence in their white and orange cars. When road accidents occcur it is the Brigada who are usually first on the scene.

Guarda Fiscal: Those who belong to the yachting fraternity are most likely to encounter the Guarda Fiscal, who are the coastguards. Always on the look out for smugglers their jurisdiction can also extend to dry land in the small coastal villages.

Guarda Nacional Republicana: The GNR are the national troubleshooters who are called in whenever violence erupts. They are a paramilitary organisation and can be spotted all over the country in vans, on motorbikes and sometimes on horseback.

RELIGION

Portugal is predominantly Catholic; and the signs of fervour are greater here than in many other Catholic countries. Approximately 95% of the Portuguese population is nominally Roman Catholic. However, it is estimated that less than a third of the population regularly attends mass and whilst the church has always played an important part in people's everyday lives, this appears to be slowly diminishing. Traditional religious beliefs are far stronger in the north of the country than in the traditionally anti-clerical south. The devotion of many Portuguese runs in tandem with older religions. Superstition has never really died out in the remote villages where pagan and Christian beliefs exist side by side. Whilst the church has never approved of these beliefs, it has tended to tolerate them as a means of maintaining popular devotion to Catholicism.

There are thousands of annual *festas* across the country celebrating a galaxy of saints, some of whom have ceased to be or who have never been recognised by Rome. Portugal's most celebrated place of devotion is Fátima, where the Virgin is alleged to have appeared several times between May and October 1917 to three shepherd children. She apparently made three prophecies known as the secrets of Fátima. The first appeared to prophesy the Second World War, the second the end of Communism and the third was locked away by the Vatican and is consulted only by each successive Pope thus giving rise to wild speculation that it is too portentous for lesser mortals to hear. Pope John Paul II visited Fatima in May 1991, which lent some of these ideas credence; and the purpose of his visit was to give thanks for the end of Communist rule in Eastern Europe. Hundreds of thousands of the faithful gather there each year in pilgrimage.

The end of Salazar's regime saw a new constitution that separated Church and State and approved religious freedom. Since then, the Catholic Church in Portugal has not played such a fundamental role in the governing of the country, and has long given up on trying to influence politics. Divorce laws have been liberalised and the only real issue that is still influenced by Catholic mores is abortion. The abortion laws are currently amongst the strictest in Europe, allowing terminations only in cases where the mother's life is in danger and in cases of rape, incest or foetal impairment. As a result thousands of illegal and dangerous back street abortions are believed to be carried out every year. However, at the time of writing the Portuguese parliament, led by the new socialist government, has agreed to hold a referendum on relaxing the country's abortion laws. Voters will be asked: 'Do you agree that abortions, carried out in the first ten weeks of pregnancy, with the woman's consent, in a legal medical establishment, should no longer be illegal?'. In a referendum in 1998, the Portuguese population voted against a similar motion, but the country has taken a dramatic swing to the left in recent years.

Those who belong to other denominations will probably be able to find other practising members of their religion in Portugal. The constitution guarantees religious freedom and within the expatriate communities there are often numerous Protestant churches, and in the country's cosmopolitan capital there is a mosque and a synagogue.

SOCIAL LIFE

In common with other Latin countries, Portugal has a lively and colourful ambience and it is up to the foreign resident to make the most of it. Traditional beliefs play a greater part in the fabric of life in Portugal than in most other EU countries and community life frequently revolves around centuries' old religious and secular festivals celebrated by the inhabitants of every town and village.

Expatriates tend to live in well-defined areas and have their own social networks organised around clubs and associations, many of which announce their forthcoming events in the English-language publications. Turning up at the bridge circle, drama society, bowling or archaeological club is an excellent way of meeting new faces. There are some useful addresses for expatriate clubs and organisations in the *Retirement* chapter which follows.

Making friends with fellow expatriates is a lot easier than meeting the Portuguese, who do not have an organised social life along the same lines as the foreign community and are not as 'clubbable' as, say, the Danes or Germans. Social life often revolves around meals with close friends and family at home or in a restaurant. For foreign residents living in country areas it will be essential to make contact with some Portuguese neighbours in order not to feel socially isolated. This requires a concentrated effort as the Portuguese, although extremely friendly and helpful, are naturally reserved and it is not usual to be invited into their homes. If such an invitation were to be offered, it should be regarded as a privilege and a major step towards being accepted into the community.

The Portuguese Attitude to Expatriates

The Portuguese seem to have no difficulty in accepting the ever increasing number of expatriates who choose to live in their country. Perhaps this is not surprising in view of their history as maritime explorers, and their links with most of the world's peoples from Africa to South America. It is part of Portugal's inheritance as a trading nation that the country's prosperity and well-being has been traditionally associated with contacts with people from other countries and the continuation of traditional ideas of hospitality in the countryside means that welcoming strangers is important here as well.

This applies especially to British visitors. The Anglo-Portuguese connection predates even Portugal's great era of maritime exploration and there has been an English presence in Portugal for centuries. There are British hospitals, schools, churches and even a British cemetery. In Porto the ancestors of some of the famous families associated with port wine came from England six generations ago. Then the French arrived in the nineteenth century, principally to carry out engineering projects. More recently American culture has made an impact: American companies participated in the 1970's in the building of the magnificent suspension bridge over the Rio Tejo among other projects, and have since invested heavily in Portuguese industry, in this way cementing a bond that exists through the many Portuguese who settled in America at the turn of the century.

Perhaps as a result of their wide dealings with foreigners, the Portuguese – like the Dutch – are also often able linguists; and it is common to find educated people speaking three or more languages fluently. However, due to the marked difference in the levels of sophistication in town and country, it would be virtually impossible to make social headway in English or other foreign languages in the remoter areas.

Whether one lives in the cities or in the countryside, one will find the Portuguese attitude to foreigners easygoing and remarkably tolerant.

The Portuguese are very proud and friendly hosts – John Carey

John Carey worked for KPMG in Lisbon during the summer of 2004, and through his work colleagues was able to make friends and immerse himself in Portuguese culture.

I found the Portuguese to be generally friendly, whether I was working with them, meeting them in a social setting or spending money with them – they were genuinely interested in speaking to a British guy. I was lucky enough have a couple of colleagues that really helped in this respect. Having Portuguese friends was particularly important when there were various festivals or key dates in the calendar as the Portuguese are very proud to show off their history and tradition. The only challenge I would note was the Portuguese language, which understandably is preferred in social settings. My lack of practice meant that I found it difficult at times to engage in group conversations.

Social Attitudes

For years Portugal lagged behind the rest of Europe in almost every respect. Forced into obedience by the Salazar regime, the people were kept in ignorance of the true state of the country and their deprivation compared badly with the rest of western Europe. Social attitudes in Portugal were shaped to a great extent by repression and hardship and by the feudal divisions between rich and poor. During the years of repression, corruption and nepotism were developed into an art and loyalty to the family and one's immediate circle were stronger than interest in the fate of the country, let alone the outside world.

In the past, this concern with parochial affairs above national ones was due to the pessimism with which the majority of Portuguese viewed their lot: without powerful friends and connections they saw themselves as the hapless pawns of the ruling regime. Today a passionate concern with local reform is seen in a more positive light, as a way to influence and improve one's prospects and environment.

Thanks to political upheaval and progressively better education, attitudes and aspirations are changing fast. Improved technical training for young people aged 18 to 25 has given them lucrative job prospects in an economy that is bounding forward to catch up with that of its EU partners. For the many Portuguese whose families have lived at subsistence level for generations, things are at last improving. But unfortunately, despite the changes brought about by the Revolution and the transition to democracy, old habits of nepotism die hard; even today it remains largely true that it is not what you know but who you know that counts.

These sometimes inward-looking attitudes affect even the foreigners living in Portugal, who claim that knowing the right people and having the right connections can have a startling, galvanising effect on some of the bureaucratic procedures. Attitudes to women can also sometimes be old-fashioned but these have improved substantially from the dictatorship days when the female half of the population was firmly relegated to the home by legislation. Contemporary women have won the right to independence largely through academic ability: over half of all university graduates in Portugal are female and their increasing entry into the professions can no longer be ignored. Once again, however, there is a gap between the cities and the countryside, where the stereotypical drinking, moustachioed machoman is unfortunately much in evidence.

Whatever their background and social status, all Portuguese share a love of family. Their consciousness of ancestry is acute, no matter how far away individual members of families may have strayed: the homing instinct is still strong enough to bring many back from the Americas, Australia etc. for long visits. On these occasions the red carpet is rolled out and reunions are celebrated in the most lavish style that can be afforded.

With such familial devotion, it comes as little surprise that families are traditionally large and extended in Portugal and parents indulge their children (boys, more than girls) to excess. However, the role of the family is currently undergoing a period of change. These days, so many women are working, and contraception has become so widely available that birth-rates have reduced drastically, and large families are no longer the norm.

Culture and Entertainment

For anyone living and working in Portugal, the rich and ancient culture and the lively entertainments are one of the main attractions. Apart from traditional art forms, particularly folk music and village *festas*, Portugal is increasingly on the international circuit for world-renowned musicians and singers as well as contemporary rock stars.

Architecture. To a lesser extent than Spain, Portugal inherited a legacy of architecture and design from the Arabs. This can be seen in the magnificent Moorish palace at Sintra and throughout the Algarve, where there are many ancient fortifications and houses built in the Moorish style. Also a legacy of the Moors are the tiles (*azulejos*) which ornament the doorways of churches and mansions, as well as the walls of countless houses. A uniquely Portuguese form of architecture, the Manueline, flourished during the early fifteenth century. In form, the Manueline also drew inspiration from Moorish architecture, but the decoration consists of maritime motifs: ships in full sail, armillary spheres (a representation of the globe constructed of metal rings), crossed anchors, and knotted ropes. This indigenous Manueline style was blended with the more classical Renaissance architecture which developed later here than in Italy or France, from around 1530.

Like Catalonia or the Basque country in neighbouring Spain, Portugal celebrates its maritime traditions in architecture as in many other areas of its life and culture.

Painting. During the Renaissance, a Portuguese school of painting also flourished. Among the Portuguese masters are Cristóvā de Figueirido, Francisco Henriques and António de Holanda. The main art musueums in Lisbon include the Museu Nacional de Arte Antiga in the Rua das Janelas Verdes and the Museu Nacional de Arte Contemporânea in Caldas da Rainha.

Literature. Portuguese literary culture is rich in novelists, poets and historians; the more flowery and romantic the style the greater their popularity. The Portuguese equivalent of Shakespeare is probably Luís de Camões (1524-1579). Not only was he contemporaneous with Shakespeare and Cervantes but his works dealt with national history told in epic verse. In addition to his plays his most enduring work is the lyric poem *Os Lusíadas*. Much of Portuguese literature is devoted to the voyages of discovery: some of the best known works on this theme include *Peregrinação* (Pilgrimage). Some Portuguese books have been published in English, notably the nineteenth century writer Almeida Garrett's *Viagens na Minha Terra (Travels in my Homeland)*. There are are a number of avidly read modern writers whose names are little known outside Portugal, including Maria Velho, António Lobo, João de Melo and Clara Pinto Correia. Those wishing to find out more about literature in Portuguese can consult the *Babel Guide to the Fiction of Portugal, Brazil and Africa* (Boulevard Books; £9.95), which has reviews, excerpts and a database of all fiction translated into English from Portuguese since 1945. A list of recommended titles can be found in the *Guides and Literature* section at the end of the *General Introduction*.

In Portugal, in common with many European countries, there is a wide range of translations of foreign writers available. Expatriates with limited Portuguese will be pleased to know that literature in English is not difficult to find in the bookshops of the capital and main towns, albeit at inflated prices.

Theatre. Although there is a long tradition of theatre in Portugal, drama outside Lisbon is far from being the most popular form of entertainment. Actors are not well paid, but subsidies and grants from the government keep a reasonable range of plays from Sophocles to Alan Bennett on offer. Gil Vicente is Portugal's most pre-eminent contemporary playwright. One of the best known theatres is the Teatro Nacional Dona Maria II in Praça Pedro IV in Lisbon.

Cinema. Portugal has its own famous film directors including the grand old master Manoel de Oliveira, who began his film career in 1931. However the biggest box office hit ever in Portugal enticed only a total audience of 150,000. In order to be commercially viable, therefore, Portuguese films have had to be international co-productions like the 1990 *Aqui d'El Rei* a Portuguese-Spanish-French production. Many foreign films are shown in the towns and cities, usually subtitled. Both national and foreign films are shown in Lisbon at the Cinemateca Portuguesa, Rua Barata Salgueiro 39, Lisbon; ☎213-546085. Expatriates unable to locate a British or American film showing in the original language will have to make do with the television which puts out many old black and white movies as well as more recent films in the original language, with Portuguese subtitles.

Music. Portugal has its own unique folk music traditions about whose origins the scholars are still arguing. It can however be said with certainty that the medieval troubadors were a great early influence. The most famous Portuguese music is *Fado* which means fate or destiny. Its conception (but not sound) is probably similar to the American blues, i.e. both grew out of the laments of African slaves. Characterised by its haunting sound which is full of melancholy and yearning, fado has male and female exponents. The repertoire varies with the region. In Lisbon the best places to hear fado are in the restaurant-cafés of the Alfama and Mouraria districts of Lisbon where, as a travel journalist has put it, 'the chip lady and the waiters sing'. For a more academic approach – the (male) students of Coimbra university are also renowned for their performances.

International classical music is also widely listened to in Portugal: Opera seasons are brief and the most notable one is based at the São Carlos Theatre on Largo Picadeiro in Lisbon. Concerts are a real joy, not least because they are often held in magnificent historical settings including palaces and monastery cloisters. Music festivals are held in summer in the Lisbon area, Sintra and the Algarve. Details can be obtained from the local tourist offices. The mammoth Gulbenkian

Foundation in Lisbon, although chiefly renowned worldwide for its art museum, also organises, concerts and recitals in its three concert halls.

Contemporary music in Portugal has taken its influence from around the world – especially Brazil and the former African colonies. Portuguese rap and hip hop, made more acceptable by the father of Portuguese rap: Pedro Abrunhosa, now dominate the underground music and club scene, featuring popular artists such as Da Weasel and General D. Portuguese rock and pop groups are also gaining wider recognition around the world, especially as many choose to sing in English. Bands to look out for include Coldfinger, Silence 4 and Os Delfins, not to mention veteran singer/songwriter Rui Veloso who has achieved cross-generation popularity in Portugal.

Bullfighting. As in Spain, bullfighting is not considered a sport but a cultural event. The season starts officially on Easter Sunday and finishes in October. In Spain the matador is the star; in Portugal it is the *Cavaleiro* a splendidly caparisoned rider complete with eighteenth century ruffles and a tricorne hat. This romantically dressed figure wears down the bull in a series of encounters which permit a dazzling display of dressage and other riding skills. Successful cavaleiros traditionally come from the same families (e.g. Caetano and Telles) whose names are familiar to generations of afficionados.

Unlike in Spain, the bull is not usually killed in the arena as part of the spectacle, but slaughtered out of sight following the *tourada*. Officially it is illegal for the bulls to be publicly killed but the closer you get to the Spanish border, the more likely this is, and action has rarely been taken by the authorities. However, the town of Barranco, close to the Spanish border now has special status, allowing it to conduct lethal bull-fights, following a recent court case brought by animal rights campaigners.

Ticket prices for bullfights start at about £15 and can rise to £60 for the best seats.

Nightlife. Apart from restaurants and impromptu and staged fado concerts there are numerous nightclubs in Lisbon and the Estoril and Lisbon coasts. The Algarve too has its share of hotspots where things only get going at 11pm and finish at dawn. For less brain-numbing entertainment there are a growing number of places to hear African and South American music, not only from local bands whose players' nationalities correspond to Portugal's former colonies, but also touring bands particularly from West Africa. The tourist office can provide details. Portugal's most celebrated jazz nightclub which has been going for at least forty years, is the Hot Clube de Portugal, Praça da Alegria, off the Avenue da Liberdade in Lisbon.

Even though the Algarve is catching up as far as entertainment is concerned, Lisbon and Porto are still the best places as regards the range and excellence and quantity on offer.

> **Lesley Keast was surprised at how easy it is to become embroiled in the Portuguese nightlife**
> *Although my social life was relatively quiet, on the occasions when I went out to bars and clubs, I often found myself getting home at 6 or 7 in the morning because the energy of the night just kept me going. It's like a time vortex exists on a Friday night. Bars are very low key and comfortable – people dressed how they liked and it was a very pleasant atmosphere.*

Holidays

For a nation whose early voyagers pushed back the frontiers of the known world and whose menfolk travelled across the world and Europe in search of prosperity in the nineteenth and twentieth centuries, remarkably few Portuguese take holidays abroad. Those who do are from the main urban areas. The fact is that the Portuguese would rather accumulate household appliances than holiday memories. This is perhaps an understandable obsession for those who have gone without these things for so long. They can now afford them (mostly on hire purchase) and the rate of acquisition particularly of automobiles and satellite dishes is phenomenal.

Portugal, in common with France and Italy, tends to take August off. Factories close and the Portuguese sport themselves at local beaches, campsites, or at friends' homes.

PUBLIC HOLIDAYS AND FESTIVALS

In addition to the national holidays (below) every region has its own calendar of feasts (*festas*), fairs (*feiras*) and pilgrimages (*romarias*). These festivals are made up of an array of traditional dances, religious processions, firework displays, music, bull-running/fighting, markets, pilgrimages, literature and generally more food and drink than is altogether necessary. Some of these festivals have been in existence for many centuries in some form or another and have their origins in ancient rituals and traditions, whereas others are far more contemporary. There are far too many celebrations to list here, but a comprehensive list is available at www.portugal.org/tourism/calendar.shtml.

One of the more important events on the festival calendar is **Carnaval,** which takes the form of numerous Rio-influenced parades around the country, particularly in Lisbon and various towns in the Algarve. A more traditional example of Carnaval can be seen at the *Entrudo dos Comprades*, near Lamgego. **Easter** is a good excuse for celebrations on a national scale, but the most impressive religious processions and displays are to be found at Braga and at the *Festa das*

Tochas at São Brás de Alportel in the Algarve. The **Santos Populares** (popular saints) festivities are also not to be missed if possible. These are festivals, largely made up of religious processions held throughout the country in honour of Santo António (12-13 June), São João (23-24 June), and Pedro (28-29 June). In Lisbon the celebration of St. Anthony is an excuse for a giant street party, and in Porto the festivities run for a week and include a bizarre ritual whereby people hit each other over the head with plastic hammers!

PUBLIC HOLIDAYS

Portugal has thirteen statutory public holidays (*Feriados Obrigatórios*) which are celebrated nationally. During public holidays all shops, banks, and offices are closed. The public holidays in Portugal are:

1 January	*Ano Novo* (New Year)
Shrove Tuesday	varies
Good Friday	varies
25 April	*Dia da Liberdade* (commemorates the 1974 revolution)
1 May	*Dia do Trabalho* (Labour Day)
10 June	*Dia de Portugal* (National Day)
Corpus Christi	during June
15 August	*Assunção de Nossa Senhora* (Feast of the Assumption)
5 October	*Dia da República* (Commemoration of the founding of the First Republic in 1910)
1 November	*Festa de Todosos Santos* (Feast of All Saints)
1 December	*Dia de Restauração* (Commemoration of the restoration of the Portuguese crown from Spanish rule in 1640)
8 December	Feast of the Immaculate Conception
25 December	*Natal* (Nativity)

FOOD AND DRINK

Although Portuguese cuisine is largely unknown throughout the rest of the world, it is famous for two things above all: Port wine and fish. The Atlantic Coast and its abundant fishing grounds has led, at least along the coasts and the hinterlands, to a largely sea-based cuisine. In addition, aspects of the cuisine of its former colonies in Africa, India and the Far East have been added, and these influences have helped make Portuguese food markedly different from that of other Mediterranean countries. The Portuguese introduced coriander, pepper, ginger, curry, saffron and paprika into Europe and brought back from their seafaring many other exotic products which were unknown to Europe such as rice and tea, coffee and peanuts, and pineapples, peppers, tomatoes and potatoes. In Lisbon there are Brazilian-style juice bars and restaurants that still specialise in the cuisines of the former colonies.

Portuguese cuisine is mainly based on regional produce, fish, meat, olive oil, tomato, infused with spices. Soups, cheeses, and combinations of meat and shellfish also feature. Regional differences aren't as marked as in neighbouring Spain but the Algarve, with its Moorish influences has a tradition of producing excellent almond and fig sweets. The spiciest dishes are to be found in the Azores and Madeira.

The best attitude to take with Portuguese cuisine, is simply to open your mind and try everything, as there are some little-known delights to be discovered. This was certainly the approach that John Carey took during his time in the country's capital:

> *I was lucky enough to sample a lot of Lisbon's restaurants and am happy to report that there are many great places to eat. Some of the dishes are not for the faint hearted (such as chicken cooked in its own blood), but on the whole the food is very tasty. Portuguese wine is also great. I knew about port before I went, but I never really had a grasp on how serious the table wine industry is. I had great fun working my way through it all, making sure that I tried as much as possible, as most of it never makes the UK shores.*

Fish

Salted cod or *bacalhau*, is the most famous of the Portuguese fish dishes and has proved to be a versatile and staple ingredient for many, many dishes in Portugal. As early as the 16th century, the Portuguese fishermen learned to salt cod at sea to last them during the long voyage home from the Americas. They would sun-dry the fish into stiff slabs that kept for months, which could later be soaked in water before cooking. Cod is still sun-dried on racks on some of the northern beaches and Portugal now imports much of its *bacalhau* from Norway to meet annual demands. *Bacalhau* dishes include *bacalhau á gomes de sá* (a casserole with thinly sliced potatoes and onions, garnished with hard-boiled eggs and black olives – a speciality of Porto), *bacalhau à brás* (a speciality of Estremadura) and *bacalhau dourado* (scrambled eggs, onions and potatoes), *bacalhau á conde de guarda* (salted cod creamed with mashed potatoes) and *bolinhos de bacalhau* (codfish croquettes – a particularly popular hors d'oeuvre). Sardines (*sardinhas*) are almost as popular as *bacalhau* in Portugal and the smell of grilled sardines (*sardinhas assadas*) is up there with the smell of Eucalyptus as olfactory memories of Portugal.

Shellfish, including clams (*amêijoas*) and mussels (*mexilhões*) are enjoyed in Portugal, as is crab and squid – often stuffed. *Lulas recheadas à lisbonense* (stuffed squid Lisbon-style) is a great example of Portuguese seafood. In Lisbon there are still traditional shops by the docks selling snails (*caracóis*). Anchovy, swordfish, sole, sea bream, bass and salmon are also popular items on the menus.

As far as freshwater fish is concerned, you can savour the lamprey (*lampreia*) and the salmon (*salmão*) from Minho, trout (*truta*) from the Serra da Estreia and Madeira, and the shad (*savel*) from the Tagus and the Douro rivers.

Meat

Pork meat is also very popular in Portugal, and pork from pigs reared among the cork groves of Alentejo is renowned for its taste. *Carne de porco a alentejana,* made with diced marinated pork meat with red peppers and clams, and roasted piglet (*Ieitão assado*) are popular dishes. Smoked ham (*presunto*) and smoked sausages (*chouriço*) such as the *paio* and the *salpicão* varieties are worth trying. Pork is also cooked with mussels in a wok-like *cataplana* to seal in the flavours. *Cozido à portuguesa*, the national dish, is a one-dish meal of beef, pork, sausage and vegetables; *Espetada*, grilled skewers of beef with garlic, is also popular. In Porto *tripa à moda do Porto* (Porto-style tripe) is favoured. Broiled chicken (*frango grelhado*), seasoned with peri-peri, garlic and olive oil, is highly aromatic and often served in restaurants.

Soups

These feature large in traditional cooking in Portugal, with all kinds of seasonal vegetables, fish and meat used to create a variety of soups, stews and chowders. *Caldo verde* (literally, green broth), originated from the Minho and is considered a national dish and is a soup made from kale thickened with potato and a slice of *salpicão* or *chouriço* sausage. Another staple is *canja de galinha* (chicken broth) and *sopa de marisco* (shellfish soup cooked and served with wine). *Caldeirada de lulas à madeirense* (squid stew) features a characteristically Portuguese combination of seafood, curry and ginger. Another typical dish is the *açorda* where vegetables or shellfish are added to thick rustic bread to create a bread soup. *Açorda á Alentejana* is a bread soup made with coriander and garlic with a dollop of poached egg. *Caldeirada* is made with water (sometimes sea-water) with added tomatoes, onions and garlic, fish in roughly equal proportion. The ingredients of a *caldeirada* traditionally varied from day to day depending on a fisherman's catch.

Cheeses

Portugal produces a number of cheeses, the most celebrated being *Queijo da Serra,* made from the milk of sheep grazing in the Serra da Estrela. Properly ripened this cheese is runnier than the finest Brie. The *Serpa* cheese, from the Alentejo town of the same name, is ranked as the nation's second best and is aged for a couple of years, brushed regularly with paprika-laced oil.

Also available are miniature rounds of sheep's milk cheese resembling compressed cottage cheese but firmer and drier and the delicious creamy little cheeses of Azeitão, especially popular in the spring. The *queijos frescos* are uncured cheeses, often sprinkled with cinnamon and eaten in place of sweets. The *cabreiro* is a strong goat's cheese; the *queijo da ilha*, a cheese from the Azores that is used grated (like parmesan) in numerous regional dishes.

Desserts

A staple of restaurant menus is chocolate mousse – richer than we are accustomed to back home; and crème caramel is served just about everywhere. Other favourites include *arroz doce* (lemon and cinnamon-flavoured rice pudding), Madeira pudding, *nuvens* (egg custard), and the rich, egg-yolk and sugar-based cakes, influenced by Moorish cooking and perfected by Guimerães nuns in the sixteenth century. You will come across one or more variations on *pão de Ló*, a rich yellow sponge cake made with egg yolks that may be flavoured with orange juice, lemon, cinnamon, vanilla, port wine, or Madeira.

For a uniquely Portuguese experience, head for a *pasteleria* or *confeitaria* to try the myriad varieties of cakes and confectionary, as well as savoury delicacies such as *bolinhas de bacalhau* (cod balls); in Lisbon, the Antiga Confeitaria de Belém, where the legendary *pastéis de nata*, delicious custard-filled tarts, are baked, is a must. Nearby Sintra has its own traditional pastry, *queijadas de Sintra* (a type of cheese tart), which street vendors sell in packs of six. Try the Belém tarts or any pastry filled with *fios d'ovos* or *ovos moles*. In Évora the *pão de rala* is made of white pumpkin candy wrapped in almond paste.

Coffee

Coffee houses and cafés are national institutions and popular meeting places. There are several types of coffee on offer, unsurprisingly, considering that the cash crop of many of Portugal's former colonies is the coffee bean.

ORDERING COFFEE	
Black coffee	*café*
Espresso	*bica*
Short shot of espresso	*ristretto / bica curta / curto*
Double shot of espresso	*bica dupla / café duplo*
Long shot of espresso	*bica cheia*
Shot of espresso with hot water	*abatanado*
Espresso with a dash of milk	*pingado / garoto*
Espresso and milk	*meia de leite / café com leite / café branco*

Espresso and hot milk in a glass	*galão*
Tea	*chá*
Boiling water with lemon peel	*carioca de limão*

Wines & Beers

Two thirds of the cork used in the world for stopping wine bottles comes from Portugal. The Portuguese produce some fine wines yet these remain relatively untried outside of Portugal. Portuguese wines may be divided into two basic categories: *vinho verde* and *vinho maduro*. *Vinhos maduros* are made for aging and maturing in the bottle, while *vinho verde* (green wine) is unique to Portugal and produced in Minho, in the northwest corner of Portugal. *Vinho verde* is not really green (though it is wine!) and can be either red (*tinto*) or white (*branco*) and often has a light fizz to it, which can vary – depending upon age, technique and storage – from light to fierce.

Among table wines the most popular regional names are Dão (for red wines) and Bucelas and Colares for white wines. Sparkling rosé wines are mostly produced for export; Mateus Rosé is one of the most famous. In the Bairrada region, to the west of Dão, the bulk of the white is being used to make rather good sparkling wine. Colares, located between Lisbon and the shores of the Atlantic, makes some of the most unusual red wine in the world. Here vines are planted in the sand of the Atlantic shoreline through exceedingly labour intensive methods. Moscatel de Setúbal is a fine dessert wine grown south of Lisbon. Portuguese brandy is available in two varieties, *Macieiera* and *Constantino*, and is cheap.

The fortified wines (*vinho do Porto*) and madeira (*vinho da Madeira*) are by far the best known of Portuguese wines. Port has an alcohol content of 19%-22% and is subject to very strict production regulations. Port wine is classified according to the grape crops, the sugar content, the amount of added alcohol, the age, and the type of wood of the barrels used in the aging process.

The two most common local beers (*cervejas*) are Sagres and Super Bock served both on tap and by the bottle. You can order many other bottled foreign brands in most bars. Order *um fino* or *um imperial* if you want a small glass; *uma caneca* will get you a half-litre.

Eating Houses

Restaurants usually offer a three-course *ementa turistica* which is usually the most economical way to eat. Note that restaurant servings tend to be so enormous that you can often have a substantial meal by ordering a *meia dose* (half portion), or sharing one portion between two.

You will come across a whole range of dishes on offer in cafés with favourites including *tosta mistas* (cheese and ham toasties), *prego* (steak sandwich, often served with a fried egg), *bifoque* (steak, chips, fried egg), *rissóis* (deep-fried meat patties);

pasteis de bacalhau (codfish cakes), and *sandes* (sandwiches). Food displayed on café counters, often shellfish, can be tasted by asking for *uma dose* (a portion). It is always worth taking stock of the *prato do dia* (dish of the day) and, if you are on the coast, going for fish and seafood.

At the end of a meal, do not miss the hot burning *bagaço* (distilled liquor) or the local liqueurs, such as the *amarguinha* (made from sour almonds).

Meal times in Portugal

Breakfast (*pequeno almoço*) is often nothing more than a cup of strong coffee and a roll with butter and jam. Lunch (*almoço*) is usually taken from noon-3pm; and dinner (*jantar*) from 7.30pm. The evenings in Portugal don't go on into the small hours as they do in Spain and outside of the larger cities and tourist spots eating establishments aren't open much after 10-11pm.

SPORT

One might be forgiven for thinking that the sole spectator sport in Portugal was *futebol* (football) which is also the national pastime with every small village having a team of its own. Football fever reached a new peak in 2004 when Portugal hosted Euro 2004. The government invested heavily, building ten new stadiums and improving the country's infrastructure allowing it to cope with the hundreds of thousands of fans feverishly supporting their national teams. Although the Greeks were eventually victorious in the tournament, Portugal got to the final and proved that the beautiful game, said to have been in steady decline in Portugal since the heady days of the sixties, was still a platform on which the Portuguese could shine. The two most famous teams are Benfica and FC Porto. The latter managed to snatch defeat from Monaco in the 2004 European Championships. However, many consider Portuguese football to have gone considerably downhill – there are regular allegations of corruption within the sport, many clubs are in severe financial crises, attendance figures for matches have never been lower, and the most talented players tend to leave to play for more lucrative European clubs. Further information on Portuguese football can be obtained from the *Federacão Portuguesa de Futebol* (Praca da Alegria 25, 1250-004 Lison; ☎213-252700; fax 213-252780; www.fpf.pt).

However there are plenty of other popular sports ranging from Formula One racing in the famous Autodrome in Estoril to golf tournaments in Porto and the Algarve, and tennis at Roger Taylor's Tennis Centre at Vale do Lobo. The Portugal Golf and Portugal Tennis Opens are fixtures now on the international sporting calendar. Further information is available from the *Federacão Portuguesa de Golfe* (Avenida das Tulipas 6, Edificio Miraflores, 17°, Miraflores, 1495-161 Algés; ☎214-123780; fax 214-107972; www.fpg.pt) and the *Federacão Portuguesa de*

Ténis (Rua Actor Chaby Pinheiro 7a, 2795-060, Linda-a-Velha; ☎214-151356; fax 214-141520; www.fptenis.pt).

Water sports along the coast are also popular, including offshore fishing, water-skiing, sailing and windsurfing. Surfing is also extremely popular in Portugal as the country boasts 600km of Atlantic coast, complete with many well known surf beaches. The best surf on the coast is allegedly at Nazaré, and the best time for surfing in Portugal is winter/spring. Further information on the best surfing clubs can be found on the website of the Portuguese Surf Federation (*Federacão Portuguesa de Surf*, Complexo Desportivo de Ouressa, 2725-320 Mem-Martins, Sintra; ☎219-228914; fax 219-228915; www.surfingportugal.com).

Those for whom life is not complete without the crack of willow on leather will find plenty of fellow fanatics in Lisbon and Porto where cricket is pursued with expatriate fervour. There is even a Portuguese Cricket Federation, based in Estoril (*Federacão Portuguesa de cricket*, PO Box 76, 2766-901, Estoril; ☎214-446446; fax 219-243004; email mail@portugalcricket.org).

Sports clubs are common in the cities; and many of the smarter developments have their own shared facilities including swimming pools and tennis courts. Squash has not yet caught on, perhaps because indoor games are not a priority in a country with such a mild climate. Keen yachties will find a very smart marina at Vilamoura just west of Faro and other smaller boating facilities along the Algarve coast. Nearly all the main coastal towns have a yacht club. Contact the Portuguese Sailing Federation for further details: *Federacão Portuguesa de Vela*, Doca de Belém, 1300-038 Lisbon; ☎213-658500; fax 213-620215; www.fpvela.pt). Portugal's best kept sporting secret is probably the ski resort at Malhão da Estrêla in the province of Beira Alta which is better known as a hiking area in summer.

In areas of high expatriate concentration there are often sports and social clubs which offer the opportunity both to socialise and enjoy good facilities in an English speaking environment. Mary Sworder recommends a popular club for expatriates:

As a way of getting to know people I suggest joining a club like the Lisbon Casuals (contact details given in the Retirement chapter), a sports club which operates from the grounds of St. Julian's school in Carcavelos on Wedesday evenings and all weekends. It has cricket, football, rugby, hockey, badminton and basketball sections and has probably the cheapest sports facilities available in the Lisbon area. There is also a convivial bar.

SHOPPING

The quality, range and style of the local shopping depends on where you are in Portugal. Well known international chains and large supermarkets (*supermercados*), unknown there twenty-five years ago, are very plentiful in the main cities, and the towns of the Algarve. Enormous hypermarkets representing the big European food retail chains (Carrefore, Continente, Lidl etc.) are now common on the outskirts of towns and cities, as more and more people own cars. Shop opening hours vary, but in smaller towns they are likely to close for two hours from 1pm to 3pm and remain open until about 7pm in the evening. Except for supermarkets and department stores, shops close at 1pm on Saturdays. Wherever you shop, the cost is not necessarily any less than it would be in the UK.

Food Shopping

Serious foodies are probably best catered for in Lisbon and Porto where there are dozens of enticing delicatessens (*Charcutaria*) where foreign and national produce including cheese, meats and wines are sold. However, delicatessens are also on the increase in the Algarve, where the range of available products until a few years ago was fairly basic. A *padaría* is a bakery and *talho* is a butcher. Portuguese meat can be disappointing, not to say tough, so it is advisable to ask for local recommendations. The big supermarkets are excellent; and prices are comparable to the UK. The frozen pre-cooked meals, especially Portuguese-recipe seafood and meat dishes are especially good; and it is worth investing in a freezer to stock up on such items. Dairy products, yoghurt, milk, cheeses etc. are sold in supermarkets or sometimes in open-air markets (see below).

Those who have not become reliant on convenience foods will presumably not mind living in the remoter areas where the choice of items is dependent on the season and subject to other variables: transport strikes and crop damage being two of the more usual. Your shopping list will have to be flexible here. Many Portuguese as well as foreign residents lament the fact that although Portugal produces superb fruit, the best quality often goes for export. Others maintain that finding what you want is just a matter of shopping around, especially in the town centre and open-air markets.

Many familiar international brand names are made under licence in Portugal which also imports many foreign food products. Those who cannot find their favourite British or American foods (which is fairly unlikely unless you are living in a rural area) have a number of internet options open to them. Websites such as www.expatshopping.com and www.expatdirect.co.uk will ship your favourite foods direct to your door, wherever you are in the world, at fairly reasonable prices. Those who simply cannot live without their Heinz baked beans should try www.heinz-direct.co.uk. Increasingly, however, the Portuguese are manufacturing their own brands of yoghurts, breakfast cereals, canned pet food and so on. Whichever version one buys they are often more expensive than one expects. Alcohol is usually good value, especially local wines (which can still be bought for less than

£3 for a bottle of country wine) and cigarettes are less than half their UK price.

Shopping Centres. The main towns of the Algarve including Faro, Loulé, Portimão, Albufeira, Tavira, and the main towns of the Estoril Coast like Cascais; all have traditional shopping centres located in their small pedestrianised streets. In addition to the famous old shopping area of the Baixa (lower town), the capital Lisbon has what is undoubtedly the most architecturally interesting shopping mall in Portugal: the Amoreiras, looking like a castle from the covers of a science-fiction novel; its immense sugar pink towers are a landmark for miles around.

Inside are several floors of shops including a giant supermarket. Other facilities within the Amoreiras include a ten screen cinema, a post office, travel agent, dozens of restaurants and a hotel.

Open-air Markets. Open-air markets are held weekly in almost every sizeable town. Some can be a little drab and uninspiring, with their motley second-hand clothes stalls. Some expat residents may be able to sell craft and other products here. A licence is usually negotiated through the local town hall. Others specialise in live animals (chickens, songbirds, rabbits, lambs etc.) while others are full of life and colour, selling everything from porcelain to tomatoes in a mix familiar in many Mediterranean countries. Among the Portuguese, the best markets are reckoned to be in the fertile northern half of the country: two well-known ones include Barcelos in the Minho province and Caldas da Rainha in the Estramadura province near Lisbon. It is worth doing some research to find out where the best ones are for the provisions or handicrafts that you want (or would like to sell) and driving the extra miles for the best home-grown and cured hams and sausages, fresher fruit and vegetables and local cheeses, honey and cakes.

Fish markets are held on the quaysides at dawn in Cascais and other coastal towns; this is one itinerary for those wishing to explore the country by car. The Portuguese claim that there are over 200 kinds of fish and crustaceans available there, which go into specialities like the *caldeirada,* a mixed fish stew, as well as soups. *Sopa de marisco* is a shellfish soup cooked and served with wine. Some of the commoner varieties includes the *peixa espada* (swordfish), *salmonete* (red mullet), and the *eiroz* (conger eel). To shop in fish markets you need an alarm clock, some courage, and the ability to haggle, preferably in Portuguese.

Non-Food Shopping

Clothes. Imported goods are increasingly available in the shops, where they are often quite expensive. However, the country has for many years produced good quality shoes (which are exported around the world) and is working hard at upgrading its textiles and fashion industry for international markets. There are dozens of fashion boutiques in Lisbon's Baixa, and all the famous names, but Portugal's capital has some way to go before it compares with Rome or Paris as a place to shop for smart clothes. There is no home-grown equivalent of the international fashion chains like Benetton yet. The best known Portuguese shop for children aged 0-12 years is Cenoura, which has about sixty shops nationwide. High class Portuguese fashion designers are mostly found in Porto; and include Ana Salazar, Olga Rego and the Nuno Morgado collection.

Chemist *(Farmácia):* As in France and Switzerland the pharmacist can be consulted on treatments for minor ailments. As pharmaceutical products are extremely expensive in Portugal, and the brand names are unfamiliar, it is advisable to bring a supply of your regular medicaments from the UK until you have identified the Portuguese equivalents.

Household: Kitchen gadgets and electric household appliances are only a little more expensive in Portugal; some may choose to bring these from the UK, though. Decorative tableware, including colourful glazed pottery and embroidered fine linen, are some of the traditional national wares to look out for. The best quality pottery (based on the complexity of its hand painted decoration) is not cheap. However it is possible to find lower priced versions in some of the open-air markets. Table linen is of extremely fine quality. One famous shop for this and other house ware is a private house in Porto (Porto) run by Beatris Perry Sampaio (Rua do Campo Alegre 713). One has to ring the doorbell to be admitted. Linen can also be found in the shop Alecrim, in the Amoreiras shopping centre in Lisbon.

Generally speaking, handcrafted items made in Portugal are much cheaper than they would be in the UK or the USA, including leather goods like belts and shoes, copper and ceramic items (decorative plates, vases, etc.), handmade silver and gold jewellery, embroidery and tapestry work, every kind of cork product, crystal and glassware, and porcelain, which souvenir sellers and outdoor markets all stock.

METRICATION

Portugal uses the metric system of measurement in all respects. Those who are used to thinking in the imperial system will find that in the long run it is much easier to learn and think in metric rather than to always try to convert from metric to imperial. To facilitate this process a metric conversion table is given below.

CONVERSION CHART

LENGTH (NB 12inches 1 foot, 10 mm 1 cm, 100 cm 1 metre)

inches	1	2	3	4	5	6	9	12	
cm	2.5	5	7.5	10	12.5	15.2	23	30	

cm	1	2	3	5	10	20	25	50	75	100
inches	0.4	0.8	1.2	2	4	8	10	20	30	39

WEIGHT (NB 14lb = 1 stone, 2240 lb = 1 ton, 1,000 kg = 1 metric tonne)

lb	1	2	3	5	10	14	44	100	2246
kg	0.45	0.9	1.4	2.3	4.5	6.4	20	45	1016

kg	1	2	3	5	10	25	50	100	1000
lb	2.2	4.4	6.6	11	22	55	110	220	2204

DISTANCE

mile	1	5	10	20	30	40	50	75	100	150
km	1.6	8	16	32	48	64	80	120	161	241

km	1	5	10	20	30	40	50	100	150	200
mile	0.6	3.1	6.2	12.5	19	25	31	62	93	124

VOLUME

1 litre = 0.2 UK gallons   1 UK gallon = 4.5 litres
1 litre = 0.26 US gallons   1 US gallon = 3.8 litres

CLOTHES

UK	8	10	12	14	16	18	20
Europe	36	38	40	42	44	46	48
USA	6	8	10	12	14	18	

SHOES

UK	3	4	5	6	7	8	9	10	11
Europe	36	37	38	39	40	41/42	43	44	45
USA	2.5	3.3	4.5	5.5	6.5	7.5	8.5	9.5	10.5

Retirement

CHAPTER SUMMARY

- The most popular areas for retirees are the greater Lisbon area, including the coasts north and south of the capital, and the Algarve.
- **Residence permit.** Pensioners require a residence permit to live in Portugal. In addition to the documents required by all EU citizens, you will be required to present proof of your income (pension or otherwise).
- **Social life.** Many expats in Portugal testify to the opportunities for out-door pursuits of every kind and well-organised expatriate socialising for retirees.
- Retirement developments with 24-hour medical facilities on site as well as home-cleaning, laundry and grocery assistance are beginning to appear on the Algarve.
- **Pensions.** If you move to Portugal before reaching retirement age, you should continue to pay national insurance contributions in the UK in order to qualify for a British state pension once you reach 65.
  - If you have paid fifteen years worth of social security contributions in Portugal, you will be eligible for a Portuguese state pension.
- **Portuguese healthcare** standards are uneven and in some cases inadequate.
  - Most people in Portugal who can afford it go to private hospitals (for which the fees can be very high). It is advisable to take out private medical insurance to cover the costs of private treatment.
  - Portugal has a long tradition of caring for the elderly within the family home. There are therefore very few state or private residential nursing homes in Portugal.
- **Wills.** For those with assets in Portugal, it is advisable to draw up a Portuguese will in order to reduce the costs and the amount of time involved in the execution of the will.
  - Inheritance and gift tax in Portugal has been abolished and replaced with a stamp duty at a flat rate of 10%.

OVERVIEW

Retiring abroad has such an allure that one in five of us will take this route by 2020 according to research by the Centre of Future Studies. Twenty years ago Portugal was still considered a European backwater. Picturesque but desperately backward, it lacked sufficient amenities and infrastructure to make it a comfortable place for retirement. Its main attraction in those days was the long historical association with Britain and the presence of a longstanding British community; also an exceptionally pleasant climate, and an unspoilt coastline. Property prices were extremely low as were taxes. Since then a political and economic revolution have taken place which have changed many aspects of life there beyond recognition. Portugal is no longer a cheap paradise: property prices in the most popular places have soared to levels that in many instances are higher than in the UK and taxes are rapidly reaching parity with other EU countries. The cost of living is rising generally.

However, as a result of being rocketed into the twentieth century, roads and communications are now reasonably efficient; and the quality of life can be exceptional for those with sufficient means to keep pace with the rapidly rising cost of living. However, away from the main expatriate areas you can still find places which seem untouched by most of the changes that have taken place elsewhere in Portugal.

The most popular areas for retirees are the greater Lisbon area, including the coasts north and south of the capital, and the Algarve. It is the Algarve above all that has been transformed from being a poor, under-populated and remote province of Portugal to an area where the British can feel at home; its exceptional coastline is being rapidly lined with condominiums, resort complexes, villas, marinas, and other developments, all designed to entice those who wish to holiday or live in Portugal. Unfortunately for permanent and long-term residents, the holiday-makers are arriving in ever increasing numbers causing the kind of traffic problems and overcrowding that one is used to back in the UK. Furthermore, there are plans afoot to promote the Algarve as a winter destination, making the tourist invasion a year-round occurrence.

However anyone looking for somewhere to retire to will almost certainly find the advantages of Portugal outweigh the disadvantages. The excellent climate and the easy-going people, the upgrading of the infrastructure, the lively expatriate community, and the proximity to the UK (useful for family visits in both directions), are just some of the reasons why this is an increasingly popular country for retirement.

The Decision to Leave

First and foremost, anyone considering retiring to Portugal must be able to afford the move financially. Until recently the relatively low living costs in Portugal and the affordable property prices have been the main draws for retirees. However, in the Algarve, property prices are now far from bargain levels and although many aspects of life in Portugal are still cheap, overall the cost of living is not too far removed from that in the UK. It is vital to calculate what your retirement income will be, allowing for exchange rate fluctuations and inflation. This involves requesting a Retirement Pension Forecast (see below), if you are not already receiving your pension; finding out which other benefits you may continue to claim once in Portugal; and seeking independent tax advice regarding your investments.

Older people should also consider health issues before deciding to move to Portugal. Portugal's climate certainly allows older people to lead a healthier, relaxed lifestyle and also offers the possibility of taking part in active outdoor pursuits. However, the public health system is currently in a state of flux and although healthcare in the larger cities is more than adequate, in more remote areas the quality of the service is something of a lottery. It is also important to consider the future, and what might happen if you were to become seriously ill or no longer able to care for yourself. The Portuguese have great reverence for their elderly and as a result older people are almost always cared for by their families and there has not been the need for networks of nursing homes or personal home care services. In fact these things barely exist and it should be borne in mind that once you have become resident in Portugal, you cannot simply nip home to the UK to take advantage of the NHS – as a resident of an EU country you will only be eligible for emergency treatment.

You will also need to possess copious amounts of energy and enthusiasm to deal with the move practically and emotionally. Problems often arise when children and grandchildren are left behind. Women often feel this wrench much more than men and for some the homesickness can have a very negative effect on the new life in Portugal. For this reason and because many decisions to move abroad are based on a love of the country discovered through past holidays, it is quite a good idea to consider a long stay of say six months which includes the winter period, in the area in which one is interested, before moving permanently.

But enough of the caveats! Most people who decide to retire abroad have the enthusiasm and energy required to cope with the challenges ahead. For those whose interests can be pursued just as easily in Portugal as in the UK there is a range of possibilities from travelling around, by car or train, to studying Portuguese history, or enjoying the sports facilities, and the climate.

Preparation and Research

If one has friends who have already moved to Portugal, the temptation to join them is very great. But retiring abroad does not suit everyone. The emotional as well as physical upheaval of moving from the UK can be a great strain. Once there, additional stress will be imposed by the unfamiliarity of everything, at least initially, and the inevitable frustration of the necessary bureaucratic procedures.

When it comes to buying property or deciding to live abroad a great many people do so without the faintest idea of what this process entails, from winding up their UK affairs to the problems of getting stung by the ever alert Inland Revenue for thousands of pounds of back taxes if you overstay on a visit to the UK. What's more, the same normally sober citizens frequently throw their caution, learned from hard experience, out of the window, when it comes to buying property and making financial deals with builders etc. abroad, thereby tumbling into all manner of obvious pitfalls. It is therefore essential to take expert financial and legal advice. There are no shortcuts to dealing with the procedure for buying property in Portugal; and it is pointless trying to find one, whatever you may hear to the contrary. For details of buying property in Portugal see *Setting up Home*.

Entry Requirements

Applications for permanent residence in Portugal should begin a few months in advance of the date on which you are planning to move there, as the process is convoluted and time-consuming. Applications are processed through the Portuguese consulates in the UK. The basic regulations regarding applications for permanent residence, and a list of Portuguese consulates in the UK and the USA, can be found in *Residence and Entry Regulations*. This chapter also contains details of the residence application procedure once you have arrived in Portugal.

Additional documents required by the Portuguese Consulate for pensioners/ retired persons are as follows:

O   Proof of retirement or old age pension indicating the amount received monthly (proving that you have sufficient means to support yourself).
O   Proof from the bank that you are dealing with in Portugal that a bank account in Portugal has been opened. The monthly balance should not be inferior to the minimum gross earnings index in the UK, per member of the family.
O   A document that proves you are covered for healthcare – eg. An insurance policy, or a social security card.

HOBBIES AND INTERESTS

Apart from financial worries, the main problems facing retired people living abroad, especially those who have never lived in foreign parts, is adapting to the different lifestyle, difficulties with the language, and not finding interesting ways of occupying spare time. Especially hard hit are couples, who until they retired led busy lives and did not see much of each other during the week. If one is not going to start a business to keep busy then it is essential to have some mind stretching and therapeutic hobbies and interests in order to prevent lassitude or murderous frustration from taking over. Endless bridge and cocktail parties are not sufficiently stimulating for everyone; and you do not have to look far in the English-language press in Portugal to find out where this leads: sadly, meetings of Alcoholics Anonymous are held in profusion. It is therefore vital to have some enthusiasms. Many people in their seventies enjoy golf, swimming, walking and fishing; and these are just a few of the outdoor pleasures readily available in Portugal. Some of the sporting activities available in Portugal are dealt with in *Daily Life*. However, it is worth mentioning that Portugal has an increasing number of gyms, especially in the larger towns and cities, where it is possible to find fitness, yoga, martial arts etc. clubs. These can be found in the *Yellow Pages*.

Research has shown that the primary reason that prompts people into retiring abroad are the need to have a completely different life after work. So for many people, retiring to Portugal is a chance to create and enjoy to the full a new lifestyle with all the challenges that this entails. Portugal certainly has much to offer, although if it's ultra sophistication that you seek you will have to look elsewhere. But for outdoor pursuits of every kind, and well-organised, lively expatriate socialising there is no better place to come as many of the habitués will testify. Those who are contemplating moving to Portugal, but have so far only been there on holiday might like to join the Anglo-Portuguese Society (Canning House, 2 Belgrave Square, London SW1X 8PJ; www.canninghouse.com) before they move to Portugal, as a way of building up contacts in advance.

Once you have arrived, an invaluable publication is the *Anglo-Portuguese News*, as well as the *British Community Handbook* they also publish: APN (Apartado 113, 2765253 Estoril; ☎214-661423; fax: 214-660358). In the Lisbon area there is a free publication available from bars and hotels, called *Follow me Lisboa* – this often contains adverts for courses and activities.

Ideas for Hobbies and Interests

Once the business of settling in and all the relevant permits and documents have been obtained, thoughts will necessarily turn to socialising and the pursuit of hobbies and interests for which there are many possibilities.

A good place to start looking for contacts is the Association of Foreign Property Owners (AFPOP – *Associação de Proprietários Estrangeiros em Portugal*, Apartado 728, 8501-917 Portimão, Algarve; ☎282-458509; fax 282-458277; www.afpop.com). AFPOP specialises in providing information and support to foreign residents and membership is open to anyone over the age of 18. Members are provided with a regular newsletter, updating them, among other things, about social events of interest. Another useful contact to new residents of Portugal is the

British Community Council of Lisbon (c/o Mrs Hilary Heger, Apartado 3762, Malavado, 7630-584 S. Teotonio; e-mail info@bcclisbon.org; www.bcclisbon. org). The BCC brings together English speaking people in Lisbon to enjoy a wide variety of social, sporting and cultural activities. They also organise a busy programme of events throughout the year.

Keen gardeners will find that plants need no encouragement; and the creation of an exotic garden provides endless pleasure for some. The Garden Studio of Sintra (see below) holds regular gardening classes.

Wherever in the world the British congregate it seems that animal charities proliferate and Portugal is no exception. There are dogs' homes and animal sanctuaries run by Brits from Sintra to the Algarve and you will find out about them soon enough, if indeed you do not decide to start one of your own.

Travelling around Portugal will give you a better perspective on the country in which you are living. Accommodation prices vary but simple pensions are very cheap. Camping is also becoming popular in Portugal. If you do not have your own transport, the trains are cheap and go to most places of interest. What is more, pensioners are entitled to half fares. Portugal also has some wonderful steam train journeys which the local Turismo (Tourist Office) will be happy to tell you about. No doubt other expatriates will give recommendations. For serious travellers there are a number of guidebooks on the market including *Fodors Guide to Portugal* and *The Rough Guide to Portugal* available in most general bookshops, as well as travel bookshops and public libraries.

Painting is one of the most soothing occupations and scenically Portugal is a painter's paradise. If you move to the Lisbon area, the Sintra Garden Studio (Quinta dos Quatro Ventos, Rua da Ribeira, Azoia 2710, Sintra; ☎ 219-280042) offers painting courses both for beginners and experienced painters. The studio also lays on transport from Lisbon. Alternatively, photography is a hobby that can bring a lot of pleasure. A collection of pictures taken of a disappearing way of life in the remote parts of Portugal could become a valuable record for future historians. Elsewhere in Portugal, the best place to look for artistic clubs or classes is the nearest university. Occasionally art and photography classes are available to non-faculty members. Alternatively, in the expat areas, you will often come across noticeboards in shops, bars and cafes, advertising art and craft courses.

There are numerous English-language amateur dramatics groups, and they are usually keen to find new members. In the Lisbon area, the international theatre group, known as the *Lisbon Players* (Rua da Estrela 10, 1200 Lisbon; ☎213-961946; www.lisbonplayers.com.pt) has been treading the boards since 1947. The Players regularly put on plays and musicals and are keen to recruit new members for acting and production roles. The Algarve also has its own theatre group – *The Algarveans*. Contact details can be found at the company's website: www.valegrifo.com/algarveans.

Those looking for places of worship in Portugal where they can meet like-minded expatriates are fairly well served in the Algarve and in Lisbon and Porto. Although most churches in Portugal are Catholic, the areas with a high concentration of expatriates have established churches of other denominations. Lisbon boasts an Anglican church (St George's Church, Rua São Jorge, 1200 Lisbon; ☎213-906248); a synagogue (Shaaré-Tikvá Synagogue, rua Alexandre Herculano 29, 1250-010 Lisbon; ☎213-858604); a Muslim temple (Mesquita Central de Lisboa, Avenida José Malhôa, 1070 Lisbon; ☎213-874604; and the Church of Scotland (St. Andrew's Church, Rua Arriaga 13, Lisbon ☎213-957677). Porto also has an Anglican Church: St James's Church, Largo da Maternidade Júlio Dinis, 4050 Porto. In the Algarve, St. Vincent's Anglican Church has three separate congregations, details of which can be found on the website (www.geocities.com/stvincents2002) or by telephoning ☎289-366720.

Useful Addresses

The British expatriate tends to be a clubbable creature and there are various associations which retired people are welcome to join in Portugal, some of them familiar from the UK, like the Royal British Legion. Some of them will change addresses as their representatives change or are re-elected. Some of the main clubs and organisations are:

Association of Foreign Property Owners: AFPOP – Associação de Proprietários Estrangeiros em Portugal, Apartado 728, 8501-917 Portimão, Algarve; ☎282-458509; fax 282-458277; www.afpop.com.

British Community Council of Lisbon: c/o Mrs Hilary Heger, Apartado 3762, Malavado, 7630-584 S. Teotonio; e-mail info@bcclisbon.org; www.bcclisbon.org.

The British Historical Society of Portugal: c/o St Julian's School, Quinta Nova, Carcavelos, 2777-601; Carcavelos; email info@bhsportugal.org; www.bhsportugal.org.

Lisbon Casuals Sports Club: c/o St. Julian's School, Quinta Nova, Carcavelos, Nr. Lisbon. A good value sports club with a congenial bar.

Royal British Club: Apartado 126, 2766-902 Estoril; ☎214-822495; fax 214-822496; e-mail rbclx@mail.telepac.pt; www.royalbritishclub.pt. A private members club which organises social and networking events, and includes a golf section

Royal British Legion: http://portugal.legionbranches.net/.

The Royal Society of St. George: c/o Mrs. B. Neasham MBE, Les Arondes, Rua do Jasmin, Birre, 2750-241 Cascais; tel/fax 214-871303; www.royalsocietyofstgeorge.com/portugal.htm.

CHOOSING AND BUYING A HOME FOR RETIREMENT

The main and very obvious point to make regarding buying a retirement property in Portugal is to choose something which is both within your scope financially and which, unlike a holiday home, is suitable for year-round living. However, you will also need to take into consideration the running and upkeep costs of the property in question. Buying an apartment within a block of flats, for instance, can help ease some of the budgeting costs involved in house maintenance. Proximity to facilities is also an important consideration for anyone reliant on public transport. The availability of buses, and general accessibility – even if you yourself own a car – should be part of your decision to buy or not to buy. Once you have decided on your new home you will need to follow all of the procedures regarding property purchase, which are explained in full in *Setting Up Home*.

Where to Buy
Older people planning to retire to Portugal should bear the following factors in mind when deciding on a place to live:

Medical Facilities. What is the medical facilities provision in the area where you are hoping to buy? Are there English-speaking staff? The British Consulate advises older people to look ahead when considering where to buy their retirement home. Although none of us like to think about the possibility of ill health in our later years, these facts have to be faced, and whilst it may be ideal to live in a beautiful but remote spot in your fifties, in your sixties the long trek to the nearest health centre may become a real burden. A good place to find out this sort of information (if you are hoping to buy in the Algarve or around Lisbon) is the English-language magazines and newspapers as well as from other expat property owners. Your local lawyer may also be able to give you an idea of what is offered and local bars are often founts of useful local information for the newcomer. Depending on how well run the town hall (Câmara) is, you may find that local facilities are very well run and efficient.

Ease of Access. If you are looking to buy to rent, you need to be aware that if a property is more than an hour's drive from the nearest airport, potential tenants are likely to think twice about staying with you. This will also be an important factor in the purchase price of a property, both when you buy it and when it comes to selling on. Ease of access to communication networks, be they rail or road links are of considerable importance when weighing up the cost against the location of a place. Add to this local and regional transport in the area and the ability for you or a tenant who hasn't a car to get to areas of interest, the beaches and the commercial centres.

Climate. The only place where you will be guaranteed sunshine and warm sea temperatures throughout the year is in Madeira. Elsewhere, even along the Algarve, winter temperatures, though pleasant, are mild rather than baking. Further north, along the west coast, winter can get distinctly chilly, and if you are buying up in the mountains remember that even in summer the highest peaks are capped with snow. You will need to pack warm clothes and make sure that the property has adequate insulation and heating. Another point related to climate is the risk or otherwise of flooding and forest fires, which in some parts (mainly in the north) of Portugal are yearly occurrences.

Leisure Facilities. Depending on what your leisure interests are – golf, sailing, equestrianism, water sports, bridge – how close are these facilities to the property? Distances can be deceptive, especially when the tourist season is in full swing and the coast roads are packed. If you are addicted to golf why not consider buying property in one of the golf resorts, or as close as possible to one of the courses along the Algarve.

The Manageability and Security of a Property. Do you really need a large property with an inordinate number of bedrooms that requires a great deal of ongoing maintenance to the house and garden? A beautiful view is wonderful for a time, but it will eventually merge into the general scenery and become everyday and you will take it for granted. If you are buying an isolated property how are you going to fill your days? If you are only planning on visiting the property for a few weeks or months a year then you should consider whether you really need a garden or whether you should get it paved over and add pot plants. Likewise a swimming pool will need continual maintenance and if a property is to be left unattended for lengthy periods of time this can become an inconvenience and an expense. Most properties will already have security grilles fitted on ground floor windows and doors but depending on how much use is going to be made of a property you will need to look into how secure it is. Grand isolated properties may be expensive to insure, especially if they are only occupied for a certain number of weeks or months a year.

Seasonal Population Fluctuations. The summer crowds versus the quiet winters. If you decide that you want to buy a property in town is it near a main thoroughfare that gets a lot of tourist traffic, or just a lot of traffic? Remember that during the height of the tourist season the evenings will bring swarms of revellers out onto the streets, partying into the early hours. If you are looking to buy in a busy downtown area are you prepared to put up with noise below your flat through the night?

Is your property part of a development where neighbouring properties are let out continually to holiday-makers intent on a raucous two-week knees-up throughout the high season (when you may well want to enjoy some peace and quiet away from the stresses of your life back home) and then left entirely empty over the winter? During the tourist season finding a parking space near to your property may prove difficult and the demand for increased services (sewerage, water, electricity) may lead to temporary shortages and restrictions that, though you may find them tolerable for one season, may begin to annoy you if endured year after year. For those seeking peace it may be better to look for property inland in order to avoid the tourist hordes.

Living Amongst Compatriots. Proximity to amenities and the best services, particularly English-speaking services will probably also mean living in one of Portugal's pockets of foreign residents. Because of the volume of foreigners who have bought property in Portugal over the years, unless you buy away from the coasts and the Algarve, you will be unlikely to find a property too far away from another owned by someone from Germany, Holland, Britain or Scandinavia. Even houses in the villages up in the hills and hinterland behind the Algarve are increasingly being bought up by foreigners. These villages remain very Portuguese and because the foreigners have moved there for precisely that reason, they try to integrate into the local community as best they can. Don't be under any illusions that you will find a 'traditional' and culturally intact village where you will be the only foreigner – those days are long gone, or if not, fast disappearing.

If you are buying an off-plan property, find out if there are likely to be further buildings planned – a possible Phase 2 or 3 where your bijou set of apartments is going to be reduced to being merely one of a number of such apartments, part of a small town complete with café, clubhouse and social centre. There are *urbanizaçãos* where all the owners of the villas or apartments are foreign and where the only native Portuguese face you see will be that of the gardener. Much like the compounds for foreigners found in Saudi Arabia these places are often insular worlds where there is no need, and no desire, to mix with the local community.

Water Shortages. Areas that get little annual rainfall will naturally succumb to periods of drought when water restrictions come into force. Bang goes your dream of a house with a pool, of beautiful lawns irrigated by the soft pulse of sprinklers. Are there alternative water supplies at hand, e.g. a well or a storage tank? Such considerations are particularly important if you are looking to buy in the Algarve and the southern reaches of the country where water is an expensive and precious commodity. It is a good idea to talk to the locals and other foreigners who have lived in the area for some time to find out possible pitfalls.

Retirement Villages

Although retirement homes do exist in Portugal they are relatively rare, and almost all are located along the Algarve to cater for expats rather than the Portuguese – who tend to look after aged relatives in the family home. In addition, there may be something of a worry still about the medical provision for the elderly in Portugal, adequate though it is and although it is often augmented with private medical insurance. The lack of residential care in Portugal leads many retirees to eventually return home when they become less capable of living an independent life. However, this gap in the market has led some developers to build top-end retirement homes and sheltered housing with 24-hour medical facilities on site, and such properties have much the same features as similar outfits back home – swimming pools, restaurants, medical block, shopping centre, gym etc., and as with *urbanizações* there are additional service charges payable on top of the purchase price of the flat.

Retirement villages cater to those in the 55+ age group. In some of these villages personal care and support services are provided, for a fee. The range and amount of care varies from place to place, with some villages offering both independent living and serviced apartments. Residents pay a premium giving them the right to live in the village and benefit from its amenities. They also pay a weekly maintenance fee for any services. However, these arrangements are quite different from buying or renting and you are unlikely to make any money on the property, as although your premium may be returned at the time that you decide to leave the village, this is minus deductions stated in the contract, and does not make allowances for the property value having increased. Residents pay their own telephone, electricity, gas, insurance etc., and their own general living expenses.

Depending on what you are looking for – whether you are happy to live out your last years away from your family back home – nursing costs in Portugal are likely to be lower and residential nursing homes far more appealing than those in, for instance, the UK. If you are only a temporary resident in Portugal you may even be able to generate some income by renting out a sheltered property to other senior citizens from back home in need of a bit of sun, a view of the sea, and soft evening breezes.

One such residential resort home, with 24-hour medical service, being advertised at the time of going to press was the Monte da Palhagueira Retirement Village in the hills near Santa Barbara de Nexe in the Algarve, available through Fifty5plus Property Search (Lower Green, Inkpen, Hungerford, Berkshire RG17 9D2, UK; ☎01488-668 655; fax 01488-668 930; www.fifty5plus.com). Set in 22 acres of landscaped gardens, the 'village' comprises 32 properties and offers a wide choice of one-bedroom apartments to three bedroom luxury villas all surrounded by colourful landscaped gardens. A one-bedroom assisted apartment costs around €125,000; while a two-bedroom close care apartment starts at €220,000; a three-bedroomed independent house costs €510,000.

PENSIONS

Portugal's pension system is currently in a state of crisis. As in most of Europe, the rapidly ageing population is placing enormous pressure on the social security fund. The percentage of the population aged 65 or more has almost doubled over the past thirty years to around 14% and emigration has seriously depleted the number of workers making social security contributions. Portugal now has one pensioner for every 1.7 actively employed people and independent studies indicate that without major reform the current pension system will start to collapse between 2010 and 2020. Whilst the previous government began to make changes to the pension system, the change of government in February 2005 has created confusion – nobody is sure what will happen to the pension system in the future. Clearly the current system is too expensive to sustain, and future reforms will have to allow the private sector to play a greater role. However, the private pension sector in Portugal is as yet not as fully developed as in other EU member states. Expats would therefore be well advised not to rely on the Portuguese state system, but to transfer their foreign public and private pensions if eligible.

Receiving a UK State Pension in Portugal

According to latest government figures, there are approximately 5,000 people receiving their British pension in Portugal. This figure is low compared to the total number of those receiving their pensions in Spain (50,000), Italy (28,000) and France (21,000). Nevertheless, the procedures for transferring your state pension to Portugal are fairly straightforward.

Those planning to start receiving their UK state pension in Portugal should request a Retirement Pension Forecast, which will tell you the amount of state pension you have already earned and the amount you can expect to receive at pension age. This will help you to plan exactly how far your pension will go in Portugal. To receive a forecast, obtain form BR19 from your local social security office or contact the Retirement Pension Forecasting and Advice Unit (DWP, Newcastle-upon-Tyne, NE98 1BA; ☎0191-218 7585; fax 0191-218 7293). If you are already in Portugal, you should contact the Inland Revenue and ask for form CA3638.

Remember that if you move to Portugal before reaching retirement age, you should continue to pay national insurance contributions in the UK in order to qualify for a British state pension once you reach 65. Failure to do so may result in your not being eligible for a UK pension – depending on the number of years' contributions made. This is a thorny issue and it is best to seek advice from the Inland Revenue National Insurance Contributions Office (Benton Park View, Newcastle-upon-Tyne NE98 1ZZ).

UK and other EU state pensions can be paid to you in Portugal. In order to receive your pension, contact the Pensions and Overseas Benefits Directorate of the Department of Work and Pensions (Newcastle-upon-Tyne, NE98 1YX; ☎0191-218 7147), before moving to Portugal, to obtain a couple of forms. These forms must be completed in order to arrange the transfer of your UK pension to either an address in Portugal or a bank account in either the UK or Portugal. Note that pensions are not frozen at the level they reached on arrival in Portugal instead the pension will rise in accordance with any increases which take effect in the UK. The DWP Overseas Benefits Directorate office in Newcastle also publishes Leaflet SA29 (available on receipt of an s.a.e.) which provides details on EU pension and social security legislation. This leaflet can also be downloaded from http://www.dwp.gov.uk/international/sa29/index.asp. Further help and advice is available from the International Pension Service (☎0191-218 7777).

You will receive exactly the same amount of pension as you would have done in the UK. This pension can be paid directly into your UK bank account or into your account in Portugal. Alternatively you can choose to receive payment by payable orders sent by post.

UK company pensions are paid as per the rules of the individual company. They may say that your company pension may only be paid into a UK bank account, in which case it will be necessary to set up a standing order from your UK account to your Portuguese account.

It is important to examine your payment options when receiving a pension from abroad as the bank abroad may charge for making the transfer, and your bank in Portugal may also apply a commission. It therefore pays to shop around. Those living on the Algarve sometimes use the banks in Gibraltar to avoid the charges that Portuguese banks make on sterling payments. It may also be more sensible to have the money transferred in quarterly instalments rather than monthly, as the charge is often less. Alternatively a currency dealer, such as Currencies Direct (Hanover House, 73-74 High Holborn, London WC1 6LR; ☎020-7813 0332; fax 020-7419 7753; www.currenciesdirect.com) will allow you to make an annual arrangement that fixes the exchange rate for a year, insuring you against currency fluctuations.

One final thing to consider is your tax position. In Portugal your UK pension may well be considered as income and therefore taxed as such. In order to avoid paying more tax than you need to contact the Inland Revenue (Inspector of Funds, Lynwood Road, Thames Ditton, Surrey KT7 0DP).

Further information regarding UK pensions is available from the following websites: www.thepensionservice.gov.uk and www.dwp.gov.uk.

Exportable UK Benefits

On top of your UK pension, once you have received Portuguese residence, you are still entitled to some UK benefits such as any Bereavement Allowance (payable for up to one year), and Widowed Parent's Allowance. However, there are a number of benefits which you can no longer receive once living abroad. These include Disability Living Allowance, Income Support, Pension Credit, Attendance Allowance, and Carer's Allowance. Some pensioners therefore find their income substantially reduced upon moving to Portugal.

Winter Fuel Payments abroad have caused some confusion, but the situation currently is that anyone who received a Winter Fuel Payment in the UK before moving to Portugal may continue to receive the payments (£200 per year, per household for people over 60, with an extra £100 for people over 80). If you left the UK before January 1998, you will not be able to receive this benefit outside the UK. For further information contact the Winter Fuel Payment Centre (Southgate House, Cardiff Central, Royal Mail, Cardiff, CF911 1ZH; ☎029-2042 8635; help line 08459-151515; fax 029-2042 8676; www.thepensionservice.gov.uk).

Further information is available in two leaflets; '*Going Abroad and Social Security Benefits*' (GL29), available from your local social security office, and the DWP's leaflet SA 29, mentioned above. A useful source of advice and information on any of the above issues is the International Pension Centre (DWP, Tyneview Park, Benton, Newcastle-upon-Tyne NE98 1BA; ☎0191-218 7777; fax 0191-218 3836; www.dwp.gov.uk).

Receiving a Portuguese State Pension

If you move from the UK to Portugal for employment, and then retire there, you may be eligible for a Portuguese pension. As the current pension is under half that of the UK pension this is not an inspiring prospect. Indeed with the cost of living in Portugal rising fast it is probably due to ingenuity alone that any Portuguese pensioner can manage on such a small amount.

The retirement age in Portugal is 65, and upon reaching this age those who have completed at least fifteen years of work (either continuously or at different times throughout their life) and hence paid fifteen years' worth of social security contributions, are entitled to a state pension. However, these stipulations have become more flexible in recent years, in schemes to encourage early retirement. Those who reach the age of 55 and can prove that they have worked for 30 years can choose to retire on a reduced pension.

For EU employees and self-employed workers in Portugal exactly the same rules should apply and if you meet the Portuguese qualifying conditions you should be eligible for a state pension. For those who have not worked for fifteen years in Portugal, it is possible for contributions made previously in another EU country to be transferred and to count towards your entitlement. UK citizens should obtain certificate E301 from the *Department of Social Security Overseas Branch* (Newcastle-upon-Tyne NE98 1YX; ☎0191-225 3963), showing the exact amount of social security contributions that they have made.

FINANCE

Anyone considering retiring to a foreign country is strongly advised to take specialist financial advice regarding their personal situation. Many people who are in the happy position of being able to retire overseas have a certain amount of income to invest, or at least will have once they sell their UK property; and it is essential to take good advice on how and where this may best be done. Moreover, those who intend to maintain connections with both the UK and Portugal will need advice on how their taxation affairs can most advantageously be organised. Usually there is no reason why one should not continue with bank accounts or investments already established in the UK and in most cases interest will be paid on deposits without deductions of tax where one is non-resident. For those who wish to sever all financial connection with the UK, except for the receipt of a UK pension and possible allowances, the situation is relatively straightforward in that they will only be liable for Portuguese taxes (see *Daily Life*).

One of the major issues regarding your investments is currency fluctuations. If you have investments which are sterling based or dollar based, then as you will be spending euros from now on, the value of your investments may go up and down with the exchange rate. Of course, the value of your investments will not crystallise until such a time as you sell them. However, any revenue generated from these investments *will* fluctuate in value. It is therefore best to consider offshore options for your investments, or to think about obtaining investments that pay out in euros. For all of these considerations, you will need a tax adviser who has expertise in both your home country and Portugal. Further details of fiscal advisers can be found in *Daily Life*.

Taxation

Taxation is inextricably linked with investment considerations. Generally speaking, if their affairs are properly managed, most people will be neither substantially better nor worse off under a Portuguese tax regime than a UK one. It is best to take advice either from your local Inland Revenue office – who should provide fairly impartial advice, or a specialist in overseas taxation issues such as Blevins Franks (www.blevinsfranks.com).

Because the UK tax year runs from April to April and the Portuguese tax year follows the calendar year from January to December, there are certain advantages and disadvantages to choosing a particular date to move to Portugal. Whereas employees are not usually able to indulge in such freedom of choice, the retired person should consider this seriously. The issue of double taxation also arises, as during your first year of residence in Portugal, there may be an overlap between the UK tax year and the Portuguese tax year and your income may be taxed in both countries. In order to avoid this, contact HM Inspector of Taxes (Public

Department 2, Management Unit 2, Ty Glas Road, Llanishen, Cardiff CF14 5XS; ☎029-2032 5000; fax 029-2032 6342).

Trusts

One important tool for the retired investor moving to Portugal is the trust. Shares, bonds, funds, bank deposits etc. can all become free from Portuguese income tax, inheritance tax and capital gains tax, simply by putting them into trust. This should only be done with expert advice. The concept of a 'trust' only exists in countries with common-law legal systems, e.g. the UK, USA, Canada and British colonies. However, there are moves by the government in the UK to make trusts less effective as a way of evading taxes.

The concept of a trust is simple enough: you give or lend your money to a trustee; this money is then treated by the taxman as though it were not yours anymore. The trustees appointed to run the trust invest the money as they see fit, or you have specified when making the initial gift. Income generated by the trust is taxed under a special regime in the UK depending on the type of trust. The two basic categories of trust are:

- ⭘ Interest-in-possession trust: this gives a person or persons the right to income from the trust or the equivalent of income (e.g. the right to live in a rent-free property). The trustees have to hand over the income to the beneficiaries stated in the trust.
- ⭘ Discretionary trust: the trustees decide which beneficiaries should receive income or capital from the trust. Where no money is paid out until the end of the trust, this is known as an *accumulation trust.* If money is paid out for the education, maintenance or benefit of beneficiaries until they get an *interest-in-possession,* then the trust is an *accumulation-and-maintenance* trust.

The income from trusts may be used as decided by the trustees, which means that though you may receive some income from the trust (which will be subject to taxation) other income may be invested or spent by the trust as they wish. If the trust company is based in a place where taxes are low or non-existent then the income from the investments will have low or no tax payable on them. Additionally, on death, the money put into a trust, as it is not 'yours' anymore, will not be subject to inheritance tax.

HEALTHCARE

Health and Insurance

In order to benefit from the state healthcare system, it is necessary to apply for a national insurance card at the local health centre. Those who are retired and in receipt of a UK state retirement pension are in an advantageous position as they can apply for a health card and enroll with a state GP upon arrival, simply by producing their passport and pension receipts. Others have to wait until they receive their residence card before they can receive routine check-ups and non-emergency medical treatment.

Before leaving the UK to retire abroad it is a good idea to have a thorough medical check up and make sure that all your inoculations are up-to-date (you will require no new ones) and that you take with you a supply of any regular medicaments to last until you find out what the Portuguese equivalents are. It is also advisable to have a dental and eye check up and take spare sets of dentures and spectacles/contact lenses with you.

Although it is to be hoped that the beneficial climate in Portugal will induce good health generally, the possibility of serious illness or accident requiring hospitalisation cannot be ruled out. The standards of state health care in Portugal are uneven and in some cases inadequate. There are however an increasing number of swish, new, private medical centres such as the modern Clínica Europa in Carcavelos which offers both medical and dental treatment. Most people in Portugal who can afford to, go to private hospitals for which the fees can be astronomic. For this reason it is extremely advisable to take out private medical insurance to cover the cost of treatment. Insurance companies specialising in expatriate health cover normally offer special 'senior' policies for those over 55 years old. Such policies are normally taken out annually. Two leading providers of medical cover are *Expacare:* (email: info@expacare. net or visit www.expacare.com) who are specialists in expatriate healthcare offering high quality health insurance cover for expatriates of all nationalities worldwide, and BUPA International; ☎01273-208181; fax 01273-866583; www.bupa-intl. com. The policy should cover the insured for private medical expenses including hospital inpatient care, local ambulance services, home nursing for a limited period, consultants' fees and technical diagnostic procedures. Further providers of private medical cover in Portugal and worldwide are listed in *Daily Life.*

When dealing with the health service, remember to keep all receipts – either to offset against any taxable income in Portugal, or to claim against medical insurance.

It is important to remember that as soon as you become a resident in Portugal, simply returning home to the UK for free healthcare is not an option. Upon visiting the UK, as in any other European country, you are only entitled to emergency treatment under the provisions of the E-111, and non-emergency treatment will cost you. Whilst the rules on this may not have been strictly enforced previously, these days controls are getting tighter as the EU's ageing population creates more of a burden on member-states' public health services. However, those with a holiday home in Portugal, who spend less than six months a year there, will still be entitled to free UK NHS treatment.

Care in the Home and Residential Care. Portugal has a long tradition of looking after its old people in the family home and this has presented a major problem for many retired expatriates who have reached the stage where they can no longer care for themselves. In most areas of Portugal the infrastructure for caring for the elderly is simply not in place. There are very few either state or private residential nursing homes in Portugal and there are even fewer hospices. Social services care in the home services are also very much in their infancy. Therefore in the case of serious illness, then it is really best to consider returning home. The only real alternative is to move into one of the few retirement villages (mentioned above) that are appearing on the Algarve, and paying for twenty-four hour medical services. However, this can be very expensive.

The E121 and E106

The first step for retired UK citizens, before moving to Portugal, is to obtain the form E121 from the Pension Service (Tyneview Park, Newcastle-upon Tyne, NE98 1BA; ☎0191-218 7777; fax 0191-2183836; e-mail tvp-ipc-customercare@thepen sionservice.gsi.gov.uk). This form gives access to the Portuguese health system for British state retirement pensioners, their spouses and dependent children, and for anyone receiving the UK Incapacity Benefit. Without it, you will be charged for treatment. Your form must be registered at the local social security office.

Many retired British people simply rely on their E-111 for healthcare. However, the E-111 is really intended only for emergencies, and is valid only for your first three months in Portugal. Until recently the authorities did not really bother to control this, and the E-111 was sufficient (many hospitals barely bothered to look at it). These days the rules are far more likely to be enforced, and patients may well be asked for flight tickets as proof of when they arrived in Portugal. It is therefore far more sensible to obtain and register the E121.

Those who move to Portugal before UK state retirement age are able to obtain temporary cover for healthcare for up to two and a half years by filling in form E106. This form is also available from the Department of Work and Pensions, or the Inland Revenue.

WILLS, BEREAVEMENT AND LEGAL CONSIDERATIONS

Wills

According to John Howell and Co. International Lawyers, over 100,000 British people have an interest in a holiday home in Portugal. Many more live there permanently and when they die, most will leave assets in Portugal that will need to be transferred to their heirs. Many people who are approaching retirement age have already made a will. An English will is valid under Portuguese law. However, in the case of property and land in Portugal, Portuguese law applies and provides for only limited freedom for disposal of assets (the husband/wife and children have priority rights which, if not reflected in the will, can allow them to challenge it). Although this rule applies, generally the Portuguese do accept that English law should pertain to property assets located in Portugal and that English people can dispose of their assets as freely as they could in England. Because there is this contradiction, it is advisable to draw up a Portuguese will, with a Portuguese lawyer, to cover the assets that you hold in Portugal. There are other reasons for obtaining a Portuguese will. Firstly it avoids having to apply for probate in Portugal and secondly the cost of having a foreign will recognised in Portugal will be far greater than dealing with a Portuguese will, and the execution of the will may take far longer.

Before making the will, it is strongly recommended that you seek the advice of a Portuguese lawyer, and a lawyer in the country where your other assets are based. This will avoid any mistakes which may prove costly and time-consuming for your heirs. If you have both a Portuguese will and a foreign will, it is essential to ensure that they do not conflict in any way. The names of English-speaking lawyers who can arrange for the drawing up of a Portuguese will, can be obtained from the British Embassy or Consulates in Portugal. Alternatively one can ask for recommendations or contact a British legal firm that has Portuguese associates. The Portuguese-UK Chamber of Commerce in London (☎020-7494 1844) can also provide a list of suitable law firms. A few British-based lawyers have associates in Portugal and can arrange for a Portuguese will to be drawn up. One such firm is Bennett & Co Solicitors (144 Knutsford Road, Wilmslow, Cheshire, SK9 6JP, UK ; ☎01625-586937; fax 01625-585362; www.bennett-and-co.com).

In Portugal there are two types of will. A **public will** must be written in Portuguese and signed in front of a notary with two other witnesses present. This will be recorded in the notarial books and you will be provided with legalised photocopies. A **private will,** on the other hand, may be written in any language, but must be signed before a notary and two witnesses. The private will must be written in the testator's handwriting. Although this will is not entered into the notarial books, the notary will draw up a minute of approval (*minuta de aprovação*) which will be given to you to keep safe, along with the will. This document testifies as to the validity of the will. A private will may be drawn up by an English solicitor, but must be copied into the testator's handwriting and then notarised in Portugal.

You will need to appoint an executor for your Portuguese will. As under English law the executor is appointed in the will. However, unlike in England, it is not a good idea to appoint lay people to act as executors – this can prove extremely onerous. Therefore it is common to appoint a solicitor or other suitably qualified person.

Useful Contact:
The International Property Law Centre: Unit 2, Waterside Park, Livingstone Road, Hessle, HU13 OEG; ☎0870-800 4565 fax 0870-800 4567; e-mail internationalproperty@maxgold.com; www.internationalpropertylaw.com. Specialists in the purchase and sale of Portuguese property and businesses, wills and probate, and litigation.

Inheritance and Gift Tax

In 2003 Portuguese tax authorities introduced reforms to abolish Inheritance Tax and Gift Tax (*Imposto sobre as Sucessões e Doações*). The new ruling came into force from 1 January 2004. Previously, Inheritance Tax and Gift Tax was payable on any assets deemed to be located in Portugal (i.e. real estate, securities) at the time of the deceased's death or at the time of their making of the gift. Rates varied from 3%-50% depending on the relationship between the recipient and the deceased or donor. With the abolition of these taxes a Stamp Duty with a flat rate of 10% will now apply, there will be exemptions available for transfers to spouses, descendants and ascendants.

Bereavement

Morbid though it may seem, this book would be incomplete without mentioning death since it affects us all sooner or later. Dying abroad complicates matters slightly in that one's near relations are often not on the spot to deal with the formalities surrounding burial: they may not even know the wishes of the deceased as regards the place of burial, i.e. in Portugal or the UK. It is therefore advisable to make ones wishes concerning this matter known in advance.

In Portugal deaths must be registered within 24 hours at the town hall, and for Britons it is advisable to also notify the British Consulate in Lisbon. In terms of tax obligations, the death must be reported to the tax authorities within 30 days if the deceased lived in the area, or 180 days if the person lived overseas.

The British Embassy points out that the famous British Cemetery in Lisbon is short of space and only the regular worshippers at St. George's Church Lisbon, St. Paul's Church Estoril, St. Vicente's Church, Portimão or the United Church of Scotland are eligible for burial there. There is usually no problem arranging for the internment of Catholics or Protestants in a Portuguese Catholic cemetery. Cremation is another possibility, although Portugal still has only three crematoriums – the *Cemitério do Alto de São João* located in Lisbon; the *Cemitério do Prado do Repouso* in Porto; and the *Cemitério do Ferreira do Alentejo* in the small town of Ferreira do Alentejo.

The British Embassy warns that air-freighting a coffin back to the UK is an expensive business. Freight charges depend on weight but the minimum cost is about £3,000. It is advisable to get some quotations from Portuguese undertakers who offer such a service.

Section II

WORKING IN PORTUGAL

EMPLOYMENT

BUSINESS AND INDUSTRY REPORT

STARTING A BUSINESS

EMPLOYMENT

CHAPTER SUMMARY

○ **The employment situation.** Unemployment in Portugal is below the EU average at just under 7%. Unfortunately this figure has been rising in recent years.
  ○ Portuguese workers are paid some of the lowest wages in the EU and living costs, although much lower than in the UK, are not as cheap as they once were.
○ **Job hunting.** Your best bet for speculative applications is likely to be your local Jobcentre, which, under the EURES scheme, can help you complete an application form to be forwarded to the employment service in Portugal.
  ○ State run job centres in Portugal (*Centros Emprego*) operate a placement service, although they are unlikely to be able to help anyone who is unable to communicate in Portuguese.
  ○ The best prospects for work are in multinational, British or American companies, English language teaching, working for expatriates, or working in tourism.
○ All employees on full-time contracts are entitled to twenty-two days of paid holiday per year – increased to twenty-five days if the worker has 3 or fewer justified absences.
○ Opportunities for women in the professions and in business have increased dramatically in recent years – but their wages are still only 75% of men's.
○ **Working etiquette.** Foreigners coming into Portuguese companies describe a profound unwillingness to challenge authority and remark upon a lack of teamwork.
  ○ The Portuguese tend to be fairly formal when it comes to dress code in the working world.
○ **Business and industry.** The economy of Portugal is that of an industrialised country, but one where the service sector is ahead of industry as the major contributor to its GDP.
  ○ The biggest industries in Portugal are foodstuffs, beverages, textiles, clothing and leather goods.

THE EMPLOYMENT SCENE

Twenty years ago, even those accustomed to working in European countries would probably have found themselves driven to distraction by the antiquated business methods and lack of amenities in Portugal. For the various reasons outlined in the *General Introduction*, Portugal was simply in the dark ages as far as working conditions and the economy were concerned. The chaotic state of national finances was having an extremely destabilising effect on the government which was changing every few months. There was a terrible time at the beginning of the 1980s when public-sector workers did not know when or how they would be paid and as late as 1990 there were still 12,000 workers awaiting settlements on wages delayed from this time. Since Portugal's entry into the EU, the prospects for international workers have happily improved but the locals are still some of the poorest paid in the EU.

Since EU entry, the economy has stabilised and contemporary technology has made the country compatible with its other European partners. The *Business and Industry Report* below will give an idea of the main sectors of the Portuguese economy, including textiles, pottery, shipbuilding, agricultural products, paper, and glassware among its more traditional industrial activities; and then there is tourism which – along with public sector and infrastructure projects, the expansion of the capital's underground system, and of the national road network, will provide most of the specific employment opportunities for international and UK workers.

Unfortunately for job-seekers, the Portuguese economy has taken a turn for the worse in recent years and consequently unemployment is on the rise. The official figure, at just under 7%, is still lower than the EU average, but the rate of unemployment has been rising consistently since 2002 when unemployment was just 4.1% (one of the lowest rates in the EU). This makes the Portuguese job-market even more competitive. Even during periods of economic boom, the opportunities available to foreigners in Portugal have never been plentiful. Theoretically EU citizens enjoy equality in the Portuguese labour market, and any discrimination against a person on the ground of their nationality is strictly forbidden. However, given that the Portuguese rely heavily on personal connections and networks for recruitment, and that perfect Portuguese will be a prerequisite for the majority of jobs, foreigners will instantly find themselves at a disadvantage.

Another disadvantage of the Portuguese labour market is that the country has the lowest per capita income in the euro area and until the recent enlargement, it also had the lowest in the EU. Income per head has remained at around 73% of the EU average ever since 1996 and the average salary currently works out at just £8,000 per annum. Low labour costs have traditionally been Portugal's method of luring the large multi-national companies to establish subsidiaries and plants there. However, foreign investment has taken a massive downturn, tumbling by over €5 billion per annum in the last four years. It is also very likely that the accession of ten new states to the EU in 2004 will grab the attention of the multi-nationals, who will be able to set up new operations there with even lower overheads.

Although the cost of living in Portugal is lower than in northern Europe, and activities such as eating out are still reasonably cheap, workers are justified in complaining that wages have lagged far behind prices. The cost of living has been rising for a number of years and this looks set to continue.

All in all then, the prospects for finding work in Portugal do not, on the face of it, appear to be terribly good. The problem is the conditions of the Portuguese economy, where there is strong competition from local and other EU staff. A traditional way around this, as in many other countries, for those seeking employment there, is to find an area (like English-language teaching) where your language or other skills will put you at an advantage. In financial services and banking, now that this sector has been modernised and brought more into line with other EU countries, as well as in the field of business advice, UK workers may often have expertise which is at a premium in this rapidly changing economy. Certainly, in most areas of work, you will require a high degree of specialised technical knowledge and probably Portuguese language skills as well.

Residence and Work Regulations

EU nationals do not need a work permit to work in Portugal, but a residence permit is obligatory for those working there (see the chapter on *Residence and Entry Regulations* where full details are given). Non-EU workers however, will require a work permit. There are at present certain categories of worker who may come from outside the EU and who are also exempt from work permits: au pairs, academics employed by Portuguese universities, teachers employed at international or American schools etc.

An exception to the above is that for jobs lasting up to 30 days, no permit is required; but the worker must have his or her passport stamped at the *Serviço de Estrangeiros e Fronteiras* (Avenida António Augusto Aguiar 20, Lisbon; ☎213-143112; offices also in Porto, Coimbra, Faro, Madeira and the Azores). This minimal regulation may be appropriate for construction workers etc. on short contracts.

For artists, freelance journalists, photographers and those who handmake things to sell, and other small business operations, the tax office (as in Britain) requires a record of payment. The usual way to do this is to obtain a book of receipts (*Cadernata de Recibos*) from the tax office. It is advisable to consult an accountant at the outset on the correct way to maintain records as regulations are liable to change.

PROFESSIONAL MOBILITY

Mutual Recognition of Qualifications

Anyone with a professional qualification, that they wish to use for employment purposes in Portugal will need to have that qualification recognised under Portuguese labour law. In recent years, the recognition of foreign qualifications for EU citizens has been rationalised. The General System for Mutual Recognition of Professional Qualifications was introduced to enable fully qualified professionals from one EU country to join the equivalent profession in Portugal without having to re-qualify. If you hold a qualification entitling you to practice a regulated profession in your Member State of origin, this is sufficient to establish that you are eligible for consideration under the general system.

There are two EU directives regarding this. To be eligible for assessment under EU directive 89/48/EEC you must have successfully completed a degree level course of at least three years' duration and also successfully completed any professional training required to enable you to practice the profession concerned. The second directive is 92/51/EEC which covers those educated below degree level (i.e. qualifications gained through any post-secondary course of more than one year, such as NVQs or SVQs, or work experience).

The requirements for the recognition of qualifications varies according to profession. For some areas, such as medical or nursing studies, the Portuguese authorities claim that recognition is almost immediate. However, in other cases (such as lawyers for example) the system is far more complicated and may require a trial period. Further information is available from Portuguese job centres (see *Sources of Jobs* below), or from the National Academic Recognition Centre (NARIC), whose head office in Portugal is at NARIC, *Direcção-Geral do Ensino Superior*, Avenida Duque D'Avila 137, 1069-016 Lisboa (☎213-126000; fax 213-126001; www.naric.org.uk). You should not contact NARIC in the UK if you are going to work in Portugal. Those who require recognition of a post-degree level qualification should contact the IEFP (*Instituto do Emprego e Formação Profissional*, Departamento de Certicação, Rua de Xabregas 52, 1949-003 Lisbon).

Those who require an equivalence of their school qualifications in order to continue studying in Portugal, should be able to do so at the school at which they enrol in Portugal. If not, they can apply to CIREP (*Centro de Informação e Relações Públicas, Direcção-Geral do Ensino Secundário*, Avenida 24 de Julho 134 C,k 1350-346 Lisbon (☎213-932860; fax 213-951776).

British crafts or trades people such as hairdressers or construction workers who wish to work in Portugal can apply to have their experience certified under the UK Certificate of Experience scheme administered by the Department for Education and Skills. Their role is to implement Directive 99/42/EEC (the so called Third Directive) concerning the mutual recognition of experience gained in a profession in EU member countries. A certificate costs £105 and takes fifteen days to process. Contact DfES, Certificates of Experience Team, Qualifications for Work Division, Room E3B, Moorfoot, Sheffield S1 4PQ; ☎0114-259 4237; www.defs.gov.uk/europeopen. A great deal of information on professional bodies and EC directives can be found on the EU website http://citizens.eu.int.

Those looking to transfer professional qualifications, may well be hoping to operate as a self-employed worker (*trabalhador por conta própria*). Further information about self-employment can be found in the following chapter, *Starting a Business*.

SOURCES OF JOBS

Unfortunately, in Portugal, personal contacts are incredibly important for job-seeking. Recruitment is often conducted through informal networks such as family and friendship ties, and word of mouth. This is especially the case in the lower-skills end of the job-market, and many of these jobs do not even reach the job pages. To a large extent this reflects the dominance of small employers in Portugal. The importance of networking cannot be over-emphasised, and although it is more difficult for a foreigner, the effort will be appreciated. Word-of-mouth information about a potential employee and references can be extremely helpful in supporting an application.

As already mentioned, one of the most promising areas for jobs for those who have not been posted there by their company (and who may not speak Portuguese) is among the expatriates, or in teaching English as a foreign language (otherwise known as TEFL). Newspapers and magazines can be a useful wellspring of vacancies in these fields. One of the best ways of going about looking for a job is to make a speculative trip to make contacts, especially among the foreign residents and the language schools, who are likely to be the most useful source of information about jobs and may even offer you employment on the spot.

The relative ease of air communications makes this a good approach to getting a job there and will help you make some practical preparations for your move as well (finding somewhere to live, or familiarising yourself a little more with the country). Making a reconnaissance trip is not as extravagant as one might think: in spring 2005 return flights to Faro were as little as £110. This can also help you avoid making more expensive mistakes further down the line, and to find out more about Portuguese life and culture. Job prospectors, once there, can also consult the English-language press as another possible source of temporary or permanent employment; or visit the various high street employment or accommodation agencies, or the local British Council office. If you are unemployed in the UK and have been receiving contribution based Jobseeker's Allowance it is also your right to go to Portugal, or the other EU countries, to look for work, and still receive your benefit while you are there. Contact your local Job Centre, or fax the Overseas Benefit Directorate on 0191-218 7652 or ☎0191-218 7777. They have a Factsheet No. 1 with information on how to do this.

Any UK citizen who has a sufficient level of Portuguese (or Portuguese friends who can help) can also consult the *emprego* (work) columns of Portuguese newspapers like the *Diário de Notícias* or *Público*.

USEFUL WEBSITES

Increasingly the trend for job-hunters is to use the internet. A wealth of online databases and resources exists, but as is often the case with the internet, some resources are very useful, whereas others are out-of-date or poorly maintained. Some of the best websites are listed below, but it is a necessary evil to trawl the net for new and specialised sites which may be of greater use to your specific circumstances.

www.iefp.pt: The website of Portugal's national employment institute (*Instituto do Emprego e Formação Profissional*). Website in English currently under construction.
www.jobpilot.co.uk: More than 56,000 vacancies worldwide, searchable by sector, country and language.
www.anyworkanywhere.com: Mostly jobs with tour operators in Portugal.
www.eurojobs.com: Pan-European job-search facility.
www.hays.pt: Portuguese page of Hays recruitment specialists, specialising in jobs in accountancy, IT, telecoms, engineering, construction, logistics, and sales & marketing. English translation available.
www.manpower.pt: International recruitment agency with offices throughout Portugal – searchable website.
www.adecco.pt: International recruitment agency with offices throughout Portugal – searchable website.
http://empregos.online.pt: Portuguese language site claiming to display the most recent job offers in Portugal gathered from numerous recruitment websites.
www.net-empregos.com: Portuguese language site. Allows you to upload your CV and apply for vacancies online.
http://superemprego.sapo.pt: Portuguese language site listing jobs throughout Portugal.

Newspapers
Newspapers and Directories Published in Britain. It is most unlikely that you will find a great many general vacancies in Portugal advertised in major national UK newspapers, or even international ones. There may be advertisements for specialists in law, accountancy, computing, and so on, which will generally be

found in the relevant issue or section, but very few will be based in Portugal. The only exception is vacancies for English language teachers, which are advertised from time to time in the *Times Educational Supplement* and the Education pages of the *Guardian*. The summer is the best time to look as language schools recruit staff for the next academic year.

For anyone interested in working in a specialised area, the relevant trade magazine (*Caterer and Hotelkeeper* for catering, *Certified Accountant* for accountancy, and so on) will probably be your best bet, and a visit to your local library (before you decide to take out a subscription) will be a way of finding out how many vacancies in Portugal are offered. Newspapers and magazines, needless to say, can also keep you in touch with your chosen area of work or business. In the UK, *The Financial Times* carries the most European (and Portuguese) news, with occasional special reports on Portugal which will certainly be worth tracking down, again probably through your local library which should keep back copies.

Also, there are all the books published by Vacation Work, especially *Teaching English Abroad, Work Your Way Around the World*, and the annual *Summer Jobs Abroad*, each of which contain a range of information about Portugal and recruiters of English teachers, in temporary or summer jobs like hotel work and summer camps. Contact: Vacation Work, 9 Park End Street, Oxford OX1 1HJ; fax 01865-790885; www.vacationwork.co.uk.

English-Language Newspapers and Magazines Published in Portugal. Job vacancies (e.g. au pair, private English tutors) often appear in the weekly *Anglo-Portuguese News* published on Thursdays in Lisbon (Apartado 113, 2766-902 Estoril; ☎214-661423; fax 214-660358). In the Algarve, these are also to be found in *The News* (Apartado 13, 84021 Lagoa, Algarve; ☎282-341100; fax 282-341201; www.the-news.net). These are both on sale at most news-stands where foreign newspapers are to be found. You can also place job-wanted advertisements in either of these papers.

Portuguese Newspapers and Magazines. Portugal has a surprisingly large selection of situations vacant in its national newspapers, e.g. *Diário de Notícias, Público, Journal de Notícias*, and the weekly business and politics magazine *Expresso* (Jobs are listed under *Emprego* – employment). *Expresso,* published on Saturdays, is the most important newspaper for specialist and management vacancies – the job supplement, *Expresso Emprego*, contains up to twenty pages of quality jobs. Amongst the daily newspapers, the Lisbon-based daily, *Diário de Notícias*, carries the most vacancies, especially on Sundays. The more popular morning daily, *Correio da Manhã*, which is widely read in the south, also carries job advertisements, mainly for skilled and unskilled staff in the services. The *Jornal de Notícias* carries jobs primarily for Porto and the northern region. The monthly publications, *Exame*, is also a useful resource as it provides employer information and a good background to business in Portugal.

Evidently you will need some knowledge of the Portuguese language (although occasionally some of these ads appear in English); and a large degree of optimism is also required if you apply for many of these jobs, which include restaurant workers, cooks and other domestic staff, shop assistants etc. Competition with Portuguese nationals is an obstacle of some magnitude, so it is better to aim higher, or at the general vacancies where speaking English, or some other experience or skill which you have, is specified. Portuguese newspapers will probably have to be consulted on the spot as they are not easily obtainable outside Portugal but may be available in some London newsagents, in specialised libraries, e.g. university and business libraries, and in the Canning House library in London (2 Belgrave Square, London SW1X 8PJ). Alternatively you may consult their online editions: www.correiomanha.ot; www.dn.pt; www.Diárioeconomico.com; http://online. expresso.pt; www.jNotícias.pt; www.publico.pt.

Professional Associations

Many professional associations do not provide official information on working overseas as such. However, many of them will have knowledge of their counterpart associations in other EU countries acquired during negotiations involving the recognition of qualifications, as required by the EU directives (see above). Such associations, when pushed, should provide some help to individuals.

Details of all professional associations are to be found in the directory, *Trade Associations and Professional Bodies of the United Kingdom*, available at most reference libraries. There is also a *European Directory of Trade and Business Associations* available in some business libraries. It is certainly worth trying to contact the Portuguese equivalent of UK professional associations: the UK body may be able to provide a contact. Some of the main associations are given below.

Additionally some trade unions have contacts with their counterparts in Portugal, so it is worth contacting them for information. A list of Portuguese trade unions can be found under *Sindicatos* in the Portuguese yellow pages (*Paginas Amarelas*).

Portuguese Professional Organisations:

Ordem dos Advogados (Lawyers): Largo s Domingos 14, 1º, 1169-060 Lisbon; ☎218-823550; www.oa.pt.

Ordem dos Medicos (Medical Staff): Avenida Almirante Gago Coutinho, Nº151, 1749-084 Lisboa; ☎218-027100; www.ordemdosmedicos.pt.

Ordem dos Arquitectos (Architects): Edifício Banhos São Paulo, Tr. Carvalho 23, 1200 Lisboa; ☎213-241140; fax 213-241101; e-mail cdn@aap.pt; www.aap.pt.

UK Employment Agencies/The EURES Scheme

Only a few UK-based international employment agencies will consider handling job vacancies in Portugal. Your best bet, somewhat surprisingly, for a speculative application, is likely to be your local Jobcentre which, under the EURES scheme, can help you complete an application form (if you have suitable language and other skills) to be forwarded to the employment service in Portugal. The Euroadviser at the Jobcentre will also have access to the useful *Eurofacts* leaflets on Portugal, and vacancies which UK Jobcentres have been notified of, through EURES, in Portugal. See the EURES website (http://europa.eu.int/jobs/eures) for contact details for the EURES Advisers in Portugal and for registered vacancies (only 10 in all of Portugal at the time of writing). The exceptions, so far as private agencies are concerned, are entertainment agencies which send dancers, magicians, disc jockeys and so on abroad on two or three month contracts and will arrange work permits and also some au pair agencies.

Employment Organisations in Portugal

Private Portuguese Employment Agencies. These exist for all categories of workers, but they are less useful for finding blue-collar work – there are more for specialists and executives. Agencies may undertake all stages of the recruitment process, from advertising to testing and selecting a candidate.

Employment agencies are probably not much use for finding a job unless one is proficient in Portuguese. However they are listed in the *Paginas Amarelas* under *Pessoal Temporário* (Temporary Personnel) and *Pessoal – Recrutamento e Selecção* (Personnel Recruitment and Selection). The majority are based in Lisbon and Porto although some of the larger chains have offices all over Portugal. For example, *Manpower* (head office: Rua Jose Fontana 9C, 1050 Lisbon; ☎213-129830; fax 213-129849; www.manpower.pt), Adecco (head office: Av. Duque de Loulé, 47A, 1069-154 Lisboa; ☎213-117700; fax 213-117749; www.adecco.pt), and Randstad (head office: Rua Joshua Benoliel 6, Edificio Alto das Amoreiras, 9ºB/10ºB, 1250-133 Lisboa; ☎213-715250; fax 213-715252; www.randstad. pt) all have offices throughout Portugal. The individual office addresses can be found on their websites.

Temporary Employment Agencies. These are fairly widespread throughout Portugal, and may be worth contacting as *trabalho temporário* is a good way to get a foot in the door at a particular company. These agencies are licensed under Portuguese labour law to place workers at the disposal of another enterprise. The maximum duration of a temporary work contract is 12 months, depending on the motive for using a temporary worker. Portuguese law has adopted a fairly restrictive position regarding these agencies – the situations in which temps may be employed are strictly limited to the following scenarios:

O   To replace existing employees who are absent or prevented from working.
O   To fill jobs which are temporarily vacant.
O   To cope with a temporary or exceptional increase in workload.
O   For short-lived and seasonal tasks.

Portuguese Government Job Centres. The Portuguese equivalent of the UK Jobcentres are the *Centros Emprego* of which there are about 84 countrywide. They are unlikely to help anyone who is unable to communicate in Portuguese. In addition to operating a placement service they also give assistance to entrepreneurs. Although primarily a service for Portuguese nationals, the job centres have an obligation, imposed by EU regulations to be of assistance to nationals of other EU countries. However, as in France, where the government employment offices are notoriously unhelpful to foreigners, do not expect them to bend over backwards to help you even if you do speak the language. Government job centres come under the *Ministério do Emprego e Segurança Social* (Ministry of Employment and Social Security) who publish a list of addresses and telephone numbers of the Centres in the *Anuário dos Serviços Públicos*. The main regional offices of the Portuguese job centres are listed below.

Useful Addresses
Delegação Regional do Alentejo: Rua do Menin Jesus 47-51, 7000-601 Evora; ☎266-760500.
Delegação Regional do Algarve: Rua Dr Cândido Guerreiro, 45-1º, Edifício Nascente, 8000-318 Faro; ☎289-980100.
Delegação Regional do Centro: Avenida Fernão de Magalhães 660; 3001-174 Coimbra; ☎239-860800.
Delegação Regional de Lisbon e Vale do Tejo: Rua das Picoas 14, 1069-003 Lisbon; ☎213-307400.
Delegação Regional do Norte: Rua Engº Ezequiel Campos 488, 4149-004 Porto; ☎226-159200.

Other Sources of Information
Chambers of Commerce: Chambers of Commerce exist to serve the interests of businesses trading in both Portugal and the UK; they do not act as employment agencies. Nevertheless, their repositories of information about member companies could prove invaluable if one wanted to know which companies customarily employ UK nationals. It is possible they may even know which companies currently have vacancies. Thus it is worth consulting these chambers of commerce and business associations on the off chance that they can be of assistance: *Associação Industrial Portuguesa (Portuguese Industrial Association):* Praça das

Indústrias, 1300-307 Lisbon; ☎213-601000; fax 213-641301; e-mail aip@aip.
pt; www.aip.pt.
Câmara do Comércio Luso-Británica (The British-Portuguese Chamber of Commerce):
Rua da Estrêla 8, 1200-669 Lisbon; ☎213-942020; fax 213-942029; e-mail
info@bpcc.pt; www.bilateral.biz.
The Portuguese-UK Business Network: 4th Floor, 11 Belgrave Square, London
SW1X 8PP; ☎020-7201 6638; fax 020-7201 6637; www.portuguese-chamber.
org.uk.
ICEP Portugal: Av. 5 de Outubro, nº 101, 1050-051 Lisbon; ☎217-909500; fax
217-935028; e-mail icep@icep.pt; www.icep.pt.
Portuguese Trade and Tourism Office (UK): Portuguese Embassy, 11 Belgrave
Square, London SW1X 8PP;   ☎020-7201 6666; fax 020-7201 6633; e-mail
trade.london@iecp.pt; www.portugalinbusiness.com.
Portuguese Trade Commission: 590 Fifth Avenue, 3rd Floor, New York, NY 10036-
4702; ☎212-354 4610; fax 212-575 4737; www.portugal.org.

The Hispanic and Luso Brazilian Council (Canning House, 2 Belgrave Square,
London SW1X 8PJ; ☎020-7235 2303; fax 020-7235 3587; www.canninghouse.
com) publishes a well-researched leaflet called *Portugal: A Guide to Employment and
Opportunities for Young People* aimed primarily at the younger worker/traveller.

Advertising in Newspapers

It is sometimes possible to attract a job offer from an employer by placing an
advertisement in either the Portuguese press or the English-language newspapers
published in Portugal. Advertisements in the Portuguese press can be placed
through the agents Powers International in London (100 Rochester Row, London
SW1P 1JP; ☎020-7592 8325; fax 020-7592 8326) who deal with the following
newspapers and magazines: *Diário de Notícias* (Lisbon daily), *Jornal de Notícias*
(Porto daily), *Expresso* (weekly newspaper), *Negocios* (biannual business magazine),
and *Público* (a national daily published in Lisbon and Porto).

On a more local level, both the Algarve based publication, *The News* (☎282-
341100; e-mail classads@the-news.net) and the *Anglo-Portuguese News* (☎241-
661423) accept adverts.

The Application Procedure

Speculative letters of application are very common in Portugal and are often
successful. A useful source of potential companies for you to target is provided
at the end of this chapter. Another useful resource is *The Directory of Jobs and
Careers Abroad* (Vacation Work Publications), which has a list of British companies
with Portuguese connections and subsidiaries. The British Portuguese Chamber

of Commerce website (www.bilateral.biz) also lists numerous companies with interests in both countries as part of its fully-searchable members database. Remember that all multi-national companies have their own websites and the majority of these will have a careers section, advertising any current vacancies.

Speculative letters targeting specific companies may seem like a long shot, but in fact many companies prefer to recruit this way and the European Employment Service (EURES) advises people to take this approach in Portugal.

Applications, spontaneous or otherwise, usually take the form of a covering letter, with a CV and a recent photograph. Copies of educational or professional certificates are not required until interview stage. Covering letters are usually short and simple and certainly no more than one page of A4. The covering letter should highlight the most relevant aspects of your CV and should be tailored to each specific company. Portuguese recruiters tend to value professional experience most of all, followed by practical training.

Application forms are also fairly widespread for both blue-collar and white-collar positions and whilst some are fairly standardised, others use more open questions. Discriminating questions regarding sex, race, country of origin, ideology or religious belief are forbidden.

A CV in Portugal should run to no more than two pages, and should be clearly presented and structured. All of the features of a standard British or American CV should be included: personal details, education, professional training, work experience, leisure activities etc. One difference is that whereas the British tend to put their most significant experience, or most recent experience first, Portuguese CVs tend to be in chronological order. You should be aware of the fact that non-vocational degrees do not hold much status in Portugal. The Portuguese are more accustomed to degrees that are directly relevant to the job to which you are applying. Most employers therefore require graduates of economics, business studies, law, or relevant scientific, engineering or technical disciplines. Model CVs and advice on how to write your CV are available on most public employment websites in Portugal (see above).

If you feel that the covering letter, application form and CV should be in Portuguese, then you may need to employ the services of a translator. The *Institute of Translation and Interpreting* (Fortuna House, South Fifth Street, Milton Keynes MK9 2EU; ☎01908-325250; fax 01908-325259; e-mail info@iti.org.uk; www. iti.org.uk) can put people in touch with freelance translators who will provide a fluent translation, for a fee.

A short-listed application will always lead to an interview, as this is the primary selection technique in Portugal. Take copies of your CV, any relevant qualifications, employer recommendations and any other documents which may prove useful along with you to interview. In every interview, but especially in an interview in Portugal, first impressions and appearances count. However many interviewers there are, the meeting is still likely to be a formal one in Portugal

– you will find that a casual approach to interviews has yet to become fashionable. Companies will invariably want to know how good your Portuguese is, and if you have lied on your CV, you are sure to be caught out at interview. Language ability may prove to be as much of a challenge as proving your suitability for the job in general, whether you are going for a high-flying position or a more basic job.

It is important, before an interview, to find out as much background information as possible about the company and the position for which you have applied. An interest in the company and its activities (based on knowledge and hard facts) is more likely to impress your potential employer than your general enthusiasm. It is also a good idea to show an interest in Portuguese culture, and a knowledge of the country in general. It is advisable not to mention anything to do with salary until you are asked, which is usually during the final stages of the interview procedure.

It is not unusual, as in the UK, for the interview procedure to involve aptitude and psychometric testing. Such tests are used for candidates up to middle level management, especially when recruitment consultants are involved. Assessment centres however, are still a relatively rare phenomenon in Portugal.

JOB OPPORTUNITIES

CASUAL/SEASONAL WORK

During the summer season casual positions for English-speakers are fairly plentiful. There is an estimated population of 12,000 expat Britons in Portugal, a great many of whom run bars, restaurants, bookshops, etc. catering mainly for an Anglophone clientele and therefore staffed by English speakers. The majority of expatriate businesses are small (and therefore have only occasional job vacancies) and located in the Algarve or on the Lisbon coast from Setúbal to Cascais. Entertainers and watersports instructors may find on-the-spot openings. Ask expatriates for help and advice in your search for a job.

The thousands of Britons and other Europeans who take their holidays on the Algarve create many job opportunities in bars and restaurants. Generally speaking, jobs in bars, restaurants etc. can most easily be found by making a reconnaissance trip to Portugal. The majority of expatriate businesses are located on the Algarve and the Lisbon coast from Setúbal north to Cascais.

According to Emma-Louise Parkes, Albufeira and the surrounding area is the place to head

I arrived at Faro Airport in June last year, and went straight to the Montechoro area of Albufeira. A job hunter here will be like a kid in a sweet shop. By 12.15pm I was

> *in the resort, by 12.30pm I had found somewhere to stay and had been offered at least four jobs by the evening, one of which I started at 6pm. All the English workers were really friendly individuals and were a goldmine of information. Jobs-wise, I was offered bar work, touting, waitressing, cleaning, packing ice cubes into bags, karaoke singing, nannying for an English bar owner, timeshare tout, nightclub dancer...I'm sure there were more. Touts can earn £16 a night with all the drink they can stomach while waitresses can expect a little less for working 10am-1pm and 6pm-10pm. Attractive females (like myself!) will be head-hunted by lively bars, whereas British men are seen by the locals as trouble and are usually kept behind bars (serving bars that is) and in cellars.*

Alternatively jobs may occasionally be advertised in the local English-language press (see *Sources of Jobs* above). Scan the advertisements in the weekly *Anglo-Portuguese News* (Apartado 113, 2766-902 Estoril; ☎214-661551) or place your own advert in this paper, though the rates are fairly expensive.

Up-to-date guide-books and hotel guides are as good a source as any for finding expatriate-run hotels and restaurants which may employ UK staff in the summer. The four-star Monte do Casal Country House Hotel in Estoi on the Algarve has been seen advertising recently for a receptionist and other staff (Cerro do Lobo, Estoi, 8005-436, Faro, Algarve; www.montedocasal.pt). The Frog at Expo, a popular brew pub, part of the French chain of Frog Pubs (Rua da Pimenta 17-21 Parque das Nações 1990-280 Lisboa; www.frogpubs.com) employs English speakers as bar staff, shift managers, pub managers, chefs, brewers, waiting staff etc. year round.

ACADEMIC STAFF

Another area of employment where English-speaking staff are likely to be indispensable is in providing education based on the English curriculum. There are several British schools in Lisbon, Porto and the Algarve which follow the British National Curriculum and offer GCSE/A-level exams etc. There are also schools that offer the American-style curriculum, as well as international schools preparing pupils for the International Baccalaureate. As a result there is a high demand for suitably qualified staff (i.e. those with full teaching qualifications – a PGCE or a B.Ed.), especially as staff turnover tends to be quite high in these schools. Interested parties should make enquiries about possible vacancies direct to the schools concerned. Their addresses can be found in Chapter Four, *Daily Life*. The weekly English-language newspaper on the Algarve, *The News*, often carries advertisements for teachers as well as offering frequent education reports. These are also available online at www.the-news.net.

An applicant who already lives on the spot is likely to be favoured, making this kind of work popular with the spouses of those who are already living and working there, as is also often the case with English language teaching (see below). However, those applying from abroad should send their speculative applications between January and June for jobs beginning in September.

One way of getting a foot in the door at a Portuguese school, or of testing the water before making the move permanently, is by applying for the British Council's Teacher Exchange Programme. An exchange can last for six weeks, one term, or a full academic year. Those eligible for the programme are teachers of modern languages with a minimum of two years experience working at secondary school level. To take part in the exchange, teachers must find an exchange partner in Portugal. Contact the British Council for advice and guidance as to how to do this: *Teacher Exchange Europe,* The British Council, 10 Spring Gardens, London SW1A 2BN; ☎020-7389 4447; fax 020-7389 4426; e-mail teacher.programme s@britishcouncil.org; www.britishcouncil.org.

TEACHING ENGLISH

Relations between Portugal and Britain have always been warm and the market for English tuition is as buoyant as it is anywhere in Europe, especially in the teaching of young children. Most schools cater for anyone over the age of seven, so you should be prepared to teach little ones. In fact some schools organise courses in nursery schools for children from the age of four. Furthermore Portugal's economy has taken considerable strides over the past two decades which has created a bigger demand for English for Special Purposes, especially business. One school has even run an 'English for footballers' course.

The vast majority of British tourists flock to the Algarve along the southern coast of Portugal, which means that many Portuguese in the south who aspire to work in the tourist industry want to learn English. Schools like the *Centro de Linguas* in Lagos and *Interlingua* in Portimao cater for just that market. But the demand for English teachers is greatest in the north. Apart from in the main cities of Lisbon and Porto, both of which have British Council offices, jobs crop up in historic provincial centres such as Coimbra (where there is also a British Council) and Braga and in small seaside towns like Aveiro and Póvoa do Varzim. These can be a very welcome destination for teachers burned out from teaching in big cities or first-time teachers who want to avoid the rat-race. The British Council (www. britishcouncil.org/portugal) has English language centres in a number of towns,: Almada, Alverca, Cascais (the prosperous seaside suburb of Lisbon), Coimbra, Foz do Douro, Maia, Miraflores and Parede.

Fixing Up a Job

Most teachers in Portugal have either answered adverts in the educational press or are working for International House which has nine affiliated schools in Portugal.

About three-quarters of all IH students in Portugal are children, so expertise with young learners is a definite asset. Outside the cities where there have traditionally been large expatriate communities, schools cannot depend on English speakers just showing up and so must recruit well in advance of the academic year (late September to the end of June).

The *Bristol School Group* offers the only possibility of which we have heard for working in the Azores, so if you want to work in the most isolated islands in the Atlantic Ocean – over 1,000km west of Portugal – this is your chance. Small groups of schools, say six schools in a single region, is the norm in Portugal. A number of the schools listed below belong to such mini-chains. One of the most well-established is the *Cambridge Schools* group which every year imports up to 100 teachers.

The British Council offices may have lists of local English language schools in their region, but they probably won't be willing to send them to enquirers. Many schools are small family-run establishments with fewer than ten teachers, so sending off a lot of speculative applications is unlikely to succeed.

As is true anywhere, you might be lucky and fix up something on the spot. In addition to calling at the British Council, check the English language weekly newspaper *Anglo-Portuguese News* which occasionally carries adverts for private tutors.

The Cambridge CELTA is widely requested by schools and can be obtained at International House in Lisbon (or part-time in Porto).

Conditions of Work

The consensus seems to be that wages are low, but have been improving at a favourable rate in view of the cost of living which is also low. Working conditions are generally relaxed. The normal salary range is €700-€1,000 net per month. Full-time contract workers are entitled to an extra month's pay after 12 months, which is partly why most teachers are employed on 9/10 month contracts. Some schools pay lower rates but subsidise or pay for flights and accommodation. Several provide free Portuguese lessons. Salaries in Lisbon are significantly higher than in the small towns of northern Portugal. Teachers being paid on an hourly basis should expect to earn €10-€15, but they will of course not be eligible for the thirteenth month bonus or paid holidays.

Contracts are for a minimum of nine months though some are for a calendar year. Several International House schools have flats for their teachers. On average teachers spend about a quarter of their net salary on rent which is lower than in some other European countries. In fact the cost of living in Portugal is among the lowest in the European Union. For example the three-hour journey Lisbon-Porto on a high-speed train costs only €30.

Since most teachers working for nine months are working on a freelance basis, they are responsible for paying their own taxes and contributions, which amount to about 20% of gross salary. Tax is paid on a sliding scale and most teachers on nine-month contracts with no other source of income will not necessarily be liable for tax. By law, all employers must insure their employees against work-related accidents. For eventualities outside work, teachers should insure themselves.

Teaching English in Portugal – Lesley Keast

Lesley Keast was an English teacher in Italy when she spotted an opening at a school in Setúbal, south of Lisbon. The job appealed to her because it gave her the chance to work with students that she had not previously worked with (children aged 10-13). She thoroughly enjoyed the experience:

I had a great time teaching in Portugal. I found Portuguese children full of life and fun. Some of them are also quite serious about study and realise it's important. Children have a lot of tests at school and often have a lot of homework to do so that restricted my expectations of giving them homework – they are, after all, only young and were getting English input in their schools as well as the private school I worked at. Children get lessons in English from the age of 8 so by the age of 10 they already have a good grasp of present and past tenses, and basic vocabulary, but more importantly have some confidence in using the language and want very much to use it to communicate.

Having lived in Italy I was expecting to have to wade through a lot of paperwork to get myself official and working. Surprisingly it was very easy to get things organised, but I think a lot of that was down to the fact that my employers (who were Portuguese) knew the systems and helped new teachers out beyond the call of duty i.e. taking me down to the bank to open an account and the office to organise my national insurance contributions/organise tax documentation.

My working conditions were very good. I taught a 24-hour week Monday to Friday, and because I was only teaching children most evenings I finished teaching at 19.30. My salary was the same as my salary in Italy, which was attractive as the cost of living is much lower in Portugal and my accommodation was provided free.

I found my job on the internet but you don't see many jobs advertised for Portugal. Whereas for a lot of EFL jobs there are always people moving on, people seem to settle in Portugal and stay in their post for a while. At my school there were people who had been there for 15, 5 and 4 years – much longer than the regular EFL teacher, who considers 2 years as a 'good stint'.

Useful Addresses – Training Centres

International House Lisbon: Rua Marquês Sá da Bandeira 16, 1050-148 Lisbon; ☎213-151493/4/6; fax 213-530081; e-mail ttraining@ihlisbon.com; www. international-house.com. CELTA courses 10 times a year (€1,280). Also part time DELTA course (€2,000) and IH Younger Learners Certificate (€630).

Useful Addresses – Schools that Regularly Recruit English Teachers

American Language Institute Lisbon: Av. Duque de Loulé 22-1°, 1050-090 Lisbon; ☎213-152535; fax: 213-524848; e-mail ali@netcabo.pt; www.americanlangu ageinstitute.com.

Bristol Schools Group: Instituto de Línguas da Maia, Trav. Dr. Carlos Pires Felgueiras, 12-3°, 4470-158 Maia; ☎229-488803; fax: 229-486460; e-mail bsmaia@bristolschool.pt; www.bristolschool.pt. Group of 9 small schools in Porto, inland and in the Azores.

CAFLI: Praceta Paulo Emilil 100, R/Ch, 3510-723 Viseu; tel/fax: 232-426266. e-mail: cafli7@hotmail.com.

Cambridge School: Avenida da Liberdade 173, 1250-141 Lisbon; ☎213-124600; fax: 213-534729; e-mail info@cambridge.pt; www.cambridge.pt. Portugal's largest private language school with 8 centres in Lisbon and other major cities.

Centro de Ingles de Famalicao: Edificio dos Correios, n° 116 - 4° Dto, Rua S. Joao de Deus, 4760 V.N. de Famalicao; tel/fax: 252-374233; e-mail cif@esoterica. pt.

CIAL – Centro de Linguas: Avenida Republica 14-2, 1050-191 Lisbon; ☎213-533733; fax: 213-523096; e-mail linguas.estrangeiras@cial.pt; www.cial.pt.

Citania Centro de Ingles: Av. Conde de Margaride 543, Sala 34, 4810-535 Guimãraes; ☎253-513757; e-mail citania-_ingles@msn.com.

Encounter English: Av. Fernão Magalhães 604, 4350-150 Porto; ☎225-367916; fax: 225-366339. Also at Avenida Boavista 80, 5°-D-s-38, 4050-112 Porto; ☎226-095410; fax 226-003453.

Instituto Britanico de Braga: Rua Conselheiro Januario 119-123, Apartado 2682, 4701-908 Braga; ☎253-263298; fax 253-619355; e-mail efl.IBB@mail. telepac.pt; www.alb-minho.pt.

Instituto de Linguas de S. Joao da Madeira: Largo Durbalino Laranjeira S/N, 3700 S. João da Madeira; ☎256-833906; fax 256-835887; e-mail institutodelingua s@hotmail.com or instituto.de.linguas@netvisao.pt.

Interlingua Instituto de Linguas: Lg. 1° de Dezembro 28, 8500-538 Portimao; ☎282-427690; fax 282-416030; e-mail interlingua@mail.telepac.pt.

International House (Lisbon): Rua Marquês Sá da Bandeira 16, 1050-148 Lisbon; ☎213-151493/4/6; fax 213-530081; e-mail info@ihlisbon.com; www. international-house.com.

International House (Porto): Rua Marechal Saldanha 145-1°, 4150-655 Porto; ☎226-177641; e-mail info@ihporto.org; www.ihporto.org. Also Leça da Palmeira, Rua Oliveira Lessa 350, 4450 Matosinhos; ☎229-959087.

Lancaster College: Praceta 25 de Abril 35-1°, 4430 Vila Nova de Gaia; ☎223-772030; fax 223-772039; e-mail info@lancastercollege.pt; www.lancastercollege. pt. Also at Covilhã, Estarrega, Santa Maria da Feira, Fafe, Oeiras, Arcozelo, Vizela and Estoril.

Manitoba Instituto de Linguas: Apartado 184, 4491-909 Póvoa de Varzim; tel/fax 252-683014; e-mail manitoba@aninet.pt.

Novo Instituto de Linguas: Rua Cordeiro Ferreira, 19C 1°Dto, 1750-071 Lisbon; tel/fax 217-590770; e-mail admin@nil.edu.pt; www.nil.edu.pt.

Oxford School: Rua D. Estefania, 165-1°, 1000-154 Lisbon; ☎213-546586; fax 213-141152. Also: Av. Marques Tomar 104-4°dto, 1050-157 Lisbon. ☎217-966660; fax 217-951293; e-mail oxford-school@mail.telepac.pt. Also Av. Bons Amigos, 37-1° Dto, 2735-077 Cacém; ☎219-146343; www.oxford-school.pt.

Pombalingua Escola de Ingles: Rua 1° de Malo, 6-1° Dto, 3100-477 Pombal. ☎236-214319; fax: 236-211064.

Royal School of Languages – Escolas de Linguas, Lda.: Rua José Rabumba 2, 3810-125 Aveiro. ☎234-429156/425104; fax 234-382870; e-mail rsl@royalschool oflanguages.pt; www.royalschooloflanguages.pt. Schools also in Porto, Agueda, Guarda, Ovar, Viseu, Mirandela, Macedo de Cavaleiros, Iihavo and Albergaria-a-Velha.

Sintralinguas Centro de Linguas: Avenida Movimento das Forças, Armada 14-3D, 2710-431 Sintra; tel/fax 219-234941; e-mail sintralingua@mail.telepac.pt.

Speakwell Escola de Linguas: Praça Mário Azevedo Gomes, N° 421, 2775-240 Parede. ☎214-561771; fax 214-561775; e-mail speakwell@speakwell.pt; www.speakwell.pt.

TOURISM

B ecause of Portugal's situation on the western side of the Iberian peninsula where the sea water is colder than the Mediterranean, it has not been mobbed to the same extent as Spain, with the exception of the Algarve coast between Faro and Lagos, which is lined with tower blocks. Other areas of Portugal such as Lisbon, Porto and the north attract a more up-market clientele. Hotels tend to be luxurious and self-catering villas have their own swimming pools and maids. However, none of the major UK camping tour operators includes Portugal sites, partly because of the great distance for motorists.

Tourism in Portugal employs around 6.5% of the active population and produces 8% of the country's GDP. Chances of finding work are best with tour operators or in hotels, restaurants and clubs along the Algarve coast. Portugal had a bonanza year in 2004, mainly due to Euro 2004, which took place across eight cities and created a range of employment opportunities for job-seekers. The resulting boost to the economy and to Portugal's prestige as a tourist destination, has meant that many of these opportunities did not end when the tournament did. However, the Portuguese are protective of their tourist industry and this has been formalised in law. For example foreign tour managers in charge of a coach must ensure that they pick up an official Portuguese guide at major tourist venues.

The mass-market beach resort operators (e.g. *Thomson, MyTravel, CT2* and *First Choice)* employ reps in Portugal. *Style Holidays* and *Open Holidays* both employ resort reps every year to work between April and October. Part-season short-term contracts may also be available. First Choice have about 100 staff in place who speak another language (not necessarily Portuguese). Apart from these and some of the Europe-wide tour operators like *Driveline Europe, Erna Low, Headwater* and *Solo's,* many of the tour operators that feature Portugal are specialisits. The founders of the well-known Travel Club of Upminster (54 Station Road, Upminster, Essex RM14 2TT; ☎01708-225000; www. travelclubofupminster.co.uk) virtually started tourism to Portugal from the UK when they fell in love with the country after the war. Occasionally they and other specialist tour operators like *Mundi Color* (276 Vauxhall Bridge Road, London SW1V 1BE; ☎020-7828 6021; www.mundicolor.co.uk), *Caravela Tours Ltd* (Chapter House, 22 Chapter St, London SW1P 4NP; ☎020-7630 5148) and *Destination Portugal* (Madeira House, 37 Corn Street, Witney, Oxon. OX8 7BW; ☎01993-771555; www.destination-portugal.co.uk) may need staff, but only if they can speak Portuguese. For links to UK tour operators to Portugal see the website of the Portuguese Trade & Tourism Office (www.portugalinsite.com).

A number of up market villa companies employ English staff to oversee the properties. Anyone applying for such a job would have to have a driving licence since the properties are often scattered. Note that these are plum jobs so there is little turnover:

Bonaventure Holidays, 6 Putney Common, London SW15 1HL (www. bonaventure-holidays.com).

Casas Cantabricas, 31 Arbury Road, Cambridge CB4 2JB (☎01223-328721; www.casas.co.uk).

CV Travel's Mediterranean World, The Manor Stables, West St, Great Somerford, Chippenham, Wilts. SN15 5EH (☎020-7581 0851; www.cvtravel.net).

Individual Travellers (Spain & Portugal), Manor Courtyard, Bignor, Pulborough, West Sussex RH20 1QD (☎01798-869485; e-mail portugal@indiv-travellers. com).

North Portugal Travel, Foxhill, Gambles Lane, Woodmancote, Cheltenham, Glos. GL52 4PU (☎01242-679867; www.northportugal.com).

Most tours from Brazil use Lisbon as their gateway to Europe, and people who can speak the language and know about European culture may be hired by one of these. One of the biggest is the Portuguese-owned company Abreu Travel (109 Westbourne Grove, London W2 4UW; ☎020-7229 9905) which handles incoming groups from Brazil.

Wine Tours

For over 600 years the British have drunk the wines of Portugal, and many companies offer specialist wine tours of the Porto region. Many of the families that work in this industry are of British ancestry. Summer jobs often become available showing visitors around the wine cellars and offering a history of winemaking.

The Douro River, lined by port wineries, is a hive of activity during the annual September barge event, when the *caravels* glide down the river. To work on these you would need to know both the language and the wine trade. There is also a hotel barge that operates on the river and occasionally needs staff.

Other Special Interest Tours

The lush countryside makes for some wonderful golfing facilities. Anyone who has worked at a golf club in the UK or US might try to work for a specialist operator in this field. Two companies to consider are Longshot Golf Holidays (Meon Travel, Meon House, College St, Petersfield, Hants. GU32 3JN; ☎0870-609 0995; www.longshotgolf.co.uk) and Supertravel Golf (Sandpiper House, 39 Queen Elizabeth St, London SE1 2BT; ☎020-7459 2984; golf@lotusgroup. co.uk). Many others can be found via the Association of Golf Tour Operators or AIGTO (www.aigto.com).

Portugal is a highly religious country and many religious pilgrimages are made, especially to the site of Our Lady at Fatima. The enormous piazza in front of the Basilica is said to hold a million people on the two main religious festivals (May 12/13 and October 12/13, the dates of the first and last appearances of the Virgin). Catholic church newspapers carry adverts for companies organising tours. Contact them if you speak Portuguese and want to work as a tour guide.

Walking and nature holiday operators take groups to the National Park of Peneda-Geres in the remote northern Serra da Peneda, e.g. Sherpa Tours (www. sherpa-walking-holidays.co.uk).

Useful Addresses

Bike Riders: PO Box 130254, Boston, MA 02113, USA; ☎617-723-2354; fax 617-723-2355; e-mail info@bikeriderstours.com; www.bikeriderstours.com. Bicycle tour holidays in Portugal. Recruit 20 tour guides for April to October.

CV Travel: 43 Cadogan St., London SW3 2PR; ☎020-7591 2800; fax 020-7591 2802; e-mail cv@cvtravel.net; www.cvtravel.net. Upmarket villa holiday company. Require overseas reps for the summer season.

Open Holidays: The Guildbourne Centre, Chapel Road, Worthing BN11 1LZ; ☎01903-201864; fax 01903-201225; e-mail recruitment@openholidays. co.uk; www.openholidays.co.uk. Villa and apartment holidays. Reps required March to October.

Scott Dunn: Fovant Mews, 12 Noyna Road, London SW17 7PH; ☎020-8682 5005; fax 020-8682 5090; e-mail recruitment@scottdunn.com; www.

scottdunn.com. Require summer resort managers, chefs, hosts, nannies etc.

Style Holidays: Coomb House, 7 St. John's Road, Isleworth, Middlesex TW7 6NH; ☎0870-442 3653; www.style-holidays.co.uk. Resort holidays in the Algarve and Madeira. Reps required April to October.

Travelsphere Ltd.: Compass House, Rockingham Road, Market Harborough, Leics LE16 7QD; ☎01858-410456; www.travelspehere.co.uk. Major coach tour operator. Require tour managers.

AU PAIR WORK

European au pairs are much less common in Portugal than nannies and childminders from former Portuguese colonies such as Mozambique and Brazil, as well as other developing nations. Virtually no British agencies undertake placements there. Yet the last few decades have seen very fast growth in the Portuguese economy and there may yet come a time when well-to-do Portuguese families look to British and other agencies for childcarers.

However, there are such sizeable expatriate British communities in the two main cities of Lisbon and Porto as well as on the Algarve, that there is some demand for English-speaking nannies and mother's helps in these households. Summer openings are most likely to occur in the school holidays between the end of July and the end of September. A few positions may be advertised in *The Lady* magazine (www.lady.co.uk). Another place to look for vacancies, or perhaps sign yourself up as a candidate is *Greycoat Placements Ltd* (Grosvenor Gardens House, 35-37 Grosvenor Gardens, London SW1W 0BS; ☎020-7233 9950; fax 020-7592 0096; e-mail info@greycoatplacements.co.uk; www.greycoatplacements. co.uk) who specialise in finding domestic staff of all kinds for families and have a *Greycoat International* department, which sometimes has positions with ex-pat families in Portugal. Other websites currently advertising positions in Portugal include www.greataupair.com, which serves 140 countries and has over 6,400 jobs available worldwide; and www.nanny-agency.com. Keep an eye also on the website of the *Instituto Portugues da Juventude* (www.juventude.gov.pt) which occasionally runs au pair programmes and international exchanges.

In Portugal there are currently two agencies worth trying for nanny, au pair, mother's help and general domestic work:

Babete & Avental Lda.: Travessa da Conceição a Lapa 11, 1200-633 Lisbon; ☎213-944010; fax 213-94 4011; www.babeteavental.pt.

Tagus: Rua Amilo Castelo Branco 20, 1250 Lisbon; ☎218-925454; www. viagenstagus.pt.

VOLUNTARY WORK

Portugal's voluntary movement is still in its infancy – its development stunted by the fact that Portugal spent most of the twentieth century under a fascist dictatorship. However the voluntary sector is growing and widening in scope, finally moving away from a reliance on parochial and inward-looking organisations. Recent years have seen a definite increase in the number of associations and voluntary work organisations, especially those involved in youth work. This is at least in part thanks to the state-supported *Instituto Portugues da Juventud - IPJ*, (Av. da Liberdade No. 194, 1269-051 Lisbon; ☎213-179200; http://juventude. gov.pt) which was established in the 1990s in order to promote voluntary work amongst young people, and which overseas a programme of heritage protection and other short-term voluntary projects. Information detailing IPJ voluntary programmes can be found at www.voluntariadojovem.pt. EU programmes such as the European Voluntary Service have also played a role in stimulating Portugal's development in this area.

There is certainly a need for voluntary programmes within Portugal – one in five people still lives beneath the EU's poverty line. Those who have the resources to involve themselves in voluntary projects will find that they are welcomed, especially if they can offer a particular skill, and speak adequate Portuguese. Bear in mind however that many of these organisations remain under-funded and often unprofessional. Nevertheless, big business has started to become involved in donating money to help fund solidarity programmes and some well-known NGOs such as Amnesty International run programmes in Portugal. Those interested in Portuguese NGOs should visit the website of *Plataforma Portuguesa das Organizações Não Governamentais para o Desenvolvimento* (www.plataformaongd. pt) which lists around fifty NGOs, mainly based in Lisbon. Unfortunately the website is only available in Portuguese.

Useful Addresses – Voluntary Work
Associação Abraço: Rua da Rosa 243, 1º, 1200-385 Lisbon; ☎213-425929; http://abraco.esoterica.pt. A non-profit, charitable association involved with HIV/AIDS. Always recruiting volunteers for fund-raising, information dissemination, and personal care.
Aldeias Internacionais de Crianças: Rua Anchieta 29-4º, 1200 Lisbon; ☎213-477647. Charitable organisation offering a home for disadvantaged and abandoned children.
Amnistia Internacional: 13, 1º Andar, 1070-128 Lisbon; ☎213-861664; fax 213-861782; www.amnistia-internacional.pt. Worldwide campaigners for human rights. May well need volunteers.
Banco Alimentar Contra o Fome: Estação de CP de Alcântara Terra/Armazem 1,

Avenida de Cueta, 1300-125 Lisbon; ☎213-649655 (Lisbon); ☎229-983140 (Porto). Institution devoted to redistributing food to the needy. Often looking for volunteers.

Fundação AMI: R. José do Patroncínio 49, 1949-008 Lisbon; ☎218-362100; fax 218-362199; www.fundacao-ami.org. Non-governmental international medical assistance organisation based in Portugal that runs a number of volunteer programmes.

OIKOS – Cooperação e Desenvolvimento: Rua de Santiago nº9, 1100-493 Lisbon; ☎218-823630; fax 218-823635; www.oikos.pt. NGO that runs voluntary projects fighting poverty and inequality.

Portuguese Association for Victim Support (APAV): Rua do Comércio 65-5º, 1100-150 Lisbon; ☎218-854090; fax 218-876351; www.apav.pt. Charity that provides confidential and free services and social support to victims of crime throughout Portugal.

Quinta das Abelhas: e-mail abelhas@pureportugal.co.uk; www.pureportugal.co.uk/abelhas. Alternative lifestyle/organic farming/low-impact living. Offer free camping and food in return for work.

Rotajovem: Largo do Mercado, 2750-431 Cascais; ☎214-862005; www.rotajovem.com. Youth projects.

ASPECTS OF EMPLOYMENT

Many people feel tempted to uproot themselves from Britain and live abroad, particularly when they have encountered unemployment at home; or to move on in their career; or to start a new one; or to experience a different way of life and culture. They may decide to move to Portugal on the basis of a marvellous two-week holiday spent on the Algarve coast, or a longer connection with the country. However, unwinding and relaxing in Portugal is not at all the same as living and working there. Working, especially, highlights quite another aspect of the country and potential employers in particular will not be impressed if your desire to live and work there is seen as a kind of extended holiday. A serious attitude to the job in hand is much more important for most than your wish to meet people and see the world, however much you enjoy travel, or living abroad. If you work in travel and tourism, though, it is better if this is one of your interests and if you do not enjoy meeting people, English language teaching – which often involves getting to know your students, and sometimes the interpersonal skills of knowing which ones not to get to know – may also be not quite your thing. In these shorter term areas, in particular, you can expect to work long hours for wages which are enough to live on, but usually not sufficient for a particularly high standard of living.

If working conditions in Portugal do not match up to British standards, then you can reflect that things – for the Portuguese at least – are getting better. It is true that in Portuguese-owned companies wages are generally low; but up until the year of Portugal's entry into the Common Market, even as the tourists cavorted happily in the resorts and on the golf courses of the Algarve, the economy was in such chaos that 150,000 Portuguese workers had no idea when, if at all, they would receive their wages. Times were so bad that they were providing their labour free on the mere promise of payment at some unspecified future date. Since then, changes have been made. For nearly twenty years employment contracts were the bugbear of Portuguese companies trying to adapt to the mechanisms of the market. These contracts had the force of state legislation in protecting the rights of employees, many of whom had security of tenure, regardless of the prevailing economic conditions. Although employers are marginally freer to dismiss and lay off workers, this is still an area that causes grave dissatisfaction to employers and economists. But there is nowadays some measure of protection for workers, in line with the social chapter of the Maastricht Treaty, which does not however always benefit foreign workers.

If the Portuguese government follows this path of improved efficiency, training and investment – and not just a low wage economy – the prospects for international workers, and working conditions generally, will be good. Such considerations should of course be weighed against the local cost of living, but there are increasing signs that wages are keeping pace with inflation. In the short-term, the situation vis-á-vis working conditions in Portugal is likely to improve in the next few years as the economy reaps the benefits of an expanded market, industrial modernisation and increased output, as well as continuing foreign investment and the arrival of more UK and international companies. But in the medium-term, competition from the central and eastern European countries could have a negative effect on growth and investment.

Useful Address

Institute for the Development of Working Conditions (IDICT): Instituto do Desenvolvimento e Inspecção das Condições de Trabalho, Serviços Centrais, Prãça de Alvalade 1, 1749-073 Lisboa; ☎ 217-924500; fax 217-924-597; www. idict.gov.pt.

Types of Contract

Employment contracts in Portugal can be made either for an indefinite term or for a specific duration. Whilst indefinite contracts have always been the norm in Portugal, fixed-term contracts are gradually becoming more common. An employee in possession of a contract has far greater protection of his rights. For example, the employer can only transfer the worker to a different place of work if this does not cause serious inconvenience to the employee. If the move does cause inconvenience then the worker has the right to end his contract and demand compensation. If, however, the worker accepts the transfer then he or she is entitled to any expenses incurred as a result of the change. Also, if ownership of the company is transferred, then employees hold all of their previous rights and their work contract remains valid with the new owner, unless otherwise agreed.

Indefinite Contracts do not have to be made in writing, as Portuguese labour law will generally regard the relationship between employer and employee as legally binding, regardless of whether there is a written contract. Such contracts do not involve a time limit, and once they have been entered into they can be terminated only with the mutual consent of the employer and the employee, on the employee's initiative, or for 'just cause' (see *ending a contract* below).

Fixed-Term Contracts *must* be written and should contain the following information:

O Name, address and profession of the parties.
O Job description of the employee.
O Remuneration agreement.
O Start date and termination date of the contract.
O Legally framed motivation for the term of the contract (see below).
O Place and weekly schedule for the work.

The new Portuguese labour code (*Código do Trabalho*) determines that there must be a specific reason for a fixed-term rather than an indefinite contract. This is strictly regulated and must be recorded in the contract. Only the following circumstances officially justify a short-term contract. If the justification does not fit any of the categories below then the contract is automatically deemed indefinite-term:

O Temporary replacements for absent employees.
O Temporary or exceptional increase in workload.
O Seasonal work.
O Irregular labour requirements due to fluctuations in activity or for limited temporary projects.
O Launching a new activity of uncertain duration or a new enterprise.
O Development of new projects not normally part of the normal activity of the employer.
O Contracting workers looking for their first job, or long-term unemployed or particular situations included in special legislation on employment policies.
O Construction activities, public works, industrial construction and repairs carried out on a contract basis or by direct administration.

The new labour code also states that fixed term contracts may be renewed twice within a period of three years, for a minimum of one and a maximum of three years (total maximum of six years). If the employee continues working beyond the end of the contract and it has not been renewed, then it automatically becomes an indefinite period contract.

This type of contract cannot be made for a duration of less than six months unless it is for a strictly defined job of a clearly temporary nature, seasonal work, temporary or exceptional increase in workload or for the temporary replacements of an absent employee. Contracts with a duration of less than six months cannot be renewed.

Part-time Contract. Employees who work weekly hours making up 75% or less of a full-time contracts are entitled to exactly the same rights and protection as full-time employees. Remuneration of part-time workers may not be less than the fraction of the wage of a full-time employee. The contract must be made in writing and must detail the normal daily and weekly working hours.

Temporary Employees are those workers contracted through a temporary employment agency for a specific period. The contract must be in writing and signed by both parties. If the employee continues to provide their services for ten days after the termination of the contract, without a new contract, their work is considered to be provided on the basis of an open-ended employment contract.

Probationary Period. This is the preliminary phase of contracts of employment in which parties are free to terminate the employment relationship. For indefinite contracts, probationary period last for 90 days (most workers), 180 days (positions with a high level of responsibility), or 240 days (for senior managerial staff). For fixed term contracts of less than six months the probationary period is fifteen days, and for longer fixed term contracts it is thirty days.

Ending a Contract

A contract of employment may cease due to its expiry, termination by agreement, cancellation, or notice of termination. When the contract of employment ceases the employer must provide his or her worker with a certificate of employment stating the posts occupied and the dates of employment.

Redundancy. Portuguese workers are fairly safe from being made redundant as the procedure that employers must follow is quite complex, and redundancy is only permitted in extreme circumstances. In order to end a contract of employment on economic grounds, the employer must be able to demonstrate that they are risking bankruptcy and that the redundancy of specific employees is the only way to prevent it and safeguard the jobs of others.

Resignation. Workers who have been with a company for less than two years need only give one month's notice. Longer-service employees must serve a two month period of notice (unless otherwise specified in the contract). However, a worker may resign his position immediately as long as he/she can demonstrate 'just cause'. It is considered justified to resign as a result of one of the following:

- Failure to pay wages on time.
- Violation of the legal or conventional guaranties of the worker.
- The imposition of an abusive sanction.
- Breach of safety/hygiene regulations by the employer.
- Offence to the integrity, liberty, honour or dignity of the worker.
- Lasting and substantial alteration of working conditions.
- Legal obligations that are incompatible with continuing to work.

In any of the above cases, the worker must provide a written summary of the grievance to his or her employer, within fifteen days of an infraction.

Dismissal. There must be a legitimate reason for dismissal. Objective reasons such as a worker's lack of ability, or the need to lose workers for economic reasons are accepted only to a limited degree as justification for terminating a contract. However, the law does accept dismissals for legitimate reasons such as inappropriate behaviour on the part of the worker, which due to its severity renders continuation of the employment relationship impossible. In such cases the burden of proof lies with the employer, who must be able to demonstrate that the grounds for dismissal are justified. The employer must give the worker written notice detailing the infractions and the intention to dismiss him/her along with a 'note of guilt' *(nota de culpa)*. The worker then has five days to respond.

If a court decides that the dismissal is unfair, then the employee has the right to an indemnity for the damages suffered due to the dismissal and to be reinstated. All of the remunerations from the moment that he/she was sacked must be fully paid. The employee can choose not to be reinstated, in which case the courts will arbitrate a compensation based on between fifteen and forty-five days remuneration for each year of the duration of the contract.

Trade Unions

Under the Salazar regime, workers' unions *(sindicatos)* were controlled by the dictatorship, under which striking was illegal. Since the introduction of democracy they seem to have been making up for such a long deprivation of their rights: long hours, and comparatively low wages – except for politicians who award themselves regular phenomenal pay rises which have fuelled the sindicatos outrage to the extent that the past few years have seen hundreds of strikes amongst almost every kind of worker but especially in the public sector. The unions are also engaged in a long-running dispute with the government over the unemployment figures which the unions claim do not include those on temporary government training schemes, which in the unions' view do not constitute bona fide employment. In Portugal, strikes tend not to drag on for weeks as they have a habit of doing elsewhere in Europe, but can be extremely disruptive, involving just a small section of the key staff within a company: for instance by bringing public transport, or the process of justice, to a grinding halt. Portuguese law forbids any repercussions for strikers, although workers will miss any payments for the days that they were on strike.

There are currently five trade union confederations registered with the Ministry of Employment and Social Security. However, only two of them are members of the Economic and Social Council – the CGTP and the UGT. The *CGTP-Intersindical*, General Confederation of Portuguese Workers (Rua Vitor Cordon 1-2, 1249-102 Lisboa, ☎213-236500; fax 213-974612; www.cgtp.pt), is a trade union federation of about 300 unions, comprising just over half the total trade union membership. This powerful federation is still dominated by the Communists. The *UGT*, General Union of Workers (Rua de Buenos Aires 11, 1249-067 Lisboa; ☎213-931200; www.ugt.pt), is moderate and mainly white-collar led. Trade Unions have the right to negotiate with the employer on any matter relating to the relationship between the employer and any member of the organisation under their employment.

Workers also have the right to create Commissions of Workers to defend their interests. Commissions of workers are established in order to gather all of the necessary information to perform their activity, carry out the management control of their companies, get involved in the reorganisation of productive activities, and manage or participate in the management of social work within companies.

Salaries

Average Portuguese salaries are around two to two and a half times lower than in the richer European countries such as the UK or Germany. The average rate of pay provides barely enough to live on and many Portuguese workers are deeply in debt. The average salary currently works out at around £8,000 per annum, and even top hospital doctors in the national health service earn less than £12,000 per annum. Professionals who wish to work in Portugal are therefore likely to experience a much lower standard of living than they might be used to as the slightly lower cost of living certainly does not compensate for these low wages. Those who have the opportunity should therefore seriously consider working for a British or American company in Portugal and earning a UK or US salary.

Portugal has a statutory inter industry minimum wage (currently around €356 per month – although slightly lower for domestic workers.) This wage is reviewed every year in the light of price and wage increases and developments in the various economic sectors. As in Spain there are two 'extra' months' salary paid at Christmas and before the summer vacation, a kind of bonus to deal with these extra expenses, so that the annual salary is usually paid in fourteen 'monthly' installments. These extra payments should not really be seen as a bonus however, as it simply means that your annual salary is divided by fourteen rather than twelve.

Working Hours and Holidays

The maximum working week in Portugal is forty hours. However, the duration of weekly work is calculated as an average over four months, so it is in fact possible to work more hours in any one given week. Any hour worked in excess of the maximum counts as overtime and should be paid as such. The first hour of overtime should be remunerated at a rate of 150% of the normal salary and the remaining hours at 175%. Those who work overtime on a day of rest or a public holiday should be paid a minimum of 200% of their normal salary. Only 200 hours of overtime may be worked per year. Pregnant women, disabled people and minors are not obliged to work overtime.

In many sectors Sunday is a compulsory day of rest. Portuguese law also allows for breaks of 1-2 hours in order to ensure that no more than five consecutive hours may be worked in any one day. This does not apply to management.

During the first year of employment, employees may take two days of paid holiday for each month they have worked, up to a maximum of twenty days. However, this holiday cannot be taken until the employee has worked six consecutive months. Thereafter all employees on full-time contracts are entitled to twenty-two days of paid holiday per year. This may be increased to twenty-five days if the worker has three or fewer justified absences. Most Portuguese people take their holiday in one block during the month of August. Those who decide to split their holiday must ensure that at least one of the periods lasts a minimum of ten days. Other non-working days include the thirteen statutory national holidays (listed at the end of *Daily Life)* plus one local one.

Health Issues

It is generally accepted by Portuguese employers that you may call in sick for up to three days. However, from the fourth day, most employers will require a note from your doctor. Should you call in sick for four days in a row or for eight days during the year without proper justification then companies are entitled to fire you. This may seem fairly draconian, but with Portuguese productivity levels being amongst the lowest in Europe, the Labour Ministry has decided that it is time to crack down on a working culture in which employees take an average of 18 sick days per year (the highest rate in the EU). Those who do not take sick leave are allowed to take an extra three days of holiday per year.

Those who are actually ill, and not simply taking a 'sickie' are provided for by the social security system. The sickness insurance fund provides employees with 65% of their average pay, or 70% if they have not taken any sick days in the 365 days before falling ill. The maximum amount of sick leave that a person may take is 1095 days. Thereafter they must undertake a medical examination establishing their inability to work, in which case they would receive an invalidity pension. The Portuguese social security system is dealt with in *Daily Life*. However, it is worth reiterating that employees (and the self-employed) are covered for all medical contingencies by their social security contributions. Contibutions ensure that you are covered for free visits to your doctor at the local *centros de saúde*. Essential prescription medicines are also provided free of charge. However, the system is currently suffering from severe under investment and as a result most people choose to take out private health insurance.

According to Portuguese labour law, the employer must provide adequate working conditions in terms of safety, hygiene and health. Additionally, every enterprise should have elected representatives for these matters. The employer is also responsible for taking out accident and injury insurance for his employees. An employee left with a permanent handicap following an accident will be paid a handicap indemnity.

Leave of Absence

Leave of absence is granted to employees for a number of reasons, mostly personal. These include getting married, the death of a spouse or other family member, illness of a child under ten years of age (30 days a year), illness of a child over ten years, a spouse or close relatives (15 days a year). Representation leave (unpaid) must also be granted for those who have trade union or works council commitments. In all cases, if the employee knows in advance when he or she will be absent from work, then they must notify the employer.

Maternity leave is fairly generous in Portugal. Women are entitled to 120 days, including up to six weeks before the birth should they require it. Thereafter the mother has the right to leave work for one hour twice a day for breast-feeding purposes until the child reaches one year old. Fathers do not receive such generous treatment, being entitled to only five days after the birth. Alternatively mothers or fathers may choose to suspend their contracts for a period of two years in order to raise their child.

WOMEN IN WORK

After a long history of discrimination, the status of women in the workplace is rising, although outside professional circles Portuguese womanhood does not seem to have made much progress. As late as the nineteenth century it was legal for a husband to kill his wife for adultery, but not the other way around. With the rise of republicanism the opportunities for women began to improve: the first women to qualify as doctors in Portugal did so in the late nineteenth century. After the overthrow of the monarchy in 1910, the first woman university professor was appointed. The clock was however turned back by the Salazar regime as women were relegated to the home by retrogressive legislation.

The end of the dictatorship brought a more enlightened approach, regarding the equality of women. However lofty the intentions, though, the reality is that many Portuguese women are still little better off. Better education and increasing prosperity are probably the long-term solution to these problems. Until recently, schooling was only compulsory until the age of fourteen. The situation for women is exacerbated by the fact that over three million Portuguese live below the poverty line (as defined by the EU). The result is that many Portuguese men have traditionally become itinerant jobseekers leaving behind their women in childrearing isolation.

Women are affected more by unemployment than men and the opportunities available to them are often unskilled and poorly paid. Many Portuguese women work as *criada* (maids) but the job title has been changed to *mulheradias* (daily woman) or *empregada doméstica* (domestic employee). Domestic service is still a relatively common form of employment for women.

Amongst the better off, full advantage has been taken of the opportunities on offer: over half of Portuguese university students are women, giving them a passport to all the professions from law to engineering. Careers in the army and the police force are open to them. Since 1989 the Portuguese air force has been training women as pilots, while one year previously in 1988, the first civilian woman pilot was taken on by the internal airline *Linhas Aéreas Regionais (LAR)*. In addition there are opportunities for women entrepreneurs (e.g. in the fashion trade, as art gallery proprietors etc.) However, women are still under-represented in the upper levels of the administration, in political parties and parliament (although Portugal did have a woman prime minister for six months in 1979, a circumstance which did not continue for as long as in the UK).

Still, it is a fact that however well women are doing in the professions and as directors and executives, the vast majority of the larger industrial concerns in Portugal are still run by men and crucially women's wages are still only 75% of men's.

WORKING CULTURE AND ETIQUETTE

Portugal's working culture is quite distinct from that which the average Briton or American may be used to. This is hardly a surprise since as recently as thirty years ago, Portugal still had a backward agrarian economy, and the dramatic changes of recent years have, out of necessity, been characterised by a certain amount of improvisation on the part of the Portuguese. Foreigners new to the country report that it is easy to become frustrated by Portuguese idiosyncrasies such as the lack of respect for deadlines, the lack of team spirit within companies, a certain guardedness within individuals and a lack of willingness to share information, and general inefficiency and disorganisation. However those who display a little patience and are prepared to adapt, will find Portugal a warm and exciting place to work and do business.

The good news is that the Portuguese are used to working with foreigners. They have a long history as a trading nation and therefore have a great deal of experience of cultural differences. As a nation, they are not easily offended and it is fairly difficult to make a serious gaff! The issues discussed below are necessarily generalisations, as with any country there are considerable differences between regions of Portugal, between the generations, and depending on the amount of international experience a particular company has.

Working Hours

Obviously this will vary from business to business, but normal working hours tend to begin at nine in the morning and end at around six. However, the Portuguese are notoriously flexible in their time-keeping and it is common for people to arrive at the office nearer to 10am and finish fairly late. In more modern companies it is increasingly expected of employees to stay at their desk until 8pm or later. Whilst there is no 'siesta' tradition in Portugal as in Spain, lunch is an important aspect of the working world and Clive Veigas Bennet of Veigas Bennet Consulting (www.businessinportugal.com) suggests that most deals are made at lunch. The lunch break usually starts at around 1pm, and a lunch-time business meeting will take anything from an hour and a half to three hours. The custom of going home for lunch is gradually dying out and colleagues often spend their lunch breaks eating out together.

Apart from the long lunch break, the working day is also punctuated with numerous coffee breaks. The best time of day to make an appointment with someone is around 11am, which allows them enough time to be late for work and to have consumed a strong coffee. Organising a meeting earlier than 10am is a fairly pointless exercise.

Punctuality

Time-keeping is generally on the relaxed side, and whilst the Portuguese have a lightly better understanding of punctuality than their Spanish neighbours, late arrivals and last-minute cancellations are far from uncommon. If you are late for a meeting or an appointment yourself, it is always best to ring ahead to apologise, but bear in mind that an associate probably won't notice unless you are more than half an hour late. Equally, you should not be surprised if you are kept waiting for up to half an hour, although any longer would be considered rude.

This 'flexible' approach to punctuality can also be seen in deadlines. Even if everything seems to be on track, bear in mind that terms such as 'tomorrow' and 'next week' are relative in Portuguese. You should never expect to be told in advance if deadlines are going to be missed.

Formality

The Portuguese tend to be fairly formal when it comes to dress code in the working world. Dress for men is based around the jacket and tie and it would rarely be out of place to wear a suit. Despite the heat in the height of summer, short-sleeved shirts are not really acceptable. Casual dress is very uncommon in Portugal, even in the newer hi-tech/software industries, although the Americanisation of the work place has led some companies to operate a 'dress-down Friday ' policy.

Women are also expected to dress fairly conservatively, with the trend being to wear a suit in the business arena, although trouser suits are perfectly acceptable. Again, long-sleeve blouses are a safer option.

Any business introduction demands a formal handshake, regardless of whether this is a first meeting. Be aware that the Portuguese tend to maintain eye-contact for longer, and stand closer to one another than you might be accustomed to.

Working Relationships

The key to successful business in Portugal lies in developing good personal relationships with your colleagues and business associates. Portuguese business and industry was forced to develop rapidly in the wake of the 1974 revolution, and as such the new generation of entrepreneurs that emerged, necessarily relied on personal contacts to build their empires. These relationships are maintained through frequent socialising and informal meetings, and work issues are often resolved outside of the office environment. The relationship that you have with a client will almost always be as important as the product or service that you are offering.

Nevertheless, developing these relationships will take time and effort. The Portuguese show great personal warmth, but they can also be very quiet and understated. It is not within the bounds of the national character to be assertive and direct, and there is little humour or banter within general business conversations. However, the importance of oral communication cannot be overstated. It is considerably more effective to come to an agreement with someone via a conversation than via e-mail or post.

Entertaining and eating out are important aspects of the Portuguese working world. As mentioned above though, lunch is the time to discuss business. Breakfast meetings are generally viewed with disdain, and dinner is for socialising rather than working. The Portuguese rarely hold dinner parties and work contacts are rarely invited into the home. If you are invited home to meet the family, it should be taken as a compliment and not considered a business meeting. During a lunchtime meeting, business should only be discussed towards the end of the meal. The purpose behind a business lunch, is the fostering of a personal relationship and until the coffee is served and the conversation turns to the real reason for the invitation, it is best not to appear overly formal. The Portuguese will usually attempt to pay for the meal as you are a foreign guest, so be firm.

Negotiations

As a rule Portuguese business meetings are badly run, poorly chaired and fail to stick to any kind of timetable. However, meetings are not generally used as a forum for decision making or delegation, and often no clear outcome of a meeting is anticipated. They are simply used for briefing and for convoluted discussions to which everybody makes a contribution. Whilst the Portuguese shy away from confrontation in everyday life, during a meeting they become incredibly competitive and like to express their point of view as emphatically as possible. This is the one arena where the Portuguese are not averse to self-assertion. Indeed, John Mole, in his book *Mind Your Manners* (Nicholas Brealey Publishing, 2003) argues that the only way to obtain agreement or support for a proposal within a meeting is to lobby the participants in private beforehand. Otherwise they are likely to disagree on principle.

Because of the nature of Portuguese hospitality, and the instinctive wish to please, as a foreigner you should be aware of the tendency to tell you exactly what you want to hear, even if it is not altogether true. Something which is agreed at a meeting may well be reneged on at a later date. Where possible get it in writing. The Portuguese are also wary of laying all of their cards on the table during meetings. The lack of transparency is perhaps a result of an innate unwillingness to appear weak, so always persevere with your requests for facts and figures.

Language

It is fairly common for professionals and businessmen to speak English to a fairly advanced level. However, it is always best to ensure that you speak slowly and clearly to avoid misunderstandings. The ability to speak some Portuguese will certainly be an advantage in any working situation, and if Portuguese and English fail you, you could try French, the third language in Portugal. The Portuguese can understand Spanish, but most could not give you a response in Spanish and even if they could they may be unwilling to do so, due to historical antipathies between the two countries.

As with many other romance languages, Portuguese has familiar and polite forms of the word 'you': *tu* and *voce*. The informal 'tu' should be used with family and friends and not really with colleagues, unless you have more than a working relationship with them and you are equal in status. In the working environment 'tu' should never be used when talking to superiors as it shows a distinct lack of respect. Nor should it be used when talking to subordinates unless you have known them for a very long time, as it might be taken as a slight.

Company Structures

Portuguese organisations tend to be run from the top-down by almost dictatorial leaders. Foreigners coming into Portuguese companies describe a profound unwillingness to challenge authority and remark upon the lack of teamwork. Managers tend not to look for consensus amongst their subordinates, preferring to appear decisive and authoritative, and colleagues tend to be individually competitive and fearful of losing out to their peers. As a result, very few Portuguese workers and middle managers are prepared to take individual responsibility for work. This can lead to a situation where commitments are simply not fulfilled.

Forms of Address

Status is of the utmost importance in the Portuguese business world, and it is therefore very important to at least attempt to address people in the correct manner. This can take some time to master as the rules are fairly peculiar, but it will always be appreciated if you persevere. The first and most important rule is that you should never use a person's first name unless you are invited to do so. However, hereafter it gets more tricky. The Portuguese use a range of titles, such as *Doutor, Engenheiro, Arquitecto, Profesor, Senhor* etc. For example, Doutor is used indiscriminately for anyone suspected of having a degree. You may not introduce yourself as Doutor – as this is considered bad form. However, being titled Dr. is an advantage in the working world and will gain you respect and leverage you might not otherwise have had, so it is best to subtly let people know that you have a degree. Generally you will be safe using Senhor, or Senhora for a woman, until you have mastered the more subtle formalities.

Portuguese names can be very long indeed, with as many as five or six family names built up over several generations. Not all of these names will be used, except in official documentation and generally you need only concern yourself with the very last one or two names. It is unlikely that addressing somebody by the wrong name will cause offence, but even so this can be avoided simply by listening to how a person is referred to by others.

BUSINESS AND INDUSTRY REPORT

Up to the present both the number and type of vacancies, as well as the level of salaries in Portuguese businesses and industries, have proved a disincentive to those considering this as a place in which to live and work. But the situation is improving as the economy develops and trade with the UK and other EU countries grows; certainly the Portuguese are optimistic about their future as an industrially dynamic nation and the recent liberalisation of the banking and financial services sector as well as the government's programme of privatisation and deregulation are signs of the country's progress towards a more modern economy, as is the relative decline in the importance of agriculture.

Anyone thinking of working in Portugal, in whatever field, ought to have some idea of the main industrial concerns, and the economic trends which may influence their development; this may help you decide where the best employment opportunities will be found. It is a good idea to know the locations of the main areas of economic activity which, it will become apparent, are mainly Lisbon and Porto, with tourism the most important industry in the south. The following is an overview of the Portuguese economy today, the domestic market (which is boosted every year by the large number of tourists and other visitors to Portugal), and trends in some of the main sectors of industry, followed by a list of the main international concerns and companies in Portugal.

The most developed manufacturing areas of the country are Porto in the north, which is the traditional centre of the port wine and textile industries, and the Porto hinterland, where fish canning, oil refining, vehicle components, light engineering, paints, tyres, earthenware, shoes, cork and jewellery are the main types of industry. The other major industrial zone is the area extending 25 miles/40 kms south of Lisbon to Setúbal which is a national development region containing steel, shipyards, engineering, textiles, cement, chemicals and automobile assembly plants. The main commercial and trade centre is also Porto. Most UK and international companies are based in these areas.

As will be seen from the data below, Portugal is in the process of upgrading its products from mainly raw materials to finished goods, thus increasing their export value. This is a traditional activity too. The port wine industry and food processing have always been based on its primary agricultural products; food and beverages today are an important part of Portuguese exports as they have always been, with other secondary industries based on raw materials like wood and cork also playing an important role in Portuguese trade.

Over 60% of its exports go to EU countries and the annual amount of direct investment in the Portuguese economy doubled in each of the four years after its accession to the EU, with Britain playing an important role, alongside Spain, as its main trading partner. In Portugal UK direct investment is nearly twice as much as that of France and nearly three times that of Germany. Of the EU countries, Spain is still the most important partner. Other trading partners are the USA and Canada, and the former Portuguese colonies in Africa.

Although Portuguese industry is expanding, statistics show that among the active population of under five million, a smaller percentage is employed in industry than in services. The economy is that of an industrialised country, but one where the service sector is ahead of industry as the major contributor to its Gross Domestic Product, not unlike that of Britain. A common history of trade around the world, as well as a centuries' old tradition of commerce between the two countries, is one of the things which unites the two countries. Both Portugal and Britain, with their former colonial interests, are international in their outlook as well as European. For Portugal, as for Britain nowadays, continued prosperity will depend on developing these international trading links alongside contacts with its European partners.

The Portuguese UK Chamber of Commerce in London was set up (only fifteen or so years ago) to encourage trade and investment in both directions; it is a useful source of information about trends in the Portuguese economy, and trade and investment prospects there, as well as for those wishing to find out more about the leading Anglo-Portuguese companies. It represents Portugal's leading business association (AIP) in Britain, the Bolsa de Valores de Lisboa (the country's expanding stock exchange), regional development organisations in Portugal, and a variety of other bodies, as well as having links with the Câmera de Comércio Luso Britânnica. It also promotes seminars and networking meetings; and is a source of information about EU funding in Portugal: *Portuguese UK Chamber of Commerce*, Fourth Floor, 11 Belgrave Square, London SW1X 8PP; ☎020-7201 6638; fax 020-7201 6637; www.portuguese-chamber.org.uk.

Food and Drink

Portugal's food and beverage manufacturing industries represent a significant source of wealth for the economy. The sector accounts for 8% of Portugal's GDP and employs around 100,000 workers. The bulk of production is for the home market, but many of the wares are familiar outside Portugal, including fish and fish products, tomato concentrate, olive oil and wines. The latter is responsible for much of the £50 million or so of beverages from Portugal imported into the UK.

Portugal is ranked 11th in the world as a wine producing country and vineyards cover approximately 258,000 hectares of the country. Perhaps the most famous Portuguese wine is port – produced exclusively in the Douro River Valley in the north east of Portugal, sixty miles from Porto. However, beer is actually the main product of the beverages sector, and the major player in this industry is *Unicer*, whose main brewery in the north produces the *Super Bock* and *Cristal* brands.

The most important home-grown manufacturer of food and beverages is *Compal* (mostly fruit juices), which is only beaten by coca-cola in terms of sales in Portugal. Other key players in this industry include *Milaneza* (pasta) and *Vasco de Gama* (fish). However, there are numerous international companies with important operations in Portugal. These include Cadbury Schweppes, United Biscuits, Nestlé and Unilever (contact details listed in the directory below).

Further information regarding aspects of the food and beverage industry in Portugal can be obtained from the following organisations:

○ *ANIRSF* (Portuguese Association of the Soft Drinks and Fruit Juices Industry): www.anirsf.pt/eng/.
○ *Casa do Azeite* (Portuguese Olive Oil Association): www.casadoazeite.pt.
○ *ViniPortugal* (Inter-professional Association for the Promotion of Portuguese Wines): www.viniportugal.pt.

Textiles and Clothing

Over 17,000 companies work within the textiles and clothing sector in Portugal, employing some 250,000 people. This is a highly export-oriented industry with 60% of products being sold abroad, mainly within the EU. This is by far the most important sector in terms of exports to Britain.

The products of this sector are woolen yarns, cotton yarns and other textiles, as well as knitwear, lace and embroidery. The majority of the production centres are situated in the north of the country, especially in the Porto and Braga districts, however, there is also a concentration of plants in central Portugal.

Leather is also a traditional Portuguese export, although in recent years there has been a shift into quality products for export, such as high fashion footwear. Indeed, the Portuguese footwear industry ranks second in exports in Europe, with 90% of production being exported. This sector has certainly been the area of the Portuguese economy registering the greatest growth in the last twenty years, transforming itself from a traditional, labour-intensive industry into an aggressive industry that has invested heavily in state of the art technology.

Whilst this industry is currently very healthy and reports year-on-year growth, it is estimated that in the longer term, cheaper production in the new eastern European EU members could damage Portuguese trade with EU partners.

Further information regarding the textiles industry in Portugal can be obtained from the following organisations:

○ *ANIVEC* (National Association of Clothing Manufacturers): www.anivec. com.
○ *APIC* (Portuguese Leather Association): www.apic.pt.
○ *APICCAPS* (Portuguese Footwear, Components, Leather Goods Manufacturer's Association): www.apiccaps.pt.

Porcelain and Faience (decorated, glazed earthenware), Glassware, Cement, Ornamental Stone

Between them, these industries represent about 6% of the industrial product. Items include the famous Portuguese tiles which are sought after abroad for kitchen and bathroom wall decorations. The porcelain sector includes industrial ceramics for the building trade. Glass includes not only receptacles for foodstuffs but plate glass. Expansion is likely to occur as production is shifted to windscreens for the car industry.

As these are quality products traditionally associated with Portugal, there is scope for UK importers with the right Portuguese contacts. Demand for Portuguese marble is increasing, also for granites and similar minerals. Carved, ornamental stone is produced by efficient, factory methods and there are a number of modern companies operating in this field.

One of the major companies that has recently been partly privatised is the leading cement producer *Cimpor (Cimentos de Portugal)*, which has 58% of the home market, some interests in Spain, and is keen to expand overseas.

Chemicals

The chemicals sector in Portugal is made up of 850 (mostly small) companies, employing 22,500 workers. The industry makes up 3.6% of Portugal's GDP and has an annual turnover of €4.1 billion. The main sectors of the industry are inorganic chemicals, petrochemicals, fertilisers, and light chemicals. The petrochemical sector is currently expanding, particularly in the field of polymers for the plastics industry. There are also good prospects in the production of synthetic resins for paints, varnishes and wood adhesives. The fertiliser industry is also expanding in relation to increasing demand from Portuguese agriculture.

The industry is concentrated in the region of Porto (spreading south to Aveiro) and Lisbon (up to Setúbal), where around 90% of the workforce is situated. Some of the key players in this industry are *Borealis, CIRES, ADP, DOW, Colgate, Palmolive, Bayer, CIN, Solvay and Robbialac.* UK companies in the chemical sector represented in Portugal include *BP, Glaxo Smithkline, ICI* and *Unilever.*

Motor Vehicles and Components

The automotive industry in Portugal has developed into the main export sector, contributing to 7% of the Portuguese GDP and worth €6.3 billion per annum. The industry currently employs over 45,000 workers and estimated growth over the next two years is 16%.

Although there are some home-grown companies with locally developed technologies, this industry relies heavily on partnerships with foreign industrial companies. The sector leaders in this industry are *VW, Mitsubishi, Opel, Toyota* and *Citroen*, which between them produce 240,000 vehicles per year in Portugal. Over 160 companies feed the assembly lines with a wide range of components. Most of the main component suppliers in the world are present in Portugal, including *Visteon, Delphi Automotive Systems, Robert Bosch, Faurecia, Lear,* and *Johnson Controls.*

More than seven million euros are currently being invested in the industry by a government keen to develop the technological, research and organisation capabilities of the automotive cluster in Portugal.

Further information regarding the automotive industry can be obtained from the following organisations:

○ *ACAP* (Portuguese Motor Vehicle Trade Association): www.acap.pt.
○ *AFIA* (Portuguese Component Manufacturer's Association): www.afia-afia.pt.
○ *INTEL* (R&D for the Auto Industry): www.inteli.pt.
○ *CEIIA* (Centre for Exellence and Innovation): www.ceiia.com.

Timber, Cork and Furniture

Over one third of Portugal is forested. The most important species of trees are the pine, cork-oak and eucalyptus. The pine trees are exported via the sawmills as timber for making pallets. Over the last few years however, there has been a growing tendency to produce more sophisticated wooden goods (e.g. furniture) with a higher export value.

Portugal produces over half the world's cork, which is no mean feat for so small a country. This is mainly exported in the form of bottle corks; but cork products and agglomerates also find a ready market. The bulk of exports go to the EU and a small proportion to the USA; and the main area for cork production is the Alentejo region, north of the Algarve.

An example of the diversity of the Portuguese economy, and of the development of many of its companies is Grupo Amorim, traditionally a cork producer, which expanded in the 1980's into real estate, tourism, telecommunications and even banking. 'In a small country, you have to be in three or four activities to get bigger,' its chairman says. And the company is also developing no less than 26 joint ventures with foreign partners.

Wood Pulp and Paper

Portugal is a significant player in the European market in the production of wood pulp and paper. Exports total over €1.4 billion, nearly 5% of all Portuguese exports, placing Portugal in fifth place behind such countries as Finland and Sweden. There is an increasing trend towards producing paper as the finished product for export and the Portuguese are able to undercut the prices of the Nordic countries. As a result Portugal now produces some leading office and printing paper brands.

The leading company in Portugal, boosted by recent major acquisitions of pulp producing companies and paper mills, is *Portucel*. The company now controls around 20% of Portugal's eucalyptus forests and is one of the world's biggest producers of bleached eucalyptus Kraft pulp for packaging. Other key companies are *Caima* (pulp), *Stora Enso-Celbi* (pulp), *Companhia de Papel do Prado* (specialist printing and packaging products), *Renova* and *Nisa* (sanitary paper products).

Despite frequent forest fires during Portugal's hot summers, the industry is very healthy and sales continue to increase by around 3% per year as demand increases. The future of the industry is therefore very good.

Electrics and Electronics

The electrics and electronics sector in Portugal has undergone a dramatic transformation in recent years to become innovative and dynamic. Companies such as Blaupunkt, Bosch and Siemens have settled in Portugal, helping to drag the industry into the twenty-first century. Indeed, 60% of production and 90% of exports are generated by foreign companies in Portugal. The top ten electronics companies in Portugal (in order of number of employees) are *Visteon* (USA), *Blaupunkt* (Germany), *Siemens* (Germany), *Efacec* (Portugal), *Tyco Electronics* (USA), *Vulcano* (Germany), *Alcatel* (France), *Visay* (USA), *Grundig* (Germany) and *Infineon* (Germany).

With a turnover of €4.6 billion per year, this sector employs 42,500 people, spread over 674 companies. The industry in Portugal may be split into the following subsectors: semiconductors, auto-electronic, consumer electronics, telecoms, IT.

Portugal has an important semiconductor sector, which is based largely in the Porto region. Many of the trained electronics workers in this subsector work for *Infineon Technologies*, the 6th largest semiconductor company in the world. In late 2003, Infineon doubled the production at its plant in Vila do Conde, creating 584 new jobs in the area. The automotive electronics sector has seen a huge amount of foreign direct investment in recent years.

Portugal has increased its production of consumer electronics for the home market, especially in terms of products such as car radios, information technologies, video cameras and remote control systems. This branch of the electronics industry is characterised by the presence of several multinationals. For example, the German company, Blaupunkt produces four million car radios in Portugal every year, employing over 2000 workers.

Further information regarding the Portuguese electronics industry can be obtained from the following organisations:

O *ANIMEE* – Electric and Electronic Portuguese Enterprises Association: www. animee.pt.
O *ANETIE* – Portuguese Association of IT and Electronics Companies: www. aneties.pt.
O *Instituto Pedro Nunes* at Coimbra University: www.ipn.pt.

Tourism

Tourism is booming in Portugal. This is hardly a surprise. The country boasts 800kms of beautiful coastline, a wide diversity of landscapes and fascinating historical and cultural traditions. However, there had been several years of fairly lacklustre demand, and it is only in the last year or so that the industry has picked up. One of the reasons for this turnaround was the European cup in 2004 that helped promote the country as a travel destination world-wide. The turn-around that began in 2004 looks set to continue. In 2005 the industry, which represents 7.2% of Portugal's GDP, is expected to generate €32.1 billion, and this is expected to have grown to €58.2 billion by 2015.

Tourism is certainly an enormously important industry for employment in Portugal, providing one in every five jobs in 2005. As a result of recent growth, the number of jobs generated by the industry is expected to grow by around 11,000 per annum – good news for foreign expats, for whom tourism is a staple source of employment.

There is also enormous scope for development within the industry and the Portuguese government is giving every encouragement by offering financial incentives to build new tourist developments. ICEP, the Portuguese Government Trade and Tourism Office in London can provide further information (ICEP UK, Portuguese Embassy, 11 Belgrave Square, London SW1X 8PP; ☎020-7201 6666; fax 020-7201 6633; e-mail trade.london@iecp.pt; www.portugalinbusiness.com).

REGIONAL EMPLOYMENT GUIDE

The number and type of jobs available will vary from region to region. The information provided here gives some idea of the dominant industries and the types of jobs that are readily available in each area.

NORTE

Provinces: Minho, Douro Litoral, Tras-os-Montes.
Main Cities: Porto, Braga, Bragança, Vila Real.
Population: 3.7 million.
Regional Newspapers: *Maia Hoje, Jornal de Matosinhos, Diário de Tras-os-Montes, Diário do Norte, Maia Hoje, O Primeiro de Janeiro, Semanario Transmontano, Correio do Minho, Jornal de Notícias.*
Unemployment Rate: 8.3%

Employment Prospects. The northern region of Portugal offers a diverse array of employment opportunities, from the predominance of services in Porto, to its surrounding areas (Cavado, Ave, Tamega and Douro-e-Vouga) where industrial employment is the norm, to the rural areas of Minhou-Lima, Douro and Alto Trás-os-Montes where more than half of the employment is concentrated in agriculture.

Around 45% of the employed population in the north of Portugal is employed within the service industry. Retail trade and the restaurant industry continue to play an important role in the region's economy. Tourism has also been a growth area within services, and the region has kept pace with the country as a whole. However, finding a job within tourism is only really an option in the major towns on the Costa Verde due to the low population of the region. The tourist hotspots such as Porto, Braga and Bagança offer many jobs during the tourist season, especially in bars, cafés and hotels.

43% of people are employed in the region's highly specialised industrial sector. The main industries in northern Portugal are cork (this region is the world's biggest producer of cork), the textile and dressmaking industry, footwear, wood products (especially furniture production), and the manufacturing of materials and accessories for the country's automobile sector. Other areas of industrial production in this region include: ceramics (Barcelos is the ceramics capital of Portugal), iron and steel, paints and dyes, paper and cardboard, naval construction and oil refineries.

Agriculture is still an important force in the region, employing around 11% of the population. Particularly important are dairy farming and cattle breeding and wine cultivation. In the coastal areas there is some horticultural production and inland cereals, cattle feed and nuts are grown. Wine production is particularly important in the north, especially in the areas of Douro, Minho, Lima and Cávado, which between them produce 29% of Portugal's wine, and famously, port. Port is the most important Portuguese agricultural export.

According to EURES, this area of Portugal is not likely to prove fruitful for young university graduates looking for a first job. However, there is great demand for less academically qualified workers. For example, in civil construction, there is such a demand for workers that the sector has resorted to employing immigrants from non-EU countries. In the hotel and restaurants sector there is a great demand for cooks and waiting and counter staff. Finally, there is a shortage in the area of assembly and machine operators.

CENTRO

Provinces: Beira Alta, Beira Litoral, Beira Baixa.
Main Cities: Viseu, Guarda, Aveiro, Coimbra, Leiria, Castelo Branco.
Population: 1.8 million.
Regional Newspapers: *Diário as Beiras, Diário de Aveiro, Diário de Coimbra, Diário Regional Viseu, Gazeta do Interior, Jornal de Coimbra, Jornal do Centro, Nova Guarda, O Interior, Reconquista, Terras da Beira.*
Unemployment Rate: 4.3%

Employment Prospects. 43% of employment in this region comes from the services, especially the social and public services, commerce, hotels and restaurants. However, the central region does not have such a well established British expatriate community as other parts of Portugal and it therefore offers less English-speaking jobs.

The hub of the central region is Coimbra, which has a buoyant tourist trade, catering for Spanish and Portuguese tourists. The city therefore offers the potential to find work in cafés, shops and restaurants for those who speak Spanish or Portuguese.

Coimbra is also a university city and as such offers a number of associated jobs for lecturers, librarians, canteen workers, security guards and housekeepers. These posts are often advertised on the university website or in local newspapers.

Industry and civil construction employ around 30% of the working population in the central provinces. The region is Portugal's leader in the pulp/paper integration process and in related industries such as industrial paper recycling and wood products. There is also a large ceramics, pottery, tiling and glassware industry in this area. Other important industries in the central provinces include: manufacturing metal equipment for the home, such as metal furniture, ironware, kitchen goods; the plastics and moulds industries; the transport material industries; and textiles.

Much of this region is agricultural, so it is possible that you mind find work in one of the many orchards, vineyards and farms. Bear in mind though, that this work is very seasonal and is poorly paid.

The main skills in demand in this region are in civil construction – there is a dearth of bricklayers, plumbers, carpenters and electricians. There is also demand in the hotel and restaurant sector for cooks, waiting staff, kitchen assistants and bakers.

LISBOA E VALE DE TEJO

Provinces: Lisbon, Estremadura, Ribatejo.
Main Cities: Lisbon, Sétubal, Santarém.
Population: 3.5 million.
Regional Newspapers: *Jornal o Setúbalense, Vida Ribatejana, O Mirante, O Templario, Diário de Notícias.*
Unemployment Rate: 7.5%

Employment Prospects. Employment in this region is based mainly around the services. Lisbon in particular has a highly developed service sector which includes, public administration departments and social services provided mainly by the state. Education is also a big employer and this area has the greatest concentration of higher education establishments (39% of the country's total) and a large number of research and development institutions. However, there is an excess of teachers in this area and most of the jobs in these institutions are to be found in administration. Other important service industries in the region include financial departments, services provided to companies (such as engineering and computer services, advertising etc.), private health services, telecommunications, commercial services, hotels and restaurants, and tourism. The workers particularly in demand in this sector include shop assistants for the increasing number of supermarkets and shopping centres, qualified doctors and nurses, and cooks, waiting staff and kitchen assistants. There is also a shortage of IT workers in the region, such as computer analysts and programmers and systems designers.

In Lisbon and the towns along the coastline to the north and south of the city, there are job opportunities within the tourist trade, if only as a stop-gap until you can find less seasonal employment. These opportunities range from joining a tour guide agency or working as an English-speaking helper in a tourist office. There are also many tourist-orientated shops, cafés and services that may be looking for English-speaking help. However, it will always be vastly useful to have some grounding in Portuguese, even for these jobs.

Employment in the industrial sector in the Lisbon region is much lower than the national average (at around 30%). Much of the industry is based on manufacturing and goods that are produced here include: automobiles and their components, materials for railways, ships and aeronautical equipment, and a range of products based on forestry exploitation. Agro-food industries also play a large role in the regional economy. Agriculture itself however employs only 4% of the working population and is characterised by subsistence cultivation.

The main unfilled positions in this region are computer programmers/analysts, cooks, waiters, bartenders, shop sales persons, bricklayers and stonemasons.

ALENTEJO

Provinces: Alto Alentejo, Baixo Alentejo.
Main Cities: Portalegre, Evora, Beja.
Population: 0.54 million.
Regional Newspapers: *Diário do Alentejo.*
Unemployment Rate: 9.1%

Employment Prospects. Agriculture is still a mainstay of the economy in Alentejo. The region is renowned within Portugal for its natural resources, particularly cork, eucalyptus and pine; fields cultivated with cereals and plants rich in proteins and vine and olive tree plantations. It may therefore be possible to find work in the primary sector. However, data from EURES suggests that there is a surplus of non-qualified workers in agriculture, which represents 22.2% of the total unemployment in the region.

Mineral resources are also abundant in the Alentejo, in the form of copper and other non-ferous minerals and ornamental stone. There is a thriving marble trade in the region, which has been known for its abundance of quality marble since Roman times.

The main industrial specialisations in the Alentejo region include wood, non-metal products and minerals, chemical products, petroleum by-products, and plastic materials. Recently the region has benefited from the establishment of new factories producing automobile parts and electronic components.

The services sector is the most significant in terms of employment, and has seen dynamic growth in recent years. Tourism in the area is showing great potential. However one area of enormous growth is the building and carpentry trade, due to second-home buyers coming inland from the Algarve in search of lower prices. As a result there are various opportunities to work on new-builds or renovation projects, and the region is crying out for qualified bricklayers, plumbers and electricians.

Other skills in demand include doctors and nurses, qualified agricultural workers, and various hotel and restaurant skills. There is however a surplus of non-specialised administrative workers in the area.

ALGARVE

Main City: Faro.
Population: 0.4 million.
Regional Newspapers: *Região Sul, The Resident, Correio da Manhã, The News, The Anglo-Portuguese News.*
Unemployment Rate: 5%

Employment Prospects. The economy of the Algarve region is heavily reliant on tourism. Thousands of tourists visit the area every year between June and September leading to a massive increase in the demand for workers in the commercial and services sectors. This is therefore the easiest area to find work without needing to learn Portuguese. However, the short-term nature of this demand leads to precarious and highly seasonal working conditions. The main labour requirements during the summer season include qualified kitchen assistants, cooks, waiting staff, chamber staff and counter assistants. The fast pace of golf-course construction in recent years has also thrown open opportunities for those with experience in gardening and green maintenance. Other tourist related jobs can be found on the beaches. There are openings for lifeguards and water-sports experts.

An increasingly dynamic industry in this region is construction and related activities, perhaps largely due to the influx of holiday and second-home buyers. The last few years have been a boom-time for builders, plumbers, carpenters, electricians etc. and also for retailers of furniture, construction materials, ironworks, as well as those providing services such as landscaping and gardening, and building swimming pools. The civil construction sector is undergoing such development that there is still a great shortage of bricklayers, masons and other qualified professionals.

Around 70% of employees in this region work in the tertiary sector (with tourism employing the majority). Only 20% work in industry and just 9% work in the primary sector. Part of the problem is that this region has a low level of qualified workers and a high illiteracy rate. As a result the business structure is fragile and made up of small and very small enterprises, often with poorly qualified employees. The lack of qualified people is also reflected in the poor expansion of information technology in the region. Many companies require computer engineers, programmers, analysts and hardware and software experts. Electronics and telecommunications engineers are also in demand.

Apart from those jobs in demand mentioned above, the region is also crying out for both specialised and general medical doctors, especially in the inner region of the Algarve. It is also very difficult to find sufficient nursing and midwifery professionals.

MADEIRA AND THE AZORES

Main City: Funchal.
Population: 0.25 million.
Regional Newspapers: *Diário de Notícias, Açoriano Oriental, Diário dos Açores, Diário Insular, Expresso das Nove, Correio da Horta, Jornal da Praia, Jornal Diário, Tribuna da Madeira.*
Unemployment Rate: 3% (Madeira); 3.8% (The Azores)

Employment Prospects. The regional economy in the Autonomous Region of Madeira depends largely on the tertiary sector (60.2% of jobs), with the tourism industry being the main source of income. Madeira's climate makes it a popular year-round destination and English-speaking workers are always in demand in the bars, cafes and restaurants. There are also occasional vacancies in the tourist offices around the island, although this will require speaking Portuguese.

The secondary sector (26.6% of jobs) is mainly characterised by construction and manufacturing. Industry is mostly small scale and relies upon artisan production such as Madeira tapestry, embroidery and basketwork. In the primary sector (13.2% of jobs) banana production, flower growing and Madeira wine are significant. Most of Madeira's business is concentrated in Funchal, but as with mainland Portugal, small enterprises predominate.

Unemployment in the area is low. However, the job market is largely made up of poorly qualified workers, and supply outstrips demand when it comes to unqualified workers in the services and commerce sector and general clerks. On the other hand there is a great demand for mathematical and engineering science professionals. The autonomous region also suffers from a dearth of building trades professionals and hotel and restaurant professionals.

Opportunities for finding work in the smaller and more secluded Azores are far more limited. Nevertheless, the increasing popularity of eco-tourism and activity holidays offers opportunities to find employment, or to set up your own business.

DIRECTORY OF MAJOR EMPLOYERS AND COMPANIES WITH AN INTERNATIONAL PERSPECTIVE

Accountants and Consultants
AJL Praceta Simões Almeida Junior 6-r/c: Dto Abraao, 2745-332 Queluz; ☎214-377112.
Deloitte Touche: Edifício Atrium Saldanha, Praça Duque de Saldanha, 1 -6°, 1050-094 Lisboa; ☎210-423000; fax 210-423190; www.deloitte.com.
Ernst & Young: Edifício República, Avenida da República 90 - 3°, 1649-024 Lisboa; ☎217-912000; fax 217-957590; www.ey.com.
Gesbanha – Gestão e Contabilidade S.A.: Rua 7 de Junho de 1759, N°

1, 2760-110 Caxias; ☎214-416460; fax 214-417387; www.gesbanha.pt.
KPMG: Edificio Monumental, Avenida Praia da Vitoria, 71A-11, 1069-006 Lisboa; ☎210-110073.
PriceWaterhouseCoopers: Palácio Sottomayor, Rua Sousa Martins 1-2°, 1050-217 Lisboa; ☎213-599000.
Rentipar, Sociedade Gestora de Participações Sociais S.A.: Av. Barbosa du Bacage, 85-5°, 1050-030 Lisboa; ☎217-910495; fax 217-959529.

Agriculture and Food Processing
António Xavier de Lima: Rua 25 de

Abril, Lote 18 Paivas, 2845-389 Amora; ☎212-260200; fax 212-248455; www.empreendimentosxav ierlima.com. Horsebreeding.

Cadbury Portugal: Praça do Campo Pequeno, n--° 48 – 4th floor, 100-081 Lisbon; ☎217-817350; fax 217-950324; www.cadburyschweppes.com.

Cockburn Smithes & Cia Lda: Rua D. Leonor de Freitas 182, 4400-099 Vila Nova de Gaia; ☎223-776545; fax 223-776599.

Compal S.A.: Rua General Ferreira Martins, Lote 6 – Miraflores; ☎214-129400; fax 214-120381; www.compal.pt.

Croft & Co: Largo Joaquim de Magalhes 23, 4400-187 Vila Nova de Gaia; ☎223-772950; fax 223-742899; www.croftport.com.

Milaneza Messas e Bolchas S.A.: Rua Manuel Gonçalves Lage, 988, 4425-122 Aguas Santas; ☎229-014505; fax 229-011991; www.milaneza.pt.

Nestlé Portugal: R. Alexandre Herculano, 8-8A Linda-a-Velha, 2795-010; ☎214-148500; fax 214-143700; www.nestle.pt.

Ramirez & Ca (Filhos) S.A.: Rua Oscar da Silva, 1683 – PO Box 2050, 4451-953 Matosinhos; ☎229-997878; fax 229-997879; e-mail ramirez@ramirez.pt; www.ramirez.pt.

Schweppes Portugal: Edifício Central Park, Rua do Central Park N°16, 1c, 2795-242 Linda-a-Velha; ☎214-209800; www.cadburyschweppes.com.

Unicer Bebidas de Portugal, S.A.: Via Norte – Apartado 1044, 4466-955 S. Mamede de Infesta; ☎229-052100; fax 229-052300; unicer_international@unicer.pt; www.unicer.pt.

United Biscuits Iberia: Rua de Proletariado 14, 2795 Carnaxide, Lisboa; ☎214-249730; www.unitedbiscuits.com.

Unilever/Fima Lda: Largo Monterroio Mascarenhas 1, 1000 Lisbon; ☎213-892413; www.unilver-jm.com.

Vasco da Gama SA: Rua de Almeiriga, n.1192, 4450-609 Leça da Palmeira – Matosinhos; ☎229-983480; fax 229-983428; www.vascodagama.pt.

Architects

Arquitraco: Calçada Tapada 143, 1300-541 Lisboa; ☎213-610250; e-mail arquitraco@arquitraco.com; www.arquitraco.com.

Giad Gabriela Iglesias: B3 Pinhal Concelho-Olhos Ag, 8200-636 Albufeira; ☎289-502408; e-mail central@giad-portugal.com; www.giad-portugal.com.

Luis Pedra Silva: Rua da Fonte, 22A 1 esq., 1600-460 Lisboa; ☎217-516210; www.pedrasilva.com.

Ponto I Lda.: Travessa Fiuza 39 – pt 5, 1300-249 Lisboa; ☎213-660912; fax 213-660914; e-mail pontoi@mail.telepac.pt; www.pontoi.pt.

Risco: Travessa Conde da Ponte, 16-A, 1300 141 Lisboa; ☎213-610420; fax 213-610422; e-mail risco@risco.org.

Banking & Finance

Barclays Bank plc: Av. Barbosa du Bocage, 54D, 1000-072 Lisboa; ☎217-911301; fax 217-911390; www.Barclays.pt.

Banco BPI S.A.: Rua Tomás de Fonseca

– Torres de Lisboa Torre H-3, 1600-209 Lisboa; ☎213-181548; fax 213-181627; www.bancobpi.pt.

Banco Comercial Portugues S.A.: Rua Augusta 62, 1149-023 Lisboa; ☎213-211000; fax 213-211739; www.millenniumbcp.pt.

Banco Espirito Santo: Av. Da Liberdade 195, 1250-142 Lisboa; ☎213-501000; fax 218-557698; e-mail info@bes.pt; www.bes.pt.

Banif – Banco International do Funchal S.A.: Av. José Malhoa 1792, 1099-011 Lisboa; ☎217-211236; fax 217-211237; e-mail info@banif.pt; www.banif.pt.

Caixa Geral de Depósitos: Av. João XXI 63, 1000-300 Lisboa; ☎217-953000; fax 217-905050; www.cgd.pt.

Financetar, Sociedade de Serviços Financeiros, Empresariais e Imobiliários S.A.: Rua S. João de Brito 605-3°, 4100-455 Porto; ☎226-197940; fax 226-107890.

Construction

A.M. Mesquita & Filhos S.A.: Rua do Souto 1, 4470-215 Maia; ☎229-431200; fax 229-431290; www.ammesquita.pt. Civil construction and public works.

Arsol Plasticos, Lda.: Devesa Velha – Apartado 363, 3700-913 S.João da Madeira; ☎256-202310; fax 256-202319; www.arsolplasticos.com.

OPCA – Obras Públicas e Cimento Armado S.A.: Rua Professor Fernando da Fonseca – Edificio Visconde de Alvalade 5°, 1600-616 Lisboa; ☎217-522100; fax 217-591347; e-mail opca@opca.ot; www.opca.pt.

Somague SGPS: Sintra Cascais Escritórios, Rua da Tapada da Quinta de Cima – Linhó, 2714-555 Sintra; ☎219-104000; fax 219-104001; e-mail somague@somague.pt; www.somague.pt.

Turiprojecto S.A.: Rua António Sérgio, Lote D, 2615-040 Alverca do Ribatejo; ☎219-938400; fax 219-938458.

Electrics and Electronics

AEG Portuguesa SA: R. João Saraiva, 4/6, 1700 Lisboa; ☎218-491171; fax 218-497128.

A.J. Fonseca Lda.: R. Herois Mucaba 32, 4470-056 Gueifões (Porto); ☎229-023868; fax 229-023852; www.masterguardian.com.

Blaupunkt Auto-Radio Portugal: Apartado 2458, 4710-970 Braga; ☎253-606100; www.blaupunkt.com.

EFACEC Capital, SGPS, S.A.: Apartado 1018, 4466-952 S. Mamede Infesta; ☎229-562300; fax 229-562740; www.efacec.pt.

EID S.A.: Quinta dos Medronheiros, 2826-851 Caparica – Portugal; ☎212-948600; fax 212-948700; www.eid.pt.

Electrolux Lda.: Est. Paco Darcos, 85, Edif. Gonçalves Zarco, 2870 Porto Salvo; ☎214-412639; fax 214-413887.

Hoover Eléctrica Portuguesa Lda: Rua D Estefánia 90A, 1000 Lisbon; ☎213-145349; fax 213-537805.

Infineon Technologies S.A.: ☎252-246000; fax 252-246001; www.infineon.com.

Leica S.A.: Apartado 69, 4761 Vila Nova de Famalicão; ☎252-312404;

fax 252-300710; www.leica.com.

Nokia Electrónica Consumo S.A.: Est. de Alfragide; ☎214-717006; fax 214-717302.

Rober Bosch Lda.: Av. Infante D. Henrique, 2-E/3-E, *1900 Lisboa;* ☎218-500000; fax 218-513810.

Samsung Electrónica Portuguesa S.A.: R. Mario Dionisio 2-1, 2795 Linda-a-Velha; ☎214-148100; fax 214-148128.

Sanyo Portugal Electrónica S.A.: R. Faustino Fonseca 1, 2720 Amadora; ☎214-717524; fax 214-713866.

Siemens S.A.: Rua Irmãos Siemens, 12720-093 Amadora; www.siemens.pt.

Sony Portugal Lda.: R. Tomas da Fonseca, Empreendimento Torres Lisboa, 1600 Lisboa; ☎217-204000; fax 217-204090.

Tefal Portugal: Av. da Republica, 90-96-4 dto., 1600 Lisboa; ☎217-956848; fax 218-682547.

Vulcano: Av. Infante D. Henrique – Lotes 2E e 3E, 1800, 220 Lisboa; ☎228-500300; fax 218-500301; www.vulano.pt.

Energy

EDP – Electricidade de Portugal S.A.: Praça Marques de Pombal 12, 1250-162 Lisboa; ☎217-263013; fax 217-265029; www.edp.pt.

Galp Energia SA: Edificio Galp, Rua Tomás da Fonseca (á Est. da Luz), 1600-209 Lisboa; ☎217-242500; fax 217-242965; www.galpenergia. com. Oil and gas.

REN – Rede Eléctrica Nacional S.A.: Av. Estados Unidos da America, 55, 12°, 1749-061 Lisboa; ☎210-013500; fax 210-013310; www.ren.pt.

Insurance Companies and Agencies

Companhia de Seguros Fidelidade Mundial S.A.: Largo do Calhariz 30, 1249-001 Lisboa; ☎213-232424; www.fidelidademundial.pt.

Companhia de Seguros Império S.A.: Rua Augusta 62, 1149-023 Lisboa; ☎213-211000; fax 213-211739; www.imperio.pt.

Companhia de Seguros Tranquilidade: Av. Da Liberdade 242, 1250-149 Lisboa; ☎213-503683; fax 213-503612; www.tranquilidade.pt.

COSEC – Companhia de Seguro de Créditos S.A.: Av. Da República 58, 1069-057 Lisboa; ☎217-913700; fax 217-913720; www.cosec.pt.

Legal Profession

A.M.Pereira, Sáragga Leal, Oliveira Martins, Júdice e Associados: Avenida da Liberdade n° 224, Edifício Eurolex, 1250-148 Lisbon; ☎213-197300; fax 213-197400; www. plmj.com.

Ana Maria Silvestre: 1°C Beco dos Caldeireiros, 8500-520 Portimão, Algarve; ☎282-415672.

Braganca Bruno & Associados: Av. Eng Duarte Pacheco 143/145 2 Dto., Almancil Codex; ☎289-390080; fax 289-390081; www.bbassoc.pt.

Ferreira Pinto Olavo Cunha & Associados: Av. Praia da Vitoria, 71A-7E, Lisbon. ☎210-303190; fax 210-303199.

Fiona Swainston: Rua 5 de Outubro 174, 8135 Almancil, Algarve; ☎289-399181; fax 289-395710.

Grupo Legal Português: Rua Castilho 32 - 9°, 1200-070 Lisbon; ☎213-131500; fax 213-131501.

Linklaters: Avenida Fontes, Pereira de Melo, Lisbon; ☎218-640000; fax 218-640001. London office: 43-45 Gower Street, London WC1E 6HH; ☎020-7580 2066; fax 020-7580 2067.

Lita Gale Solicitors: Rua Ataide de Oliveira, No. 57, Faro, Algarve; fax 289-880559. London office: Chancery House, 53-64 Chancery Lane, London WC2A 1RA; ☎020-4042899; e-mail info@litagale.com; www.litagale.com.

Lusojurist: Rua Almeida Brandão 19, 1200-602 Lisboa; ☎213-975180; e-mail info@lusojurist.pt; www.lusojurist.pt.

Maria Teresa Silva e Dra. Sandra Qudario: Edificio Altis 2°L, Rua do do Indico, 8200-139 Albufeira; ☎289-585162; fax 289-585163.

Neville de Rougement: Avenida Praia Da Vitoria, No. 5, 1ˢᵗ Floor, Lisbon; ☎213-191290; fax 213-527619. www.ndr.pt.

Ronald Swyer: Rua do Comercio-4, Almansil 8135-125, Algarve; ☎289-399362; fax 289-397208.

Simmons & Simmons Rebeldo de Sousa: Rua Castilho no. 32-9, Lisbon; ☎213-132000; fax 213-132001.

Uria & Menendez: Av Duque d'Avila 141, 1050-081 Lisbon.

Manufacturing

ACO – Fábrica de Calçado S.A.: Rua Padre António Ferreira 599, 4770-350 Pousada de Saramagos; ☎252-990410; fax 252-921585. Footwear and leather products.

ADP – Adubos de Portugal S.A.: Estrada Nacional n. 10A, 2615-909 Alverca do Ribatejo; ☎210-300400; 210-300500; e-mail adubos. portugal@adubos-portugal.pt; www.adp-adubosdeportugal.com. Chemical products.

Alvaro Cunha e Ca, Lda.: Lugar dos Carvalhais – Santa Maria Oliveira, 4765-339 – Santa Maria Oliveira; ☎252-900500; fax 252-900509; www.alvarocunha.pt. Clothing.

Alvaro Coelho & Irmãos S.A.: Ap. 56, Zona Industrial de Prime, 4535-902 Mozelos VFR; ☎227-470050; fax 227-470079; www.acoelhoirmaos. pt. Wood and cork products.

Arsol Plasticos, Lda.: Devesa Velha – Apartado 363, 3700-913 S.João da Madeira; ☎256-202310; fax 256-202319; www.arsolplasticos.com.

Arspoi S.A.: Apartado 10, 3730-901 Vale de Cambra; ☎256-426100; fax 256-426101; www.arsopi.pt.

BP Portuguesa SA: Lagoas Park, Edificio 3, 2740-244 Porto Salvo; ☎213-891429; fax 213-891482.

Casfil – Industria de Plásticos S.A.: Apartado 20, 4796-908 Aves; ☎252-820100; fax 252-820109; www. casfil.pt. Plastics/packaging.

Crispim Abreu & Ca Lda.: Lugar de S. Barolomeu – Serzedelo; 4765-918 Riba de Ave; ☎252-900850; fax 252-900859; e-mail info@crispimabreu. pt; www.crispimabreu.pt. Textiles.

Dielmar S.A.: Largo do Chafariz Velho, Ap-8, 6005-999 Alcains; ☎272-900900; fax 272-906679; www. dielmar.pt. Clothing.

Fábrica de Cerâmica de Valadares S.A.: Rua Manuel Moreira da Costa Jr – Apartado 3 EC Valadares, 4408-951 V.N. GAIA; ☎227-150000; fax

227-150091; www.valadares.com. Ceramics.

Flor Textil S.A.: Lugar da Gandara – Soutelo, 4730-570 Vila Verde; ☎253-310380; fax 253-312898; www.flortextil.pt. Clothing.

Glaxo Smithkline Portugal: Rua Dr. António Loureiro Borges n°3, Arquiparque - Miraflores, 1495-131 Algés; ☎214-129500; fax 214-120438; www.gsk.pt.

Gomes & Mendes, Lda.: Rua do Emissor, 208 – Apartado 2511, 4400-436 Canidelo V.N. Gaia; ☎227-723434; fax 227-723432; www.gmshirt.com. Clothing.

Grupo Calvelex: Monte do Calvelo, 4620-249 Lustosa; ☎255-880320; fax 255-880326; www.calvelex.com. Women's clothing.

Grupo Portucel: Apartado 55 – Mitrena, 2901-861 Setúbal; ☎265-700570; fax 265-700553; www.portucel.pt; pulp, paper and stationery products.

Guialmi SA: Apartado 1 – Aguada de Cima, 3754-908 Aguada de Cima; ☎234-660600; fax 234-666906; e-mail guialmi@guialmi.pt; www.guialmi.pt. Office furniture.

Malhas Sonicarla S.A.: Boavista, Mogege, 4770-350 V.N. Famalicão; ☎252-990670; fax 252-990671; www.sonicarla.com. Clothing.

M. da Costa e Silva S.A.: PO Box 17, 3721-904 São Roque; ☎256-870230; fax 256-871427. Footwear.

Mertalúrgica do Levira S.A.: Oiã – Apartado 11, 3770-951 Oliveira do Bairro; ☎234-729300; fax 234-729301; www.mlevira.pt. Furniture.

Metalúrgica Progreso de Vale de Cambra S.A.: Apartado 6, 3730-952 Vale de Cambra; ☎256-460050; fax 256-460051; www.progresso.pt. Metallurgical and light engineering.

MG Rover Portugal: Lagoas Park, Edifício 8 – piso 1, 2740-244 Porto Salvo; ☎219-406000; fax 219-406097; www.mg-rover.com.

Norcor – Industria de Cortiças S.A.: Ap. 26, Porto Region, 4509-908 Flães VFR; ☎227-471000; fax 227-471009; e-mail norcor@norcor.pt; wwwnorcor.pt. Wood and cork products.

Oliveira & Irmão S.A.: Apartado 705, 3801-851 Aveiro; ☎234-300202; fax 234-300212; www.oliveirairmao.com. Bathroom accessories.

Papelaria Fernandes S.A.: EN – 249 – 3 Sitio do Cotão, 2735-307 Cacém; ☎214-268507; fax 214-268607; www.papelariafernandes.pt. Pulp, paper, stationery.

Plasmeriz – Fabrica de Plásticos de Meães Lda.: Meães – Esmeriz Apartado 226, 4764-901 Vila Nova de Famalicão; ☎252-300050; fax 252-375785.

Plimat S.A.: Rua da Alemanha, Lote 35 Zona Industrial, 2431-959 Plimat; ☎244-572323; fax 244-572320; www.plimat.pt. Plastics/packaging.

Recer SA: Vila Verde – Apartado 20, 3770-953 Oliveira do Bairro; ☎234-730500; fax 234-730501; www.recer.pt. Ceramics.

SECIL S.A.: Av. Das Forças Armadas, 125-6°, 1600-079 Lisboa; ☎217-927100; fax 217-936200; www.secil.pt. Cement.

Shell Portuguesa SA: Av da Liberdade 249, 1250-143 Lisbon; ☎210-970620; fax 213-534441; www.shell.com.

Soporcel - Sociedade Portuguesa de Papel

S.A.: PO Box 5, 3081-851 Figueira da Foz; ☎233-900108; fax 233-941650; www.soporcel.pt. Pulp, paper and stationery products.

Sousa Dias S.A.: Lugar de Cimo de Vila, 4765-459 Guardizela; ☎252-900740; fax 252-900749; www. sousdias-sa.pt. Textiles.

Termolan S.A.: Carvalheiras – Apartado 11, 4796-908 Vila Aves; ☎252-820080; fax 252-820079; e-mail termolan@termolan.pt; www. termolan.pt. Thermal insulation.

Tintas Robbialac S.A.: Manjoeira, Santo Antão do Tojal – Apartado 104 – EC Loures, 2671-901 Loures; ☎219-739600; fax 219-739697; www. robbialac.pt. Chemicals (paint).

Vicaima – Indústria de Madeiras e Derivados S.A.: Apartado 9, 3730-953 Vale de Cambra; ☎256-426300; fax 256-426301; e-mail vicaimaind@vicaima.pt; www.vicaima. com. Wood and cork products.

Real Estate

Algarve Real Estate Centre: Rossio Grande, Alto do Poço, Lote E/F Loja A, Apartado 110, 8501-906 Alvor; ☎282-420970; fax 282-420979; www.algarve-real-estate-centre.com.

Algarve Realty: Rua 25 de Abril, 7 r/c, 8300-184, Silves; ☎282-442471; www.algarverealty.com.

Atlantic Estates: Mediacao Imobiliaria Lda., Av. da Marina, Vila Lusa, Loja 7, 8125-401 Vilamoura; ☎289-315324; fax 289-315325; www. atlantic-estates.com.

Beltico – Emprendimentos Turisticos S.A.: Vale de Janelas – Apartado 2, 2510-451 Obodps; ☎262-905000;

fax 262-905003; www.praia-del-rey. com. Managers of a 200 hectare golf and residential resort.

Caldeira & Stevenson: Rua da Carreira 92, 9000-042 Funchal, Madeira; ☎291-228 435; fax 291-220206; www.caldeirastevenson.com.

CerroNovo: Centro Comercial, Cerro Grande, Albufeira; ☎289-510790; fax 289-510799; e-mail allan@cerronovo.com; www. cerronovo.com.

David Headland (Portgual) Lda.: Edifício Twin Stars, Rua Cristovao Piers Norte 362, Almancil 8135-117; ☎289-351790; fax 289-391079.

Grupo Parque Expo: Av. D João II – Lote 1.07.2.1, 1990-096 Lisboa; ☎218-919898; fax 218-919878; www.parquedasnacoes.pt.

Hamptons International: Avenida das Comunidades Portuguesas, Edificio Lapinha A, 8600-501 Lagos; ☎282-789336 & 0870 414 0444; fax 282-788184; e-mail portugal@hamptons-int.com; www.hamptons.co.uk. Also have offices in London: 18/21 Cavaye Place. London SW10 9PT; ☎020-7244 4740; fax 020-7244 4701.

Knight Frank: Edifício Taurus, Campo Pequeno n° 48 – 4 Dt, 1000-081 Lisbon; ☎217-999960; fax 217-999965; www.knightfrank.com.

Lusotur II SA: Apartado 501, 8125-851 Quarteira; ☎289-310900; fax 289-310909; www.vilamoura.net. Managers of real estate in the tourist resort of Vilamoura (Algarve).

Proprium – Mediação Imobiliária S.A: Rua S. João de Brito, 605-3°, 4100-455 Porto; ☎226-197940; fax 226-107890.

Turiprojecto SA: Rua António Sérgio, Lote D, 2615-040 Alverca do Ribatejo; ☎219-938400; fax 219-938458.

Shipping, Transport and Freight

AIM Removals: Parque Indsutrial Do Infante, Unit 8, EN 125, Torre, 8600-256 Odaixere; ☎282-799141; fax 282-799146.

ANA – Aeroportos de Portugal S.A.: Rua D – Eidficio 120, Aeroporto Lisboa, 1700-008 Lisboa; ☎218-841500; fax 218-403547; www.ana-aeroportos.pt.

CTT – Correios de Portugal S.A.: Rua S. José 20, 1166-001 Lisboa; ☎213-185803; fax 213-229937; www.ctt.pt.

DHL Transp. Rap. Int. Lda.: Rua Cidade de Liverpool 16, 1199-009 Lisbon; ☎707-505606; www.dhl.pt.

Grupo ETE: Largo do Corpo Santo 21, 1200-129 Lisboa; ☎213-226100; fax 213-226279; www.ete.pt.

Grupo Tertir: Terminal do Freixiero – En 107, Apartado 5144, 4456-901 Perafita; ☎229-991200; fax 229-58926.

K&R Transportes Lda.: Cerro do Ouro, 8200-468 Paderne, Albufeira; ☎289-368 879; fax 289-368881.

Metropolitano de Lisboa EP: Av. Barbosa du Bocage 5, 1049-039 Lisboa; ☎213-558457; fax 213-574908; www.metropolisboa.pt.

Rede Ferroviária Nacional, REFER, EP: Estação de Santa Apolónia, 1100-105 Lisboa; ☎211-022000; fax 211-022439; www.refer.pt. Management of rail infrastructures, transport equipment.

SPC – Serviço Portugues de Contentores

S.A.: Parque Industrial Salgados da Póvoa de St. Iria; ☎219-568300; fax 219-568308; www.sapec.pt. Transport, distribution and logistics.

Transporta – Transportes Porta a Porta S.A.: Av. Frei Miguel Contreiras, 54-1°, 1749-017 Lisboa; ☎218-424700; fax 218-405278; www.transporta-sa.pt.

Vendap – Soc. Portuguesa de Aluguer e Venda de Equipamentos, Lda.: Estrada Nacional 118 ao km 22, Vil Figueiras – Apartado 107, 2135-111 Samora Correia; ☎212-349150; fax 212-349159; www.vendap.pt. Transport equipment, hire and maintenance.

Telecommunications

Alcatel: Estrada Malveira Serra 955 Aldeia, Juzo, 2750-782 Cascais; ☎214-859000; www.alcatel.pt.

Ericsson Telecomunicações Lda.: R. da Barruncheira 4, 2795 Carnaxide; ☎214-249300; fax 214-182901.

Portugal Telecom S.A.: Av. Fontes Pereira de Melo 40-11°, 1069-300 Lisboa; ☎215-002000; fax 213-562624; www.telecom.pt.

Telepac II Comunnicações Interactivas S.A.: Rua Dr. António Loureiro Borges 1, 1495-131 Algés; ☎217-907000; fax 217-907001; www.telepac.pt.

TMN Telecomunicações Móveis Nacionais S.A.: Av. Alvaro Pais 2, 1649-041 Lisboa; ☎217-914400; fax 217-914500; www.tmn.pt.

TV Cabo Portugal SA: Av. 5 Outubro 208, 10, 1069-203 Lisboa; ☎217-914800; fax 217-914850; www.tvcabo.pt.

Vodafone Telecel: Parque das Nações, Av. D. João II – Lote 1.04.01 - 8° E Piso

– Ala Sul, 1990-093 Lisboa; ☎210-915252; fax 210-915480; www.vodafone.pt.

Travel and Tourism

Air Luxor: Luxor Plaza, Avenida da Republica 26, 1050-192 Lisboa; ☎210-062200; www.airluxor.com.

Casino Estoril: Praça José Teodoro dos Santos; 2765-237 Estoril; ☎214-667700; fax 214-667966; www.casino-estoril.pt. Hotels and casinos.

Dom Pedro Hotels: Av. Eng. Carte Pacheco – Amoreiras, Torre 2 – 13 – B, 1070-109 Lisboa; ☎213-896600; fax 213-896601; www.dompedro.com.

Ipanema Park Hotel: R. Serralves 124, 4150-702 Porto; ☎225-322100; fax 226-102809; www.ipanemaparkhotel.com.

Lusotur II SA: Apartado 501, 8125-851 Quarteira; ☎289-310900; fax 289-310909; www.vilamoura.net. Managers of the tourist resort of Vilamoura (Algarve).

Pestana Hotels & Resorts: Rua Jau 54, 1300-314 Lisboa; ☎213-615665; fax 213-647537; www.pestana.com.

Portugália Airlines: Aeroporto de Lisbon, Rua C. Edf. 70, 1749-078 Lisboa ☎218-425559; www.flypga.com.

Pousadas de Portugal S.A.: Av. Santa Joana a Princesa 10, 1749-090 Lisboa; ☎218-442000; fax 218-442081; www.pousadas.pt.

Solverde – Soc. de Invest. Túristicos da Costa Verde S.A.: Rua 19, n°85, 4501-858 Espinho; ☎227-335500; fax 227-313193; www.solverde.pt. Hotels and casinos.

TAP – Transportes Aéreos Portugueses S.A.: Edifício 25 – Aeroporto de Lisboa, 1704-801 Lisboa; ☎218-415000; fax 218-416690; www.flytap.com.

Other

AdP Aguas de Portugal, SGPS, S.A.: Av. Da Liberdade 110 - 7°, 1269-042 Lisboa; ☎213-230700; fax 213-460110; www.adp.pt. Environment and water supply management.

Edinfor Sistemas Informáticos S.A.: Alameda dos Ocenos – Vila Expo, Edif. Ico Rock One, Lote 4.62.01, 1990-392 Moscavide; ☎210-018300; fax 210-018430; www.edinfor.pt. Information technology.

INCM – Imprensa Nacional-Casa de Moeda S.A.: Av. António José de Almeida, 100-042 Lisboa; ☎217-810700; fax 217-810732; www.incm.pt. Printing, graphic arts, minting.

ParaRede SGPS S.A.: Rua Laura Alves 12-3°, 1050-138 Lisboa; ☎217-235000; fax 217-235001; www.pararede.com. Information technology.

Quidgest: Rua D. João V, 2 - 6° Esq, 1250-090 Lisboa; ☎213-870563; fax 213-870697; www.quidgest.pt. Software and services to businesses.

Select Recursos Humanos Lda.: Av. João Crisóstomo 52, 1069-079 Lisboa; ☎707-202010; fax 210-105401; www.vedior.pt. Staffing agency.

Searasoft – Desenvolvimento de Software, Lda.: Cais das Pedras, 8/9 1° Esq., 4050-465 Porto; ☎226-075670; fax 226-075677; www.seara.com.

STARTING A BUSINESS

CHAPTER SUMMARY

- ○ The Portuguese government actively encourages inward investment. There are several good governmental sources of information available to the potential entrepreneur.
  - ○ Business formalities centres (CFEs) have recently been established as an integrated system providing all of the facilities for setting up a business in a single location.
  - ○ The government aims to promote the diversification of tourism in Portugal and there are numerous incentives available to innovative business start-ups in this sector.
- ○ **Residence regulations.** A work permit is not required for either EU or non-EU citizens who enter Portugal to set up their own business and are self-employed.
- ○ The **self-employed** and sole traders are required to pay into the social security system and can choose between the minimum rate of 24.5% and 32% (which offers extended cover).
- ○ **Starting vs. buying.** Before deciding which type of business to run you will have to decide whether to buy an existing business or start a completely new one. There are pros and cons to both options.
- ○ **Starting a new business.** The minimum time it will take to incorporate a new company is approximately 23 business days.
  - ○ The cost of incorporating a new company is approximately 10% of the initial share capital.
  - ○ There are several types of corporate entity that a Portuguese business may assume. Choosing the right structure for your business should be the subject of extensive study.
- ○ **Buying an existing business.** Obtain an independent evaluation. It would be foolish to take actual or projected turnover or profit figures at face value.
- ○ **Taxation.** Corporation tax is levied at 25% on the profits of companies covered by the general taxation regime (cut from 30% in 2004).
- ○ **Employing staff.** Bosses are required to make two extra payments to their staff at Christmas and during the annual summer holiday.

INTRODUCTION

Many emigrants from the UK and other European countries who choose to live in Portugal will do so with the intention of starting a business there. Indeed many are already doing so. Generally this is only a realistic proposition for those with previous experience of running a business in the UK or elsewhere, and who have located a demand for a similar enterprise in Portugal. Those without any hands-on knowledge of business practices may be heading for disaster. It is all very well to have been nourishing a retiree's pipe dream of a little bar or restaurant in a sunny place but before embarking on such a project it would be advisable to get first hand accounts from those who are already running catering establishments in Portugal. The alternative is to go into business with someone whose business credentials are already well established. Advice from old hands will almost certainly counteract the idealistic tendencies of the uninitiated. Inevitably long hours and hard work are the lot of anyone in the catering business.

Anyone wishing to escape the professional rat race and use their qualifications (e.g. medical, architectural, legal etc.) to start a practice in Portugal can realistically expect a less pressured working atmosphere and a healthier lifestyle than working in the metropolises of the UK. There will of course always be some expats who have emigrated with a single notion: to live a life of ease with no stimulation except golf, sailing, and the pursuit of pleasure. After initially enjoying the relaxation, boredom might well set in and the need for a challenge arise. Setting up a business in Portugal is certainly that – an obstacle course crammed with trials in the form of endless red tape and regulations. Generally speaking, the bulk of the red tape is reserved for larger business structures requiring substantial startup capital. There are less elaborate procedures for those who are self-employed for which fewer permits are needed.

One is tempted to suppose that the mass of paperwork and the snail's pace bureaucracy that has to be endured exist to deter the ambitions of entrepreneurs. It is therefore good news that positive encouragement exists in the form of the Portuguese Trade Office (ICEP) and the Portuguese UK Chamber of Commerce (see below), which are both indefatigable in their production of leaflets, booklets and in the case of the Chamber of Commmerce a useful newsletter (*Tradewinds*), which contain much information pertinent to business creation in Portugal. Another useful source of information is the British-Portuguese Chamber of Commerce, Rua da Estrêla 8, P1200 Lisbon; ☎213-961586. The following sections detail the necessary procedures for setting up different kinds of businesses, namely:

- Preparation and groundwork in order to select a type of business.
- Raising finance and investigating the possibility of claiming grants and incentives.

O   Selecting the most appropriate legal/corporate business structure.
O   Submitting a prior declaration of intent to start business.
O   Starting the company formation/branch registration procedure.
O   Registering the chosen entity for tax and social security purposes.

Residence Regulations for Entrepreneurs

A work permit is not required for either EU or non-EU citizens who enter Portugal to set up their own business and are self-employed. A residence permit, however, will be required. Although the need for a work permit is waived for the self-employed, many of those who fall within this group will be forced to obtain a licence before setting up in business; this includes any concern which deals with food, the maritime industries, or renting out property in Portugal.

SELF-EMPLOYMENT

If you want to become self-employed (*trabalhador por conta própria*) in Portugal, as a surveyor, lawyer, plumber, carpenter, journalist, language teacher etc., or if you run a business in your own name as a sole trader (*empresário em nome individual*), the procedures are fairly simple. This is a popular option for many, as finding a stable employment contract in Portugal is not easy. Those who have a skill that naturally leads to freelance work, such as translation, feature writing, photography and so on, will be aware of the potential pitfalls. Freelancing can be terribly unstable, and your life swings from being totally inundated with work, to being bored senseless waiting for the next job to come in. However, working for yourself does allow you to organise your own time, hopefully leaving you free to enjoy the relaxed lifestyle that Portugal can offer.

If you practice a profession such as medicine or the law, the EU General System for the Mutual Recognition of Professional Qualifications allows workers to join the equivalent profession in Portugal without having to re-qualify. However it is necessary to have your qualifications checked by the relevant Portuguese body which will grant permission to practise based on the authenticity of these qualifications. Those with crafts or trades qualifications, can also apply to have these recognised in Portugal. Further details are supplied in the *Professional Mobility* section of the *Employment* chapter.

Once you have obtained your residence permit (see *Residence and Entry Regulations*), you will be required to register as a self-employed worker with the tax authorities, who will supply you with a tax card (*cartão de contribuinte*) and a receipts book (*caderneta de recibos*), in which payments received should be recorded. This will be incredibly useful when it comes to filling in your tax forms. As in the UK, it is possible to deduct business expenses from your taxable income, but, as in the UK, there are strict regulations regarding what may be considered a tax-deductible expense. In general, deductions may not exceed 32.5% of gross income.

A self-employed person must also be registered for social security (*segurança social*). The contribution rates are currently 25.4% for compulsory coverage (covers retirement, disability, death and old age) or 32% for optional extra coverage (includes sickness benefits and additional family benefits). Unlike workers on a contract with a company however, the self-employed do not receive paid holidays, nor are they able to claim any form of unemployment benefit if their business fails or if the freelance work dries up. Further information on social security for the self-employed is provided in *Daily Life*.

Those who do decide to become self-employed in Portugal, or are running their own businesses without having formed an incorporated entity, should certainly seek the advice of a good accountant to make sure they are making the most of their tax situation, and paying the appropriate social security contributions. Self-assessment declarations can be difficult enough in English, let alone in Portuguese!

TALKING TO THE RIGHT PEOPLE

Preparation

Before launching into the formalities involved in starting a business, solid preparatory groundwork is essential. This undoubtedly means spending some time in Portugal. Prospective entrepreneurs can rent accommodation in the Algarve, Lisbon, Cascais and other expatriate playgrounds while they do their reconnaissance. The Portuguese National Tourist Office in London and the Portuguese-UK Chamber of Commerce, can provide a list of UK-based property-letting agencies and other useful information. It is advisable to rent outside the main tourist areas, or out of the summer season, as seaside, summer rents tend to be astronomical. Whilst out in Portugal the aspiring businessman or woman should carry out a thorough survey of the areas in which they are interested. It is advisable to assess carefully the potential of any proposed business, and in particular the general viability of any scheme (e.g. supplies, supporting infrastructure) they have in mind. Demand is also a vital factor in the success of any business: for instance, can the area support another bar, restaurant, horticultural centre, bookshop etc.? Is income purely seasonal, or all year round?

Sources of Information

The Portuguese government actively encourages inward investment. There are several good governmental sources of information available to the potential entrepreneur, and these organisations will be happy to deal with initial enquiries and provide general orientation. The websites of these organisations are provided below. The most important of these organisations for initial guidance and information are:

The Portuguese UK Chamber of Commerce: 22-25A Sackville Street, London W1X 1DE; ☎020-7494 1844, fax 020-7494 1822; www.portuguese-chamber.org. uk.

ICEP: 22-25A Sackville Street, London W1X 1DE; ☎020-7494 1844; fax 020-7494 1822; www.portugalinbusiness.com.

API: Edificio Peninsula Praça do Bom Sucesso 126-131, Sala 702, 4150-146 Porto; ☎226-055300; fax 226-055399; e-mail api@investinportugal.pt; www.investinportugal.pt.

Additionally, useful online 'business in Portugal' guides are provided at the following locations:

○ www.investinportugal.pt/MCMSAPI/HomePage/InvestingInPortugal/ BusinessSetUp/ (under *Investor's Guide* select *English*).
○ www.hlbi.com/DBI_list.asp (select *Portugal* for the PDF document).
○ www.deloittewebguides.com (under business guides – select *Portugal*).

USEFUL WEBSITES

www.prime.min-economia.pt: Portuguese Ministry of Economy.

www.portugalinbusiness.com: Portuguese Investment Tourism Institute.

www.investinportugal.pt: API – Portuguese Investment Agency (*Agência Portuguesa para o Investimento*).

www.portuguese-chamber.org.uk: The Portuguese-UK Business Network.

www.portugaloffer.com: Business club promoting trade with Portuguese companies around the world.

www.iapmei.pt: IAPMEI – Portuguese Institute for Small and Medium Sized Enterprises and Investment (*Instituto de Apoio ás Pequenas e Médias e ao Invetimento*).

www.cfe.pt: CFEs – *Centros de Formalidades das Empresas* – procedures for registering a business.

www.portugalinbusiness.com: ICEP – The Portuguese Investment Tourism Institute.

www.port-chambers.com: Lisbon Trade Association.

www.ifturismo.min-economia.pt: Portugal Tourism Institute – has details about tourism businesses.

www.adi.pt: Portuguese Innovation Agency (*Agência de Inovação*).

On a local level there are also numerous organisations that will be able to offer advice or at least point you in the right direction. These include your local municipal council, your local citizen's shop (*loja do cidadão*) and your local employment services. In some towns and cities there are also Business Formalities Centres (CFEs – see below) that can provide you with advice regarding the setting up of a new business entity.

If you are thinking of buying an already established business then you will have far less red tape to deal with, but you are running a completely different set of risks and should still obtain professional advice.

Professional Assistance

Lawyers. Inevitably the prospective businessman will at some point during the setting up, buying or running of the enterprise, need specialist legal advice from a qualified, English-speaking lawyer. If you are willing to spend the money, it is possible to give a lawyer power of attorney to deal with all of the necessary procedures involved in establishing a business presence. It is well worth investing the money in seeking professional advice since the authorities are becoming increasingly vigilant and will not hesitate to close down or heavily fine a business that does not have the correct papers to trade.

Lawyers' fees can vary enormously in Portugal, depending on the amount of work involved. It is best to ask in advance and try to agree on a fee before choosing a lawyer.

There are a number of UK law practices with knowledge of Portuguese company law and some international firms with offices in Portugal. However, many small businesses will be best served by a local Portuguese practice, and although these are numerous, English-speaking lawyers are relatively rare. A list of Portuguese law firms is provided at the end of the *Employment* chapter. Those looking for legal advice in the UK, should approach one of the following companies, both of which have experience of commercial law in Portugal:

The International Property Law Centre: Unit 2, Waterside Park, Livingstone Road, Hessle, HU13 OEG; ☎0870-800 4565; fax 0870-800 4567; e-mail internatio nalproperty@maxgold.com; www.internationalpropertylaw.com. Specialists in the purchase and sale of Portuguese property and businesses, wills and probate, and litigation.

John Howell & Co Solicitors & International Lawyers, The Old Glass Works, 22 Endell Street, Covent Garden, London WC2H 9AD; ☎020-7420 0400; fax 020-7836 3626; e-mail info@europelaw.com; www.europelaw.com. Team of lawyers specialising purely in foreign work.

Accountancy Firms. Anyone intending to go into any form of business in Portugal will need expert advice to guide them through the fiscal jungle. There are several

UK accountants with branches in Portugal and the Portuguese UK Chamber of Commerce in London, or the British Embassy in Lisbon, will supply a list on request. International accountancy firms with branches in Portugal include:

PricewaterhouseCoopers: Palácio Sottomayor, Rua Sousa Martins 1-2°, 1050-217 Lisboa; ☎213-599000.

Deloitte Touche: Edifício Atrium Saldanha, Praça Duque de Saldanha, 1 -6°, 1050-094 Lisboa; ☎210-423000; fax 210-423190; www.deloitte.com.

Ernst & Young: Edifício República, Avenida da República 90 - 3°, 1649-024 Lisboa; ☎217-912000; fax 217-957590; www.ey.com.

KPMG: Edificio Monumental, Avenida Praia da Vitoria, 71A-11, 1069-006 Lisboa; ☎210-110073.

Corporate Relocation. Those who would like to transfer an existing business from the UK to Portugal can employ the services of a corporate relocation specialist. Relocation specialists are widely used in the USA but are a relatively new concept elsewhere. These will offer services similar to, but more extensive than, a lawyer or accountant. Smaller businesses will usually take the option of setting up a new business from scratch in Portugal; and it may be better then to seek your legal and accountancy advice on the spot.

IDEAS FOR NEW BUSINESSES

Starting a business from scratch requires thorough background research, preferably on the spot, and if possible conducted for longer than a few weeks. If you have already lived in the area where you wish to start a business, so much the better, particularly if you have made a point of getting on good terms with anyone who can use their influence in your favour. In Portugal knowing the right people can make the difference between falling over every obstacle in your path or negotiating each stage painlessly. One aspect of doing business in Portugal is worth noting: the Portuguese have a relaxed attitude to business dealings; deals are more likely to be struck over a drink in a bar than from either side of a desk. So part of your business plan should certainly be to cultivate new contacts.

Those thinking of starting a business in Portugal, should really approach it from the point of view of an entrepreneur, rather than an expat. There are always bars and restaurants for sale and these may seem very appealing. However, the truth is that these businesses often struggle out of season, and owners can be forced to work horrendously long hours just to scrape together a living. It is therefore always better to be a little bit creative in your choice of business; to come up with an original idea and fill a gap in the market. The most important consideration when deciding on the type of business you will open is whether or not it is viable. Is there a market for your product or service and will you be able to compete against similar products or services in the area? This is not to say that a bar or restaurant will certainly not succeed. On the contrary, there are many bar-owners making a comfortable living. Entrepreneurs should however, try to ensure that their business has a unique selling point to distinguish it from the competition, and they should always do a comprehensive study of the market before entering into anything. Once you look beyond the bars and restaurants that are for sale, you will find a wealth of business opportunities, from selling handicrafts to practising medicine. Small garages, plumbers, gardeners, legal advisory services, caretakers, delicatessens, bookshops, desktop publishers, dairy farms, trout farms and English language publications are just some of the businesses being operated by expats at present. There are a number of other possibilities connected with Portugal's burgeoning tourism trade, which is moving up-market and towards more independent holidays.

Tourism

Portugal is a country of stunning natural resources. Aside from the 800 kilometres of coastline, the country also offers the discerning traveller a variety of striking scenery and an array of historical and cultural traditions. Around 12.5 million visitors are attracted to Portugal each year, providing vast employment and entrepreneurial opportunities, and Euro 2004 undoubtedly helped to focus international attention on Portugal as a tourist destination.

The Portuguese government, aware of the importance of this industry, is currently working to create a business environment conducive to encouraging start-ups, with relevant incentives schemes and favourable government support to the tourism industry. One of the government's main targets is to promote the diversification of tourism in Portugal. Whilst the Algarve beach holiday is undoubtedly still very popular, Portugal is keen to promote some of its more hidden delights inland and in the north. Rural tourism is becoming very popular, and international tour operators are beginning to offer packages which include cruises on the Douro River in northern Portugal and wine tasting tours.

As tourism continues to diversify in Portugal, other possibilities for holidays-with-a-difference will arise. For example there is certainly a market for walking and riding holidays in areas of natural beauty. Alternative holidays are also beginning to attract attention in Portugal, with a sharp rise in the number of spas and health centres, as well as yoga centres. Those with artistic flair could also consider offering painting and arts and crafts holidays.

In addition to mainland Portugal, the Azores are being promoted for walking and big game fishing holidays and there are openings here too for adventure holiday organisers.

The most popular sport with visitors to Portugal is golf. There are signs that the existing facilities are under pressure and that there is scope for additional golf courses, and many more permanent developments for visitors and expatriates are growing up around golf courses. Tennis and water sports facilities, and marinas are also current growth areas.

One area that looks promising for the future is the provision of tourist accommodation and facilities. The Portuguese Tourist Board is keen to promote Portugal as a year-round destination. The Algarve is also becoming more popular with those (like elderly and retired people) who stay there over the winter because of its mild climate. This means that businesses in this area, hitherto dependent on a seasonal tourist trade, may in future be able to benefit from a more regular income. The Tourist's Board's other aim is to increase the number of Pousadas and manor house holidays available around Portugal. Pousadas are historic hotels run by the state, but manor houses are privately owned and usually less grand than pousadas. This is a growing sector of the market.

Those who wish to establish a tourism-related business, be it hotels and accommodation, or leisure complexes, will need to follow the steps outlined in the box below in order to obtain a tourism licence from the Directorate General for Tourism.

STEPS FOR OBTAINING THE LICENCE FOR A TOURIST ACTIVITY

Step 1 – Visit the local council office, who will advise you as to the relevant requirements for your particular activity (*pedido de inormação prévia*). On your behalf, the municipality will consult the Directorate General of Tourism (DGT) and the Regional Coordinating Commission. These entities will come to a decision on your proposal within thirty days.

Step 2 – Should you require a **building permit**, the building plans and safety measures will need to be examined by the local council (*Câmara Municipal*), who will also consult the DGT. The local council will issue a building permit after a detailed assessment of the project. Entrepreneurs should bear in mind that building regulations for tourist businesses are fairly strict regarding provision of disabled access.

Step 3 – Permit for Tourism Use (*Licença de utilização turística*). The local council will send a representative to visit the location and inspect the site, as soon as the business is ready to open.

Step 4 – The entrepreneur then has two months after the above permit has been issued to request the final approval of classification of the tourism activity (*Vistoria de aprovação definitive da classificação*). This will involve a representative of the DGT visiting your business and officially approving it.

Car Hire

Another possibility for new businesses connected with the increase of tourism, and in particular independent and tailor-made holidays, is car hire. This has experienced something of a boom recently, particularly in Lisbon, Porto and the Algarve. Many UK tour operators book cars for their clients at very competitive terms, so the market is operating on low margins. However it may be possible to compete with on-the-spot rentals for casual customers in the Algarve, or land a lucrative contract with a tour operator. Car maintenance is another need, as more British people live there or choose to travel around by car.

Shops and Services

Over the last fifteen years, Portugal has developed the kind of consumer culture that we are used to in the UK and the USA. The new consumer class amongst Portugal's young and affluent now pursues shopping as a pastime, rather than out of necessity, and whilst fashionable boutiques and multinational chains were unheard of previously, they are now appearing rapidly in Portugal's towns and cities. However, despite this 'progress', over half of all shops in Portugal are still small and often family-run businesses, peddling the traditional wares that they have sold for generations. Small outlets with an unusual product will therefore be able to flourish in a retail environment that as yet has not been completely consumed by supermarkets and international chains.

Many entrepreneurs have chosen the route of setting up shops to sell goods imported from the UK to homesick Britons who miss their marmite and digestive biscuits, or are in need of a good English-language book. There is also a market amongst the local population for everyday British items which may appear quite exotic to the Portuguese.

Wherever there are expatriates, there is also a need for services in English, including builders, carpenters, electricians, plumbers, piano tuners, removals, TV installation, insurance, central heating specialists, kennels and catteries, hairdressers and so on. If you have experience providing a service elsewhere, there is no reason why it should not translate to the expatriate market in Portugal. Ex-pats who have not yet got to grips with the language will be far more comfortable dealing with services that they can understand. Once you have mastered the language yourself, then you should be able to offer such services to the local population.

Property Related Businesses

The property market in Portugal is currently faring well, remaining buoyant throughout 2004 and continuing to rise in 2005. Interest rates remain low, the euro remains stable, there is still a great deal of property available throughout the country and international interest in buying property in Portugal is high. Certainly amongst UK residents, interest in property investment in Portugal has been encouraged by a strong economy and buoyant UK housing market, as well as other factors such as the increasing ease of travel to and from Portugal. All of this suggests that there are many business opportunities available to the entrepreneur within this sector, including setting up as an estate agent, property management companies (who manage the properties of absentee landlords), gardening and maintenance services, and of course private rentals. Property developing has traditionally been one of the ways that the British have earned a living in Portugal. Many small developers have built up extensive business empires by building properties and selling them on. Others run thriving property management companies or have built up holiday rental portfolios.

Renting out property is one of the more obvious ways for second home owners to exploit their recurring visits to Portugal. Terms and conditions of rent agreements and the tax implications of renting out second homes are detailed in the earlier chapter, *Setting up Home*. However, it is worth pointing out here that the buy-to-let market can be extremely lucrative. And buy-to-let investors are snapping up properties, especially those on or near to golf courses and marinas, and those in resorts that are close to a beach and are well served by local shopping and leisure facilities. It is also worth reiterating that the recent introduction of new taxation laws in the property market (see *Setting up Home* for further details) has been very favourable to investors. Changes to tenancy laws are also expected in 2005 and it is believed that these will create greater flexibility in the long-term rental market (long-term rentals must currently last for a period of five years).

The availability of property management companies in Portugal are also an encouragement to those looking to let property. These companies take care of your rent collection and bill payments, and are able to resolve any problems that the tenant may have, allowing you far greater freedom. Property management companies usually take a commission of around one month's rent for introducing a new long term tenant, but this is money well spent if you are not going to be available yourself to select tenants and iron out difficulties during the tenancy.

STARTING A BUSINESS VS. BUYING A BUSINESS

One decision that you will have to make before deciding on the type of business that you want to establish is whether to start up from scratch or to buy an existing business. There are pros and cons to both options and these are summarised in the table below. The reality is that it is quicker and easier to buy an existing business but this has to be balanced against the fact that when buying you are limited to the businesses that are on sale, you have a greater chance of being targeted by conmen and you may buy a business that has very little chance of success because the books were pure fiction. The international legal expert

John Howell argues that:

'Existing businesses come with too much baggage such as differing management styles, décor, staff policies and a possibly undesirable customer base. People find that it takes them a lot of hard work, changing things around, before they get it right. Starting a business from scratch allows you to establish the business exactly as you want it, from the outset'.

Of course, balanced against this is the fact that the legal fees relating to starting from scratch are higher and it can take much longer.

Ultimately, it will come down to a purely personal decision based on the type of business that you wish to establish. If the business you hope to start is fairly original and there is nothing like it on the market, then you will have no choice but to start from scratch.

STARTING VS. BUYING

Advantages of buying an existing business	Advantages of starting a new business.
Most new businesses fail within the first two years of operation. Existing businesses have already gone through this difficult period and hopefully established a good reputation, recognised products, loyal clientele, proven management techniques, a place in the market and a clear and visible profit margin.	The business will be entirely your own project – you are free to open exactly the business that you want to open, where you want to open it and you are free to run it exactly as you wish. It will not have any of the baggage that goes with buying an existing businesses.
Existing businesses involve less paperwork. Legal fees are therefore much lower and you should be up and running in a matter of weeks.	All of your options are still open. There are a number of legal entities available, which allow you to minimise your personal liability.
Disadvantages of buying an existing business	**Disadvantages of starting a new business**
It is very difficult to value an existing business. How do you know how much the 'intangible assets' such as client base and reputation are really worth? Many people fail to keep proper tax records and their official accounts may bear little resemblance to the reality.	Start-ups can fail due to a host of reasons that could not possibly have been foreseen and the majority of new businesses take around a year or even more to show a profit. During the initial period, all your time energy and funds must be invested into the business. You may need to cover the business's expenses without taking a salary for yourself.

Your choice of business is limited to those which are on the market. Quite often, especially in the coastal resorts, these businesses are for sale because they are struggling to survive in a saturated market.	Starting a new business involves a lot of bureaucracy, paperwork and hence legal fees. Even if you decide not to incorporate a company, you could find yourself waiting six months or so for the town council to approve an opening licence.

PROCEDURES FOR STARTING A NEW BUSINESS

Creating a New Business

In order to create a new business it is necessary to find a gap in the market that has a realistic prospect of success. For instance a bar situated in an isolated village would almost certainly be doomed to failure. We have already mentioned that the task of assessing what kind of business is likely to be profitable can only be done on the spot. Many businesses started by northern Europeans in Portugal are aimed either at the foreign residents or the tourists. Despite the fact that Portugal has one of the lowest per capita incomes in the EU and a quarter of its population lives below the poverty line, the better off local Portuguese residents are also a potential target for goods and services. The aspiring entrepreneur should therefore include the needs of local Portuguese residents when canvassing ideas (e.g. self-service launderette, film processing laboratory, fax bureau etc.).

The type of person intending to create a new business will probably fall into one of three main categories:

Firstly those who are already experienced in running a particular type of business, (e.g. a restaurant or boarding kennels) and would want to find out whether a similar enterprise would be viable in Portugal.

Secondly those whose entrepreneurial flair will help them to spot a lucrative gap in the market. This usually means supplying a product or service familiar at home but not available in Portugal. Food outlets are often successful. Homemade sausages, pies and bread are some of the products that have so far resulted in nostalgic expatriates keeping their fellow nationals in business in Portugal.

The third category is professional services (e.g. legal, medical) for which there is always a demand.

Advice and Assistance

The Portuguese-UK Chamber of Commerce and the Portuguese Government Trade Office (ICEP) are two invaluable bodies for the aspiring investor and entrepreneur to know about. Although they share the same address and work closely together, they have different objectives. Both the Chamber of Commerce and the Trade Office are invaluable sources of information for the prospective business entrepreneur. These two organisations have at their disposal up-to-date information on all aspects of the economic and business scenes in Portugal. They can provide appropriate contact addresses in Portugal for all types of commerce. Booklets on investing in Portugal, including how to start up a business, are available free on request. Enquiries which comprise a range of questions are better submitted by post or fax.

The Portuguese-UK Chamber of Commerce: 22-25A Sackville Street, London W1X 1DE; ☎020-7494 1844, fax 020-7494 1822; www.portuguese-chamber. org.uk. The PUCC is an independent body which exists to promote two-way trade between Britain and Portugal and to promote UK investment in Portugal. A list of companies who are members of the PUCC is kept by the Chamber; and many of its other invaluable services are outlined in the previous chapter.

ICEP: 22-25A Sackville Street, London W1X 1DE; ☎020-7494 1844; fax 020-7494 1822; www.portugalinbusiness.com. The Portuguese Investment, Trade and Tourism Institute is a government agency under the umbrella of the Ministry of the Economy. The ICEP's role is primarily to promote Portugal's image internationally as a producer of high quality goods and services. However, they also provide information and assistance for potential investors in Portugal. The Tourist Office provides fact sheets and leaflets on the different regions and the Trade Office can supply much trade and commercial information. The head office of ICEP in Portugal is: Avenida 5 de Outubro, 101, 1050-051 Lisbon; ☎217-950500; fax 217-937521; website www.icep.pt.

API. Edifício Peninsula Praça do Bom Sucesso 126-131. Sala 702, 4150-146 Porto; ☎226-055300; fax 226-055399; e-mail api@investinportugal.pt; www. investinportugal.pt. The Portuguese Investment Agency (*Agência Portuguesa para o Investimento*) has recently been set up with the mission to promote foreign investment in Portugal. Although their remit is to attract larger companies, they may well provide you with some useful advice and direction, depending on the type of project you have in mind. Further information is available from their website.

Centros de Formalidades das Empresas (CFEs). Portugal has a network of business formalities centres designed to facilitate the setting up of companies. Staff at the CFE are able to explain the complete set-up procedure to potential entrepreneurs. They can tell you exactly which documents you will need, advise as to the most appropriate corporate structure for your business, inform you about the different types of incentive available, and put you in contact with the appropriate government bodies.

CFEs have the legal capacity to incorporate the following type of companies:

O   Private limited liability companies and single-person quota companies.
O   Public limited companies.
O   Limited co-partnership companies.
O   General partnership companies.

CFEs are essentially 'one-stop shops for business' – an integrated system providing all of the facilities for setting up a business in a single location, precluding the need to travel great distances and produce an inordinate number of duplicated documents. The following services are represented and available at all CFEs:

O   Technical information services from the IAPMEI (Institute for Small and Medium-sized Enterprises and Investment).
O   The national commercial registry (DRGN).
O   A notary.
O   The Directorate-General of Taxation (DGCI).
O   The Social Security Financial Management Institute (IGFSS).
O   Company Registry support office (GARC).
O   Licensing Office.
O   A branch of the CGD bank.

The national network of CFEs has offices in the majority of Portugal's major towns and cities. However, it is currently expanding and several new centres are due to open in the near future. The addresses of the main offices are given below. There is also a central helpline: ☎808-213213; and further information is available from the CFE website: www.cfe.iapmei.pt.

CFE Lisboa I: Av. Columbano Bordalo Pinheiro 86, 1099-063 Lisbon; ☎217-232300; fax 217-232323; e-mail cfelisboaI@iapmei.pt.
CFE Lisboa II: Rua da Junqueira, No.s 39-39A, 1300-342 Lisbon; ☎213-615400; fax 213-615423.
CFE Porto: EXPONOR – Feira International of Porto, Portaria C, 4450-617 Leça da Palmeira, ☎229-994000; fax 229-994023.
CFE Coimbra: Complexo Tecnológico de Coimbra, Rua Coronel Veiga Simão, 3020-053 Coimbra; ☎239-499700; fax 239-499717.
CFE Setúbal: Avenida Luísa Todi 379, 2900-464 Setúbal; ☎265-547300; fax 265-547333.
CFE Braga: Edificio da Associação Industrial of Minho, Rua Dr. Francisco Pires Gonçalves, 4710-911 Braga; ☎253-202900; fax 253-202923.
CFE Loulé: Edificio of NERA, Zona Industrial de Loulé, 8100-285 Loulé; ☎289-420600; fax 289-420623.

Researching the Market

Whatever the size of the business, making a comprehensive study of the proposed market is the best way to avoid failure and disappointment. Good market research is necessary for the entrepreneur to ascertain who are the potential consumers for his product or service, both their quantity and their qualities. This will include information on the target population's location, needs and tastes, buying power, age, sex etc. This information is also very useful when deciding how to target your marketing strategy.

However, clients and consumers only make up around half of the market research. It is also necessary to make a thorough study of the competition. The type of questions that need answering include:

O   Who are the market leaders and what are the reasons for their success?

O   Which businesses in the sector are having difficulties and what are the causes?

O   How can we offer our products in a form that is perceived as more attractive than the competition?

O   Which products perform similar functions to ours or satisfy the same need?

O   Which businesses offer products or services that are complementary to ours and is collaboration possible?

Finally a good study of the market should include information on possible suppliers of materials or stock for your business. Often suppliers can be an important source of information regarding the characteristics of the market.

If there is a deficient market, then it really is necessary to abandon the project before you've even started, or at least modify it dramatically. Therefore it is sensible to put as much time and effort as possible into identifying your potential customers, suppliers and competition.

There are a number of specialised market research companies who will do the work for you, but they are expensive and for a smaller business, usually unnecessary given the amount of information publicly available and on the internet. The type of research that you do and the questions that you ask will vary enormously depending on the business. If, for example, you are starting a country hotel then you need to consider the variables affecting the number of visitors you are likely to have such as the traffic throughput, the weather conditions, local attractions and so on. If your business is fairly small scale, then all of this information will be available simply by asking local businessmen and observing trade in the area. If your business is on a larger scale, you may need to do some more in depth investigation.

Consumer associations, trade publications and trade fairs and exhibitions are all good ways of investigating the market, and your local ICEP office or the British Embassy in Portugal will supply details of these.

Making a Business Plan

Producing a business plan is not obligatory for new businesses as in France, nor will it guarantee your business success. However, what it will do is to force you to examine the viability of the business proposal in a realistic way. According to John Howell & Co. Solicitors and International Lawyers, one of the main reasons for people going bust is that they do not have a realistic business plan. It will also provide you with a useful document to present to third parties when for example asking for the opinion of a business advisor, looking for private investment or applying for public subsidies, and also when looking for collaborators for the business. Even if you are planning to take over a business which is already up and running, the business plan will help you to consider the logical and viable steps for development in the future.

It will involve a great deal of work, speaking to potential clients, gathering information regarding the competition, making a projection of all the possible costs that the business will have to confront, and of the capital needed to start up. Maximising the depth of your investigation should mean minimising the risks involved later on.

A mistake which people often make, even if subconsciously, is that they fool themselves. They are very optimistic about their income and tend to minimise their projected outgoings. It may well be worth seeking the help of a qualified accountant to help you to avoid these pitfalls and to make sure that your plan follows an accepted format and is realistic. In the UK, solicitors John Howell and Co. (The Old Glass Works, 22 Endell Street, Covent Garden, London WC2H 9AD; ☎020-7420 0400; fax 020-7836 3626; www.europelaw.com) have a lot of experience drawing up business plans in Portuguese and in the format expected by Portuguese banks and other institutions.

Necessary Steps to Establish and Incorporate a New Company

In order to create a new business entity from scratch, perhaps the most important prerequisite is an enormous amount of time and patience. It is often necessary to visit an array of offices and departments such as the national tax agency, the social security office, your lawyer and so on. Whilst the labyrinthine bureaucracy associated with incorporating a business entity in Portugal may seem off-putting, this section attempts to break the procedures down into more straightforward, manageable stages.

According to the CFE the average time that it takes to set up a company is currently 23 business days. However, the time required by the Company Registry to register the company must be added to this and can vary depending on the efficiency of your local branch.

The total cost of the incorporation process varies depending on the company's share capital and the extent of the articles of association. However, an example cost of setting up a private limited liability company with a share capital of €5,000 is given below.

EXAMPLE COST OF SETTING UP A PRIVATE LIMITED LIABILITY COMPANY

Step 1 – RNPC	Validation Certificate	€56.00
	Provisional Company Identity Card	€14.00
Step 2/3 – Notary	Deed of Incorporation	€130.94
	Stamp Duty (0.4% of the share capital)	€20.00
Step 4 – DGCI	Company Identity Card	€15.96
Step 5 – Company Registry	Initial Registration	€56.00
	Fee	€3.74
	Certificate Application	€16.00
	Fee	€1.25
	Registration in the Company Archive	€20.00
	Publication in the *Diário de República* (3 paras)	€216.00
TOTAL	**€549.89**	

(Source: *Centro de Formalidades das Empresas*)

Step 1 – Provisional Registration of the Company Name. The first step on the path to obtaining the deed of incorporation is to apply for approval of the company name at the National Registry of Companies – *Registo Nacional de Pessoas Colectivas* (www.dgrn.mj.pt). The company name must reflect the activities that the company intends to perform and cannot be misleading or easily confused with another company name that is already registered. Having decided upon a name it is necessary apply for a Validation Certificate – *Certificado de Admissibilidade* (application form Mod. 11 in duplicate) and a Provisional Company Identity Card – *Cartão Provisorio de Pessoa Collectiva* (application form Mod. 10). The approval application will require that you propose two alternative company names. The applicant must be one of the company's future shareholders and the forms must be signed by the applicant or his/her legal representative.

The Validation Certificate currently costs €56, and the provisional identity card costs €14.

Step 2 – Request a Date for the Signing of the Deed of Incorporation. As soon as you have received the Provisional Company Identity Card, it is possible to arrange a date for the signing of the notarial deed, which must within 180 days of receiving the Validation Certificate. The following documents must be taken to the Notary's office:

- Validation Certificate – *Certificado de Admissibilidade.*
- Provisional Company Identity Card – *Cartão Provisorio de Pessoa Collectiva.*
- Copies of each of the shareholders' identification documents.
- An official auditor report for the different asset (non-cash) participations of the shareholders.

Step 3 – Execution of the Public Deed of Incorporation. Once the articles of incorporation have been drawn up, and on the agreed date, the company deed must be signed and sealed by the Notary Public. It is necessary for all of the shareholders or their legal representatives to attend the incorporation and the Notary Public will require those who appear before him to demonstrate evidence of their identity and, where applicable, power of attorney. All notarial fees should be paid at the moment of incorporation.

Step 4 – Declaration of Start of Activity for Tax Purposes. Following the execution of the deed of incorporation, and within 90 days of the Provisional Company Identity Card being issued, the commencement of business activities (*Declaração de Inicio de Actividade*) must be registered at the Government tax office – the *DGCI, Direcção-Geral dos Impostos* (www.dgci.min-financas.pt). The official form (Modelo 1698) must be filled out in triplicate and will require details of the company's official accountant as well as his/her signature. The following documents will also be required at this stage:

- The Provisional Company Identity Card.
- A copy of the Deed of Incorporation.
- Copies of the Identification Documents and Tax Cards of the shareholders and the company's official accountant.

You should now be provided with the full business identity card.

Step 5 – Registration of the Company at the Commercial Registry. The Company's constitution should be registered at the *Registo Nacional de Pessoas Colectivas* (RNPC) within 90 days of the incorporation of the public deed. There is no central registry, so companies are required to register at the local Commercial Registry. To register officially you will be required to fill out an official form (*Impresso Modelo 232*) and present the following documents:

- The company's Deed of Incorporation.
- The company's Validation Certificate.
- The Declaration of Start of Activity.

The commercial registry will then arrange for the company's publication in the Portuguese Official Journal (*Diário da Republica*) or in a local or regional newspaper where the company is based. This applies to private limited liability companies, public limited companies and limited co-partnership companies. Payment will be required of registry office fees, RNCP tax, and a publication fee.

The company should also be registered at the Commercial or Industrial Record Office (*Cadastro Comercial ou Industrial*) within thirty days of the opening of a commercial establishment, or at the start of operations.

Step 6 – Registration at the Regional Social Security Office. Finally the new company must also register with the regional Social Security Office, within thirty days of starting business activities. To do this, the following documents are required:

- The Company Tax Card.
- An authenticated copy of the Deed of Incorporation.
- The RNPC Identity Card.
- Company minutes naming the members of the statutory board and the form in which they will be paid.
- Copies of the Tax Cards of the members of the statutory board.
- The tax declaration of the start of activity.

Companies are obliged to register their employees into the social security system. The statutory board members may ask to be exempt from payment of contributions, if they have paid contributions for another activity and still do not receive any salary or remuneration as director.

WHICH BUSINESS STRUCTURE?

One of the first decisions that the entrepreneur should make, having analysed the viability of his business, is which form of business enterprise he should adopt. There are several types of corporate entity that a Portuguese business may assume and choosing the right structure for your business should be the subject of extensive study. Taking legal advice, or CFE advice, is a must. The most frequently adopted company structures are the private limited company (*Limitada*) and corporations (*Sociedades Anónimas*).

One of the main considerations is finding a good balance between keeping the administration simple and protecting your personal assets. It is impossible to establish general criteria to determine the legal form that your business should take, as each particular project will have its own characteristics and requirements. Remember that the decision that you do make will determine aspects such as the individual liability of share/'quota'-holders, the form of taxation payable and the amount of capital to be invested.

Business Structures for Individuals

There are two forms of business possible for individuals:

Unlimited Sole Trader. this type of sole trader is responsible without limit for debts which he may incur as a result of his trading activities.

Estabelecimento Individual de Responsabilidade Limitada (EIRL –Sole Trader With Limited Liability). Under this the trader can safeguard his personal assets by limiting liability to the company's assets only. The registration procedure is the same as for companies (see below). An EIRL requires a minimum investment capital of 5000 euros.

It is also possible for a single shareholder to form a limited company (see below)

Business Structures for Companies

Sociedade por Quotas (Lda). An Lda is a private limited liability company and is the most widely used form of company for small and medium-sized enterprises. It is suitable for small businesses generally because the administrative and supervisory control by overseeing bodies is kept to a minimum. The main characteristic of an Lda is that all partners are liable not only for their own contributions but also for all contributions required to realise the full amount of the company's share capital. The minimum capital investment is 5000 euros. The minimum value of each quota is 100 euros (i.e. no less than 2% of the share equity). The Articles of Association by which an Lda is bound to operate must include by law, shareholders' names and contributions. Contributions must always be in cash. However as a transitional measure 50% of capital contributions may be postponed to fixed or determinable future dates. Contributions must be lodged with a credit institution (*Caixa Geral de Dépositos*) in the period prior to notarial registration of the Articles of Association. This is by way of a deposit.

Deferred contributions ultimately fall due at the expiry of a five-year period from the signing of the Articles of Association. An Lda is required to maintain a legal reserve of a minimum of 1,000 euros. The governing bodies of an Lda are the shareholders and director(s). Shareholders' meetings may decide on supplementary provisions of capital, disposal and reorganisation of contributions (quotas), expulsion of members, dismissal and appointment of managerial staff, approval of accounts and distribution of profits and handling of losses. The Shareholders' meeting can also arrange the alteration of the Articles of Association, and approve

mergers, demergers and any other transformations of the company.
The management of the company is attributed to one or more directors, who may or may not be shareholders. If a legal entity is elected as a director it must nominate an individual to represent its name.

One good piece of news for smaller businesses is that auditing is optional in private limited companies. However, if such companies do not have an auditing board, they are required to appoint a qualified auditor (*Revisor official de Contas*) if two of the following three limits are surpassed in two consecutive years.

- Total net assets of €1,500,000.
- Total net sales and other profits of €3,000,000.
- More than fifty employees.

Individual Shareholder Company (*Unipessoal*). This is a form of private limited company which is either incorporated from the beginning by a single shareholder, or an ordinary private limited company which is subsequently transformed into a single shareholder company by concentrating all of the capital in a single shareholder. Other than the fact that it is entirely owned by an individual, this form of entity is identical to the Limitada described above, with a minimum start-up capital of €5,000. However, the name of the company must include the word *unipessoal* before the word *limitada*.

Sociedade Anónima SA Corporation. An SA has a more complex system of supervision and administration than the all-purpose Lda. It is suitable for large and international concerns. The SA form is essential for companies who wish to have their shares quoted on the Lisbon Stock Exchange. Shareholders' financial obligations differ from an Lda in that they are only liable for the amount equivalent to their individual contributions to realise the shares subscribed by them. A minimum of five shareholders who may be either individuals or corporations, is required for the incorporation of an SA. The procedures of incorporation are broadly similar to those of an Lda. There are however additional regulations and larger financial considerations in the structure of an SA.

The minimum capital required is 50,000 euros and the shares must have a value of not less than 1 cent of a euro each. Not less than 30% of the share capital must be deposited with a credit institution (see Lda's above) before the final registration of the Articles of Association.

The incorporation of an SA is usually made partly by private and partly by public subscription when individual promoters subscribe for shares (*acções*). Commercial law requires the existence of at least five shareholders. The shares represent the capital of the company and their issue price cannot be less than their nominal value. Except in exceptional circumstances it is forbidden for the company to own in excess of 10% of its own share capital.

Definitive conditions governing SA's are set out in the statute entitled *Código das Sociedades Comerciais*. The promoter(s) must prepare a draft of the Articles of Association in which should be included, a precise description of the activities in which the company will be involved and the number of shares not yet subscribed for. The draft Articles should then be submitted for provisional registration. When this has been carried out the promoters place the shares for private subscription and offer the others for public subscription. Upon completion of these preliminaries each promoter and subscriber is entitled to one vote per share at a meeting for all promoters and shareholders. The minutes of the meeting are registered with a notary and incorporated into the deed. A copy of the minutes is also filed with the *Conservatória do Registo Comercial* (Commercial Register).

The final articles of Association should include details of the categories of shares, the procedure (if applicable) for the issue of bonds or debentures, and the organisation and supervisory structure of the company, and the conditions, if any, governing the transfer of shares. A share register must be kept at the head office of the company and be available for inspection by any member.

The supreme governing body of an SA is the Shareholders' Meeting presided over by a *Mesa da Assembleia Geral* (Board). A chairman of the board is elected for a maximum period of four years. Ordinary Shareholders' Meetings must normally be called annually by means of a public announcement in the Official Gazette and a daily newspaper of Lisbon and Porto. Extraordinary Shareholders' Meetings are instigated on the advice of the Company's Board, Management, or Audit Board. They can also be called by the President of the Shareholders' Meeting or by the Courts if the shareholders' request is ignored. The Board is subject to dismissal by shareholders' meetings at any time.

The supervision of a corporation is handled by an Audit Board or a single statutory auditor if the capital does not exceed 99,759 euros. The Audit Board must meet at least quarterly and minutes of meetings must be recorded and signed by all present. Disapproval of resolutions must also be summarised in the minutes.

Although the traditional form of the administrative and supervisory structure of an SA consists of a Board of Directors and an Audit Board, a new structure is also available, comprising a General Board, an Auditor and the Management.

Sociedade em Comandita (SC) (Partnership Association). This form of business comprises two categories of partners: *Sócios Comanditários* (dormant partners), whose liability is limited to the amount of their shares. *Socíos Comanditados* (Full Partners) who are liable without limit for company debts jointly with other partners. Public corporations and private limited liability companies are usually partners of the latter sort. There are two types of Sóciedades em Comandita depending on the form in which their capital is represented.

Sociedades em Comandita por Acções (Partnerships by Shares): when the capital is in the form of shares. Partnerships by shares require a minimum of six partners i.e. at least one full partner and five dormant ones. Only full partners can contribute services in exchange for their share in the partnership.

Sociedades em Comandita Simples (Simple Partnerships): when the capital is not represented by any shares. Simple Partnerships require a minimum of two partners (i.e. at least one full and one dormant partner) and do not require any minimum capital.

In both types of SC it is normally only full partners who may be appointed managers. The partners' resolutions are adopted in general meetings and the partners' voting rights are in proportion to their stake in the company. However the full partners together, cannot be granted less than 50% of the votes to which the dormant partners are also jointly entitled.

Sociedade em Nome Collectivo (SNC), (General Partnership). A General Partnership is one based on personal relations and mutual trust. Partners are jointly liable without limit for the company's debts except where they have no financial stake i.e. partners may contribute services in exchange for their share in the company without liability for debts. Each partner is entitled to one vote. All partners are managers and each may represent and bind the company.

Branch Office of an Existing Foreign Firm. This form of enterprise is a possibility for foreigners wishing to create a branch office in Portugal of an existing UK-based firm. Opening a branch office requires presentation of a translation of the foreign company's Articles of Incorporation, a certificate of the company's legal existence, a translation of the minute that includes the board's decision to create a branch in Portugal and the appointment of a legal representative empowered by the head office to administer the affairs of the branch. The translation should be duly legalised and posted in the *Portuguese Official Gazette*. When all the necessary documents have been assembled the branch office must be registered at the local Commercial Registry. The branch requires no minimum capital to operate.

BUYING OR LEASING AN EXISTING BUSINESS

Since the paperwork involved in setting up a business is both prolific and time-consuming, it is no wonder that some prospective proprietors look for a going concern which they can take over. Small businesses are, on the whole, cheaper to buy in Portugal than in the UK or USA. It is still possible to sell your house in the UK, buy a home in Portugal and still have enough surplus to invest in setting up a small business. The variety of businesses for sale is quite staggering. Whilst the majority are undoubtedly bars, cafés and restaurants, at the time of writing, one agent was offering a traditional cheese factory for €750,000, an enormous campsite for €350,000, a hairdressing salon for €150,000, and a vineyard for €995,000. Almost every imaginable business comes up for sale at some point.

In order to get some idea of the price range of the type of enterprise in which one is interested, it is advisable to ring and check with a few UK-based property bureaux; many are listed in the overseas property columns of national newspapers. Alternatively a list of agents who deal with commercial properties in Portugal is given below; some of the estate agents listed in *Setting up Home* also deal in commercial properties. Anyone buying a business should note that about 10% will be added to the price by transfer tax and an additional 23% by the notary and registration fees. For details of purchase procedures, please see *Setting up Home*.

Buying an established business can be less risky and much easier than setting up a new one. The obvious advantage is that you are buying a business that is already producing an immediate cash flow and has an established customer base. The risk is also reduced because studying the accounts of a business will allow you to analyse the past performance of a business before buying.

As well as reduced risk, an immediate cash flow and an established clientele, there are numerous other advantages. These include an established location, existing licences and permits, existing suppliers and equipment and sometimes even trained employees.

In spite of all of these apparent advantages, buying a business that is a going concern is not by any means easy and the need for comprehensive research cannot be over-emphasised. Thriving Portuguese businesses are not usually sold without good reason. It is imperative that the buyer finds out what this is before signing anything. It may well be that the business is failing, or there may be a hidden motive such as imminent construction works, which would adversely affect the performance of the business. You should always check local planning permissions for roads, housing developments, rival businesses, factories and anything else that may affect your business.

Anyone planning to buy a business should certainly obtain an independent valuation. Never take actual or projected turnover or profit figures at face value, especially if they are provided by either the current owner or the estate agent. Theoretically the company's books will show the past performance of a business before you buy it. Unfortunately this benefit is almost entirely negated by the fact that in certain businesses, very few people keep accurate tax records. The business owner will usually tell you what they consider to be the actual turnover, but whether they are telling the truth is an entirely different matter.

There are many factors affecting the value of a business. It is fairly easy for example to put a value on the tangible assets such as equipment, fixtures, inventory and so on. However, intangible assets such as the reputation of the business, its customer base and its strength within its own competitive market, are more valuable. It is these assets which will produce your cash-flow and are the best indicator as to whether the business will sink or swim. Other factors, which a buyer should take into consideration, include location, lease terms or possible ownership of premises, competition, reputation, years in business, the industry's outlook for the future, special permits and terms of sale.

In order to ensure that you are paying the correct price for a business, it is better to take professional advice about the viability of a business from an accountant, or lawyer.

Estate Agents

Although there are few estate agents that specialise only in commercial sales and leases, there are many general estate agents with a number of businesses on their books. It may seem very tempting to buy privately, especially with so many businesses on the market, but unless you speak the language very well and have a great deal of experience in business, it is advisable to use an agent. A reputable agent will ensure that your business has all of the relevant paperwork and will make you less vulnerable to getting a bad deal.

Agents take a commission from the vendor rather than the potential buyer, so you should not hand over any money to them. Potential buyers should thoroughly check the credentials of the estate agent that they intend to use before employing them. Some agents may be prepared to sell businesses that they are fully aware are not viable, safe in the knowledge that the buyer has little or no protection against things going wrong. There are however, many more reputable and trustworthy agents who offer full support packages to their clients. What follows is merely a selection of agents for you to investigate:

Algarve Real Estate Centre: Rossio Grande, Alto do Poço, Lote E/F Loja A, Apartado 110, 8501-906 Alvor; ☎282-420 970; fax 282-420979; www. algarve-real-estate-centre.com.

Algarve Restaurants: Apartado 1161, 8401-909 Carvoeiro; ☎282-329216; fax 282-359278; e-mail info@algarve-restaurants.com.

AlgarImob: Urb. Porte da Vila Lote 2-T, 8600-642, Lagos; ☎282-769362; fax 282-763612; www.algarimob.com.

Central Portugal Properties: Tras de Figueiro, Alvorge 3240-402, Ansiao; tel/fax 236-981717; www.centralportugalproperties.com.

CerroNovo: Centro Comercial, Cerro Grande, Albufeira; ☎289-510790; fax 289-510799; e-mail sales@cerronovo.com; www.cerronovo.com and www. cerronovo.co.uk; UK Office ☎01380-831411. A government-registered estate agent, Cerro Novo has a commercial department and handles business properties.

Homes for Sale in Portugal: Couchel, 085-3350 Vila Nova de Poiares; ☎239-

422627; fax 933-171978; email martin@homesforsaleinportugal.com; www. homesforsaleinportugal.com. As well as homes they have a selection of freehold and leasehold businesses for sale.

Imatico: Ava Remigio Manuel, Edificio Palmar, 2450 Nazare; ☎262-551552; fax 551501; www.imatico.lu.

Portugal Property Group: Apt. EC 3600, 8135-902 Almancil; ☎289-994346; fax 289-994785; www.portugalpropertygroup.com. Have a range of businesses for sale and will search for a business for you to your own specifications.

Portugal Home Real Estate: Laarweg 78, 6721 DG Bennekom Nederland; ☎+31 318-630556; www.portugalhome.nl.

Sunseaker Properties: Apartado 89, Praia da Luz, 8601-926, Lagos; ☎282-697413; fax 282-697413; www.sunseaker.co.uk.

Veieranima Lda.: Centro Comercial Monumental Lido 1°, Loja 17, 9000-101 Funchal, Madeira; ☎291-765023; www.vieiranima.com.

Choosing a Business

The first question that you need to ask when analysing any business is 'why is it for sale?'. Obviously there are numerous reasons why a business could be on the market, but it is in your interests to ask searching questions of the owners. If a business has been badly run, or is simply in a poor location, then you may not be buying an asset, but a liability.

Because of the intangible nature of the 'goodwill' involved in a business transfer it is not an easy task to assess the value an existing business. The unreliability of Portuguese accounts exacerbates this problem. There is a tendency for businesses to place in the accounts only that which they want the tax inspector to see! Unlike in the UK or France, there are no hard and fast rules for valuing a business. In most cases the vendor of a business will dictate the price based not on the intrinsic value of the business's tangible and intangible assets but based on recovering what he paid for it with a little extra to cover the transfer fee to the freeholder and the agent's fee. This leads to the fairly ludicrous situation where the price of businesses snowballs by 5% or so each time it changes hands, regardless of whether or not the business has been successful. Many entrepreneurs will endeavour to sell a business on at the same price, or even higher even if the business has been failing. It is essential that the potential buyer has his wits about him as paying more than a business is worth is one of the principal reasons for businesses failing at an early stage. The majority of the businesses sold to foreigners are bars and restaurants in the resort areas and these are notorious for changing hands every six months or so. Agents have very little influence over the price of a business but the good ones will inform you if a business has been on the market for a long time, or if they consider it to be over-priced.

DUE DILIGENCE

To accurately evaluate whether you are getting a good price you will have to take into account the following factors:

- o Cost of 'goodwill' .
- o Cost of rent (for a leasehold or rental business).
- o Previous three years accounts (and their accuracy).
- o Running costs (based on previous years books and your own estimates).
- o Insurance.
- o Employee's contracts.
- o Stock / inventory.
- o Credit to customers.
- o Working capital requirements.

The 'goodwill' includes the customer base and the reputation of a business, but there are other intangible assets included in a business transfer such as the name of the business, the location, the right to continue a lease and so on. The contract should state exactly what these intangible assets are. Even something as simple as a promise from the existing owner that he will not set up a similar business around the corner has value and should be negotiated into a contract. There are numerous horror stories of former leaseholders taking all of their clients with them and decimating the clientele of the new business. The equipment needed to run the business and the stock are tangible assets and are simpler to value.

Location. The most important of the intangible assets is almost certainly location. A greengrocer's has little future if it is next door to a supermarket and bars and cafés rely on passing trade. Admittedly businesses that have built up a reputation rely more and more on people seeking them out, so location is not so important. In the early years of a business though, it makes the difference between success and failure and potential entrepreneurs should research the area and its potential, both during and outside of the tourist season. If not, you could end up losing everything.

Turnover. As mentioned previously, the Portuguese often do not keep accurate records of the business turnover. Many businesses will not even allow you to see the books and even if they do there is no guarantee as to their accuracy. However, there are ways around this. For example, many bars will have a 'day book' in which they record the takings for every single day. Such books are only for the business owner's personal use, not for the tax-man and are therefore likely to give a more accurate reflection of takings. Ask also to look at purchase invoices, see how much stock the business regularly needs to buy and the value of assets which have been invested in. Another handy tip is to look at the takings on any games machines or jukeboxes etc. in a bar or restaurant. Although you cannot investigate this personally, your agent can contact the companies that distribute and manage these machines and such information will give a rough approximation of the business's client base.

BUYING A FRANCHISE

Anyone who is tempted by the idea of running their own business, but who is deterred by the high failure rate, may consider taking on a franchise. 'Business format franchising' is the granting of a licence by the franchisor to the franchisee allowing them to trade under a specific trade mark or trade name. This licence usually includes an entire package comprising all of the necessary elements to establish a previously untrained person in the business and to run it for a predetermined period. Each business outlet is owned and operated by the franchisee but the franchisor retains control over the way in which the products and services are marketed and sold.

The cost of a franchise varies dramatically depending on the type of franchise and its location. For example, one of the most successful franchise operations of all time – McDonalds – will require a minimum investment of €450,000. However, this is one of the most expensive on the market and other less well-known franchises are available for as little as €3,000. Most franchises require a franchise fee, paid at the outset. They will also require a minimum capital investment to help get the business started. This is not a payment, rather your money which you are investing into your business, although how you spend it is usually dictated. The initial investment will vary depending on the size and reputation of the franchisor. On top of this there are usually on-going management service fees charged by the franchisor (approximately 5% of turnover), as well as a charge for marketing costs on a local, regional or even national scale. Some useful websites listing the franchise opportunities currently available in Portugal include:

O   www.franchising.pt
O   www.ptfranchising.com
O   www.infofranchising.pt

Having found a suitable franchise agreement, it is always a good idea to have it checked over by a specialist lawyer.

ADVANTAGES AND DISADVANTAGES OF BECOMING A FRANCHISEE

Advantages	Disadvantages
One of the simplest ways of running your own business if you have limited knowledge of the business world. Good franchisors will offer comprehensive training programmes.	Although it is your own business, you will be constrained by the franchisor's system.
You can talk to existing franchisees before you buy and investigate the pros and cons of a particular chain.	Your business is part of a chain and the image and reputation of that chain as a whole is in somebody else's hands.
The business already has a proven position in the market and a recognisable brand, making it easier to obtain start up capital and premises.	The franchisor has access to your figures and may run regular security and quality checks.
There is less risk because your business will benefit from the brand name and you will be following a path that has proved to be successful in the past.	You must commit to a certain number of years on the franchise contract. If you decide to quit, to re-sell or lease the franchise, you will be subject to any penalties agreed in the contract.
You will benefit from the financial backing of a large organisation. Small businesses cannot usually afford to buy in bulk or spend large amounts on research and development or marketing.	You must pay a franchise fee to join the network and then continue paying royalties throughout the contract period.
You will receive ongoing technical support.	You may be required to make publicity contributions.

Useful Addresses

The British Franchise Association, Thames View, Newtown Road, Henley-on-Thames, Oxfordshire RG9 1HG, ☎01491-578050; fax 01491-573517; e-mail mailroom@british-franchise.org.uk; www.british-franchise.org.uk. Useful for general advice on Franchises.

European Franchise Association, Bd. de L'Humanitie 116/2, 1070 Brussels, Belgium; ☎+32 2523-9707; e-mail eff-franchise@euronet.be. Promotes franchising in Europe and exchanges information between the European national federations and associations.

Portuguese Franchise Association: Associação Portuguesa da Franchise, Rua Viriato 25-3°, 1050-234 Lisbon; (213-192938; fax 213-192939; e-mail apf@apfranchise.org; www.apfranchise.org. Website lists franchise opportunities. Unfortunately only available in Portuguese.

FINANCING YOUR BUSINESS

Those contemplating opening a business in Portugal should note that UK banks in Britain will not usually be able to provide start-up loans in cases where the prospective proprietor intends to become resident outside the UK, although this is now theoretically possible within the EU and not just in Britain. Some UK banks have Portuguese branches (see *Daily Life*). Unfortunately Portuguese banks are unlikely to lend money to start up a business, except in certain circumstances (e.g. if the business deals with manufacturing and guarantees jobs for the Portuguese). But readers should check on this. In addition, Portugal has base lending rates which may be higher than those in the UK. Many of those who have founded small commercial enterprises in Portugal have had to rely on money raised from the sale of a UK home. If this proves insufficient it might be worth considering taking out a mortgage on your Portuguese home through a Portuguese bank. One of the biggest banks is the Banco Espirito Santo e Commercial de Lisboa, with branches throughout the country. Needless to say, the branches in places like Loulé, Faro and Portimão in the Algarve will be more used to dealing with such requests than branches in the back of beyond. When making enquiries one should ask to speak to the manager (*gerente*).

Government Investment Incentives

If raising finance proves a problem it is certainly worth investigating whether the proposed business qualifies for an incentive grant from one of the various Portuguese bodies empowered to allocate grants to certain types of enterprise. This should be considered as an addition to your investment, not of course something which can in itself justify starting a business, which should be viable in itself. This is how government grants are looked on in Portugal as in many other countries nowadays and the prospects for the business from a commercial point of view will usually determine whether or not you can receive an additional grant. If you cannot persuade your bank, or other investors, of this, you are unlikely to persuade the relevant Portuguese government body.

The Portuguese definitely wish to encourage foreign investment. It is to this end that the government has devised a series of incentive packages for agricultural, industrial and touristic projects. Further information regarding all of these investment incentives and grants can be found at the API website: www. investinportugal.pt.

Agriculture. Cash grant incentives for agriculture are available for schemes that contribute to the efficiency of Portuguese agriculture generally, or promote agricultural development in the less developed regions of the country. The grants are distributed by the Financial Institute for the Development of Agriculture and Fisheries (*Instituto de Financiamento e Apoio ao Desenvolvimento da Agricultura e Pescas* – IFADAP), after approval for the project has been granted by the Regional Agricultural Department (*Direcção Regional da Agricultura*). In the first instance the promoter should contact: Information Services, IFADAP, Av João Crisóstomo 11, P1000 Lisbon; ☎213-534456; e-mail ifadap@ifadap.minagricultura.pt; www.ifadap.pt. Forestry projects including afforestation, reafforestation and forest improvement are also eligible for IFADAP grants. The incentive programmes currently available are:

O POAGRO – the Operational Programme for Agriculture and Rural Development. Its aim is to improve agro-forestry, competitiveness and sustainability. Further information is available from: Gabinete do Gestor do POAGRO, Praça do comércio, 1149-010 Lisbon; ☎213-234960; fax 213-234988; e-mail poadr@min-agricltura.pt.

O POAGRIS – Part of the same Programme for Agricultural and Rural Development as above, but aimed at smaller holdings. Includes support for diversification of small holdings and for agricultural services supplied by small companies. Further information is available from Gabinete de Planeamento e Política Agro-Alimentar; ☎213-819300; e-mail gppaa@gppaa.min-agricultura.pt.

O VITIS – Support regime for the Reconversion and Restructuring of Vineyards. Further information from IFADAP (address above).

O RURIS – the Rural Development Plan. Designed to promote a competitive agricultural sector allied to sustainable rural development. Further information is available from IRDHA (*Instituto de Desenvolvimento Rural e Hidráulica*, Gabinete do Gestor, Av. Defensores de Chaves 6, 1049-063 Lisbon; ☎213-184300; e-mail dgrural@dgrural.pt; www.idrha.pt).

Industry. Although there are no incentives designed exclusively for industry, the majority of support measures envisaged under the PRIME incentive programme apply to industry. These measures are designed to attract a range of projects (e.g. mining, manufacturing, catering, vehicle hire, travel agents and transport enterprises) to less industrialised regions and the aim is to create balanced regional development and the continued growth of Portuguese industry.

PRIME was launched in 2003 and the programme's principal aim is to promote the productivity and competitiveness of Portuguese companies. There are also specific incentives for research and development and innovation. Some of the schemes included in PRIME include SIPIE, SIME, NEST and SIUPI. Further information on all of these schemes is available from the Portuguese Investment Agency: www.investinportugal.pt.

Tourism. There are a number of incentive programmes available for projects relating to tourism in Portugal. Applications for further information should be send to the Institute of Tourism Funding and Support (ITP), Rua Ivone Silva, lote 6, 1050-124 Lisbon; ☎217-810000; fax 217-937537; e-mail info@ifturismo.min-economia.pt; www.ifturismo.min-economia.pt). The ITP also provides direct financing to some projects. The current investment incentives available are:

○ SIVETUR – Incentive Scheme for Tourist Products with a Strategic Dimension. Aimed at the development of tourism products with a strategic dimension that will promote economic growth, notably through the use and development of architectural heritage, nature tourism and sustainable tourism. Eligible projects include hotels, rural hotels, spas, restaurants and bars, campsites, golf courses, marinas, theme parks etc. The maximum rate of subsidies applicable to small businesses is 50% of the investment costs.

○ PITER – Integrated Tourism Programmes with a Strategic Nature and Regional Basis. This programme aims to enhance and rehabilitate areas with strong tourism and to take advantage of tourism market niches. The maximum level of finance available is 75% of qualifying costs.

○ PIQTUR – A financial support programme for significant tourism projects, running from 2002-2006 and endowed with €180 million. It supports projects that involve structural training and the enhancement of Portuguese tourism, tourism promotion, employment and training, research, planning and quality improvements, and innovation, information and new technologies.

○ PROREST II – This scheme is designed solely for the upgrading and modernisation of restaurants and bars and is coordinated by the Portuguese Federation of Restaurants, Cafés, Coffee Shops and Similar Services (FERECA, R. Fernandes Tomás, 235-4000 Porto; ☎225-899530; fax 225-103588).

Incentives for Small Businesses. Small companies on mainland Portugal are eligible to receive incentives under the SIPIE scheme, which promotes the creation or development of SMEs (small and medium-sized companies). Industry, construction, trade, tourism and services are all covered by the scheme, which offers a 30% subsidy for investments of between €15,000 and €150,000. The organisations responsible for this project are the Institute for Small and Medium-sized companies (IAPMEI, Rua Rodrigo da Fonseca 73, 1269-158 Lisbon;

☎213-836000; fax 213-836283; e-mail info@iapmei.pt; www.iapmei.pt) and the Portuguese Tourism Institute (ITP, Rua Ivone Silva, Lote 6, 1050 – 124 Lisbon; ☎217-810000; fax 217-937537; e-mail info@ifturismo.min-economia. pt; www.ifturismo.min-economia.pt).

European Union Grants and Incentives. The European Commission also runs programmes to help finance small and medium-sized enterprises, one such scheme is run by the European Investment Bank (EIB). The EIB grants loans to intermediary banks which in turn provide funding for small-scale business initiatives. There are many types of loans and credits with varying maturities, amounts and interest rates, but generally they will cover up to 50% of the overall investment costs. Amounts awarded range from €20,000 to €12.5 million and must be repaid over a period of between four and twenty years. These loans are free of fees and other charges, except for minor administrative expenses.

To search for European Union grants and incentives visit the European Union on-line (www.europa.eu.int), select 'enterprise' and then 'grants and loans'.

RUNNING A BUSINESS

Business Taxation

Corporation tax (*Imposto Sobre o Rendimento das Pessoas Colectivas* or IRC) applies to companies and other corporate entities including public enterprises, co-operatives and non-profit making organisations. Businesses whether commercial, industrial or agricultural are subject to taxation on their profits in the form of corporate income tax. Entities which have their registered or effective headquarters in Portugal are subject to IRC levied on their global income, including income earned abroad. Non-resident entities are taxed only on income deemed by law to be earned on Portuguese territory.

The normal rate of IRC is 25% on the profits of companies covered by the general taxation regime (cut from 30% in 2004). On top of this payment is the *Derrama,* a municipal surcharge that is levied in addition to IRC and is charged at a total rate of up to 10% of the amount of IRC payable. The tax is collected together with IRC, but the revenue goes to the local municipality. The decision to levy the tax and the rate at which it is levied is taken by the municipal assemblies.

The tax is collected annually and determined on the basis of the tax return. IRC is paid in instalments – three advance payments – usually in July, September and December. Then a fourth instalment covering the period up to the deadline for submission of the periodic tax return – which represents the total tax calculated in the return, minus the advance payments. This final instalment is paid when the tax return is submitted (before 30 April). Losses made in a given financial year may be deducted from taxable profits in one or more of the following six years.

Capital gains tax will also be levied where appropriate, normally when disposal of assets takes place two or more years after acquisition.

Profits of a Portuguese branch or subsidiary of a foreign company are also liable to the above taxes.

All businesses must register a record of their company accounts with the local tax office.

Free Trade Zones: Madeira and the Azores are free-trade zones. Madeira offers long-term tax and trade incentives to foreign domiciled corporations who wish to develop their activities within the free zone. Incentives include exemptions from corporation tax until 2011 and local taxes. Further details may be obtained from the Madeira Development Company (*SDM – Sociedade de Desenvolvimento da Madeira, SA*), SDM Building, Rua da Mouraria 9, 1st floor, 9000-047, Funchal, Madeira; ☎291-201333; fax 291-201399; www.sdm.pt.

Santa Maria, the Azores 'free zone', offers similar incentives. For the Azores, requests for information should be addressed to the Governo Regional dos Açores, Rua 16 de Fevereiro, P9500 Ponta Delgada; ☎9624694; fax 9623648.

In addition to the special tax rates in these two free-trade zones, the VAT in these regions is also lower (see below).

VAT

VAT is payable, as in all EU countries, by suppliers of good and services, who charge it on every supply they make, and afterwards pay the appropriate amount to the tax authorities. Suppliers of goods and services are then allowed to deduct from the VAT that they have charged the amount of VAT included in the expenses that they have incurred, as well as the amount of VAT included in imports. However, some expenses are considered to be unrelated to the business activities and are therefore not VAT-deductible, for example, fuel expenses, business travel expenses, maintenance expenses.

VAT is collected at the following tax rates:

VAT RATES IN MAINLAND PORTUGAL, MADEIRA AND THE AZORES		
	Portugal	**Madeira and the Azores**
Reduced rate	5%	4%
Intermediate rate	12%	8%
General rate	19%	13%

Note: at the time of going to press, the Portuguese government announced an increase in the standard rate of VAT from 19% to 21% as part of measures aimed at reducing the public sector deficit to bring it back below the 3% ceiling set by the EU. No further details of the plans were available at this time.

Social Security

The self employed and sole traders are required by law to pay into the Portuguese social security system (*segurança social*) under the self employed scheme. The contribution rates are currently 25.4% for compulsory coverage (covers retirement, disability, death and old age) or 32% for optional extra coverage (includes sickness benefits and additional family benefits). However, self-employed workers can choose their own contribution base in order to determine their level of pension upon retirement. Contributions are paid on a minimum of the monthly minimum wage (€365.60) and on a maximum of twelve times the monthly minimum wage (€4,387.20). Unlike workers on a contract with a company however, the self-employed do not receive paid holidays, nor are they able to claim any form of unemployment benefit if their business fails or if the freelance work dries up.

Those who employ staff will have to register them at the social security office and pay towards their social security contributions. The social security is paid in part by the employer and in part by the employee, although the employee's contribution is withheld at source. Currently employees make a contribution of 11% of their gross salary, and the employer contributes 23.75%. Social security contributions are payable on all salaries, wages, regular bonuses and other regular income. The total amount must be paid to the caixa by the fifteenth of the month following the month for which deductions were made.

Members of the management body of a company or any other legal entity have a slightly different system: they must personally contribute 10% towards their contributions, and the entity must contribute 21.25%. However, the amount of the social security contributions is limited to twelve times the monthly minimum wage (€4,837.20).

Employing Staff

Employment regulations in Portugal are covered in detail in the *Employment* chapter. However, it is useful to look at the employment regulations from an employer's point of view. The labour code (*Código do Trabalho*) was revised in 2003 in order to create a more flexible labour market. Previously labour laws were biased heavily in favour of the employee, making his or her security of tenure almost unassailable regardless of the prevailing economic state of the company. This new legislation has made some improvements in the employer's favour, by facilitating relocation, easing restrictions on short-term hiring and making collective bargaining more flexible. Any queries regarding labour regulations should be directed to the *Institute for the Development of Working Conditions* (*Instituto do Desenvolvimento e Inspecção das Condições de Trabalho*, Serviços Centrais, Prãça de Alvalade 1, 1749-073 Lisbon; ☎217-924500; fax 217-924597; www.idict.gov.pt).

When employing staff, you have the choice between two main types of contract: indefinite term and specific duration contracts. Until recently indefinite contracts have been the norm, and these offer the worker far more protection of his or her rights. However, fixed duration contracts are becoming more common, as it is much easier for an employer to terminate such a contract without incurring heavy redundancy payments. However, officially only certain circumstances can justify a fixed term contract, which may last for a maximum of six years. All forms of contract provide for a trial period. These vary in length, but allow a worker to be dismissed at short notice if they do not meet expectations.

There is one other main type of contract, the temporary employment contract which is applicable to temporary employment firms. In such cases the employer uses a third party (the temporary employment firm) to recruit temporary labour. If however the employer maintains the temporary employee longer than ten days after the contract should have terminated, the employee may stay on permanently.

Staff are entitled to thirteen public holidays and one local holiday. In addition the minimum annual holiday is twenty-two days and the maximum is thirty days. However, under new regulations, extra days of holiday are granted when an employee has taken very few sick days. For example, if an employee has taken only one full day's absence, then they are entitled to three extra days of holiday. These regulations were brought in to counter a culture of taking 'sickies'.

The normal work period for employees cannot exceed eight hours daily or forty hours weekly. However supplementary work may be carried out when a company must respond to a work increase that does not justify hiring another worker. However, the daily limit for supplementary work is 2 hours.

Minimum wages are fixed by the government annually and are currently around €356 per month. However wages are normally agreed by Collective Labour Agreements between the employees (or trade unions) and the Employers' Associations. Two extra monthly salaries are paid annually: one at Christmas and one during the annual summer holiday. As mentioned above, all employees must be registered for social security, and the employer is charged with the lion's share of the contributions which must be made by the fifteenth of the following month.

Marketing

Whichever business you decide to establish, effective marketing is always going to be an integral part of making it a success. The internet has opened up new marketing possibilities and even the most traditional business can, so long as they have access to a telephone line and a computer equipped with a modem, an internet browser and e-mail software (which almost all computers possess as standard features these days), make good use of technology to reach a wider – and international – customer base.

The simplest of websites will act as an online brochure, announcing the business and containing information about the company's activities together with contact information. This can then be improved by adding images of products and services offered (photographs can be taken using digital cameras and then scanned onto the site) as well as logos and graphics, etc. With the introduction of a secure payment facility customers can carry out their business with the company remotely, buying online and paying by credit card over the internet. Even if the cost of providing online shopping facilities proves too high for the start-up business the speed and ease of use of e-mail, together with simple devices such as a downloadable booking/payment form, can work almost as well to make booking and buying easier.

You will want to publicise your website by putting your website address on as much business paraphernalia as possible and registering the site with internet search engines so that your website comes out on the search results page ahead of businesses offering similar services to yours. The domain name (website address) that you choose should be as distinctive as possible and should either include the name of your business or describe the product that you are offering. In addition, if you have the finance to spend, you can advertise your site on other websites. Remember that the best websites are those that are updated regularly and offer up-to-the-minute information about the company and its activities. Updating also brings return visits from existing customers.

Websites are fairly cheap to create. Registering a domain name costs between €50 and €150; site hosting around €50 a month. Site design costs range from zero (if you do it yourself) to thousands of euros depending on how flash you want the site to look. Online shop software, which will allow you to offer secure pay-online facilities, costs around €600.

Setting up your own website is a cheap and direct way to reach potential clients overseas. For even the smallest business, setting up a dedicated website or advertising on a community or commercial site is cost-effective. For larger businesses, the returns are potentially even greater. The internet has opened up whole new fields of enterprise and successful businesses can be established which would not have been possible or profitable any other way. Internet auctions are popular worldwide, and increasing numbers of people are finding they can make a good income by dealing in all kinds of goods and services by using the internet as a cyber-shop window, selling through the internet auction sites and those devoted to specific products (such as second hand books, records, DVDs, etc) and shipping products across the world.

BUSINESS GLOSSARY

Abastecer	to supply
acção	share
accionista	shareholder
activo fixo	fixed assets
activo incorpóreo	intangible assets
advogado	lawyer
caderneta de recibos	receipts book
câmara municipal	town hall/local authority
cartão de contribuinte	tax card
Cartão de Pessoa Collectiva	company identity card
Centro de Formalidades das Empresa (CFE)	Business Formalities Centre
centro regional de segurança social	social security centre
contabilista	accountant
conta bancária	bank account
contrato de arrendamento	lease
contrato de venda	sales contract
custo	costs
declaração de início de actividad	declaration to start trading as a registered business
débito directo	direct debit
dinheiro vivo	cash
domiciliação de pagamentos	standing order
empresa	business
empresário em nome individual	sole trader
estabelecimento individual de responsbilidade limitada(EIRL)	sole business trader
facturas	bills/receipts
finanças	tax office
gerente	manager
imposto sobre o rendimento das pessoas colectivas (IRC)	corporate income tax
imposto sobre o rendimnto das pessoas singulars (IRS)	income tax
imposto sobre o valor acrescentado (IVA)	value added tax
licença de abertura	opening licence for a business
licença fiscal/alvará	business licence or permit
licença de utilização	licence stating what a building can be used for
notario	notary

Registo Nacional de Pessoas Colectivas	National Registry of Companies
sociedade anónima (SA)	business corporation
sociedade em comandita (SC)	partnership association
sociedade em nome colectivo (SNC)	general business partnership
sociedade por quotas (lda)	private limited company
sucursal	branch
taxa de juro	interest rate
trabalhador por conta própria	self employed
Unipessoal	individual shareholder company

APPENDIX

PERSONAL CASE HISTORIES

PERSONAL CASE HISTORIES

LESLEY KEAST

Lesley Keast, 35, has spent the last six years teaching English abroad. A seasoned traveller, she spent her first few years teaching in Hungary, before moving to Italy, and finally to Portugal. She has now returned to the UK, lured by the prospect of a job as the Director of Studies in an international school. For Lesley, Portugal offered a unique and exciting opportunity to become completely immersed in another culture. We asked her:

Why did you decide to relocate to Portugal?
As an EFL (English as a Foreign Language) teacher you realise there is a lot of transience to the job and there are always interesting opportunities popping up. I was looking for a good job rather than a particular location and that's when I saw an advert for a job in Setúbal, a port south of Lisbon, which offered me the chance to work with students I hadn't worked with before (children aged 10-11 and 12-13). The place seemed to ring a bell with me as a school an ex-colleague had worked at and had a good experience.

The more I thought of Portugal the more I liked the idea. You don't see many jobs advertised for Portugal. Whereas for a lot of EFL jobs there are always people moving on, people seem to settle in Portugal and stay in their position for a while. I asked friends for their thoughts on Portugal and I realised that, strangely, it's not a place many people have really visited. This appealed hugely to me and I got very excited about going to live in Portugal.

Did you encounter any problems with red tape?
Having lived in Italy I was expecting to have to wade through a lot of paperwork to get myself official and working. Surprisingly it was very easy to get things organised, but I think a lot of that was down to the fact that my employers (who were Portuguese) knew the systems and helped new teachers out beyond the call of duty i.e. taking me down to the bank to open an account and the office to organise my national insurance contributions/organise tax documentation. On another level I was surprised (and amused) at the degree of bureaucracy for the simplest of things e.g. having to produce my passport to join the local swimming pool.

Was it hard to find accommodation? What is Portuguese accommodation like?

In Setúbal there is a mix of housing, with modern apartments in the suburbs, piles of concrete flats thrown up in the 60s and 70s and then antique apartments in the old town. I lived in a 70s concrete flat but would have liked to have lived in the old town, which is apparently a lot cheaper to live in as everyone wants to live in a more modern flat.

I was lucky because the school provided the accommodation for teachers. My flat was on the 7th floor, spacious and with parquet floors – cool for summer. It was open plan with a long corridor running from the living room/dining area to the 4 bedrooms and 2 bathrooms, but no balconies. I remember waking up one morning in September when it was still very hot and realised, with horror, that there was no central heating. I knew it was warmer in Portugal than many European countries but still…. And yes, even if December was relatively mild, January was indeed chilly. Most Portuguese in these type of flats seem to be content to use a plug in heater and have fleecy blankets to huddle under on the sofa while they watch TV.

My accommodation was furnished, and had a rather gaudy array of dark wood furniture and orange/brown furnishings. It reminded me a lot of accommodation in Hungary and I believe the retro look is now very popular again!

How did EFL teaching in Portugal compare to other countries that you have taught in?

I had a great time teaching in Portugal. Children get lessons in English from the age of 8 so by the age of 10 they already have a good grasp of present and past tenses, and basic vocabulary, but more importantly have some confidence in using the language and want very much to use it to communicate.

I found Portuguese children full of life and fun. Some of them are also quite serious about study and realise it's important. Children have a lot of tests at school and often have a lot of homework to do so that restricted my expectations of giving them homework – they are, after all, only young and were getting English input in their schools as well as the private school I worked at.

My working conditions were very good. I taught a 24-hour week Monday to Friday, and because I was only teaching children most evenings I finished teaching at 19.30. My salary was the same as my salary in Italy, which was attractive as the cost of living is much lower in Portugal and my accommodation was provided free.

How does the quality of life compare to other countries you have lived in?

It didn't take me long to acclimatise. As soon as I found a few friends (mostly other English teachers), located some good restaurants and cafés and got to know Lisbon, I felt very comfortable there. I think the Portuguese have a great quality of life. They seem to have a very easy-going attitude to life and enjoy the simple things like good food and wine in the company of friends and family.

I also found Portugal a very reasonable place to live. I could eat out a few times a week comfortably, pop into a café every day and go travelling. At the end of my time in Portugal I had saved a substantial amount of money, something I had not been able to do in previous jobs as an EFL teacher.

What was the social life like?

My social life was relatively quiet and involved visits to the arts cinema (I speak Italian so could work out the Portuguese subtitles), meals out and travelling. On occasions when I went out to bars and clubs I often found myself getting home at 6-7 in the morning because the energy of the night just kept me going. It's like a time vortex exists on a Friday night. Bars are very low key and comfortable, there's a variety of clubs and the one I liked had good music that wasn't too loud so you could sit and chat to friends. People dressed how they liked and it was a very pleasant atmosphere.

I didn't find it easy to make friends with Portuguese people although I found them friendly and polite. Because I worked with children there was no chance to socialise with students, which is how I've made friends in the past. One of the main problems was that although I could understand a lot of Portuguese, I was not a confident speaker of the language and that restricted my ability to interact with people, which was frustrating. I also think that Portuguese men have a very traditional attitude towards women and have questionable motives for speaking to 'foreign' women. At night it was unusual to see groups of women out in bars as you would in Hungary or the UK.

What did you like best and least about Portugal?

It's difficult to say what I liked least because overall I had a very positive experience. I didn't get ripped off as I have done as a foreigner in other countries. I suppose things like seeing a lot of very ill and poor people on a daily basis was very sad, people with drug problems. At outside cafés and restaurants people selling things can be a nuisance.

The things I liked best is much easier. I loved Lisbon and it's history. In particular I adore the Museu de Azulejos. On a different level I loved the fact that I could get a ferry to the Alentejo, walk along the beach, collect beautiful orange and pink shells, have lunch on the beach and still be back in time to teach my children in the afternoon. I did love my long nights out in Setúbal, I think because I didn't do it very often and also I wouldn't do that in the UK. Oh, yes and seeing the Benfica eagle swoop around the Stadio de Luz before a football match was fantastic, as well as being able to buy cheesecakes at half time.

PATRICIA WESTHEIMER

Patricia Westheimer is an American journalist and teacher. Patricia writes: 'In 1991 I moved from the USA to Portugal, a country I had never visited before I moved. I spoke no Portuguese, had no job and knew no-one before I moved. However, I had been a teacher in the USA and felt sure that I would be able to get a job and support myself. I am also a woman who has always achieved goals I set out to. This was my hardest, but I did it. The move has changed my life, and it was even good before I left! Now I prepare students for University and write a weekly column for the Portugal News. I also teach online courses in the USA and in Europe.' We asked her:

What were your first impressions of Portugal?
I loved Portugal from the beginning. Compared to the USA, it's calmer, more community-oriented, more beautiful, and I love the challenge of speaking a second language.

How traumatic or otherwise is dealing with bureaucracy in Portugal?
I got my papers as soon as I arrived. I'm glad I did that. I think it's harder for non-EU residents now, but not impossible, with perseverance and patience. You have to be willing to put up with inconvenience and incompetence, but that's part of the 'game' as I see it. A sense of humour helps.

How did you go about finding accommodation?
I rented at first, which was very costly. Then I bought a small, brand new apartment right in the centre of the old part of Cascais. At the time I could have purchased the apartment below as well. Now I wish I had. I'm still trying to buy it and I believe some day I will. I loved Cascais from the first day I saw it. It's animated, by the sea and quite international. I wanted to be close to the train station, post office, markets and shops so I wouldn't have to rely on my car all the time. That was a wise decision.

My apartment was almost finished when I bought it so I had few problems with builders and tradesmen. It wasn't usual for a woman on her own to buy, and so I had some clashes with male workmen in the beginning, but not many.

Have you any advice that you would give first-time buyers?
Be sure you know where you want to live. I know people who bought, quickly, in the Algarve, and then realised they wanted to be in the Lisbon-Cascais area. Rent before you buy to make sure it's where you want to live. *Have a lawyer look over your contract.* Even though they tell you it isn't necessary, it is. I did and my lawyer helped me in many important ways. It's worth the extra cost. Use a lawyer whom others recommend and who speaks your language fluently. In fact, I have a

rule: I do all of my business dealings, money matters, health issues and anything contractual in English. That way I am less apt to make mistakes. I understand Portuguese, but I will never understand it as well as English.

How traumatic was the process of moving your life to Portugal - getting things shipped over, getting settled in, etc?
I came with very little and had no home in the USA. I did have possessions in storage. After one year I disposed of them, as I knew I wanted my life to be here, not there.

Have you found it easy to make friends? What is your general impression of the Portuguese?
Yes, I am very outgoing so I have many friends but I am also involved in numerous activities as well as my work. You have to involve yourself and get out. No-one comes to you. The Portuguese are kind, formal, and not too efficient, can't say 'no' very easily, and are kind of a closed people as opposed to Americans. But the longer I am here, the more Portuguese friends I make. Still, my closest friends are ex-pats and not just Americans.

JOHN CAREY

John Carey, 28, a project finance advisor with big 4 firm, KPMG, jumped at the chance of securing a secondment to work in Lisbon over the summer of 2004. For John the move was primarily driven by the demands of his job but he soon became enamoured with Portugal's friendly atmosphere, bright blue skies, and fantastic food and wine. He was also lucky enough to live in Lisbon at a time when the city was buzzing with the excitement of Euro 2004, witnessing Portugal break British hearts with a penalty shootout defeat, first hand. John has since returned to London but looks back fondly on his time in Portugal and continues to involve himself in Portuguese infrastructure projects. We asked him:

How did your secondment with KPMG in Lisbon come about?
The process began with a request from our Lisbon office for an experienced individual who would be prepared to relocate for six months to work on a particular project. For me this was simply too good an opportunity to turn down. The project involved working for a consortium planning to build and operate a new hospital in Loures, just outside of Lisbon.

The process was fairly simple, and there was minimal red tape to deal with. There is a well trodden internal process at KPMG for organising short-term placements. I simply signed a secondment agreement which outlined my terms and conditions, and what to expect from the Portuguese practice etc. As it was only a short-term opportunity, I was able to stay on the UK payroll and my

UK tax and national insurance contributions were unaffected. The Portuguese practice agreed to pay a monthly fee for my services to the UK practice, along with other ad-hoc and daily expenses that I incurred during my stay.

Did it take you long to acclimatise to living and working in Portugal?

I think I was lucky in that I was the first secondee my team in Lisbon had received and therefore they seemed very keen to make sure I settled in. In truth it was not difficult as the people are extremely friendly which is so important when moving abroad. Moving from London meant that whilst the language is a little strange and there are other differences (eating times, going out times) overall there is not too much that feels alien.

The Lisbon office of KPMG helped me to find accommodation. I saw three apartments that were all of a decent standard, were well-organised and had a good feeling of space. In the end I stayed in a modern, serviced apartment block in central Lisbon. The quality of the apartment was high, with all mod-cons provided, plus a daily maid service.

In terms of working life, I actually found it far more straightforward than working in London. The journey to work was certainly much simpler. Living centrally meant that I could choose to walk to work or take the very efficient metro system, which is expanding all the time.

Compared to London, the cost of living was very reasonable. Essential shopping items such as food and household items were clearly cheaper than London although I would note that there are supermarkets such as Corte Ingles which are less cheap than others. Eating and drinking out was also generally cheaper.

How well were you able to immerse yourself in Portuguese culture? Was it easy to make friends?

I was lucky enough have a couple of colleagues that really helped in this respect. This was particularly evident when there were various festivals or key dates in the calendar as the Portuguese are very proud to show off their history and tradition. I found the Portuguese to be generally friendly, whether I was working with them, meeting them in a social setting or spending money with them – they were genuinely interested in speaking to a British guy.

The only challenge I would note was the Portuguese language, which understandably is preferred in social settings. My lack of practice meant that I found it difficult at times to engage in group conversations. I would recommend that anyone thinking of moving to Portugal should work as hard as they can on learning the language before they go. Many people comment that it is a difficult language to learn, but with lessons, a bit of application and practice, it shouldn't be too hard. I got the sense that a good basic grasp would have helped me more than scrambling to pick it up once I was there.

What did you like best about life in Portugal?
The quality of life in Lisbon was very high. The city certainly has a very smooth way of life and also has an amazingly consistent climate. I lost count of the number of days I awoke to find crystal-clear, blue skies which stayed that way for the entire day. Prior to moving there I had a vague idea that the climate would be better than that of the UK, but it really is remarkably good and makes a big difference to the overall experience.

As I have said, I found the Portuguese to be very proud and friendly hosts. I was also lucky enough to sample a lot of Lisbon's restaurants and am happy to report that there are many great places to eat. Some of the dishes are not for the faint hearted (such as chicken cooked in its own blood), but on the whole the food is very tasty. Portuguese wine is also great. I knew about port before I went, but I never really had a grasp on how serious the table wine industry is. I had great fun working my way through it all, making sure that I tried as much as possible as most of it never makes the UK shores.

All in all, when I think about the superb climate, easy-going people, and interesting cuisine I sometimes wonder why I am not still there.

MARY SWORDER

Mary Sworder had five years of working in public relations in London and one year working in France before coming to Portugal because her husband (then boyfriend) was offered a job there, with a Portuguese subsidiary of a British software company. Mary's husband had already worked in Portugal previously for Lloyds Bank. We asked her:

How easy was it to move to Portugal?
The move was relatively easy because it was a company move which meant most of the red tape was taken care of. There is plenty of rented accommodation available (start by looking in the *Anglo-Portuguese News*).

Was it difficult to find work?
There is always work as long as you have something to offer, for example teaching English, translating, secretarial work etc. I did a TEFL course at International House in Lisbon in order to be qualified to teach English. There is a great demand for English-language teachers so I had no problem finding a job.

How do you find living and working in Portugal compared with the UK?
Living and working in Portugal is a combination of pleasure and frustration. It is a beautiful country with a great climate and social life if you are prepared to mix in. Working is sometimes frustrating because you often come up against the bureaucracy; initially you are in unfamiliar territory so that even simple things are

time-consuming and sometimes the telephones don't work! However, for me, it is interesting working in a country which is still developing and by being flexible it is enjoyable.

TEFL teachers earn less than in some other places. Teaching privately you earn more. Rates of pay are not high compared with the UK, but they are enough to live on.

What kind of recreation is there and does it include mixing with Portuguese?
Getting to know the Portuguese is not easy, especially if you are not confident with the language. If you like the outdoor life, especially sports, and are prepared to adapt to your surroundings you should have a good time in Portugal.

Any tips for anyone considering taking the plunge themselves?
It is a good idea to spend some time learning the language. As a way of getting to know people I suggest joining a club like the Lisbon Casuals, a sports club which operates from the grounds of St Julian's school in Carcavelos on Wednesday evenings and all weekends. It has cricket, football, rugby, hockey, badminton and basketball sections and has probably the cheapest sports facilities available in the Lisbon area. There is also a convivial bar.

MARIBEL GATTEY

As a student of Spanish, Portuguese and Latin American studies, Maribel Gattey, 22, took the opportunity to spend a semester living in Porto, practising the language and experiencing Portuguese culture first hand. Maribel was able to take advantage of the ERASMUS (European Community Action Scheme for the Mobility of University Students) programme, which enables students in 31 European countries to study for part of their degree in another country. ERASMUS students receive an EC grant, and their courses and accommodation are arranged by the two universities in question. Maribel found studying in Portugal to be a very different experience from studying in the UK, and has mixed feelings about her time there. We asked her:

What were your first impressions of Portugal?
I thought that Porto was an incredibly old and beautiful city. As the centre of the city is a world heritage site, no new buildings are allowed, so the city has a very traditional air. Another thought that struck me was that Porto seems fairly poor by European standards. For example, there were a lot of dilapidated buildings and a huge number of elderly beggars.

How did the quality of life in Portugal compare to other countries you have

lived in?
In comparison to England, Portugal is a very cheap country to live in. In general I would have thought that the Portuguese have a fairly good quality of life, but I would say that it did not compare favourably with that of Spain. For example, when I lived in Spain I saw what a good quality of life elderly people had – they often went around in large groups, eating out or having coffee. I definitely did not see this in Porto, partly I think because there is not quite the same café culture. But, it could also be to do with the climate, I was there in winter and Porto gets very cold. Perhaps in the summer the atmosphere is better.

What about red tape – any problems?
As I am from a country that is in the European Community, and I was part of the ERASMUS programme, I did not need any sort of visa or permit to study in Portugal. However a Korean friend of mine did encounter numerous problems getting a visa and has found the Portuguese authorities to be overly bureaucratic.

How did you find studying in Portugal compared with home?
Studying in Porto was a very different experience from studying in England. On the whole the general feeling of the foreign students (which even included the Spanish) was that there was a real lack of organisation at the university. For example I have been studying Portuguese for 2 years and when I enrolled in a Portuguese course for foreign students at the university, they put me and other people from my university in the beginners class, as there were no spaces in the more advanced classes. Bettering my Portuguese was the main reason for studying in Portugal, so I am sure you can imagine how frustrated I felt. I even knew of one English student at the university who could not get on the course. This poor organisation was a huge problem for me but luckily I did not have to pass the exams I took in Portugal.

How did you find the social life in Porto?
This was one aspect of Porto that I did not like very much. I went there thinking that the nightlife would be comparable to that of Spain, but the reality was quite different. I found that there was a real lack of nightlife. For example there were few bars to go to for a quick drink, and there were very few clubs. Luckily for me I was as ERASMUS student, which meant that we had lots of nights out organised for us. Porto is quite a small city, so after a few months I did get a bit bored of the social life. I think that Lisbon would be a much better city to live in for a young person.

LESLEY & MIKE COLLINS

Lesley and Mike Collins and their two daughters (aged 23 and 21) are from Somerset. They have been holidaying in the Algarve since the early 1990s. Lesley writes: 'Two years ago we decided to look for a property near Silves/Monchique as this was an area we really liked. We originally started to look at ruins and plots of land, with a view to building a holiday home. After about eight months of travelling to and from Portugal looking at various sites, none of which were what we wanted, we saw the house we now own. It was in a sorry state as it had been rented out for 15 years with no work done to it at all, but the location was great. We ended up spending more than we had first intended, but this is now more a second home than a holiday home.' We asked them:

What type of property do you own and how often are you able to use it?
The house we have bought was built approximately 20 years ago and is a three-bedroom older style house built into a hillside. We would not change the choice we made, as we love the house and the area, and we are still working on renovating it.

We will not be living in our house permanently (though hopefully sometime in the future we will) as at the present time our youngest daughter has just finished her first year at University and will have two or three more years to do. I would not want to be away at this time. Therefore the house in Portugal is a second home to use as often as we possibly can throughout the year. So far, with all the building work going on, it has been approximately once a month. For us, as we live in Somerset, flying from Bristol to Faro with Easyjet has made this possible. We now also have Exeter to Faro with Flybe available.

What were the factors that influenced you on your choice of location?
The location was not really of our choice originally but we really like it now. We have bought to the south of the N125 between the coast of Benagil and the N125 in the countryside. The main advantages to us are that it only takes 40-45 minutes to drive to and from the airport in Faro. It is close to beaches (5 minutes by car) but away from the tourist resorts. It is also close to the large town of Lagoa, and close to Carvoeiro for restaurants and night life; close to the Algarve Shopping Centre and within easy reach of the west of the Algarve and Silves/Monchique.

How have you found dealing with local builders and other tradesmen?
We have used mainly Portuguese tradespeople – the builder was recommended to us by our now good friends who were the agents we went through to buy the house. We have been very pleasantly surprised at just how good and sympathetically the builder has done the work to the house. All other tradespeople have also been local except for the heating company who have put in our central heating and hot

water systems, which is English owned. All have been very good. You hear such horror stories! We have had some arguments with the local plumber to get the pipe-work done to our standards and not 'local' standards. On the whole we have found everyone we have dealt with very good and extremely helpful, although they are as expensive as tradespeople in UK.

What were your first impressions of Portugal?

In the early 90s Portugal was much quieter and less commercial, but we still like it. The climate is good and the lifestyle much slower than in the UK, which is important for us as my husband's job is highly stressful and travel orientated. Portugal to us is a place to get away to and relax at any time of the year.

The best things about Portugal are the climate, the people, the friendliness of the locals we have met so far, and the peace and quiet.

Have you any advice that you would give first time buyers?

Make sure you know the area you are moving to and that what you are buying is really what you want. Don't go into it thinking it is going to be cheap, as Portugal is not cheap when it comes to buying houses, furniture, etc., although the cost of living is still much cheaper than in the UK.

Complete guides to life abroad from Vacation Work

Live & Work Abroad

Buying a House Abroad

Starting a Business Abroad

Available from good bookshops or direct from the publishers
Vacation Work, 9 Park End Street, Oxford OX1 1HJ
Tel 01865-241978 * Fax 01865-790885 * www.vacationwork.co.uk